Diversity and Inclusion on Campus

As scholars and practitioners in higher education attempt to embrace and lead diversity efforts, it is imperative that they have an understanding of the issues that affect historically underrepresented students. Using an intersectional approach that connects the categories of race, class, and gender, *Diversity and Inclusion on Campus* comprehensively covers the range of college experiences, from gaining access to higher education to successfully persisting through degree programs. Authors Winkle-Wagner and Locks bridge research, theory, and practice related to the ways that peers, faculty, administrators, and institutions can and do influence racially and ethnically underrepresented students' experiences. This book is an invaluable resource for future and current higher education and student affairs practitioners working toward full inclusion and participation for all students in higher education.

Special features:

- Chapter Case Studies—cases written by on-the-ground practitioners help readers make meaningful connections between theory, research, and practice.
- Coverage of Theory and Research—each chapter provides a systematic treatment of the literature and research related to underrepresented students' experiences of getting into college, getting through college, and getting out of college.
- Discussion Questions—questions encourage practitioners and researchers to explore concepts in more depth, consider best practices, and make connections to their own contexts.
- Connection to Professional Standards—chapters prompt readers to connect content with the CAS (Council for the Advancement of Standards in Higher Education) standards for relevant Student Affairs functional areas and to consider how the NAPSA Professional Competencies and ACPA Statement of Ethical Principles and Standards shape practice in ways that support and include underrepresented students on college campuses.

Rachelle Winkle-Wagner is an Assistant Professor of Educational Leadership and Policy Analysis at the University of Wisconsin-Madison, USA.

Angela M. Locks is an Assistant Professor of Student Development in Higher Education at the California State University, Long Beach, USA.

Core Concepts in Higher Education

Series Editors: Edward P. St. John and Marybeth Gasman

Diversity and Inclusion on Campus

Supporting Racially and Ethnically Underrepresented Students

**Rachelle Winkle-Wagner
and Angela M. Locks**

Routledge
Taylor & Francis Group

NEW YORK AND LONDON

First published 2014
by Routledge
711 Third Avenue, New York, NY 10017

Simultaneously published in the UK
by Routledge
2 Park Square, Milton Park, Abingdon, Oxon OX14 4RN

Routledge is an imprint of the Taylor & Francis Group, an informa business

Library of Congress Cataloging in Publication Data
A catalog record for this book has been requested.

ISBN: 978-0-415-80706-7 (hbk)
ISBN: 978-0-415-80707-4 (pbk)
ISBN: 978-0-203-15380-2 (ebk)

Typeset in Minion
by EvS Communication Networx, Inc.

CONTENTS

v

SERIES EDITOR'S INTRODUCTION

I am pleased to include Rachelle Winkle-Wagner and Angela Mosi Locks' book *Diversity and Inclusion on Campus: Supporting Racially and Ethnically Underrepresented Students* as part of the Core Concepts in Higher Education Series that I co-edit with Edward St. John. Our series is focused on foundational books that can be used in higher education classrooms—books that reach back to the disciplines and provide a rich understanding of essential topics for students, scholars, and practitioners.

Diversity and Inclusion on Campus is an incredibly thorough, well-researched book on what I think is the very most important issue in higher education. As the nation's demographics rapidly change, our colleges and universities need to be ready, willing, and well equipped to support the changing student body. And, as we prepare future practitioners and scholars, it is essential that they read this book.

Winkle-Wagner and Locks are greatly adept at teasing out the most important issues related to diversity and inclusion, providing a rationale for the focuses on these issues, and showing us where the connections are to ourselves, our work, and our institutions.

Diversity and Inclusion on Campus is comprehensive and usable. It is the kind of book that a practitioner can pull off the shelf for reference but can also be used by scholars to bolster their research related to diversity. It challenges the reader in that it takes bold stances and offers fresh perspectives on issues.

It is my hope that this book is used in all higher education programs and quickly becomes a classic.

Marybeth Gasman
Professor of Higher Education
University of Pennsylvania
and Series Co-Editor, Core Concepts in Higher Education

PREFACE

We wrote this book for you. If you have long wondered why some groups of students seem to have a more difficult time getting into and out of college, this book is intended for you as a way to provide some answers to these questions. If you have struggled with the idea of diversity in higher education, pondering why some populations of students get so much attention because of their race, even while the larger social conversation seems to be moving in a direction that suggests race might no longer be an issue, this book might challenge you, but, it may also offer ideas as to why race still matters in higher education (and arguably in society more generally). If you are a student, this book is for you, it will offer you insight into some of the challenges we face in higher education, as our population of students becomes increasingly more diverse. If you are someone who wants to become (or already is) an administrator or practitioner in higher education, this book is a place to contemplate the practice of diversity and how practice can be informed by research and theory. Finally, if you are a scholar, this book provides a new synthesis of the diversity research and theory from the past 30 years, exploring ideas for future study and reminding us of the importance of practice in asking new questions.

Among numerous diversity-related texts in higher education (Brown-Glaude, 2008; Hurtado, Milem, Clayton-Pedersen, & Allen, 1999; Smith, 2009; Turner, Garcia, Nora, & Rendon, 1996), there remains a need for a compilation that bridges research, theory, and practice related to the numerous ways that institutions, and those within them (peers, faculty, administrators, staff) influence students, specifically those who are racially or ethnically underrepresented in many of the nation's institutions. This book aims to fill this gap, offering a systematic treatment of the literature, findings, and implications for practice related to the college experiences of underrepresented students.

We emphasize diversity as it relates to underrepresented students, particularly examining African American, Latina/o, Native American, and Asian American students' experiences in higher education. Diversity is central to every aspect of the college experience and accordingly, this text covers many aspects of the college experience for students, from gaining access to higher education to successfully persisting through degree programs. Central to this text are explorations into how different kinds of people and institutional/social structures influence students' experiences, and consequently, the way that students navigate these structures, interactions, and experiences.

GETTING IN, THROUGH, AND OUT: THE SCRIPT FOR STRUCTURING THIS BOOK

The purpose of this book is to cast a revealing light on how diversity and inclusion in higher education has been theorized, researched, and practiced in higher education. The concept of diversity is, in its very definition, so pluralistic and multifaceted that it would be nearly impossible to cover all aspects of the topic in one volume. We focus particularly on diversity as it relates to those students who have historically been excluded, marginalized, or disallowed from participation in postsecondary institutions because of their racial or ethnic background.

We specifically highlight the following racial/ethnic groups of students in our analysis of racially/ethnically underrepresented students: African American or Black, Latina/o or Hispanic, White or European American or Caucasian, Native American or American Indian, and Asian American or Pacific Islander. We often use multiple terms to refer to students from these groups, to represent the diversity of identifications *within* the groups. For example, students with African or Caribbean descent might self-identity as Black, while others may self-identify as African American. We opt to use both terms to include both groups of students. Among students whose ancestors hail from a huge variety of countries in regions like Latin America, Mexico, South America, the Caribbean, or Spain, they may wish to be called Latina/o or Hispanic. We use both Latina/o and Hispanic in this book in order to include all populations of students from these ethnic backgrounds and the diversity within these populations. Or, some students whose heritage harkens back to Eastern or Western Europe or Scandinavia might identity as White while other identify as European American or Caucasian. Again, we use all designations here. Finally, while they are often put into the same group, there is enormous diversity among Asian, Asian American, Pacific Islander, Indigenous, Native American, and American Indian populations. We use multiple terms to refer to students from those populations too.

We attempt, whenever possible, to connect race and ethnicity with other categories of diversity such as gender, socioeconomic status, sexual orientation, religion, or ability. We root this perspective in an intersectional approach (Collins, 2000; Crenshaw, 1991; hooks, 2000) that connects deeply with the thinking of critical race feminist scholars who initiated a call to view categories of race, class, and gender as overlapping (Shields, 2008; Zinn & Dill, 1994).

While we take an intersectional approach when possible in this book, we admittedly do not have the space in this volume to give adequate treatment to all topics of diversity. Additionally, there are many diverse actors in higher education: students, staff, faculty, administrators, policymakers, and many more. Our focus here is on the students, and particularly on students who have historically been racially or ethnically underrepresented in higher education. We refer to these students as "students of color" or "underrepresented students" throughout the book. One reason for our inability to cover the full range of diversity in higher education is that diversity, by its very definition, is such an all encompassing concept that it would be nearly impossible to represent its totality in one volume. But, another reason for our approach, considering students of color in college, is due to the way that the body of scholarship on the topic has been approached, highlighting students of color as a primary point of interest.

We organized our examination of diversity and inclusion for students in higher education around students' processes from gaining access to college until they graduate and determine their next steps. In their book, *Getting the Most out of College,* Chickering and Schlossberg (2002) asserted that this process could be considered the process of "moving in," "moving through," and "moving on." We adapt this idea here, structuring the chapters in a chronological ordering of how a student might move through higher education institutions, into three parts: getting in, getting through, and getting out. We chose this approach in part as a way to demonstrate the actionable moments of diversity and inclusion in the process of students' college going (as students enter, matriculate, and graduate). We collaborated with a few people in the practical case studies at the end of some chapters. This was in an effort to offer practitioner perspectives on some of the content.

CHAPTER AND SECTION ORGANIZATION

The first section of the book, including Chapters 1 through 3, is centered on the process of learning about and gaining access to college. We initiate the idea of "getting in" with an examination of access to college in Chapter 2. In this chapter on access, we reveal the complicated and difficult pathways that many students might have to navigate in order to enroll in college, considering such issues as how primary and secondary schooling influences student's chances of going to college, the role of families in college going, the process whereby a student decides if and where to go to college, and how a student negotiates a way to pay for college. After a student learns about college, perhaps contemplating various options for places to attend college, and finds a way to finance the degree, he or she would attempt to gain admission. Courtney Luedke, a doctoral candidate at the University of Wisconsin – Madison in the Educational Leadership and Policy Analysis department with experience in multicultural affairs and summer bridge programs for students of color, authored the case study for this chapter entitled "College Choice for One High Achieving Undocumented Dreamer." In Chapter 3, we explore college admissions and how diversity has (or has not) been fostered through admissions processes. We momentarily enter the affirmative action debate in Chapter 3 as to whether race should be a factor in admissions decisions, pondering what will become of diversity as race begins to disappear from many of the conversations about college admissions (Winkle-Wagner, Sule, & Maramba, 2012). Julie Vultaggio, Assistant Dean of the Doctor of Education Leadership Program at Harvard University in the Graduate School of Education, wrote the case study for the chapter, "Inclusivity for All Applicants: An Admissions Case Study."

Getting through college is the longest portion of the book, in part to demonstrate the many factors that can affect a student's likelihood of making it through to earn a college degree. Chapters 4, 5, 6, and 7 are targeted toward the time period after a student gains access and admission to college and begins to matriculate through a degree program. In Chapter 4, we examine the college transition process, where a student begins to adjust to a college campus, making progress toward a degree. In this chapter, we try to demonstrate the way in which students' earlier experiences in education or within their families can influence their ability to transition and adjust to college. Courtney Luedke also authored Chapter 4's case study, "The First Year Experience: Inclusivity for All Students." Chapters 5 and 6 are structured with an eye on the institutions, exploring how institutional types, scopes, and missions can affect students' experiences in college. In Chapter 5, we present information about minority serving institutions, those postsecondary campuses such as historically Black college and universities (HBCUs), that have a historical or current mission to serve students who have been historically underrepresented in higher education. We counter our review of minority serving institutions with a chapter on campus environments within predominantly White institutions (PWIs), or those institutions that have a majority White student population. Specifically, in Chapter 6, we discuss the campus racial climate, or the way that students perceive the campus related to acceptance or openness to diversity. We wrote the case study "Leveraging Demographic Shifts to Expand Services to Students" for Chapter 5, as well as "Dealing with Hate: Responding to Hostility on Campus," the case study for Chapter 6. Section 2 of the book ends with an analysis of students' identity development during college in Chapter 7. Here, we ruminate on how students' experiences on particular college campuses may either facilitate or hinder their ability to develop. Tasha Willis of California State University, Los Angeles, and Rashida Crutchfield of California State University, Long Beach, both Social Work faculty who have experiences serving diverse students of color as both instructors and practitioners, wrote "Exploring Cultural Climate and Identity at Mid-State University," the Chapter 7 case study.

The third and final section of the book is dedicated to students' progression through their degree programs and into the next stage in their lives. We begin with a chapter on students' persistence in college (Chapter 8). As we illustrate in the chapter, there are a multitude of challenges that students may face in their path toward graduating from college, but there are also some ideas as to what might help facilitate students' retention in their degree programs. The case study in Chapter 8, "A Will to Succeed," was written by doctoral candidate Aundria Green of the University of Nebraska – Lincoln; she has expertise in student support services for underrepresented students. Finally, in Chapter 9, we call the book to a close by initiating another path that students may choose to take, the path to graduate or professional school. In this final chapter, we investigate issues that seem to help or hinder students' gain access to graduate and professional programs. Carmen McCallum, Assistant Professor, Higher Education Administration, Buffalo State, State University of New York, with expertise in graduate school access and experiences, wrote "First Things First: Gaining Access to Graduate School," the case study for Chapter 9.

SPECIAL FEATURES

We separated each chapter into four areas with the goal of offering theoretical, empirical (i.e., data driven studies), and practical analyses to each of the topics in the book. Our desire in doing this was to offer readers multiple ways in which to use the book, as thinkers, researchers, practitioners, students, staff, administrators, or faculty. These areas are as follows:

1. Thinking about diversity: In this section of each chapter, we review the common conceptual, philosophical, or theoretical approaches to the particular topic;

2. Diversity still matters: For this part of each chapter, we provide a review of the extant literature on the topic, research that presented new data;
3. Summary: In each chapter we discuss what scholarly and practical work remains for the specific areas germane to the chapter's topic;
4. Discussion questions: We offer ideas as to what practitioners and/or researchers might be able to do in the future on the topic through posing questions to stimulate further thinking;
5. A case study: At the end of each chapter, we or someone with administrative experience in higher education provides a case study where the reader can practice the concepts in the chapter in a practical way.

One of the pedagogical hallmarks of this text is the inclusion of case studies for each of the content chapters. Each case study includes a description of a relevant diversity issue that may be analyzed through an inclusive lens. These cases draw on the theoretical and empirical content reviewed in the chapter. Through these cases, we prompt readers to consider best practices in their response to the discussion questions at the end of the cases. These case studies could be used by instructors to facilitate classroom discussions. Our hope is that each case study will allow readers to make connections between theory, research, and practice.

The field of student affairs and higher education is fortunate to have three sources of guidelines and standards that guide the practice of serving students. These are College Student Educators International (ACPA), Student Affairs Administrators in Higher Education (NASPA), and the Council for the Advancement of Standards In Higher Education (CAS). ACPA and NASPA are the two largest student affairs professional associations. CAS is a collective whose mission is focused on the improvement of programs and services in postsecondary education. Both ACPA and NASPA are focused on professional competencies necessary to successfully develop as student affairs professionals and provide effective services to students. Because of the importance of making connections across practice, theory, and research, we include practice-related questions in Chapters 2 through 9 that prompt readers to consider how these competencies shape their practice in ways that support and include underrepresented students on college campuses. Those new to student affairs will read these three important documents and come to learn that the structure of the CAS document is organized in a directory-like format that lists a wide variety of types of programs present on college campuses (see http://www.cas.edu/index.php/standards/). ACPA organizes their Statement of Ethical Principles & Standards around four ethical standards (see http://www2.myacpa. org/statement-of-ethical-principles-and-standards). The NASPA Competencies, jointly approved with ACPA, are a set of 10 core competencies key to the profession of student affairs (see http://www.naspa.org/programs/profdev/default.cfm). We include all three across the content chapters as these three documents collectively are meant to guide and shape how students are served in higher education and thus deserve attention in discussions of creating inclusive campus environments for students of color.

With the organization of the book in mind, we turn our attention toward our introduction where we provide a foundation for the volume and give insight into our conceptual framework for this work. We begin with a historical grounding for race and ethnicity in higher education and frame diversity as an action of inclusion. Through this introduction, we discuss why our call to action is both timely and necessary. We end with a description of the cast of characters that set the stage for future actions related to diversity-and-inclusion in higher education institutions, uncovering trends in the populations of students who are making it into, through, and out of college in the United States.

ACKNOWLEDGMENTS

As we submit the final version of the manuscript, it seems important to reflect on the many moments and transitions that transpired during this time. As collaborators on this project, we shared much more than the writing of the book because of the many transitions that occurred during this time: the birth of a new daughter, Abigail; sick and aging parents; funerals for loved ones; supporting other family members in their life transitions; the beginning of new faculty positions; changes in our current positions; moves to new cities; new relationships; and growth in our own thinking. Perhaps the one constant during this time period was the writing of this book. As we compile the final version, it somehow marks this time period and calls it to some type of end, beginning a new chapter. As we enter a new chapter, we want to take a few moments to thank the many people who supported us during this time.

We are grateful for the many colleagues who supported this project through conversations and feedback on earlier versions of this work: Leticia Oseguera, Carmen McCallum, Deborah Faye Carter, Michael Dumas, Uma Jayakumar, Bianca Baldridge, and Peter Goff. Aundria Duncan-Wagner offered research assistance early in the project, thank you. Leise Hull did editing work on early versions of this work, and we are grateful for her engagement and feedback. We are especially thankful for her dedicated referencing work, thinking, and critical feedback.

A few individuals deserve special mention. Marybeth Gasman, this project would have never happened without your encouragement for us to do it. Thanks for being such an exemplar of mentoring, the inclusion of diversity, impactful scholarly writing, and generosity, not just for us, but, for our field. Ed St. John, the other series editor, is also a personal mentor and colleague for us. Thanks to you for demonstrating in your prolific writing and through our conversations, what it means to be committed to diversity and justice. The two of you together exemplify what it means to enact diversity-and-inclusion, and we, in many ways, modeled our argument here from your examples.

Deborah Faye Carter, co-author on Chapter 4, deserves a special acknowledgement for her contributions and her continued engagement of us as a mentor, scholar, and colleague. The authors of the case studies included in this book are among the best scholar-practitioners the field has to offer, and we are grateful for their thoughtful contributions to this book. Courtney Luedke, serving as Rachelle's research assistant during the final stages of writing this book was an invaluable help in making this project come to fruition; thank you. Additionally, we are thankful to the anonymous reviewers and to Heather Jarrow for their helpful comments on crafting this manuscript. Finally, we want to collectively thank our families and close friends for their steadfast support during the development of this book.

Rachelle Winkle-Wagner thanks her colleagues in the Educational Leadership and Policy Analysis department at the University of Wisconsin-Madison, and especially, Clif Conrad, Xueli Wang, and Peter Goff. I feel so incredibly grateful to work in such an intellectually stimulating, supportive, collaborative, and kind environment. My mentoring committee, Julie Mead, Jerlando Jackson, and Clif Conrad, all offered helpful advice on this project and my larger research agenda during this time; I am thankful to have such fantastic support and "spirited dialogue." My writing group, Haley Vlach, Percival Matthews, Xueli Wang, and Peter Goff, spent hours helping me to strategize the details of writing this book (and many of you read drafts)—thanks! Finally, to my brilliant "FG" club, Peter Miller, Xueli Wang, Peter Goff, and the newest member, Nick Hillman, thanks for your smart examples of good scholarship and for your friendship and support.

Thanks to my family for your constant support: my sister, Brenda and my niece, Mya; my parents, Carola and Bill Winkle; my mom-and-dad-in-law, Marilyn and Bill Wagner; and the Hansons, Jenny, Corey, Taylor, and Brennan.

I save the last acknowledgement for those in my world who sacrificed and gave the most to the project, aside from Angela and me. Mike Wagner, choosing you as my partner in this stumbling journey through life should go down in the record books as the best decision I could have ever made (and since the record books, wherever those are, haven't captured this yet, I am marking it here). As I continue to choose you each day, I am stunned by your generosity, your brilliance, your unconditional love, and by how much you challenge my thinking. I count myself lucky that you question my arguments (and our readers probably should thank Mike for this too). Thank you for reading multiple drafts of this manuscript, and for your constant support of my career, my writing, and my thinking. Eleanor, who was between the ages of 2 and 4 during the writing of this book, my sweet girl, you inspire me daily and teach me to be a better human being (and mama-scholar). Your question, "how's your book going, mommy?" helped to remind me why I do this work. Abigail, who was born during this time, I am thankful for your presence each day. As I watch your fierce tenacity develop, it gives me courage to ask tougher questions about our world. I hope for a better, more inclusive world for you, my powerful girls.

Angela Mosi Locks thanks the Student Development in Higher Education program students at California State University, Long Beach who are a dedicated group of student affairs professionals. These students, along with my colleagues Don Haviland, John Murray, Jonathan O'Brien, Anna M. Ortiz, and William Vega have shaped my thinking about higher education and how we might best serve our increasingly diverse students. The students of CSU Long Beach's Residential College and Beachside College were constant reminders about the hope and promise intertwined with the opportunity to attend college. They reminded me often with their personal stories that so many higher education journeys are unique, and remain untold.

The National Center for Institutional Diversity (NCID) at the University of Michigan partially sponsored this project by providing me support throughout the development and completion of this project. Philip J. Bowman, Constance Bush, Patricia Ellis, Valerie Johnson, and Ana Ormsby deserve special thanks for continuing to provide me an academic and intellectual home at NCID. To my NCID colleagues: Nancy would have been thrilled that NCID supported this project. I would be remiss if I did not publically acknowledge Marvin Peterson for his support of my interest in minority serving institutions as a doctoral student at the University of Michigan.

Jeanette Maduena and Sonja Simmons, along with Peggy Card Govela, provided feedback on the proposal that led to this project. Jeanette and Sonja provided assistance with securing literature we used in this project. Vicenta Arrizon Maffris and Michael Tran were incredibly helpful with referencing and formatting work in the final stages of the development of this book.

As this project developed, Ann Sprunger and Dave Corsa generously opened their home to me so that I could spend a summer writing; they deserve a special acknowledgement. Every young student affairs professional who identifies as a person of color should be fortunate to have allies such as Ann Sprunger and Sandra Gregerman. I am deeply grateful for being able to count myself in this group.

Eric Richard is a wonderful cousin and colleague—I am grateful for the conversations about education and your support. The McCallum's have been a constant source of love, laughter, and support. Courtney Jane Gilbert—there are no words to express how much our friendship has changed my life and made me strive to be a better human being. Sandra Vallie and Tom Flagg, Mr. and Mrs. Trujillo, Pelema and Christine Morrice, Callie Corsa, Penny Pasque and Frank Kaminsky, and the Martinez family supported this project during summer 2012—the connections and conversations helped shape my thinking about this work. And finally, this book is for: LeAsia, Patrick, Jr., Emma Ruth, Ava, Elle, Hayden, Florence, Donovan, Michio, Marco, and Nia with the hopes that your journey to college and beyond brings you new learning opportunities, adventures and empowers you to change the world

SECTION I

GETTING IN

1

INTRODUCTION

The Action of Diversity and Inclusion in Higher Education

We recall that what binds this nation together is not the colors of our skin or the tenets of our faith or the origins of our names. What makes us exceptional—what makes us American—is our allegiance to an idea, articulated in a declaration made more than two centuries ago:

> *"We hold these truths to be self-evident, that all men are created equal, that they are endowed by their Creator with certain unalienable rights, that among these are Life, Liberty, and the pursuit of Happiness."*

... That is our generation's task—to make these words, these rights, these values—of Life, and Liberty, and the Pursuit of Happiness—real for every American. Being true to our founding documents does not require us to agree on every contour of life; it does not mean we will all define liberty in exactly the same way, or follow the same precise path to happiness. Progress does not compel us to settle centuries-long debates for all time—but it does require us to act in our time.

—President Barack Obama (2013)

DIVERSITY-AND-INCLUSION-AS-ACTION

Diversity. It requires thought. It requires understanding. But, mostly, diversity is a call toward *action*, a verb, something that one can demonstrate, behave, enact. Our task in this book is to call for action. We charge our readers to do something with, about, and for diversity. To ensure that all people have their right to pursue happiness, their right to be included in the fabric of the United States and the world, requires action. Inclusion is not something that happens on its own. To enact diversity in positive ways requires the act of inclusion. And inclusion assumes the deliberate act of bringing people into the group, the norms, into the opportunities that will allow for a meaningful pursuit of happiness. Our focus in these pages is on racial and ethnic diversity and inclusion in higher education. We start from the assumption that higher education is a vessel through which these goals can be enacted and then modeled into society more generally.

Left alone, diversity might simply exist with or without our approval, our tolerance, or our enacting it. All people have their uniqueness, their differences in thinking, acting, behaving, or being. We, as a larger humanity, do not really choose to be diverse; we simply are. History teaches us that left alone, diversity may exist, but inclusion may not. This is our rationale for pushing the meaning of diversity from an adjective, something that describes another object or idea, toward an action.

One lesson of history is that when diversity, the difference(s) between us, the adjective to describe us (i.e., diverse people), is left untouched and unenacted, those who were initially afforded power and privilege by way of their birthright will continue to have it and those who were not so fortunate, will be relegated to persistently disadvantaged positions. In the United States, this history includes the cancerous effects of genocide upon indigenous populations, the deep and persistent scars of slavery, the memory of concentration camps both foreign and on U.S. soil, a federal law that permits states to refuse to recognize same sex marriages performed in other states, and a constitution that allows the detention of its citizens based on race and ethnicity, and still does not explicitly grant women equal rights to men. While we simply *are* all different, our history on diversity as an adjective has not been only the well-intended metaphors for the patchwork quilt, the melting pot, or the salad bowl where people come together and make something more beautiful. Our collective human history on diversity-as-an-adjective has been messy, painful, and all too often subjugating and violent towards those who are not born into dominant groups.

We choose to acknowledge this history as we enter into such a delicate, shifting subject like diversity. Without knowing where we have been, there is no path to know where we should go next. We acknowledge diversity as the adjective, the idea that we are different. But, our task in this book is to devise ways to think about a deliberate marriage contract between diversity and inclusion. To those who read this book as philosophers and thinkers, our goal is to offer a review of theoretical notions of diversity in higher education with a call toward empowering new thinking on the topic. For those who read this text as seasoned or emerging researchers, we attempt to provide a synthesis of a vast body of research that has been done on diversity on college campuses. For those who read this book as practitioners, administrators, and do-ers, we hope to offer practical ideas, insights, suggestions, and calls for your action in order to make diversity and inclusion go hand in hand on college campuses. For those who are not sure yet where you fit in the diversity-and-inclusion action plan, our desire is that you might be able to figure out your own path toward enacting these ideas, even if only in your own life. And finally, for those students, staff, faculty, or administrators who maybe never felt like higher education legitimately included them, we hope the book can be at least one step in the process of helping you to feel less alienated, marginalized, and alone because ultimately, in order to enact diversity-and-inclusion, we must all be in this together.

We emphasize race and ethnicity in this book, highlighting action toward racial/ethnic diversity-and-inclusion in the student population in higher education. We do this not as a way to claim that other categories and identities such as gender, socioeconomic status, religion, ability/disability, or sexual orientation are unimportant; rather we attempt to bring in these categories whenever possible. But we focus on race/ethnicity here because we stand in a time when *Race [STILL] Matters* (West, 1993/2001).

Even as we craft this very argument, we cannot turn away from the current reality that skin color still imposes upon many people the script they feel allowed to enact in their lives. Examining the U.S. Census data, we learn that race and ethnicity still predicts the likelihood that a child will grow up in poverty (U.S. Census Bureau, 2012a). Black and Hispanic children are almost twice as likely to be living in poverty than are White children, and these racial gaps have not shifted all that much in nearly 30 years (U.S. Census Bureau, 2012a).[1] Race and ethnicity still predicts the students with whom a child will attend school; schools continue to be racially segregated in many cities, states, and regions (Ross et al., 2012). And the color of a person's skin continues to be a predictor of whether that child will go to college and earn a degree (Ross et al., 2012). *Race still matters.* We point our book in that direction as a way to continue our collective journey toward hopefully, one day, making race matter less as a predictor of inequity.

THOSE WHO PAINTED THE SCENERY: REFLECTIONS ON DIVERSITY IN HIGHER EDUCATION

We enter a dialogue about diversity in higher education that has been going on loudly since at least the 1960s, and arguably, in one form or another since the passage of the Morrill Act of 1890 that allocated land to some states so that colleges and universities could be constructed to serve African American students in Southern states where these students were legally disallowed to enroll in the state institutions. A review of the work that synthesizes the topic of diversity in higher education uncovers three general topics. Scholarship on diversity in higher education has explored: diversity of students and how to better understand them and serve new populations, ideas for administrators and faculty who teach and work with diversity on campuses, and structural approaches that aim to explore higher education diversity as emblematic of larger socio-structural issues.

The scholarship about student diversity generally attempts to understand unique challenges faced by students from various subpopulations or groups (e.g., African American, Latina/o, students with disabilities, gay students, etc.; Adams, Hackman, Peters, & Zúñiga, 2000). One area of research on diversity in higher education puts the spotlight on ways to teach majority group students, such as White students on many college campuses, how to better interact with students who are different from them in order to help these students work in diverse settings after college (Engberg, 2007; Jayakumar, 2008). A counterpoint to the scholarship on diversity education for majority students is to inquire into students who are not in the majority groups, called "diverse" students by some authors because of their positions as being in the minority in many campus contexts (Bonner, Marbley, & Howard-Hamilton, 2011).

Another area of discussion on diversity in higher education places campus leaders, teachers, or administrators in the lead role of facilitating a better path toward embracing diversity on college campuses. For example, some of these works primarily study administrators' experiences in facilitating successful diversity initiatives on college campuses (Bonner et al., 2011; Brown-Glaude, 2008; Hurtado, Milem, Clayton-Pedersen, & Allen, 1999). Other scholars have offered ways to move to *Multiculturalism on Campus,* asserting that higher education professionals, including staff and faculty, should adopt multicultural competencies (e.g., awareness, knowledge, and ability to work with people who are different than oneself) as a way to help campuses to be more inclusive (Cuyjet, Howard-Hamilton, & Cooper, 2011). Still others highlight ways to structure teaching to meet the needs of diversity and inclusion in the classroom and on college campuses more generally, with a faculty audience in mind (Grace & Gravestock, 2009).

A third line of research offers a view of the larger scenery of society and social structures as a way to reveal what might be happening with diversity on college campuses. Some scholars in this area call for an institutional focus on diversity instead of a gaze toward students in order for *Diversity's Promise for Higher Education* to work (Smith, 2009). For example, Stulberg, Weinberg, and their contributors (2011) provided a synthesis of the way that inequities in higher education connect with primary and secondary school inequality and larger social inequalities (racism, sexism, homophobia, poverty, etc.). Maher and Tetreault (2007) use institutional ethnography with three institutions (Rutgers University, Stanford University, and the University of Michigan) to reveal ways that *Privilege and Diversity in the Academy,* are manifested from admissions decisions for students, to diversifying the faculty, to institutional conversations about issues like excellence.

We take a slightly different approach in this book, connecting diversity with action, specifically, the act of inclusion. We root our work in an intersectional approach (Crenshaw, 1991; Collins, 2000; hooks, 2000) that initiated with critical race feminist scholars who called to view categories of race, class, and gender as overlapping (Shields, 2008; Zinn & Dill, 1994). Crenshaw's work with violence against women of color offered the word "intersectionality" to encompass this kind of thinking (Crenshaw, 1991; Crenshaw, Gotanta, Peller, & Thomas, 1996). Intersectionality is a way of making explicit the manner in which people's experiences and identities cannot be parsed out into separate categories (such as race, gender, etc.). Within this way of thinking, issues such as oppression, discrimination, subjugation, and domination are called to the forefront. In other words, as scholars using this approach, it would be important to not only think about categories like race, class, gender, or sexual orientation, but, to also consider how history and power structures might influence people's experiences of those categories. In other words, a person who self-identifies as Black in the United States may have family memories of slavery, overt racism, or racial discrimination. An intersectional approach would require that one take this history into account when thinking about race. But, it would also require that one go deeper than the racial category and think about how one's gender, class, or sexual orientation might also influence racial experiences. Part of taking an intersectional approach is an attempt not to privilege ethnicity/race over other identities (e.g., hooks, 1981, 2000; Hurtado, 1996). It is also important to note that within this approach, anyone, regardless of their group membership(s) can be marginalized, depending on the context in which one finds oneself (hooks, 1981, 2000; Hurtado, 1996).

We do want to note here that our analyses are unlikely to wholly represent all students who feel underrepresented in college. For example, many students with physical or mental disabilities may be underrepresented. Other students feel underrepresented and are marginalized because of their sexual identity as lesbian, gay, bisexual, transgender, or questioning (LGBTQ). Still other students likely feel underrepresented because of their religious backgrounds as Christian, Muslim, Buddhist, Hindu, Jewish, or other religious beliefs. While ability issues, sexual orientation and religious issues are woven in when possible, this is not our primary focus here. We do hope that future books might take up where we leave off, contemplating gender, disability/ability, sexual orientation, or religion in greater depth and detail. We also encourage future efforts to contemplate different actors in more detail such as staff, faculty, or policymakers.

A VIEW OF THE CAST FOR DIVERSITY-AND-INCLUSION: WHO GETS IN, THROUGH, AND OUT OF COLLEGE?

As we begin to grapple with the process of getting in, out, and through college, we must first turn our attention toward the cast of characters who are likely to be the next generation of college students. We take a moment to do so in this introductory chapter as a way to set the stage for the rest of this book. There is great diversity in the students who are and will be attending college, hence the issue of inclusion in higher education is of paramount importance.

The racial/ethnic demographics of the United States are shifting, relatively rapidly (U.S. Census Bureau, 2004). As these demographic shifts continue, there are painful reminders of racial and class disparities in the United States. In 2010, nearly one-quarter (21%) of children under the age of 18 were living in families who were in poverty (Ross et al., 2012). For children who grow up with only a female parent, the rates are even more staggering; 44% of children were living in poverty (Ross et al., 2012). During this same time period, approximately 22% of children spoke a language other than English at home. Many students grow up in homes where neither parent has a college degree, meaning that the students would be the first in their families to attempt to go to college (also called first-generation students). Students are much more likely to grow up with parents who hold at least a bachelor's degree if they are White (44% of parents) or Asian (59% of parents). In 2010, the percentage of parents in the home who held a bachelor's degree from other populations was as follows: 20% of Black parents, 16% of Hispanic parents, 18% of American Indian parents, and 16% of Alaska Native parents (Ross et al., 2012).

While there is great racial diversity in the United States, children may not experience this diversity during their primary and secondary schooling. As these students attend school, they are often more likely to be with children who look like them, where more than half of the student population is from the same racial/ethnic group. Even more than 50 years after the Supreme Court ruling in *Brown v. the Board of Education* (1954),[2] when racial segregation in schools was deemed unconstitutional, it appears that schools remain largely separated by racial groups. During the 2010–2011 academic year, 84% of White students attended a predominantly White school, 46% of Black students attended a predominantly Black school, 56% of Hispanic students attended a predominantly Hispanic school, and 23% of American Indian/Alaska Native students attended a predominantly American Indian/Alaska Native school (12% of Asians attended a predominantly Asian school and 13% of Pacific Islanders attended a predominantly Pacific Islander school) (Ross et al., 2012).

This is the cast of characters that will be and already are applying to college and trying to make their way towards completing their degrees. These demographics are important because they illustrate that among prospective college students, many of those students who will complete a high school degree and attempt to apply to college, are likely to be from low-income homes. These students are also very likely to be the first in their families to have attended college. Many of these students may not have grown up speaking English in their homes. Further, many of these students may not have gone to school with or interacted with students outside of their own racial/ethnic group.

Amidst these demographic shifts in the nation, the college going rates in higher education have not changed all that much. Students who are the first in their families to attend college, those from low-income backgrounds, and students of color are less likely to go college (Ross et al., 2012). Yet when asked if they have plans to attend college, most students report that they do (Ross et al., 2012). Of students who are between the ages of 18 and 24 in the United States, White students are still the most likely to enroll in college (51% enrolled in 2010), followed by Black students (43%), Hispanics (36%), American Indians (33%), and multiracial students (49%). More females between the ages of 18 and 24 enroll in college than males (Ross et al., 2012). These numbers, illustrating persistent racial and gender disparities, have not shifted that noticeably since 1980 (Ross et al., 2012).

Of those students who enroll in college, approximately 58% will graduate from a four-year college in 6 years (Ross et al., 2012). But students' chances of finishing college differ dramatically by racial/ethnic group. The chances of graduating for White students (73% completed in 6 years) and Asian students (76% completed in 6 years) are relatively high (Ross et al., 2012). For Black students and Hispanic students, only approximately 50% of students finish college in 6 years. These graduation numbers are important because they link to students' occupational opportunities. For example, nearly 85% of those people who held bachelor's degrees were employed full time in 2010 as compared to people who held only a high school diploma (67% were employed full time in 2010). Additionally, some research finds that median annual earnings increase by as much as $20,000 with a college degree; thus, there are long-term economic gains to be garnered from completing a bachelor's degree (Ross et al., 2012).

These are the students who come to the gates of higher education, hoping to gain access, be admitted, and complete their degrees. These students *are* diverse, representing multiple racial/ethnic groups; males/females; various socioeconomic backgrounds; first-generation college goers; students who grew up speaking many languages in their homes; multi-faceted primary and secondary schooling experiences, and a whole host of other characteristics (e.g., sexual orientation, religion, etc.).

Our concern here is what is being done with this diversity. Are students being offered opportunities to gain access to college, regardless (or in spite of, in some cases) their backgrounds? Are there efforts to include these students who do win access and admission to college? Do students experience these efforts as inclusive to them? What does this diversity and inclusion (or lack thereof) mean for students' chances of graduating college? There is much at stake with these questions. Higher education as we know it is at stake because this is the essence of who will be effected by and benefit from these ivory towers. But, perhaps there is even more at stake than this. Recalling President Obama's 2nd inaugural address that we cited in part at the beginning of this introductory chapter, perhaps what is at stake is the next generations' ability to participate in our country and world (Obama, 2013):

> *That is our generation's task—to make these words, these rights, these values—of Life, and Liberty, and the Pursuit of Happiness—real for every American.*

To allow full inclusion requires progress toward this goal. We argue in this book that higher education is a key player in helping to realize the goal of an educated, engaged citizenry where people can pursue their life, liberty, and happiness. However, this requires action, the action of diversity-and-inclusion.

NOTES

1. In 1980, the percentages of people living in poverty, by racial group were 10.2% White, 32.5% Black, and 25.7% Hispanic. In 2009, the percentages were 12.3% White, 25.8% Black, and 25.3% Hispanic.
2. In the 1954 Supreme Court decision, *Brown v. The Board of Education,* a combination of five cases were pulled together, all filing suit against racial segregation in public schools. The ruling maintained that racial segregation in schools was unconstitutional.

2

THE RACE TO COLLEGE ACCESS

Getting in the Starting Gate

Dominator culture has tried to keep us all afraid, to make us choose safety instead of risk, sameness instead of diversity. Moving through that fear, finding out what connects us, reveling in our differences; this is the process that brings us closer, that gives us a world of shared values, of meaningful community.

—bell hooks (2003)

Access to college is the starting gate, where the story of diversity-and-inclusion on college campuses begins. As students gain access, they take action toward bringing diversity into college campuses. Then, institutions and those within them must enable, encourage, and facilitate this access to college, particularly for historically excluded students. This enabling of access is a step toward the act of inclusion, opening the gate to diversity-and-inclusion.

In the academic literature, college access is typically separated into two categories: academic preparation and college affordability. Nevertheless, access to college is a complicated process that is bigger than these two categories. The issue of access encompasses earlier educational and life experiences that may shape a student's chances of being able to gain admission, enroll in, and matriculate through college. For many students, the road to this starting gate is long and difficult. Students begin their pathway to college in elementary school and each subsequent grade level of education carves out a path that is college bound, or, begins to diverge away from college. Sometimes these educational pathways are the choice of students. More often, within earlier levels of education, students have little choice in the paths that might begin to be laid out for them as we discuss in this chapter.

Families, parents, teachers, peers, and administrators may play a huge role in shaping students' pathways, and students eventually have to contend with whether they will stay on the paths that were created for them, or, if they will go their own way and create a path of their own that is college bound. Some students appear to be on the path headed directly toward that college starting gate, while others may not even know the gate exists.

Access also includes students' life experiences, their backgrounds related to race, gender, sexual orientation, religion, and class. There is clear and consistent evidence that some students have a greater likelihood of being able to gain access to college over others. Students of color, those who are the first in their families to attend college (first-generation students), and students who come from low-income backgrounds are far less likely to enroll in college than are White, middle- or high-income students (Ishitani, 2006; Ross et al., 2012). Examining gender trends in college going, women are more likely to enroll in college than are men (Ross et al., 2012).

This chapter is structured in a way that mirrors the literature on the topic, covering issues such as academic preparation, college choice, and college affordability. In addition to earlier educational experiences and background characteristics that we review here, the issue of access also includes the decisions that students make about whether they want to attend college (also called college choice). Students must first decide if they will attend postsecondary education (either a two- or four-year institution). Once a student has opted to go to college, then he or she must make a decision about where to attend college. Many factors influence these decisions about whether and where to attend college, as we illustrate below. Among the background factors and decisions about where to attend college, the issue of affordability may either help or hinder students' decisions. Some students may desire to be eligible for college, but they may not perceive college as something that they and their families can afford. We review the literature on financial aid and college affordability below as a way to converse about the significant role that finances play for many students, but particularly for low-income students, students of color, and first-generation students. We begin by contemplating theoretical approaches related to the idea of college access.

THINKING ABOUT DIVERSITY: THEORETICAL IDEAS ABOUT ACCESS TO COLLEGE

A few theoretical models relate to the issue of gaining access to college, particularly for underrepresented students, such as:

1. Social reproduction theory: Based in sociological theory, this theoretical work considers how some groups gain social advantages and privileges across generations. This theory has been adapted to the study of college access as a way to stress how social status backgrounds may influence students' likelihood of going to college.
2. College choice models: These models emphasize the decision-making process that students and their families undergo as they decide if and where to attend college.
3. Academic capital formation: This emergent theory contemplates the way that students gain academic, social, and financial access to college by blending together theories such as human capital, social capital, and cultural capital, all of which are explained below.

Social Reproduction Theory

French sociologist, Pierre Bourdieu (1979/1984; Bourdieu & Passeron, 1964/1979) initiated social reproduction theory in an attempt to better understand how social status and privilege were transferred from one generation to the next. Rather than continuing to study economic disparities as a way toward uncovering differences in social outcomes between groups (e.g., educational attainment, career attainment), Bourdieu was interested in lifestyles and the more implicit factors that might affect how people are rewarded or sanctioned in particular social settings such as schools or college campuses. Bourdieu's (1979/1984) social reproduction theory includes four concepts (Bourdieu & Passeron, 1990):

1. Cultural capital: the knowledge, skills, or abilities that are rewarded in particular cultural contexts such as schools or college campuses;
2. Social capital: Social networks, relationships; and obligations that can be rewarded in social settings such as college campuses;
3. Field: The social setting or context such as a particular college campus or a particular school; and
4. Habitus: A set of dispositions that relate to one's tastes or preferences. These dispositions also influence what actions or opportunities that one sees as available to take (e.g., habitus can influence whether a student feels like college is accessible or a viable opportunity to pursue).

A growing group of scholars have utilized Bourdieu's social reproduction theory, and in particular the concept of cultural capital, in research and theory about higher education (see Winkle-Wagner, 2010, for an extended discussion of research using Bourdieu's theory in education). Related to college access, as we discuss below, many scholars have used cultural capital, social capital, or habitus to inform thinking and scholarly work on the decision-making process students undergo as to whether and where to attend college (e.g., Goldrick-Rab, 2006; Lin, 1999; McDonough, 1997; Portes, 1998; Stanton-Salazar, 1997, 2001, 2004).

College Choice Theoretical Models

Theoretical models of the college going decision-making processes typically take either economic (Hossler, Braxton, & Coopersmith, 1989) or sociological (Goldrick-Rab, 2006; McDonough, 1997; Stanton-Salazar, 1997) approaches. The economic models employ a rational choice approach. Rational choice assumes that students and their families have necessary college information, weigh that information relative to the costs (e.g., costs in time, money, distance away from each other) and the benefits (e.g., making more money, gaining status, gaining knowledge or skills) of earning a college degree. Then, the student can make a decision about whether it is beneficial (outweighing the costs) to go to college. The sociological models, on the other hand, highlight economic, social, and cultural issues that may influence the decisions that students view as available to them, or, students' access to particular information that may be helpful in college going decisions.

Economic Models of College Choice. One of the predominant models of college choice decision-making processes, by Hossler and his colleagues (Hossler et al., 1989; Hossler & Gallagher, 1987), initially specified three stages in the choice process:

1. The predisposition phases when a student decides whether to attend college;
2. The search phase that occurs after a student has decided to attend college. Then, the student searches for information about specific colleges; and

3. A choice phase when the student winnows down to a single choice or top choices and makes a decision about where to go for college.

This model of college choice, which is the historically dominant model, represents an economic approach that is primarily rooted in a human capital perspective. A human capital perspective assumes that going to college is equated with gaining knowledge and skills that can be rewarded financially or in terms of upward social mobility (e.g., social status; Hossler et al., 1989; Paulsen, 2001). In this view, the choice of whether and where to go to college is a rational investment where the benefits of going to college outweigh the costs (DesJardins & Toutkoushian, 2005; Hossler et al., 1989; Paulsen, 2001).

Within this human capital perspective is an assumption that the decision-making process is linear and that students have adequate information to make wise decisions about whether and where to attend college. Additionally, there is an assumption that students have access to the information necessary to make the decision (e.g., students know about various types of colleges, such a four-year or two-year institutions, and they can compare programs and opportunities for each).

Subsequent research and theory creation has initiated some questions regarding the dominant college choice decision-making models, specifically for racially, ethnically, or socioeconomically underrepresented students. One reason for this critique is that the cost-benefit approach within the college choice model may not account for differences in social, academic, economic, or cultural influences (Kane, 2006; Paulsen, 2001). For example, Valadez's (2008) ethnographic work with high-achieving Mexican immigrant high school students found that these students did not follow a conventional, individualistic path in their decision-making process. Rather, these students made their college going decisions with full consideration of the potentially conflicting structural (e.g., finances, geography) and familial (e.g., support, lack of understanding) constraints and opportunities.

Freeman's (1999a) qualitative research about college choice for African American students in seven cities indicated that decision-making processes for these students were different than the predominant college choice models would suggest (e.g., choices were less linear and were heavily influenced by families and peers). Theoretical models should allow for differences in cultural contexts, especially for racially or ethnically underrepresented students (Freeman, 1999a). St. John (2006), one of the leaders in scholarship about financial access to college, maintained that the economic approach to college choice may disregard the role that college costs and financial aid may play in students' decisions about whether and where to attend college.

Sociological Models of College Choice. Those scholars who use a sociological approach to thinking about college going decisions attempt to connect family social class, students' individual characteristics, and larger socio-structural factors that may influence the way students decide whether and where to attend college. Many scholars who want to emphasize socio-structural factors such as the accumulated effects that family and early education have on future educational opportunity have used Bourdieu's (1979/1984; Bourdieu & Passeron, 1990) social reproduction theory as a theoretical framework (e.g., Goldrick-Rab, 2006; Lin, 1999; McDonough, 1997; Portes, 1998; Stanton-Salazar, 1997, 2001, 2004). Additionally, Coleman's (1988) notion of social capital has been used by numerous scholars who are interested in the way that familial relationships and relationships with peers, faculty, or staff might help students gain access to college (e.g., O'Connor, Hammack, & Scott, 2010; Perna & Titus, 2005; Rowan-Kenyon, 2007). Coleman (1988) was interested in how families promoted (or hindered) the status attainment of children across generations. He asserted that strong family ties and closed community social networks where people were very connected to one another (e.g., teachers, administrators, and parents are connected) were helpful to students' social capital accumulation. Social capital has been used as a way to understand how social relationships or networks of relationships might help students gain information about college (Engberg & Wolniak, 2010; O'Connor et al., 2010) through parental involvement (Perna & Titus, 2005; Rowan-Kenyon, 2007) or through links to people within the college setting (e.g., admissions officers, faculty, staff).

Academic Capital Formation

As a culmination of numerous research studies on college access, St. John and his colleagues (St. John, Hu, & Fisher, 2011) initiated the still emerging theoretical framework that they called Academic Capital Formation (ACF; also see, St. John, 2012; Winkle-Wagner, St. John, & Bowman, 2012). In particular, the initial development of ACF was rooted in research on college access intervention programs that are geared toward fostering college going for first-generation students, low-income students, and students of color (e.g., the Twenty-first Century Scholars, Washington State Achievers, and Gates Millennium Scholars).

St. John's (2003) balanced access model, which connected students' financial backgrounds and academic preparation, served as the foreground for the development of ACF. St. John was particularly interested in how the most financially disadvantaged students gained access to college. Through the idea of balanced access, St. John contemplated the way that family background and family income might affect students' plans for college; the connection between students' expectations of their high school academic preparation (i.e., the college preparation coursework that they do or do not take); the influence of college preparation coursework on students' college entrance exams (e.g., SAT, ACT) and completion of college applications; and college planning (e.g., taking coursework, applying for financial aid, etc.; St. John, 2003, p. 153). Academic capital formation was used to continue to examine these issues, underscoring students' individual agency and the way that college participation could affect the intergenerational uplift of families or entire groups (e.g., low-income or first-generation students, students of color; St. John et al., 2011).

The theoretical framework of ACF marries the theoretical ideas from the capital theories (Winkle-Wagner, 2010): cultural capital, social capital, and human capital (St. John et al., 2011). St. John and his colleagues (2011) theorize that college going is not only the acquisition of knowledge and skills (human capital). Through ACF, they also contemplate the role of students' social networks in providing resources related to college access (social capital) and the acquisition of culturally, contextually relevant competencies (cultural capital). In particular, ACF allows for the in-depth, simultaneous exploration of college access concerns such as how students gain knowledge or information about college, the way that students can benefit from their social networks in gaining access, views on college affordability, and how students need to negotiate challenges in college.

Adapting Bourdieu's above-mentioned social reproduction theory (1979/1984; Bourdieu & Passeron, 1964/1979), the theoretical concept of ACF allows for a focus on subtle parts of social status such as tastes, preferences, or the decisions people feel compelled to make. Human capital theory provided a way to think about the knowledge or skills that are acquired mostly through formal education (Becker, 1964). Human capital theory is one of the more common arguments given for the need for higher education where the purpose of college going is for students to gain knowledge and skills that can serve the economy. Social capital offered insight into the way that social relationships might be used as resources in particular situations in order to build one's status (Bourdieu, 1979/1984; Bourdieu & Passeron, 1964/1979). For example, knowing a person who has a college degree might allow a student to gain information on how to apply to college. The concept of cultural capital (Bourdieu, 1979/1984; Bourdieu & Passeron, 1964/1979) uncovered how some groups of people gained social advantages and status across generations. We defined cultural capital above as those skills, knowledge, competencies, or abilities that are rewarded in a particular social setting (or field) that gives cultural capital its value (Bourdieu, 1979/1984; Winkle-Wagner, 2010). Additionally, Bourdieu's (1979/1984) idea of habitus, a set of dispositions or expectations that influence the actions that seem possible to take, was used in the ACF theoretical framework. For instance, a student might view college going as simply an expectation, based on their background (perhaps their parents are both college educated). Or, a student may view going to college as completely foreign and out of reach.

Within Bourdieu's theory of social reproduction there is some room for transforming one's social standing in order to achieve upward mobility (Winkle-Wagner, 2010). St. John and his colleagues (2011) were particularly invested in the idea of transformation. They asserted that gaining access to college could work to transform an entire social group. One way that this might occur is through the bridging between the "field" and social context (Bourdieu, 1979/1984) of the family with the field of a college campus (Winkle-Wagner, 2012a). ACF is particularly useful for the research on college readiness and preparation, college choice and enrollment, and giving back to communities or family uplift, among other issues such as how students' achieve success in college (St. John, 2012; Winkle-Wagner, St. John, & Bowman, 2012). In a practical way, ACF allows for the theoretically grounded study of how students might benefit from their social networks of friends, mentors, staff, or faculty. Or, ACF might connect to programming that offers ways for students to develop the knowledge and skills that they need to be successful in college (e.g., summer bridge programs, orientation programs, and first-year seminars).

DIVERSITY STILL MATTERS: LITERATURE ON COLLEGE ACCESS

There are three lines of inquiry related to college access; following the chronological process whereby a student prepares, learns about, and eventually may gain admission to a postsecondary institution:

1. Academic preparation: This line of research contemplates the way that students are prepared (or not) for college in primary and secondary education;
2. College choice: Using the college choice theoretical models, this research explores how students make decisions whether to attend and where to go for college;
3. Financial aid: This scholarship examines the financial resources that students are able to acquire through families, grants, or loans in order to be able to finance their college education.

Academic Preparation for College

Scholarship on college access often relies on the notion of academic preparation, or the way that preparation for college begins in primary or secondary schooling (Tierney, Corwin, & Colyar, 2005). For students from low-income background or other underrepresented groups, this academic preparation may be extremely difficult to achieve. There is some evidence that as many as 71% of low-income high school students are academically underprepared for college (Cabrera & La Nasa, 2001). For some underprepared students, they will not attend college. Others may delay entry to college (Goldrick-Rab & Han, 2011; Rowan-Kenyon, 2007; Wells & Lynch, 2012). According to empirical work on the topic, the path toward academic preparation for college may be created by the perfect storm of family background and early educational experiences and opportunities in primary and secondary schooling.

The Role of Families in Academic Preparation.　Research in sociology maintains the importance of families in helping students to prepare academically for college (Lareau, 1987, 2003). Through their involvement in schooling, families can influence the way students are treated in schooling, and ultimately the way they are prepared for college (Lareau, 1987). Additionally, families influence students' preparation for college through the out-of-school activities in which they involve their children, many of which are increasingly geared toward preparing students with particular skills necessary for college (e.g., motivation, initiative, multi-tasking, time management, etc.; Lareau, 2003). Lareau's ethnographic work with Black and White families from both middle- and working-class backgrounds, found that families who involved their children in structured, formal out-of-school activities had children who were more rewarded in schools (e.g., the reading groups students were involved in, the treatment they received from teachers related to college preparatory coursework, etc.). Subsequent evidence based on Lareau's work found that those formal, out-of-school activities and parenting correlated with higher math and reading scores in children (Cheadle, 2008). This line of inquiry signals that academic preparation for college (e.g., the types of courses students are allowed to take, etc.) may begin very early in the education process.

Ability Grouping, Tracking, and Academic Preparation for College.　Beyond the family, academic preparation for college begins early in a student's formal educational career. The ongoing debate over ability grouping, where students are placed into particular groups based on their academic ability in certain subjects (e.g., math and reading), connects to the issue of academic preparation for college. As students are placed into particular reading or math groups, for example, there is a cumulative effect where they begin moving on the track towards college, or, they do not (Oakes, Wells, Jones, & Datnow, 1997). While some ability groups are fluid, meaning that students can change groups as their academic abilities shift, other groups are not; students who began in lower groups would remain there regardless of their change in ability (Oakes et al., 1997; Rubin, 2003; Yonezawa, Wells, & Serna, 2002). By the time a student is in middle school, he or she begins taking coursework that ultimately places the individual into college preparatory coursework in high school or into coursework that will not prepare students well for college applications. Tracking in primary and secondary education has long-term consequences, setting the course for students' educational attainment (Gladieux & Swail, 2000; Martinez & Klopott, 2005).

Ability grouping, also known as tracking, in primary and secondary schooling has been a particularly thorny issue as it relates to racial and ethnic equity and opportunity. The purpose of ability grouping is typically to place students into homogenous groups, based on some measure of their ability in a particular subject (e.g., math, reading, etc.). But, as we review below, there is great debate as to how these ability groups are constructed (e.g., are they by ability or by other factors such as socioeconomic status?), how permeable the groups might be (e.g., can a student move between groups as abilities change?), and how grouping may influence students' long-term educational outcomes.

Scholars who empirically study tracking or detracking efforts (where schools have attempted to shift away from the most inflexible forms of ability grouping) highlight large racial disparities in the tracks (Oakes et al., 1997; Rubin, 2003; Yonezawa et al., 2002). That is, tracking has historically been detrimental for Black and Hispanic students in particular because they are often placed in lower tracks that ultimately will not help them to prepare academically for college (Oakes et al., 1997). Detracking efforts in schools have often been intended to remedy the blatant racial inequities in academic groups (i.e., where students of color are consistently placed in lower ability groups; Oakes et al., 1997). Still, there remains concern among those doing empirical studies on detracking that the use of tracks in schooling still connects with students' racial groups, with students of color perpetually ending up in lower ability groups (O'Connor, Mueller, Lewis, Rivas-Drake, & Rosenberg, 2011; Rubin, 2003; Yonezawa et al., 2002).

Some of the literature on ability grouping indicates that high-achieving students in particular may experience higher academic achievement in homogenous academic groups, with students who are of similar abilities (Hallinan, 1994a, 1994b; Robinson, 2008). But, Hallinan's (1994a) pivotal longitudinal study that included over 4,000 students in two cohorts, found that while students in higher tracks had an increased rate of learning, the tracks often related to students' social origins such as class or racial backgrounds. Some subsequent studies have suggested that students may do better in homogenous ability groups (Allensworth, Nomi, Montgomery, & Lee, 2009; Robinson, 2008). But, in some cases of homogenous ability grouping, the school resources may be primarily directed toward a few high-achieving students to the detriment of other students who are not so fortunate to be in the high-ability groups (Attewell, 2001).

There is contradictory evidence to the inquiry about homogenous groups, indicating that perhaps students are treated fairer and actually achieve more academically in *heterogeneous* academic ability groups, among peers of varying abilities (Burris, Heubert, & Levin, 2006; Oakes, 1994; Welner & Oakes, 1996). A longitudinal study of heterogeneous grouping in advanced middle school math classes found that racial minority students participated more frequently (Burris et al., 2006). This line of inquiry generally asserts that ability grouping is damaging to the educational chances of students of color and low-income students (Gorman, 1998; Oakes, 1995; Welner & Oakes, 1996).

Ability grouping in primary and secondary education clearly begins to lay a path for students' academic preparation for college; students may experience differential preparation for college. Yet the research in this area seldom makes an explicit connection to college access. Many of the studies on tracking are large-scale quantitative, longitudinal projects. Making the connection with how tracking influences college enrollment and participation would be quite beneficial, both to the study of primary and secondary educational outcomes and to the understanding of academic preparation for college. In addition, future research could contemplate students' subjective experiences within ability groups, and how these experiences relate to students' expectations or plans for college.

Some students may not complete secondary education in a traditional way, opting to leave high school before they earn a diploma. While ability grouping may be one reason for this, research has not yet made this connection empirically. Yet there is evidence that students of color and low-income students have a greater likelihood of taking the General Educational Development (GED) in place of earning a high school diploma (Maralani, 2011; Murnane, Willett, & Tyler, 2000). Thus, one could make the connection that ability grouping may be one factor in students' paths toward either completing a high school diploma or taking an alternative path. Contemplating this alternative path toward access to college, there is some research on students who take the GED test as a way to gain access to higher education. Low-income students and students of color are overrepresented among those who complete a GED in place of earning a high school diploma (Maralani, 2011; Murnane et al., 2000). But students who earn a GED are far less likely to gain access to college, and for those who do begin college, they are much less likely to persist through college than those students who earned a high school diploma (Murnane, Willett, & Boudett, 2000). Maralani's (2011) study of GED recipients in comparison to students with high school diplomas found that students with a GED are more likely to attend less selective institutions. However, between ages 21 and 30, GED recipients are more likely to enroll in a two-year school than are high school diploma holders (Maralani, 2011). A surprising finding of Marlani's study was that for nontraditional students ages 22 to 26, the GED holders were more likely to enroll in four-year institutions than were diploma holders. This line of work is important because it represents a non-traditional pathway into higher education. But, it also offers ideas about nontraditionally aged students. It would be helpful to expand the knowledge base about the way academic preparation influences college access if scholars began to examine the variety of pathways that students might take to get to college. Additionally, a deeper consideration of how tracking might influence students' paths toward the high school diploma or the GED would be useful.

Finally, there is some preliminary work on college enrichment or preparatory programs that may be beneficial to consider alongside the research on tracking. While the debate may continue as to whether tracking is beneficial or detrimental to students' educational chances, some scholarship has revealed that pre-college programs might be able to mitigate the negative effects of tracking in primary and secondary schooling (Tierney & Jun, 2001). Many of these programs target students in eighth grade or higher (50%) or begin their services in middle school (12%) (Swail, 2000). Programs like the federally funded Gaining Early Awareness and Readiness for Undergraduate Programs (GEAR UP) are concerted efforts that might help detrack students. GEAR UP requires that entire cohorts be served and partnerships established between school districts, universities, and community organizations, as well as grants given to school districts to target low-income first generation students. Services to students begin in the seventh grade and end in the 12th grade, although services will extend into the first year in college in the future.

In an examination of one college preparatory program that was intended to help remedy the effects of early tracking, over 67% of the students involved not only graduated from high school, but, they also enrolled in four-year institutions (Tierney & Jun, 2001). More research on ways to mitigate racial and socioeconomic disparities in tracking, such as college preparatory programs, would be very beneficial for the future.

College Choice and Access

There are many empirical studies that emphasize the student and family decision-making process related to gaining access to college. The college choice literature can be divided into two categories whereby a student and his or her family decide whether the student will attempt to gain access to college. Then, once a student has decided to try to gain access to postsecondary education, the student must decide where to apply and ultimately attend college. College choice is a complicated process that is influenced by many issues. For example, Freeman's (1997, 1999a, 1999b), qualitative studies of African American students' college choice decision-making processes uses the theoretical concept of channeling to guide the data analysis, which cuts across financial, social, and cultural capital to predict a student's likelihood of choosing to enroll in postsecondary education. Freeman found that many factors influenced choice such as: economic expectations (Freeman, 1999b); race and culture (Freeman, 1999a); economic barriers, and psychological barriers (Freeman, 1997). Based on other studies, there are a few specific aspects of students' lives that may influence this decision-making process about college, each of which we contemplate below:

1. Social relationships with significant others such as family, friends, or mentors can influence students' decision whether and where to attend college, influencing students' aspirations for college going and the geographic locations students may consider (Freeman, 1997; McDonough, McClafferty, & Fann, 2002; Perna, 2000);
2. The financial background of a student's family may be one of the most important factors in whether and where a student attends college (Freeman, 1997; Perna, 2006; Rosa, 2006; St. John & Noell, 1989; St. John, Paulsen, & Carter, 2005);
3. High school experiences set the stage for whether a student is prepared to attend college (Freeman, 1997; McDonough, 1997; Perna, 2000); and
4. Students' perceptions about the particular campus environment may affect whether they feel welcome to enroll on certain campuses (Freeman, 1999a, 1999b; Freeman & Thomas, 2002).

Clearly, the college choice process is complicated and may be even more so for students who struggle financially, or who may experience college campuses as different from their cultural and educational backgrounds.

Social Relationships with Significant Others and College Choice. There are many people in students' lives, such as families or peers, who may influence their college going decisions. Families are critical players in the college going decisions of many students (Cabrera & LaNasa, 2001; Ceja, 2006; Perez & McDonough, 2008; Valadez, 2008). Parents of students of color have been found to hold high educational aspirations for their children (McCallister, Evans, & Illich, 2010; Tekleselassie, 2010). These expectations may relate to students' desires and aspirations to attend college, which influence their college going decisions (Goyette, 2008; Perna, 2000; Pitre, 2006). Perna (2000), expanded upon traditional econometric models by including social and cultural capital as proxies to interpret expectations, preferences, tastes, and uncertainty in college choice. Such nuanced research makes important contributions to understanding the college choice process. For example, Perna found that when one controls for factors related to college enrollment, African American students are 11% more likely than Whites to enroll in a four-year college or university (p. 136). In other words, if social disadvantages such as racism, discrimination, or financial barriers are removed, the families of students of color may be equally or even more likely to desire that their children attend college than parents of White students.

For instance, Mexican immigrant students described a significant sense of duty to their families (e.g., to support them emotionally and financially) that heavily influenced their decisions about whether and where to attend college (Valadez, 2008). For those students who decide to attend college, parents' expectations for their children have an effect on students' decisions about whether to attend four- or two-year institutions (Cabrera & LaNasa, 2001; Horn, Chen, & Chapman, 2003; Hossler & Stage, 1992). Family expectations regarding whether a students should attend college may influence the student's aspirations for college. For example, in Kiyama's (2010) qualitative study of Mexican American families, she found that families shaped students' beliefs about college going, the information about college that was available to the students, and how the students might later experience college.

Additionally, family influence has been linked to where students might go to college geographically. Some students, such as Latina/o or Hispanic students for example, have been shown to be more likely to feel compelled to attend college close to home, and this often results in students choosing community colleges (McDonough et al., 2002). Other research maintains the importance of students' relationships with high school counselors, who often are key players in helping students gain information about college applications, financial aid, and the types of postsecondary institutions that are available (McDonough, 1997, 2005).

In addition to families, students' peers influence their educational experiences and decisions about college going (Ceja, 2006; Hallinan & Williams, 1990; Perez & McDonough, 2008; Sokatch, 2006). The role of peers is particularly important to contemplate relative to the college choices for racially and socioeconomically underrepresented students. Sokatch's (2006) analysis of the National Educational Longitudinal Study (NELS:88) dataset specified that friends were the single best predictor of four-year college attendance for low-income, students of color from urban areas. In a large qualitative study with 106 high school students, Perez and McDonough (2008) used a social capital framework to understand college choice decisions finding that first-generation students in particular relied primarily on peers, counselors, extended relatives, and siblings for information about college going decisions. These scholars called for a more community-based approach toward facilitating college access for Latina/o students, specifically in order to better incorporate the importance of the many social relationships that these students may utilize in their college choice decision-making process.

Financial Background and College Choice.   There are many individual experiences or factors that influence the decision whether and where to attend college. We offer an extensive treatment of the role of financial aid in college access below. Still, it is important to note the way in which financial background has been identified as an important factor in students' decisions whether and where to attend college such as two- or four-year institutions (Kim, DesJardins, & McCall, 2009; O'Connor, 2009; Perna, 2006; Tierney & Venegas, 2009; Rosa, 2006).

Financial background may be more complicated than simply considering family income levels. For example, in a study of delayed college entry (students opting not to attend college directly after high school), Wells and Lynch (2012) found that parental education levels may be an important predictor of students' unplanned delayed college entry. There are many ways that coming from a low-income background may influence students' college going decisions. High school students from low-income backgrounds may choose not to prepare for college because they view college as unaffordable to them, according to some studies (Grodsky & Jones, 2007; Tierney & Venegas, 2007, 2009). One study of merit-based financial aid over a 10-year period of time found that many students chose to stay in their own state for college so that they would be available for the state-based merit aid scholarships (Orsuwan & Heck, 2009).

Other scholarship has corroborated this finding that financial aid and knowledge of funding options has a large impact on college choice, particularly for students of color (Kim, 2012; O'Connor et al., 2010; St. John & Noell, 1989). St. John and Noell's (1989) path-breaking study, using the High School and Beyond dataset to consider some of the variables which influence college choice for minority students, analyzed the impact of financial aid on college enrollment finding that financial aid had a positive impact on enrollment decisions. Financial barriers must be an important consideration in examinations of college going and access (St. John et al., 2005). As we explain momentarily, one way that financial barriers can be manifested is within secondary schooling, with a lack of resources toward college preparation in some schools.

High School Experiences. As we demonstrated earlier, the academic experiences that students have in primary and secondary schooling may greatly influence their ability to be academically prepared for college. Beyond the academic preparation issue, the experience that students have in high school related to college counseling or opportunities to gain information about college may be crucial to students' access. Students of color and low-income students may be more likely to attend high schools that lack the resources that aid in college preparation such as advanced placement courses or other preparatory coursework, adequate college counseling, or other school resources that relate to college access (Orfield & Lee, 2005).

Inadequate college counseling, for example, has been demonstrated to be detrimental to students' ability to gain access to college, particularly to four-year institutions (McDonough, 2005). A few studies find that first-generation students, for example, are less likely to have as much access to college preparatory college counseling and that these students are more likely to attend community colleges rather than four-year institutions (Gandara, 2001; McDonough, 1997; McDonough & Fann, 2007; Stanton-Salazar, 2001). One of the biggest disadvantages for students who come from under-resourced high schools is the availability of information about college going. For example, students with limited access to college counseling may not have appropriate information on how to apply for college or how to apply for financial aid. McDonough's (1997) qualitative inquiry used Bourdieu's theoretical concepts of cultural capital and habitus[1] to examine the college choice decision-making processes of high school students, finding that some students were taught to consider college as simply the next logical step in their lives (as if it were normal) and other students were taught to see college as inaccessible to them. Students from middle-class backgrounds and schools were more likely to choose to attend four-year institutions, suggesting the importance of considering the socioeconomic status of schools in the college choice process.

Perceptions of the Campus Environment. After a student has decided to attend college, the choice must be made as to *where* to enroll. There are numerous studies that assert the importance of a students' choice of institution (Black & Smith, 2004; Bowen & Bok, 1998; Light & Strayer, 2000; Mayhew, 2012). Students' choice of a postsecondary institution has been shown to influence everything from their moral reasoning (Mayhew, 2012) to the likelihood that they might finish their degree (Bowen & Bok, 1998; Melguizzo, 2009). This decision of the type of institution many times connects directly to whether a student finishes his or her degree program, and only those students who complete their degrees receive the benefits of upward social mobility (e.g., economic payoff; Kane, 1998). Many studies indicate that choosing a more selective institution may increase students' chances of completing their degrees (Bowen & Bok, 1998; Kane, 1998). For example, Melguizzo's (2009) research on institutional quality within selective institutions found that the African American and Hispanic students who attended the most selective institutions were most likely to complete a bachelor's degree than those who attended less selective institutions.

Financial Aid and College Access

A student's socioeconomic background is crucial to keeping the gate to college access cracked open because there are increasing financial barriers to college attendance for many students. For example, almost half of undergraduate students in 2003 were from low-income backgrounds (i.e., those from families with incomes of $37,000 or less for a family of four) and many of those low-income students (48%) were also students of color (Seidman, 2005; also see Chen, 2005). In a survey of students' first year in college, 77% of the participants reported that they were concerned about how they would finance their college degree (Ruiz, Sharkness, Kelley, DeAngelo, & Pryor, 2010).

Finances are one of the most important factors in students' access to and ultimate success during college (Perna, 2006; Rosa, 2006; St. John et al., 2005). The importance of financial resources cannot be underscored enough. Numerous studies over the course of two decades have shown that increases in college tuition lead to decreases in college enrollment (Dowd & Coury, 2006; Heller, 1997; Leslie & Brinkman, 1987). Financial aid has been demonstrated to be vital to providing access to college (Hilmer, 2001; Perna, 2007; St. John, 2003, 2006; St. John et al., 2005) and subsequently, to students' ability to engage in, perform well academically, and persist through college (Bozick, 2007; Hawley & Harris, 2005; Hurtado et al., 2008; St. John, 1991; St. John & Noell, 1989; St. John, Hu, Simmons, Carter, & Weber, 2004; Stater, 2009).

Low-income students, first-generation students, and students of color may be differentially impacted by financial aid when compared to White and middle- or high-income students. Some studies assert that financial aid is crucial for low-income students because there is evidence that students who view college as financially inaccessible will not prepare for college academically (Grodsky & Jones, 2007; Tierney & Venegas, 2007, 2009). Moreover, financial aid is particularly fundamental to providing access to higher education for low-income African American and Latina/o students (Hurtado et al., 2007; Hilmer, 2001; Kim et al., 2009; Oseguera, Locks, & Vega, 2009; Sànchez, Esparza, Colòn, & Davis, 2010). Additionally, financial aid accessibility can be very complicated for students of color who have recently immigrated to the United States (Baum & Flores, 2011). Finances may be one of the main determining factors in many socioeconomically or racially underrepresented students' decisions about whether or where to attend college

(Sànchez et al., 2010). Students of color are differentially impacted by the type of financial aid in their college choice decision-making process (Fenske, Porter, & DuBrock, 2000) and in the process of transitioning to college more generally (St. John, Paulsen, & Starkey, 1996; St. John & Starkey, 1995). For example, students of color may be more resistant to taking out loans and may therefore opt to not attend college, or to attend a less selective institution (St. John et al., 2005).

While many studies underscore the issue of financial access to four-year colleges, financial aid is also an important factor in students' ability to gain access to two-year institutions (Jaeger & Egan, 2009; MacCallum, 2008; Mendoza, Mendez, & Malcolm, 2009). In an analysis of the influence of the Pell grant and federal loans, findings maintained financial assistance positively affected access to and persistence through the first year of community college (Mendoz et al., 2009). Lacking an appropriate amount of financial aid hinders students' ability to be involved in campus activities (Cabrera, Nora, & Castenada, 1992; St. John, 1991; St John & Noell, 1989). This lack of involvement could relate to students' ability to complete their college degrees. Students who do not receive enough financial assistance, are less likely to remain in college even if they do initially gain access (Bozick, 2007; Nyirenda & Gong, 2009; Reyes, 2000).

The growing need for financial assistance is a challenge in the recent policy context. The Higher Education Act of 1965, which authorized the majority of all postsecondary financial aid available to students in the United States, was significant in that it shifted the role of federal funding from the allocation of funds primarily being allocated to institutions to the funding of individual students through federal loans and grants (Gladieux, Hauptman, & Knap, 1997; Hannah, 1996; Keppel, 1987/1997). Since the 1980s, there has been a dramatic shift from federal postsecondary funding via grants to loans (Ficklen & Stone, 2002; Hannah, 1996; Hearn & Holdsworth, 2004). Researchers have discovered that one potential way to increase need-based aid that is intended for the most financially needy students is to consider state-based aid going to students rather than institutions (Toutkoushian & Shafiq, 2010).

Since the 1990s, there has been a shift in financial assistance that emphasized financial need (e.g., grants and scholarships targeted toward low-income students) to merit-based aid (e.g., grants and scholarships awarded based on academic competition; Doyle, 2010; Toutkoushian & Shafiq, 2010). Many scholars have expressed a concern that this shift has constrained access to college, particularly for students of color, low-income and first-generation students (Heller, 2004; Long & Riley, 2007; Orfield, 1992). Empirical studies support this concern. For example, in a study on private institutional merit-based aid, Griffith (2011) found that overreliance on merit-based aid limited access for low-income students of color. In an examination of a state merit-aid program in Kentucky (Education Excellence Scholarship, KEES), Kash and Lasley (2009) found that the focus on merit-based aid over need-based aid was detrimental to student access to college, specifically for low-income students. Yet some merit-based aid programs have increased access to college for students who may not have otherwise attended (Zhang, 2011; Zhang & Ness, 2010). In an investigation of a statewide program in Florida, the Bright Futures Scholarship, Harkreader, Hughes, Tozzi, and Vanlandingham (2008) found that this program had a positive impact on the college going of students of color and low-income students.

State merit-aid programs are vastly different in how they determine students' eligibility for the financial assistance (Ness, 2010), and therefore there is a great need for more research to identify programs that are useful in providing access to college, and those that are deleterious to college going for underrepresented students. Ness and Tucker's (2008) analysis of The Tennessee Education Lottery Scholarship found that many African American and low-income students equated eligibility for the scholarship with the decision of whether to attend college. According to Ness and Tucker, a liberally awarded merit-aid program may provide college access to some students. Still, the debate will likely continue as to where federal and state financial aid should be allocated, to students with the greatest financial need, to students who have demonstrated particular abilities, or to both.

Families and Financial Aid. Many low-income and first-generation families may not have the financial resources to fund their children's college education. A disproportionate number of families of color do not have financial resources to pay for college and may be resistant to taking out loans (Burdman, 2005; Long & Riley, 2007). But a lack of financial means is not indicative of a lack of desire to see their children attend college; research asserts that many families of color have high educational aspirations for their children (McCallister et al., 2010; Tekleselassie, 2010). An analysis of the NELS 1988:2000 (National Education Longitudinal Study) dataset found that African American parents were equally dedicated to helping to finance their children's college degrees when compared to White parents (Tekleselassie, 2010). But, the way that these parents were able to assist their children financial differed based on their racial group: while White families reported that they would use their savings or have their children work during college to pay for school, African American parents reported plans to rely on financial support from their extended families (Tekleselassie, 2010).

For students who are undocumented, meaning that they do not have evidence of being U.S. citizens, financial access to college is even more limited because they will not be eligible for federal financial aid (as they must prove U.S. citizenship to apply). Families and scholarships are the primary sources of financial support for many undocumented students (Baum & Flores, 2011; Diaz-Strong, Gomez, Luna-Duarte, & Meiner, 2011; Flores, 2010; Perez, 2011; Perez & Cortes, 2011). Undocumented students who may or may not be eligible for federal loans and grants, may have to find creative ways to finance their degrees. For instance, in a qualitative study, one undocumented student became a property caretaker in exchange for room and board during college (Nuñez, 2011).

Other studies imply that there may be an information gap about financial assistance programs. For example, Latina/o parents in one study planned for their children to receive scholarships and did not demonstrate knowledge of other forms of financial aid (McCallister, McClafferty, & Fann, 2010). Families have been shown to have the greatest influence on students' understanding of finances (Shim, Barber, Card, Xiao, & Serido, 2010). For example, in a study of Asian American students' decisions about college, Kim and Gasman (2011) revealed that the students' decisions related to finances were connect to the financial situations of their families and with a desire to pay back their families for sacrifices, and this was across socioeconomic groups. But, for students who are the first in their families or communities to attend college, families may have very little understanding of financial aid that is available to pay for college. In a grounded theory study, high school counselors reported that African American and Latina/o parents in particular were often not as clear about differences in the various types of aid (e.g. loans, grants, etc.; McDonough & Calderone, 2006; also see McCallister et al., 2010).

In addition to parents, siblings have also been illustrated to be important information points related to financial aid and college more generally (Ceja, 2006).

Programs aimed at providing students with information about financial aid does lead to higher college going rates, according to many empirical studies (Bell, Rowan-Kenyon, & Perna, 2009; Murr, 2010). However, much more work is needed in this area to provide opportunities to gain information about aid. Researchers studying the accessibility of information about financial aid argue that students of color are particularly vulnerable when it comes to knowing where to find information on both the availability of financial aid and how to apply for it (Tierney, Sallee, & Venegas, 2009). For example, in an exploration of students' financial literacy in California, Gilligan (2012) found that Latina/o and Asian American reported lower levels of financial literacy when compared to White students (socioeconomic status, institutional type, and financial stress were controlled in this study).

The Type of Financial Aid Matters to Student Access. Financial aid, in the form of federal grants such as Pell grants or scholarships that do not need to be paid back, have been shown to influence college access particularly for low-income students (Rubin, 2011). Low-income students have been evidenced to be much more sensitive to the cost of college than have middle- or high-income students (McPherson & Shapiro, 1999). Students of color have been found to be particularly sensitive to the type of financial aid that is offered (Kim et al., 2009). For example, research into the type of financial aid shows that grants that do not need to be paid back are positively related to enrollment in college (Hu & St. John, 2001; St. John & Noell, 1989). First-generation students whose parents did not attend college have also been found to be more sensitive to grant aid as well as the amount of work-study funding included in their aid package; they are more likely to enroll in college when receiving grants (Lohfink & Paulsen, 2005). One reason for an aversion to loans might be that families who do not have a history of educational debt (realizing the benefit of taking this kind of debt as compared to other forms of debt such as credit card debt, for example) may not be as familiar with it. Numerous studies have found evidence that financial assistance in the form of grants or scholarships is correlated to the persistence of students of color once they gain access to college (Alon, 2007; Hu & St. John, 2001; Kuh, Kinzie, Buckley, Bridges, & Hayek, 2006).

Need-based financial aid, aimed at providing the most financially needy students with financing for college, has been evidenced to positively influence college choice decisions and enrollment of low-income students and students of color (Heller, 1999). State-based financial aid that emphasizes the most financially needy students has been linked to greater chances of enrollment in college for low-income students in particular (Perna & Titus, 2004; St. John et al., 2004). In a study using the National Education Longitudinal Study (NELS: 88/2000) to explore the effects of state-level financial aid policy on college enrollment, Kim (2012) found that need-based financial aid positively affects the odds of enrollment for all students in two-year institutions. However, perhaps alluding to an aversion to student debt, in Kim's study, there were differential effects across racial groups: increases in need-based financial aid in the form of loans decreased the likelihood that Hispanic and African American students would enroll in either two- or four-year institutions. Another reason for this finding could be limited information about state-based financial aid systems within these groups (i.e., if students do not know the financial assistance is there, they will not know to apply for it).

In recent years, there has been an attempt to provide comprehensive aid packages that offer financial assistance in the form of grants alongside academic and emotional/social support. Students involved in these comprehensive assistance programs are evidenced to be more likely to become academically and socially engaged on campus (DesJardins, McCall, Ott, & Kim, 2010; Hu, 2010, 2011; Nora, Barlow, & Crisp, 2006). One note-worthy comprehensive assistance program is the Gates Millennium Scholars program, aimed primarily at low-income students and high-achieving students of color. Three-wave longitudinal analysis of the student engagement of Gates Millennium Scholars (Hu, 2011) asserted that comprehensive financial aid packages may influence students' early engagement in college (also see Hu, 2010). Additionally, Gates Millennium Scholars have been shown to be more likely to be involved in volunteer activities (Marks & Robb, 2004) and cultural activities on campus (DesJardins et al., 2010).

While there is significant empirical evidence that grants may be important in providing access to postsecondary education for low-income students and students of color, over half of federally funded financial aid in 2007–2008 was in the form of loans that would need to be paid back, with interest (Wei, Berkner, Lew, Cominole, & Siegel, 2009). However, some students, particularly those from low socioeconomic backgrounds, may not be as willing to take out loans, according to the findings of a qualitative study on prospective college students from different socioeconomic backgrounds (Perna, 2008).

The impact of loans may be greater for some racial and socioeconomic groups. For example, African American students had a higher percentage of financial aid in the form of loans (70% of all federal aid awarded to African American students) than did other racial groups in 2007–2008, particularly Asian American students (whose loan percentage of federal aid was 37%; Wei et al., 2009). These percentages are particularly noteworthy alongside other empirical evidence regarding students' likelihood to go into debt based on their racial group. For example, there are a few scholars who have found that students of color (Native American, Asian American, Latina/o, African American) and low-income students are more resistant to borrowing money to support their college education (Burdman, 2005; England-Siegerdt, 2011; King & Bannon, 2002; St. John & Noell, 1989; St. John et al., 2005). Among that group, however, African American students are more likely than Latina/o or Asian American students to take out increased loans to pay for college tuition, according to some data (Hart & Mustafa, 2008). Students from families with higher incomes were the most likely to take out loans for college, revealing that loans may not be as useful to offering college access to low-income students (Hart & Mustafa). But, the adverse effects of high loan burdens may not just influence access to college. For instance, in a study of graduation rates, Kim (2007) found that higher loan burdens had a negative effect on the graduation rates for low-income and African American students.

In addition to grants, scholarships, and loans, many students work either on-or off-campus to help finance their college education. Some forms of employment, such as work-study (on-campus employment) have been shown to benefit college students in terms of their access to and persistence through college (Corrigan, 2003; Pascarella & Terenzini, 2005; Tinto, 1993). First-generation students are also more likely to work than are other students, according to the results of a study using the Beginning Post-secondary Study (BPS 96/01) dataset (Lohfink & Paulsen, 2005). Where and how much a student works matters. Working more than 30 hours per week (Furr & Elling, 2000) or off campus has been demonstrated to negatively impact students (Nora, Cabrera,

Hagedorn, & Pascarella, 1996). African American, Latina/o, and Native American college students are more likely to be working more than 35 hours per week than are White students (King, 2006; Tuttle, McKinney, & Rago, 2005).

The kind of financial aid that students receive influences how much they work during their time in college. In an examination of students involved in the Gates Millennium Scholars Program, results found that African American and Asian American students in this program worked far less than did their counterparts who did not receive this kind of aid (DesJardins et al., 2010). This is important because working more than 20 hours per week has been shown to reduce students' engagement on campus (Moore & Rago, 2009), course grades and grade point average (Svannum & Bigatto, 2006), and chances of persisting through college (Bozick, 2007). Some research finds that working as few as 16 hours per week may challenge students' ability to develop critical thinking (Bowman, 2010).

SUMMARY: DIVERSITY AND COLLEGE ACCESS

The gate toward college access does not swing open for all students; there continue to be racial and socioeconomic disparities in terms of which students enroll in college. College access is about *inclusion*. As campuses, the larger field of higher education institutions, and policies bend toward helping students who have historically been excluded to make their way to college, this *action* of inclusion can work to open these college gates for students. While the theory and research on college access is substantial, there remains empirical, theoretical, and practical work to be done toward finding ways to extend postsecondary opportunities to students from underrepresented backgrounds.

Think about Diversity

College access thinking is primarily rooted in a set of theories that have been referred to as the capital theories (Winkle-Wagner, 2010): human capital theory, social capital, and social reproduction theory (including the concepts of social capital, cultural capital, habitus, and field). Academic capital formation, an emergent theory, pulls together all of the capital theories, human, social, and cultural capital, in order to theoretically explore pathways toward college access for racially underrepresented and low-income students in particular (St. John, 2012; St. John et al., 2011; Winkle-Wagner, St. John, & Bowman, 2012). Collectively, these theories have provided the foundation for the majority of the studies on college access, college choice, and college affordability.

As previously mentioned, within college choice, there are economic and sociological theoretical foundations. Much early work on college choice was based on econometric models (Hossler et al., 1989; Hossler & Gallagher, 1987). The statistical development of econometric models, used to examine college choice, generally assumes that a person makes a decision about attending college by comparing the benefits with the costs for all possible alternatives and then selecting the alternative with the greatest net benefit, given the individual's personal tastes and preferences. This idea is rooted in human capital theory, the notion that college is about the acquisition of knowledge and skills, and students' must determine the costs relative to the benefits of attendance. Social and cultural capital allow for the study of other factors, such as students' cultural and social background, in consideration of who gains access to college. Academic capital formation (ACF) highlights the way that students might be able to transform their own lives, but, also those of their families and people in their neighborhoods, through college attendance (St. John, 2012).

Future theoreticians on college access should contemplate some of the limitations of the capital theories. Academic capital formation is a good step in this direction, toward re-conceptualizing the capital theories in such a way as to stress the importance of connecting students' cultural backgrounds with higher education institutions (Winkle-Wagner, 2012a). Additionally, ACF underscores the importance of agency, or students' ability to make choices that could ultimately influence their status across generations (e.g., as one student goes to college, it pulls up an entire group; St. John, 2012). But, more work on agency, students' ability to choose, and transformation (e.g., the ability to transform the life chances of whole social groups) because there are perpetual racial and socioeconomic disparities in college access that seem to infer that some groups are continuing to gain privilege over others when it comes to college going.

Diversity Still Matters

Academic preparation for college continues to be an important factor in college access, according to the empirical literature on the topic. Ability grouping or tracking in elementary and secondary school can influence students' likelihood of being academically prepared for college. But, most of the work on primary and secondary schooling is in a silo away from the research in higher education. We recommend more research that allows for longitudinal study of ways that early educational opportunities influence students' academic preparation for and ability to enroll in college. Additionally, there needs to be a serious examination of racial disparities in tracking and how this may perpetuate unequal outcomes in college access, connecting these issues specifically in research studies. Finally, inquiry into the long-term consequences of beginning one's education in lower ability groups (or higher groups for that matter) would help to inform connections between primary/secondary schooling and academic access to higher education.

Relative to college choice, many of the aforementioned studies considered the college-related decision-making process *while* students were making their decisions (i.e., during their last year of high school). It would be useful to capture students' reflections on their college going decisions after they enrolled in college, or, for those who did not attend, after they move onto something other than college. This kind of inquiry would reveal how the college choice process might influence other life chances. Additionally, students are more likely to be able to see where opportunities were gained or lost during the choice process after having time to reflect on it. Finally, while there is a growing body of research that contemplates the non-linear, complicated choices of underrepresented students, we recommend more work in this area. For example, as we alluded to earlier, the growing number of undocumented students and their college going decision-making needs further consideration in the empirical research. Additionally, explorations of ways that students' multiple, intersecting race/class/gender/sexual orientation identities might influence college going decisions would be useful.

In terms of college affordability, there is a vast body of research on the topic, indicating the finances may be one of the primary barriers to college access for many students (St. John et al., 2005). Financial aid might be one of the most important ways to ensure that the door to college access remains open for students of color, first-generation students, and low-income students (Hilmer, 2001; Hurtado et al., 2007; Kim et al., 2009; Oseguera et al., 2009; Sànchez et al., 2010). But, financial aid alone is not the solution because the type of aid matters to student access. Students are much more likely to gain access to college, particularly if they are from underrepresented groups, if they receive grants (Burdman, 2005; Long & Riley, 2007; St. John et al., 2005). Future researchers should continue to study the types of financial aid that appear to be most useful in facilitating access to college. Additionally, amidst changes in federal policies and shrinking state support for higher education in many cases, it will be necessary to identify and study creative ways that students are financing their college educations (e.g., combinations of family, state, institutional, and local support, etc.).

The changing demographics of the United States also points to a need to study ways to provide college access to new populations of students. Continued research on students of color, low-income students, and first-generation students must be done. This work should begin to ponder within-group differences in these populations in particular. For instance, are there variations in college accessibility *among* students who self-identify as African American (or Latina/o, Native American, Asian American)? The research above would indicate that there are likely to be many differences, but most of the scholarship does not focus on within-group differences. Additionally, more research is needed on college accessibility for a variety of populations: non-traditionally aged students (over the age of 21); veterans who may be coming to college after serving in the military and potentially having served in multiple deployments (see Rumann & Hamrick, 2010); students who are parenting during college; student from religious minority groups; and undocumented students who may or may not be able to negotiate a path toward U.S. citizenship during college. Finally, as we referenced earlier, more research that allows for students' multiple, intersecting identities (race, class, gender, sexual orientation, religion) to be part of the college access work would be helpful to uncover the variety of catalysts and barriers that students encounter in attempting to get to college.

Diversity Is Everywhere

Faculty and staff within postsecondary institutions have important roles to play in opening the college access gate. It is easier to let students initiate the call for help on college access; waiting for students to tell administrators and faculty what might be needed in their attempt to get to college. But, for those students who are the most underrepresented on campus (students of color, low-income students, and first-generation students), they may not even know what questions to ask. And these students are very unlikely to know *who* to ask, or *where* to go for this kind of support. We are placing the obligation for college access on federal, state, and local constituencies. Federal and state policies around financial aid, for example, are crucial to college access. These forms and information about this kind of aid needs to be made more accessible and user friendly. But, for the purposes of this discussion, we are particularly interested in what campus administrators can do regarding college accessibility.

For many students, their first experience with a college campus is with visitors from college campuses, most of whom are likely to be student affairs professionals and/or college admissions officers. These first encounters are crucial to offering students appropriate information on college access such as the application process, college admissions requirements, or how to apply for financial aid. College counselors within high schools are vitally important too, but many college counselors are overburdened with far more students than they can possibly serve. In our view, this puts more responsibility on higher education institutions to find ways to reach out to students in middle school or high school in order to educate them about college access. Summer programs, where students are invited to campus to take classes, conduct research, and begin to adjust to campus life, are an important part of this kind of outreach effort. Additionally, there may be ways to offer more community-oriented town hall meetings or opportunities for parents and their children to come to learn about how to gain access to college; these could be initiated by student affairs professional on college campuses.

There have been a few advertising campaigns in recent years aimed at providing ways to inform students about what is necessary to gain access to college (see http://www. knowhow2go.org, for an example). Campus administrators could use such efforts as a guide for how to reach out to students. Additionally, campus professionals might be able to utilize these resources in reaching out to prospective students.

Faculty could also take some responsibility in finding better ways to reach out to local high school and organizations to inform students and families about local institutions. This might be personally rewarding, but it would also be an important service to the larger community. If students felt more connection to faculty, they may experience college as more accessible to them. We offer this idea knowing that many faculty are already overburdened with research, teaching, and service responsibilities. Yet perhaps campuses need to consider ways that this kind of outreach could be rewarded for faculty.

Finally, on college campuses, students, staff, faculty, and administrators should take stock of who seems to be gaining access. Are there faces, experiences, or entire groups of students who are not represented on campus? Campus forums, seminars, and colloquiums might be one venue for discussing these issues and what to do about them. For example, if the campus is lacking certain groups of students of color, there must be a deliberate, campus wide effort to recruit and retain these students.

DISCUSSION QUESTIONS

There are many directions future practice and research could take related to college access. Below we pose some questions aimed at improving practice and stimulating future research ideas.

Improving Practice

1. Why does college access matter to the general field of higher education? Why is it important to consider this topic in a book about diversity and inclusion specifically?
2. What role do you think that student affairs professionals should play in helping students gain access to college?
3. Consider some specific activities or tasks that you might be able to do as a campus professional that would help students gain access to college.
4. Are there ways that you might be able to mitigate gaps in students' academic preparation in primary or secondary schooling? Ponder a few specific ideas that you might be able to implement.
5. How might you influence college choice processes for students who are contemplating going to college, particularly at your institution? Name a few specific activities that you could undertake.
6. Financial aid is important in facilitating college access for many students. Think about the local policies on financial aid at your institution. How accessible is the

information on financial aid? If you are having trouble finding it, for example, this is a clue that there may be an information gap. What might be done about gaps in information about financial aid possibilities for students?

7. One of the major student affairs associations, NASPA (Student Affairs Administrators in Higher Education), developed a set of professional competencies that are encouraged for all student affairs professionals. How might the NASPA professional competencies relate to the issue of college access for underrepresented students in particular?

   a. The NASPA Competencies are (see http://www.naspa.org/programs/profdev/default.cfm): advising and helping; assessment, evaluation, and research; equity, diversity, and inclusion; ethical professional practice; history, philosophy, and value; human organizational resources; law, policy, and governance; leadership; personal foundations; students learning and development.

8. Another national association for student affairs (College Student Educators International) developed a Statement of Ethical Principles and Standards. How might the ACPA Ethical Principles and Standards influence your thinking about what groups of students gain access to college?

   a. The ACPA Standards are (see http://www2.myacpa.org/statement-of-ethical-principles-and-standards): professional responsibility and competence; student learning and development; responsibility to the institution; and responsibility to society.

9. The Council for the Advancement of Standards in Higher Education (CAS) developed a set of standards for student affairs. How might these CAS Standards relate to the issues of college access that were reviewed in this chapter?

   a. The domains for the CAS Standards are (see http://www.cas.edu/index.php/cas-general-standards/): knowledge acquisition, integration, construction, and application; cognitive complexity; intrapersonal development; interpersonal competence; humanitarianism and civic engagement; practical competence.

Developing Future Research

1. Name some of the strengths and limitations of the current theoretical frameworks that are predominantly used to study college access (e.g., human capital theory, cultural capital theory, social capital theory).

2. What theories or ideas might be useful to expand theoretical ideas about college access? If you cannot think of any, how might you go about collecting this information?

3. As you consider the role that academic preparation in K-12 education plays in college accessibility, what gaps do you see in the current research? How might you construct a study that could fill some of those gaps?

4. Examining college choice, specifically for underrepresented students, what limitations do you see in the current body of research that was presented here? What studies might be useful to expand the knowledge base on college choice for these students?

5. As you look at the large body of research on financial aid, what remains to be done on the topic relative to college student access? Outline a study that you might be able to conduct on the topic of college affordability.

====================A CASE STUDY====================

PRACTICING DIVERSITY ISSUES RELATED TO COLLEGE ACCESS

College Choice for One High Achieving Undocumented Dreamer

COURTNEY LUEDKE, UNIVERSITY OF WISCONSIN

The decision of where to attend college weighs heavily for many families. Oftentimes, families have always expected college as the next step, ensuring their son or daughter took the necessary preparatory courses in high school which results in multiple admissions offers to choose from; while others who entered the college planning game in their junior or senior year may be more limited in their college acceptance choices. For the Aviles family, college had always been a dream that the parents had for their children. The Aviles family talked about college as an expectation, not a choice. Little did they know how difficult this dream would be to become a reality for their eldest undocumented daughter.

Although college was always an expectation in this family, they were less informed about what it was their eldest daughter needed to do to attend college. When Lucia enrolled in high school, Mrs. Aviles made an appointment with the college counselor to express her desire for her daughter to become prepared for college. It was 4 weeks before Mrs. Aviles was able to actually speak with the college counselor because of several cancelled and rescheduled appointments on the counselors end. During the meeting, in which Mrs. Aviles had her daughter translate for her, Mrs. Aviles wanted to learn more about what Lucia needed to do now to begin preparing for college, what courses did she need to take, and what else she could do to better her odds of admission into college.

Throughout high school Lucia had participated in 2 years of pre-college enrichment programs (which she learned about through her Advanced Placement, AP Composition teacher). In addition, she enrolled in multiple AP courses, and consistently did well in her coursework landing her in the top ten percent of her senior class.

Lucia attended a large urban high school which was short staffed, particularly when it came to college counseling. Although Lucia had been meeting with her college counselor since her freshman year (because of her initiative, not that of her high school counselors), it was not until her senior year arrived that Lucia learned about the application process for financial aid. She was disheartened to learn that she did not qualify for federal financial aid as an undocumented student, despite living in the United States since the age of 2. She was in even more shock that she was just learning about this now. Her parents, both field workers, lived on minimal incomes. Without financial aid to help offset the costs of college she did not know how she would be able to afford college. This news came weeks before application deadlines. Lucia had planned on applying to three highly ranked public institutions as well as two private colleges. Upon hearing this news, she began considering other options including attending a community college near home where tuition was cheaper and she could live at home and commute 45 minutes to avoid the additional costs of room and board. In the end, Lucia still applied to her dream school, the state's flagship, where she had been attending pre-college preparatory programs, as well as two local community colleges.

Her acceptance letters to all three institutions arrived in early spring. Later that semester she also learned that she had won $2,500 in local scholarships from her high school. Lucia's parents had also saved and scraped together (through gifts and loans from family and friends) $7,000 for Lucia's education. Her scholarship money and parents contribution could cover 2 years of tuition at the local community college, but was not sufficient for the first year of tuition and room and board at her dream school, which was 3 hours away from home. As the eldest child, and only child born in Mexico, the cost of her education was of particular concern since her younger siblings were born in the United States and would qualify for financial aid.

President Obama and the U.S. Senate have both recently released information regarding proposed immigration plans, both of which include a faster path to citizenship. Based on minimal information that has been released, it appears that Lucia would qualify for a path to citizenship if either of the plans presented were passed. Even if she did qualify for citizenship, the path toward financial aid might take more than 4 years. But, the release of this information has increased Lucia's desire to attend a university so that if she did graduate with a bachelor's degree she would have greater job opportunities and earning potential than she would expect to receive with a technical or associates degree. Lucia has 1 week left to make her college decision.

Lucia's mother scheduled a meeting with the high school counselor. During this meeting, she posed the following questions. If you were the counselor in this case, or someone from a postsecondary institution advising this counselor, how should the counselor respond? Lucia's mother asked:

1. "If you were in my shoes, what would you do? We have borrowed money from friends and family and have enough to cover Lucia's tuition at the local community college. But with an associate's degree what can Lucia really do?"
2. "Lucia applied for all of the scholarships she was eligible for through the high-school, do you know of any other ways she can apply for scholarships for college?"

In addition, Lucia schedules a meeting with the director of her pre-college program to discuss her options. The main concerns that she raises include:

1. She wants to attend the university, however she only has enough money to cover tuition for 1 year. She has crunched the numbers and even with $3,000–$4,000 in additional financial support from her family per year and working 20 hours per week, she would not be able to keep up with current tuition costs (not including the tuition hikes that she has heard about on the news). If you were the director, how might you advise Lucia on how she might be able to financially support her education?
2. Lucia has contemplated attending a community college for her first 2 years of college and saving money along the way towards transferring to a four-year university later. However, she's worried that living at home will be a distraction because of familial expectations regarding caring for her younger siblings after school and on

the weekends (when her parents frequently work). Lucia wants to know how the director thinks she can balance school and home responsibilities. How might you advise her if you were the director?

3. She also wonders about what types of college experiences (if any) she will miss out on by attending a community college. As the director, what might you say?

NOTE

1. Cultural capital is the skills, knowledge, or abilities that would be rewarded in particular contexts such as a college campus. Habitus is a common set of subjective perceptions held by all members of a group or class which shapes attitudes, expectations, and aspirations (Bourdieu, 1984; McDonough, 1997).

3

DIVERSITY AND COLLEGE ADMISSIONS DECISIONS
Adding Ebony to the Ivory Tower

I don't want nobody to give me nothing. Open the door. I'll get it myself. Don't give me integration, give me true communication. Don't give me sorrow, I want equal opportunity to live tomorrow. Give me schools and give me better books, so I can read about myself and gain my truer looks. I don't want nobody to give me nothing. Open up the door. I'll get it myself. We got talents we can use on our side of town. Let's get our heads together and build it up from the ground.

—James Brown, 1960, The Godfather of Soul,
"I don't want nobody to give me nothing." (cited in King, 2005)

As if it were a decision of which bricks to use in building the towers of college campuses, college admissions decisions have the power to determine the construction of higher education. These admissions decisions are inherently actionable choices. Admissions decisions are actions. These actions either work toward the inclusion of diversity on campuses, or, they reinforce exclusion. Diversity-and-inclusion simply cannot be manifested without contemplating the role that admissions decisions had in the process of building the campus, as if it were brick by brick, student by student.

The college admissions process epitomizes the national tension about how to diversify the student populations of college campuses. As a scholar who spent 18 months as a participant observer of admissions in an elite institution aptly noted, college admissions is a difficult, complicated process that often advantages those in society who have experienced social privilege (Stevens, 2009). Historical analysis also mirrors this point. Since the passing of the Higher Education Act in 1965, which initiated the possibility of basing part of the admissions decision-making process on race and/or gender, there have been contentious debates about how to best promote equity and diversity in institutions of higher education. Affirmative action policy was initiated with a hope of at least partially remedying past racial inequality (Bowen & Bok, 1998; Moses, 2010). On the one hand, is an argument that college admissions decisions should be based entirely on students' merits, or, the demonstrated educational potential or abilities that students bring with them to campus. On the other hand, is an assertion that past injustices related to exclusion based on race cannot be remedied without policy (e.g., affirmative action) to support race and sometimes gender as a part of the admissions process. Merit may appear to be an appropriate way to assess candidates for college admissions. But given historical and current racial injustices in education such as racial disparities in enrollment and graduation rates in college (NCES, 2011), the benchmark of merit is not equally able to be achieved by all. Ultimately, this debate over college admissions processes continues with the passage of state ballot initiatives and Supreme Court rulings that have forbidden race as a factor in college admissions within public postsecondary institutions in multiple states (Moses, 2010; Moses & Saenz, 2008; Moses, Yin, & Marin, 2009). As the debate persists, race has started disappearing from college admissions policy-making discussions in many instances (Winkle-Wagner, Sulè, & Maramba, 2012).

This chapter explores the college admissions process related to diversity. We contemplate the theoretical assumptions of the college admissions debate, whether admissions should be based solely on merit or on other factors such as background, race, or gender. We pay particular attention here toward race-based college admissions processes because this is an area that has been heavily debated and contested in the last few decades. Then, we explore alternative ways of handling admissions such as class-based affirmative action or percentage plans where students who graduate in a particular percentage of their high school class are guaranteed college admission. But, first we need to offer a bit of context related to the history of college admissions in the United States.

HISTORICAL CONTEXT OF DIVERSITY AND COLLEGE ADMISSIONS PROCESSES

Before the Civil War (1861–1865), even selective colleges in the United States were not selective in their admissions processes (Schmidt, 2007), at least if the applicants were White and male (women and students of color were still largely excluded from admissions to most institutions). Land-grant institutions, initiated by the Morrill Act in 1862[1] were, in their inception, places of open access in order to train their states citizenry, particularly in agriculture. Yet even land-grant institutions were not that inclusive to students of color in the 1800s, providing the necessity for a second Morrill Act in 1890 that provided land and money for historically Black public institutions to educate some states' Black students.

In spite of normalizing the use of standardized tests with a history of deliberate racial exclusion as the primary college admissions gatekeeper, after World War II, the GI Bill was signed into law in 1944. This policy guaranteed that college would be free for returning war veterans and led to one of the biggest booms in college admissions in the nation's history (Schmidt, 2007). In 1961, President John F. Kennedy used the phrase "affirmative action" and made an executive order to require government agencies to stop discrimination in hiring practices (Moses, 2002). Then, in 1964, the Civil Rights Act was passed, making it illegal for any federally assisted program to discriminate on the basis of race (Moses, 2002). By the mid-1960s, many public and private institutions implemented affirmative action policies for hiring of faculty and staff and aimed at diversifying their campuses relative to female and racially underrepresented students.

In 1978, in the Supreme Court case, *Regents of the University of California v. Bakke,* the decision maintained that race could be a factor in admissions as long as the use of race was for the purpose of ensuring the diversity of postsecondary institutions. Since *Bakke*, the United States has experienced a flurry of hotly contested policies, protests, state ballot initiatives, and Supreme Court rulings related to college admissions decision-making policy (Moses & Saenz, 2008). Meanwhile, starting in the 1980s, the U.S. News and World Report began to reinforce the scholastic Aptitude Test (SAT) as one of the primary markers for postsecondary institutions' selectivity and quality (McDonough, Lising, Walpole, & Perez, 1998).

By the 1990s, there were multiple state ballot initiatives (Michigan, 2006; Nebraska, 2008; Colorado, 2008) and court rulings barring the use of affirmative action in college admissions processes (Moses, 2010; Moses et al., 2009; Moses & Saenz, 2008). There is evidence that many institutions stopped using affirmative action in their admissions processes after the mid-1990s (Grodsky & Kalogrides, 2008). For example, Proposition 209, the California Civil Rights Initiative (CCRI in 1996) banned race as a factor in college admissions decisions in California (Kahlenberg, 1997). In the southern states, in the case of *Hopwood v. Texas,* 1996, the U.S. Court of Appeals for the Fifth Circuit (with jurisdiction of Texas, Louisiana, and Mississippi) ruled that quotas based on racial categories or race preferences to promote diversity was illegal (Kahlenberg, 1997; Orentlicher, 1998). In 2003, the Supreme Court ruled on a case from Michigan, *Grutter v. Bollinger,* where a White woman was denied admission into the Michigan Law School and claimed it was because she was not a person of color. The decision essentially reaffirmed that it was legal to use race in college admissions if it was used for the purpose of diversifying the student body. But, this ruling went one step farther to also consider the role that student diversity could play in the larger democratic society (i.e., training diverse individuals in higher education leads to more people who can fully participate in society). The companion case to *Grutter* was *Gratz v. Bollinger* (2003), attempted to outline the boundaries around which race could be used in college admissions decisions. For example, the University of Michigan law school had previously used a points system where students from particular demographic groups were given points for admission. The *Gratz* ruling stated that points systems like that used by the University of Michigan were unconstitutional. It is amidst this historical backdrop, that we explore theoretical assumptions related to diversity in college admissions decisions.

THINKING ABOUT DIVERSITY: THEORETICAL IDEAS ABOUT DIVERSITY AND COLLEGE ADMISSIONS

College admissions decisions center on three underlying assumptions, some of which are deeply rooted in history while others are more recent advances in thinking about admissions decisions in light of the goal to increase campus diversity. These assumptions are often implicit in the discussion about how college admissions processes should be conducted. Yet they are the driving force for much of the literature and practice of deciding who gets admitted into postsecondary institutions. These underlying theoretical assumptions are:

1. Higher education is a privilege for those who have achieved merit. College is a privilege that should be made available to only the deserving. Admissions should be based on merit;

2. Higher education should remediate social wrongs. College is the path toward social opportunity and better life chances and college admissions should attempt to remedy historical discrimination, providing opportunity to groups that have previously been left out; or

3. Diversity in higher education enhances education: When college campuses offer diversity in the student population, this argument assumes that all students will benefit educationally.

Higher Education Is a Privilege for Those Who Achieve Merit

One theoretical assumption related to the college admissions process is that admissions decisions should be based on markers of a student's merit such as scores on standardized tests (i.e., the SAT) or his or her class rank in high school (Baez, 2006; Killgore, 2009; Lawrence, 2001). These markers of merit are often considered to be objective and have been a way for postsecondary institutions to bolster their prestige. The underlying assumption of the argument that higher education is a privilege is that students have the opportunity to compete for admissions based on their abilities. The assumption is that competition is fair and that all students have the opportunity (and background) to know how to compete. Underlying this position is the idea that the absence of explicit, formal, legal discrimination is enough to create an equitable society (Geiser, 2008; Goggin & Virginia, 1999; Moses, 2004, 2010).

The idea of merit has also been a way to exclude particular groups such as students of color, Jewish, or low-income students from higher education (Karabel, 2005; Tierney, 2007). The open gates to higher education institutions began to close for many groups early in the 1900s. As Ivy League institutions began to have higher populations of Jewish students, some institutions began to put in place exclusionary policies, in large part to keep some of the Jewish students and students of color out (Karabel, 2005).

By the middle of the 20th century, the anti-Semitic and racist admissions policies became a concern to many institutions as social opinions on these groups became more welcoming (E. Anderson, 2002; Bell, 2004; Lemann, 1999). Many institutions began to adopt the notion of merit as a way to appear equitable. Although the actual practices within many institutions continued to be exclusionary (i.e., deliberately leaving out particular groups such as students of color or Jewish students), the official policies focused on competition for positions based on ability or markers of merit and were therefore hard to contest (E. Anderson, 2002). How could one raise an issue with a process that was based on the idea that everyone could have the opportunity to compete?

Stemming from the psychological "intelligence quotient" or IQ test that was crafted by psychologist Alfred Binet in 1905, the scholastic Aptitude Test (SAT) and other now-popular admissions exams (e.g., Graduate Record Examination or GRE, Medical College Admission Test or MCAT) were initiated (Schmidt, 2007). Even in their inception, these tests were embraced and promoted by those involved in the eugenics movement, the movement with a goal of demonstrating racial inferiority of those who were not White (Schmidt, 2007).[2] By 1947, the SAT and other similar admissions tests were so commonly used to demonstrate students' merit of being admitted into college and graduate or professional programs that the College Board could barely keep up with the demand. As many of the nation's most selective institutions began to turn their backs on racial exclusionary practices in college admissions, they still continued to use standardized test scores as a way to connote students' ability to do well in college (i.e., merit) (Alon & Tienda, 2007; Lawrence, 2001; Stevens, 2009).

Theoretical analyses of the concept of merit suggest that the concept is often *not* an objective measure of ability or potential (Alon & Tienda, 2007; Tierney, 2007). This theoretical argument emphasizes the larger social and institutional policies and norms that may create disadvantages for some students over others (Tierney, 2007). For example, in a theoretical critique of the concept of merit, Baez (2006) argued that many institutions, particularly the most selective institutions, use the idea of merit as a way to bolster their prestige or to defend their own interests. Scholars have called the trend toward standardized tests a "shifting meritocracy" (Alon & Tienda, 2007) because these tests have a history of exclusionary outcomes for particular groups such as students of color (Lawrence, 2001). Going one step further, Guinier and Sturm (2001) asserted that merit is a fictional concept that should be abandoned because of the dependence on tests that do not predict students' potential to perform well in college.

The notion of higher education as a privilege rests on the assumption that the United States is meritocratic and that if people work hard and follow the rules, they will be rewarded with success. Some who feel strongly about this argument may consider affirmative action to be a form of reverse discrimination where those in majority groups are now discriminated against in favor of trying to help those who were historically disadvantaged to be successful (Moses, 2001). This line of thinking offers one of the roots of the contentious debate around whether race should be a factor in college admissions decisions. The reverse discrimination argument is also the one favored by Connerly (2000, 2009) in his attempts to pass state ballot initiatives that ban affirmative action in states such as Nebraska, Michigan, and Colorado.

Higher Education Should Remediate Social Wrongs

The ideology of the United States is rooted in the concept of liberal democracy (Dworkin, 2000; Ravitch, 1995), or the perception that although people differ in multiple ways, we all are unified as a nation. The principal of equality, part of the national philosophical view in the country (Dworkin, 2000), is the foundation of the idea of higher education as a right. This idea is challenging to implement in a country that also values plurality of beliefs and values neutrality in the government where the federal government is also not meant to impose beliefs on the citizenry (Moses, 2004). Some people were deliberately excluded from full participation in the citizenry through slavery, racism, and legal discrimination (J. D. Anderson, 2002a; Bell, 2003). Thus commenced a moral argument (Moses, 2010) that higher education could repair, remediate (Moses, 2010), or offer restitution (J. D. Anderson, 2002b) for some past social wrongdoing through affirmative action, particularly as it relates to the inclusion of people of color.

The argument that higher education can play a role in repatriating past social wrongs such as the historical pathology of slavery or legal racial discrimination (e.g., Jim Crow laws) is one aspect of the debate as to whether race should be used in college admissions decisions (Bell, 2003; Feinberg, 1998). Affirmative action, race-based admissions, was initiated as a way to ban explicit discrimination of individuals (Moses, 2001, 2010). Proponents of this view argue that the use of affirmative action could help to mitigate racial discrimination, therefore increasing educational opportunity (Moses, 2001).

One part of this argument that the use of affirmative action in admissions could help repair past social wrongdoing is the idea that such a policy can help people who were disadvantaged to be able to contribute to the larger society and economy (J. D. Anderson, 2002b; Bowen & Bok, 1998). This is an effort toward the idea of social justice where people who have been historically oppressed are able to become full, contributing citizens (J. D. Anderson, 2002a; Bell, 2003; Moses, 2001). In an analysis of the way that selective institutions may reproduce racism through the idea of merit where people are deemed as good candidates for admissions based on seemingly fair markers of competition, Lawrence (2001) argued that institutions should be focused on reparations for socially disadvantaged groups in his conceptual analysis.

As affirmative action has been challenged at the Supreme Court in recent years, this moral argument of remediating past wrongdoing was found to be far less compelling as a rationale for continuing race-based admissions (Marin & Horn, 2008). According to some scholars, one reason for the general reluctance to adopt the moral view that affirmative action should be used in admissions to remediate past wrongdoing is that there has been a shift away from the social justice principles of the Civil Rights Movement (Graham, 1990). For example, in recent years, there has been a trend toward arguing that while affirmative action was necessary for equity in the past, it is no longer necessary because people of color have made so many social advances (e.g., the argument that President Obama is Black and therefore race is no longer an issue, in the United States). For example, in *Grutter v. Bollinger* (2003) Supreme Court Justice Sandra Day O'Connor implied that in the next years, the use of race in college admissions may no longer be necessary (Ogletree & Eaton, 2009). The shift away from this line of argumentation may be partially strategic, a way to bring others into the argument. Thus, the prevailing argument for race-based admissions has been that diversity on college campuses reaps benefits for all students (Moses & Chang, 2006).

Diversity in Higher Education Enhances Education for Everyone

One aspect of the argument that affirmative action can help to repair past social wrongs is a more instrumental idea (Moses, 2010) that diversity has a role to play in learning and development for students. Some scholars maintain that if students encounter diversity during college, they will be more engaged, democratic citizens (Gurin, Nagda, & Lopez, 2004). In a conceptual study of the meritocratic assumption in the affirmative action debate, Tierney (2007) argued that racial diversity should be one admissions criterion alongside others (e.g., test scores, grade point average, etc.) in large part because of the idea that diversity facilitates learning for all students. The argument that diversity benefits all students has become the leading claim for the continuation of affirmative action in recent years (Zamani-Gallaher, Green, Brown, & Stovall, 2009).

The main argument related to the outcomes of diversity on college campus is that affirmative action then has a role to play in helping to increase campus diversity, and that there will be educational benefits from this diversity (Chang, 2001; Moses & Chang, 2006). Numerous scholars have asserted benefits (e.g., better cognitive and learning outcomes) of diverse environments for the learning of students (Antonio et al., 2004; Chang, 1999, Chang, 2001; Gurin, 1999a, 1999b; Gurin, Dey, Hurtado, & Gurin, 2002). Since the mid-1990s, the view that there are educational benefits of diversity in college has served as the primary rationale for the continuation of race-based admissions (Moses & Chang, 2006).

DIVERSITY STILL MATTERS: LITERATURE ON COLLEGE ADMISSIONS AND DIVERSITY

There is a large body of research that examines the college admissions process and the role of diversity within this process. Here we explore two categories of this literature as they relate college admissions decisions to diversification of higher education institutions:

1. Markers of merit in the college admissions processes; and
2. College admissions decisions within affirmative action alternatives.

Race-Based Admissions Decisions and Diversity on Campus

Since the implementation of affirmative action policy, many higher education institutions have used race as one factor in college admissions decisions as a way to diversify institutions (Bowen & Bok, 1998; Bowen, Kurweil, & Tobin, 2005). Elite institutions in particular were often sites where affirmative action policy was particularly commonplace (Bowen & Bok, 1998). There is a long line of scholarship asserting that race-based admissions are necessary to continue racial diversity efforts within higher education institutions (Boisjoly, Duncan, Kremer, Levy, & Eccles, 2006; Chang, Witt, Jones, & Hakutta, 2003; Gurin, 1999a, 1999b).

One of the primary arguments to emerge from the scholarship about the use of race in admission policies is that diversity on college campuses is beneficial to all students (Boisjoly et al., 2006; Smith, 2009). However, other scholars argue that this argument for race-based admissions begs further examination. For instance, Arcidiacono and Vigdor (2009) did not find strong evidence that the benefits of diversity on campus were that significant for majority group students in their analysis of data from 30 selective institutions.

The empirical evidence related to how institutions have used race in their admissions processes illustrates that many institutions stopped using race as a factor in admissions decisions since the 1990s (Dickson, 2004; Grodsky & Kalogrides, 2008; Hicklin, 2007; Levey, 2004). In a study analyzing 18 years of institutional data from postsecondary institutions nationwide, findings maintained a sharp decline in race-based admissions since the 1990s, particularly at public institutions (Grodsky & Kalogrides, 2008). Some institutions began developing a class-based affirmative action policy to supplant the use of race in admissions processes (Cancian, 1998; Long, 2004b).

In light of the controversy over race-based admissions decisions, some scholars have been involved in research about the predicted effects of developing race-neutral policies that do not consider race as a factor in admissions decisions (Chambers, Clydesdale, Kidder, & Lempert, 2005; Howell, 2010). Examining what a complete elimination of race-based admissions might do to the enrollment of Black and Hispanic students, Howell's (2010) research asserted that race-neutral admissions would decrease public four-year enrollment for Blacks and Hispanics by 2% and at selective four-year institutions, the enrollment of these groups is estimated to decrease by 10%. Sander (2004) argued in the *Stanford Law Review* that race neutral admissions in law schools would lead to more Black attorneys because the students who entered law school would ultimately be more successful (assuming that the students do not merit admissions when race is a factor). However, Chambers and his colleagues (2005) reanalyzed the data from

Sander's study finding that if race was no longer a factor in admissions decisions for law schools, that the number of new Black attorneys would decrease by 30% to 40% per year.

Some research has explored the perspectives of college students related to affirmative action (Aberson, 2007; Inkelas, 2003; Park, 2009; Sax & Arredondo, 1999; Smith, 1998). Women are more likely to be supportive of affirmative action, according to some studies (Aberson, 2007; Konrad & Linehan, 1995; Sax & Arrendondo, 1999). White students have been shown to be the largest student population in opposition to affirmative action (Sax & Arredondo, 1999). As a group, Black and Latina/o students have been evidenced to be relatively supportive of the use of affirmative action (Aberson, 2007; Smith, 1998). Asian American students in one study were split in two directions as a group in their support of affirmative action with some students noting opposition to the policy and others supporting it (Inkelas, 2003). But scholars have discovered that students' ideas about affirmative action may shift during their time in college (Park, 2009; Sidanius, Levin, van Laar, & Sears, 2008). For example, in a 5-year study of students' perceptions of affirmative action, White and Asian American students were found to be more supportive of affirmative action by their fourth year in college, even if they began college in opposition to the policy (Sidanius et al., 2008). Park's (2009) study analyzed how students from different racial/ethnic groups varied in their opposition to affirmative action during a four-year time period finding that Asian American students were more likely than White students to want to abolish affirmative action, even over time. These results argued that while college may play a role in shifting students' views of affirmative action, students' backgrounds still may drive their attitudes toward the policy.

Markers of Merit in College Admissions Processes

One line of inquiry about college admissions decisions examines the factors that are used in admissions decisions. These studies underscore particular characteristics that are used to mark a student as meriting admission into college. For example, Killgore's (2009) qualitative study assessed the admissions process at 17 selective private colleges. She found an almost uniform admissions process that heavily weighted academic performance (e.g., grades, courses, standardized tests). However, she also discovered that these institutions systematically targeted students that would allow them to meet non-academic goals like income diversity and athletic competitiveness. Non-academic goals were important because they "help the college gain or maintain prestige, public legitimacy, or financial stability as well as maintaining the college's underlying traditions, identity, and endowment" (p. 478). Overall, the study specifies that elite colleges are supplementing the test-centric definition of merit in ways that benefit underrepresented students with the caveat that the institution will be rewarded for its efforts. While scores on standardized tests and grade point averages have been historical markers of merit in college admissions (Geiser, 2008), some studies have begun to examine other factors in admissions such as legacy admissions where students are granted admission to college because a family member attended the institution (Hurwitz, 2011).

There has been a shifting idea of what constitutes merit in the admissions process (Horn & Flores, 2011; Long & Tienda, 2008; Winkle-Wagner et al., 2012). There has been more discourse in recent years on the importance of holistic admissions processes where students' test scores and grade point average are considered alongside other factors such as leadership experiences, their reactions to adversity, creativity, or other personal qualities (Sternberg, 2010; Stevens, 2009; Wells, Brunson, Sinkford, & Valachovic, 2011). Yet holistic processes are hard to define (i.e., what factors should be considered and how would they be measured?) and holistic factors may be hard to implement amidst institutional desires for rankings. In other words, institutions report the test scores of the entering classes for decisions about the way institutions will be ranked nationally and this may work to the contrary of holistic admissions processes (Johnson, 2006). Nonetheless, there has been an increasing push for more holistic admissions processes.

College Admissions Decisions Based on Affirmative Action Alternatives

Amidst the threats to the use of affirmative action in college admissions decisions, began a search for race-neutral alternatives to race-based affirmative action (Orfield & Miller, 1998). These alternatives have in many cases facilitated a discourse that is absent of race, meaning that racial diversity in college admissions policy may be disappearing from some discussions as policies attempt to become race neutral (Winkle-Wagner et al., 2012). Some scholars argue that race-neutral policies may not actually have race-neutral outcomes, meaning that race-neutral policy may be detrimental to the college access process for students of color (Geiser & Caspary, 2005; Santos, Cabrera, & Fosnacht, 2010). Findings of a study of the impact of race-neutral policy on racially underrepresented students in California indicate that students of color experienced increasingly adverse impacts of race-neutral policy in their college admissions processes (Santos et al., 2010). Nonetheless, a few alternatives to affirmative action have been used:

1. Class-based admissions policy replacing the focus on racial background to an emphasis on students' socioeconomic backgrounds; and
2. Percent plans where high school students graduating in a certain percentage of their high school class were guaranteed admissions.

Class-Based Admissions Policy. As race-based college admissions policy came under fire in the 1990s, some scholars began to discuss the possibility of using socioeconomic status as a way to continue diversification efforts on college campuses (Banks, 2001; Cancian, 1998; Kahlenberg, 1997). The argument that perhaps class might be the more necessary form of inequality upon which to focus mirrored on a long-standing debate in sociology as to whether racial inequality was still as significant as it had previously been in the United States (Cancio, Evans, & Maume, 1996; Thomas, 1993; Thomas & Hughes, 1986; Wilson, 1978). Essentially, class-based alternatives to affirmative action would stress inequalities in socioeconomic status, targeting students from low-income backgrounds for college admissions as a way to diversify postsecondary institutions (Kahlenberg, 1997). Some assert that the use a class-based policy may still continue racial diversity efforts since people of color tend to be disproportionately from low-income backgrounds (Banks, 2001). Proponents of a class-based alternative offer that this was a way to continue to remedy the persistent effects of historical discrimination in the United States without the negative stigma of race-based affirmative action while opponents maintained that racial inequality would not be remedied with a class-based alternative (Darity, Deshpande, & Weisskopf, 2011).

There remains little empirical work that contemplates or predicts the outcomes of class-based affirmative action (but see, Banks, 2001). In a study using the National Longitudinal Survey of Youth (NLSY) to simulate what a shift from race-based to class-based admissions might do to college admissions processes, Cancian (1998) asserted that many, although not all, of the youth of color who would be eligible for race-based affirmative action would also be eligible for class-based affirmative action (i.e., more youth of color were low-income in that sample). Yet as Cancian found in her study, there is little consensus as to what merits socioeconomic disadvantage in the United States. Sander's (1997) conceptual analysis of the potential of class-based affirmative action corroborated Cancian's point that class-based preferences might be particularly complex because there are conflicting notions of disadvantage related to class.

Percent Plans.   One of the primary alternatives to affirmative action are percent plans, granting admission to college for those students who rank in particular percentages of their high school graduating class (Colburn, Young, & Yellen, 2008; Long, 2004a). These plans have primarily been implemented in Florida, California, and Texas (Horn & Flores, 2003). For example, in Texas, the legislature passed House Bill 588 (H.B. 588) ushering in the Texas Top Ten Percent Plan in 1998, a policy that guaranteed college admissions to state institutions for students who were in the top 10% of their high school classes. The Texas Top Ten Percent Plan was crafted with the idea that many of the high schools were racially and socioeconomically segregated. Therefore, the argument was that a policy that aimed to facilitate merit-based admission to college for students from each of the high schools would also work to create diversity in the admissions process, supplanting affirmative action policy with an officially race-neutral policy (Tienda & Niu, 2006a, 2006b; Tienda & Sullivan, 2010). In 2009, the Texas legislature passed a revision to the Texas Top Ten Percent plan (Senate Bill 175), maintaining that once an institution had admitted 75% of the first-year class based on the Texas Top Ten Percent plan, the remaining 25% of students could be admitted based on other factors such as SAT scores, extracurricular involvement, or special talents or abilities (Falick, 2009).

After the *Hopwood* (1996) decision banned affirmative action and led to implementation of the Texas Top Ten Percent Plan, the enrollment of students of color in Texas postsecondary institutions dropped dramatically (Bell, 2004; Finnell, 1998). The empirical evidence about the outcomes of the Texas Top Ten Percent Plan relative to diversification of college campuses concludes that this policy has not served as a suitable alternative to race-based affirmative action in fostering racial diversity in the college admissions processes in the state (Backes, 2012; Harris & Tienda, 2010; Long, 2004b, 2007; Tienda, Leicht, Sullivan, Maltese, & Lloyd, 2003). For example, in a study of UT-Austin and Texas A&M, findings showed that the Texas Top Ten Percent Plan was not able to help restore Black and Latina/o college enrollment to the levels from when affirmative action was used (Harris & Tienda, 2010). There are similar findings for other states that employed percent plans (Colburn et al., 2008). For example, in California, the percentage of freshmen enrollment of Black, Hispanic, and Asian students remained flat after the percent plan was initiated (Horn & Flores, 2003). In Florida, the percentage of Black students enrolled in higher education remained the same for four years after the implementation of the percent plan. While the plan has been the primary college admissions policy in Texas since the late 1990s, the University of Texas at Austin (UT Austin) was also using race-sensitive admissions since 2006 and there is evidence to signaling that this has increased Black freshman enrollment in particular (Lewin, 2007).

There have been many criticisms of the Texas plan and percent plans in other states like Florida and California. One criticism is the dependence within the policy on housing and school segregation (Tienda & Niu, 2006a). A related criticism is that the Texas

Top Ten Percent Plan does not account for inequities within K-12 education in the way that affirmative action may have done (Thompson & Tobias, 2000; Winkle-Wagner et al., 2012a).

According to some evidence, there may not be enough Black and Hispanic students in particular in the top 10% of their high school classes for the policy to be used as a way to diversify Texas institutions (Long, 2004b). Other research argues that the policy has been damaging to the college admission of those Black and Hispanic students who are still high achieving (10%–20% class rank in particular), but not in the top 10% of their graduating class in high school classes (Tienda et al., 2003). According to an analysis of 20 years of Texas postsecondary institutional data, the plan may also be detrimental to students from particular high schools, such as those in rural areas or those with a large number of students of color and low-income students (Long, Saenz, & Tienda, 2006). There is also some research asserting that financial aid might be an important supplement to the Texas Top Ten Percent Plan, particularly for helping students of color access postsecondary institutions (Long & Tienda, 2008; Tienda & Niu, 2006).

Alternatives to affirmative action not only influence admissions process at the undergraduate level. More recent work has also contemplated the way that percent plans, for example, influence admissions decisions at the graduate and professional school levels (Attiyeh & Attiyeh, 1997; Cross & Slater, 1997; Garces, 2012a, 2012b; Law-Sander, 2004). In an analysis of the impact of *Grutter v. Bollinger* (2003) on the enrollment of students of color in Texas graduate programs, Garces' (2012a) research asserted that the allowance for the use of race in these admissions decisions did increase the enrollment rates for students of color. Some scholars argue that if race-based admissions were not used in graduate programs, Black students in particular would be excluded (Cross & Slater, 1997).

Most of the studies on affirmative action alternatives such as the percent plans are quantitative. There is very limited inquiry into students' perceptions of college admissions processes and policies in the states that have the percent plans. Additionally, there is little work on the way that parents are encountering or interpreting the Texas Top Ten Percent Plan and this work would be useful because parents often play an important role in students' decision-making about college. Finally, in spite of the hotly contested terrain of law school and medical school admissions, there is a relatively small number of research studies (but see, Garces, 2012a, 2012b). There is also not much research into the way that affirmative action has been used within doctoral or master's programs.

SUMMARY: DIVERSITY AND COLLEGE ADMISSIONS

Diversity and the college admissions decision-making process make strange bed partners in many instances. While administrators and faculty in many institutions may desire to diversify their incoming classes, the details of how to make this diversity happen have been painstaking to implement. Affirmative action allowed a way to use race as one of many factors in the admissions process. But, the use of race-based admissions is and likely will be under fire, making the diversity-and-inclusion goal a difficult one to reach deliberately through the admissions process. Still, we maintain that diversity is something to continue to think about in college admissions because these decisions can represent an action toward inclusion, or, in some cases, toward exclusion.

Think about Diversity

College admissions have been predicated on divergent ideologies. The first assumes that higher education is a privilege; students have the opportunity to compete for college admissions based on their merit. While this idea seems fair, it assumes that students have equal opportunities to compete. This assumes that students are equally prepared in primary and secondary schooling so that they have the same opportunity to demonstrate their abilities through standardized admissions tests, for instance. Or, this assumes that students have the same knowledge of what they need to do to compete for admissions (e.g., taking appropriate coursework in high school, applying for financial aid, etc.). Then, there is another branch in the philosophical debate about college admissions, the idea of remediation, that higher education should play a role in repairing or remediating social wrongdoing. Affirmative action stems at least in part from this philosophy. Finally, is the argument that diversity on college campuses benefits the education of all students and should therefore be encouraged (Antonio et al., 2004; Chang, 1999, 2001; Gurin, 1999a, 1999b; Gurin et al., 2002).

There are moral and instrumental arguments within these divergent philosophical debates about college admissions (Moses, 2010). The moral arguments relate to the idea that higher education should be a right, or that society should play a role in remedying past wrongs. Otherwise society should be created in such a way as to value individual opportunity to compete (meritocracy), the notion of higher education as a privilege. The instrumental argument is about the benefits of diversity (as an educational benefit). Future theoretical work should contemplate if there are ways to marry the moral and instrumental aspects of the arguments. Additionally, is there a way to value opportunity for all students while also valuing competition and merit? This question would be interesting to ponder in a philosophical way for future thinking about college admissions and diversity more generally. Scholars have tried to do this with percentage plans or class-based admissions with less than ideal results, but more thinking and innovation is certainly needed.

Diversity Still Matters

There are persistent racial disparities in college enrollments, particularly for Black and Hispanic students (NCES, 2011). The empirical evidence related to the use of race in college admissions decisions argues that affirmative action has played a significant role in helping to provide postsecondary access for students of color (Backes, 2012; Hicklin, 2007; Hinricks, 2012). The race-neutral alternatives to affirmative action are less compelling in terms of helping to continue campus diversity efforts (Chambers et al., 2005; Howell, 2010). For example, there is mixed evidence as to whether percent plans such as the Texas Top Ten Percent plan have been successful in fostering racial diversity on campus in Texas institutions (Long & Tienda, 2008; Tienda & Niu, 2006a, 2006b). There is yet to be much empirical evidence about class-based alternatives to affirmative action. Future work could contribute by investigating the outcomes (or predicted outcomes) of these policies.

Diversity Is Everywhere

Amidst the many challenges to affirmative action, policymakers, admissions officers, faculty, and other campus administrators are going to need to find ways to deliberately contemplate how to continue diversification efforts. Campus administrators will need to think about their own stance on how college admissions should be conducted and then contemplate how this relates (or doesn't) to those used on the campuses in which they work. If diversity is a goal, administrators will need to think seriously about admissions decision-making and the role that diversity will play in the admissions process. Will race be a factor in admissions decisions? If so, administrators and policymakers must consider what role race can legally play (e.g., one of many factors, but, not quotas), given their state context and the shifting federal rulings on the topic.

If race cannot be a factor in college admissions decisions, as is already the case in many states, how will racial diversity be fostered within college admissions? Will states and campuses adopt class-based admissions policies? Or, will there be other race-neutral policies adopted, such as percent plans? Administrators and policymakers must contemplate these questions or diversity is unlikely to be a deliberate goal in admissions decisions. In our view, given the perpetual racial disparities in college enrollment, there is still a great need to consider how to provide more equitable access to college for students of color. In the absence of race as a factor in admissions decisions, campuses have to be very creative in finding ways to meet this goal. For example, the Texas Top Ten Percent Plan was dependent on racial segregation in schools in order to create diversity in admissions (i.e., if students graduating in the top 10% of all state high schools were guaranteed admissions, it was likely that there would be racial diversity if the schools were racially segregated; Tienda & Niu, 2006a). Many of the class-based affirmative action alternatives also have this in mind, that more people of color might come from low-income backgrounds and therefore, class-based affirmative action would perpetuate racial diversity (Kahlenberg, 1997). But, there remains a need in higher education to craft new, creative policies and programs that foster racial diversity and other forms of diversity (class, religion, sexual orientation, gender).

In the absence of diversity within admissions policies, practitioners are left to determine creative ways to foster diversity on their campuses. Deliberate college preparation efforts might be one way to do this; summer bridge programs, for example, that aim to give middle school or high school students opportunities to be on campus in order to understand what needs to be done to be admitted could be helpful. Additionally, deliberate recruitment efforts will be necessary to make institutions seem accessible to underrepresented students (and to help students gain access). Much of the weight of these efforts will likely fall on admissions officers and other campus administrators.

DISCUSSION QUESTIONS

Future work and study on college admissions may take multiple directions. Below we suggest some questions in the hope of leading toward improvements in practice and future research on this topic.

Improving Practice

1. From a practical standpoint, what are some of the benefits to the idea that higher education is a privilege and that students should compete for college admissions based on their merit?

    a. If you were an admissions officer, how might this make your job easier or even fairer?

    b. If you were an admissions officer, what might be some limitations to this approach?

2. If you were to consider higher education as a place where past wrongdoing could be resolved, how might this influence the way you progressed with college admissions?

    a. What are some strengths of this idea?

    b. What are some challenges to this approach?

    c. If you held this view, would you use race in admissions decisions? In what way would you use race as a factor?

3. If you were an admissions officer or someone involved in creating admissions policy, how might you apply race-based admissions in a way that seemed fair?

    a. What might be some of the strengths of race-based admissions?

    b. What might be some challenges to race-based admissions, as a practitioner?

4. If you were to create a race-neutral college admissions policy that still aimed at diversifying college campuses, what might this policy look like (e.g., percent plans, class-based plans, other plans that might be innovative)?

5. One of the major student affairs associations, NASPA (Student Affairs Administrators in Higher Education), developed a set of professional competencies that are encouraged for all student affairs professionals. How might the NASPA professional competencies inform the way you advanced in your thinking about diversity and the college admissions process?

    a. The NASPA Competencies are (see http://www.naspa.org/programs/profdev/default.cfm): advising and helping; assessment, evaluation, and research; equity, diversity, and inclusion; ethical professional practice; history, philosophy, and value; human organizational resources; law, policy, and governance; leadership; personal foundations; students learning and development).

6. College Student Educators International (ACPA) developed a Statement of Ethical Principles and Standards. How might the ACPA Ethical Principles and Standards influence the way you contemplated diversity efforts and college admissions processes?

    a. The ACPA Standards are (see http://www2.myacpa.org/statement-of-ethical-principles-and-standards): professional responsibility and competence; student learning and development; responsibility to the institution; and responsibility to society.

7. The Council for the Advancement of Standards in Higher Education (CAS) developed a set of standards for student affairs. How might these CAS Standards be applied in college admissions decision-making?

    a. The domains for the CAS Standards are (see http://www.cas.edu/index.php/cas-general-standards/): knowledge acquisition, integration, construction, and application; cognitive complexity; intrapersonal development; interpersonal competence; humanitarianism and civic engagement; practical competence).

Developing Future Research

1. What are some of the trends in the research about the contributions of race-based admissions processes? What are some of the challenges to these policies?
2. Given the race-neutral alternatives to affirmative action, what are some of the benefits and challenges to these policies, according to the literature?
3. If you were to create a research study on the use of race in college admissions decisions, what might you do in that study?
   a. What research question would you ask?
   b. What data might you use?
   c. What kind of study would you conduct (qualitative, quantitative, historical)?
   d. How might you analyze your data?
4. If you were to study race-neutral admissions policies, what might this research study look like?
   a. What question would you pose?
   b. What data would be useful for this kind of study?
   c. How would you approach this study (qualitative, quantitative, historical methods)?
   d. How might you analyze the data that you collected?

===================A CASE STUDY===================

PRACTICING DIVERSITY ISSUES RELATED TO COLLEGE ADMISSIONS INCLUSIVITY FOR ALL APPLICANTS

An Admissions Case Study

JULIE VULTAGGIO, HARVARD UNIVERSITY

With an unparalleled balance of historic buildings and lush quads surveying the Pacific Ocean, Western University is as diverse in academic options and student enrollment as it is in architectural landscape. Located 200 miles south of Los Angeles, WestU is home to students, faculty, staff, and visitors from across the globe, inhabiting the majority of a small coastal town called Baywood-Los Osos.

Though the culture is described as "driven and motivated" over "cut-throat and competitive," WestU is one of California's most selective private institutions. With a midsized enrollment of about 12,000 students (9,000 undergraduates and 3,000 graduate students), the institution boasts a 26% undergraduate acceptance rate from over 40,000 applicants each year. The average combined SAT score is 2000 (680 Critical Reading, 700 Mathematics, and 720 Writing), and the average ACT composite score is 30 (30 English, 29 Mathematics, 31 Reading, and 30 Science).

In 2011, the 2,236 entering freshmen represented WestU's most diverse incoming class yet: 53% female and 47% male; 23% self-identified students of color (of those, 52% Asian/Pacific Islander; 36% Hispanic/Latina/o; 4% Black/African-American; 1% Native American/Alaska Native, and 7% two or more races); and 12% international students. WestU undergraduates are spread over five colleges: The College of Architecture, the College of Engineering, the College of Humanities, the College of Business, and the College of Drama and Performing Arts.

As a private university, WestU generates revenue from state and federal agencies as well as philanthropic sources in addition to tuition and sponsored research funds. As such, the institution's operations are not bound by state laws, although its leaders abide by them to the extent possible, including the 2006 state proposal that banned the use of affirmative action in college admissions (Proposition 209).

Since her arrival in 2009, WestU's president Jennifer Matheson, hailed by the campus community as "an institutional game changer," has redefined the university's priorities to emphasize the following:

- Commitment to the STEM fields (science, technology, engineering, and math), which was strengthened by a recent $3 million donation from a prominent philanthropist interested in funding a new biotechnology lab;
- Promoting cross-disciplinary learning, such as the creation of a new joint-bachelor's degree option between the College of Architecture and the College of Business;
- Increasing undergraduate access and diversity, particularly with respect to geographic (both domestic and international) as well as economic diversity;
- Instituting holistic development opportunities for students, including new semester-long co-ops in which undergraduates apply their classroom learning in real-time professional environments (under the guidance of a WestU alumnus/a).

YOUR ROLE

As WestU's Dean of Undergraduate Admissions, your core responsibility is to recruit and enroll each new class of approximately 2,250 first-year students at WestU. You oversee a staff of 16 admissions representatives, which are organized into four regional committees. Each committee recruits in designated geographic locations, and subsequently reads, evaluates, and makes admission recommendations on all applications from the allocated region. The committees are all managed by a senior admissions officer, with a breakdown shown in Table 3.1.

Following the January 1 undergraduate application deadline, each committee spends 2.5 months reading and evaluating applications from their geographic region. The committees then meet every day for 2 to 3 weeks to discuss and make decisions on their region's applicants. Before committee meetings begin, you share target enrollment numbers (based on your calculation of "yield" rates, or the number of admitted applicants who ultimately elect to enroll at WestU) with the committee managers, which they are responsible for meeting—and not significantly exceeding—with the help of their committee members. Additionally, you talk with each committee about the importance of diversity, including demographic (gender, race, geography, socioeconomic status), academic (School and major), and personal (extra-curricular interests) differences.

	Committee 1	Committee 2	Committee 3	Committee 4
Region	Rhode Island, Delaware, Maine, New Hampshire, Vermont, Maryland, Connecticut, Pennsylvania, Massachusetts, Texas, Oklahoma, parts of New York, and parts of California	Michigan, Illinois, Minnesota, Ohio, Kansas, Florida, Georgia, Arkansas, Alabama, Nebraska, Louisiana, Tennessee, New Jersey, parts of New York, and parts of California	Washington, Oregon, Iowa, Wyoming, Nevada, Utah, New Mexico, Hawaii, Montana, Idaho, Alaska, Colorado, Arizona, some international locations, and parts of California	North Dakota, South Dakota, Kentucky, Wisconsin, Indiana, Missouri, North Carolina, South Carolina, Virginia, West Virginia, Mississippi, some international locations, and parts of California

While the senior admissions officers report directly to you, you report directly to President Matheson, who expects that you and your team will support the institutional priorities described above. Additionally, you work closely with other internal and external constituents—such as the Dean of Financial Aid, the Athletic Director, the Chief Diversity Officer, other administrative leaders, faculty members, donors, alumni, and of course, applicants and their families—to work toward the realization of President Matheson's vision of an academically, socially, professionally, and economically successful institution.

THE CHALLENGE

As described above, each committee manager is responsible for meeting defined enrollment targets without exceeding their projected numbers. During the committee meeting period, if managers experience particularly challenging applicant cases and need advice regarding admissions decisions, you are often asked to provide insight. Following one of Committee One's discussions, the manager approached you for consult on a difficult situation.

On the day your guidance was sought, Committee One reviewed applications from two disparate U.S. regions: the Northeast and the South. That morning, the committee began with a discussion of applicants from Maine, and later forayed into applicants from Texas. Toward the end of the day, the committee manager tallied the number of recommended "admits" to share with the group, so they had a sense of how they were faring compared to their enrollment target. When the manager noted that the team was operating slightly above target (meaning they were at risk of over enrolling, even though the final numbers from all regions are subject to your approval), they engaged in a discussion of which, if any, applicants they might want to re-review.

During the re-review process, Committee One raised questions about several applicants. According to the committee members, they were less certain about this small subset of applicants' fit with WestU—with fit incorporating various elements, from academic readiness to concentration interest. The conversation became heated between two committee members as they reflected on applicants from each of the day's states. In helping the committee decide whether to keep the applicants on their recommended admit list, the committee manager asked you to join them, listen to brief presentations by the members who read and evaluated two applicants in question, and guide the team toward a final admissions decision.

After settling into the old wooden chairs in the committee manager's office, you listen to the following presentations by two Committee One representatives.

Applicant 1. Kate Egan is the valedictorian at H.T. Greenleaf High School in rural northern Maine. Kate lists herself as a White female; her father works at a small accounting firm, and her mother is a teacher. Both graduated from the University of Maine. Kate has two younger brothers—one in middle school, and one in elementary school. All three siblings have dual citizenship in the United States and Canada, where their mother was born.

Kate's GPA at Greenleaf is a 4.0. She has two AP exams under her belt (English Language and Composition and Biology), and plans to take three more this spring (U.S. History, French, and Calculus AB). Her SAT scores are 700 Critical Reading, 680 Mathematics, and 720 Writing. Kate writes for her school newspaper (*The Leaf*), and is a member of the Key Club, as well as a reading tutor at the local middle school. She is also the star of her school's equestrian team.

As described in her application, Kate hopes to attend WestU as an English major in the College of Humanities, and eventually become a journalist. She writes, "My dream is to inform the masses—through writing, through storytelling, and through affirmation. In an age when data lies inches away from our fingertips, the world has access to any information we can dream of; the only requirements are an Internet connection and a Google prompt. However, the media relays 'truth' as they see it, define it, and choose to comprehend it. My goal is to understand how stories can be woven into written and spoken prose without sacrificing facts and reality, in effort to help the world make rightly informed decisions."

Applicant 2. Mike Barry is graduating in the top 10% of his class at West Floral Park High School in Austin, Texas. Mike self-identifies as an African American male; his father manages a local retail store, and as stated in his application essay, Mike's mother passed away just 2 years earlier after a long battle with heart disease. His father graduated from Texas A&T, although his mother did not attend college. Since his mother's passing, Mike has worked 10 hours per week with his father to help support his three younger siblings: a brother in high school, a brother in middle school, and a sister who just entered third grade.

Mike's GPA at WFP High is a 3.2, though no AP courses are offered at the school. His SAT scores are 600 Critical Reading, 620 Mathematics, and 580 Writing. Mike is the Captain of WFP High's Varsity Basketball team, as well as Captain of the Varsity Baseball team. He also volunteers, with his father and siblings, at the local parish every Sunday.

In his WestU application essay, Mike describes his interest in enrolling at the School of Engineering en route to medical school and a career as a radiologist. Mike's essay takes the form of a personal journal, including multiple entries spanning the past year. It reads: "May 15, 2011. 4:56 pm. Afternoon with Mom in the hospital. Today's another round of testing. She hates the stuff they make her drink before (I tried it once; it's pretty gross). I made friends with the guys in Radiology. I get pumped when they let me sit in the room with them while Mom's in the machine. It's cool to see what comes up on the screen, and how they can find anything from broken bones to cancer in there. It's like seeing lessons from my Bio textbook in real life! I look forward to learning more about science, technology, and Engineering at Western University, after which I hope to complete medical school and find a Radiology career of my own."

1. Based on the Committee One presentations, what other information (if any) would you want to know about the applicants before making an admissions decision?
2. What would your decision be regarding each of the applicants presented above? What factors did you consider in making the decision?
3. How would you advise the members of Committee One in terms of their next steps?
4. What would be the implications of your decision with respect to the various stakeholders to whom you are accountable?
5. What theoretical assumption of college admissions would your decision represent (e.g., higher education as a privilege for those who merit admission; higher education as repairing past social wrongdoing, etc.)?
6. How would you respond to push back on your decision from the following constituency groups?
   a. President Matheson
   b. Coaches from the WestU Athletic Department
   c. The Chief Diversity Officer
   d. The applicants and their families

NOTES

1. The Morrill Act of 1862 granted land to states in order to create postsecondary institutions to educate the state's citizens. In 1890, there was a second Morrill Act that granted land for historically Black colleges and universities in many southern states where African Americans were being excluded from the state's original land-grant universities.
2. The eugenics movement was a pseudo-scientific movement where scientists were engaged in a series of experiments (e.g., skull measuring) with the express intent of demonstrating racial inferiority for those who were dark-skinned.

Section II

Getting Through

4

THE COLLEGE TRANSITIONS PROCESS

When Many Ships Collide[1]

DEBORAH FAYE CARTER, ANGELA M. LOCKS,
AND RACHELLE WINKLE-WAGNER

We may have all come on different ships, but we're in the same boat now.

—Rev. Dr. Martin Luther King, Jr., Civil Rights Activist

After access and admissions, students make their way onto the proverbial harbors of college campuses, as if they are many ships docking at the same port. This entering process, the transition into college, is a time when the act of inclusion of student diversity is particularly crucial. The transition to college during a student's first year is a time filled with enthusiasm, hope, and sometimes, disappointment for many students (Yosso, Smith, Ceja, & Solórzano, 2009). In student affairs, most scholars and practitioners mark this time period as facilitating students' emotional, social, and identity development (Evans, Forney, Guido, Patton, & Renn, 2010). Most scholars agree that the first year of college is crucial because only approximately 20% of full-time students and 55% of part-time students will come back for their second year (Aud et al., 2012). The rates of persistence between the first-year transition and the second year of college are even more concerning for students of color who are even less likely to come back for a second year of college as compared to White students (Aud et al., 2012; Ross et al., 2012). First-generation students, those whose parents did not attend college, have also been shown to have more difficult transitions to college than their peers whose parents attended college (Padgett, Johnson, & Pascarella, 2012). Given that the first year of college is a time when many students are undergoing substantial personal development (Evans et al., 2010) and are determining whether to continue in college past the first year, scholars generally agree that the transition process is ripe for intervention from practitioners and faculty to help students succeed in college (Li, McCoy, Shelley, & Whalen, 2005; Sankar & Raju, 2011). In terms of aiding the successful transition, this first year has also been asserted to be a particularly important period of time (Reason, Terenzini, & Domingo, 2006). A response to the magnitude of this first-year transition process has been to develop programs aimed at helping students to make a successful transition into college (Inkelas & Soldner, 2011; Li et al., 2005; Passel & Cohn, 2008; Sankar & Raju, 2011). Student affairs practitioners have been a big part of making this first-year transition successful, through orientation programs, first-year experience programs, fall welcome events into the academic year, residence hall activities, and other programs and events.

While the mainstream scholarship on college student transitions often emphasizes the experiences of White students, in this chapter we focus particularly on the transition experiences of students of color, particularly Asian American, Latina/o, African American, and Native American students, and first-generation students. An examination of the transitions of students of color is particularly important because there is evidence that students of color report feeling isolated, stress about maintaining family relationships, and experiences with racial harassment (Cano & Castillo, 2010; Solórzano, Ceja, & Yosso, 2000; Winkle-Wagner, 2009a, 2009b; Yosso, Parker, & Solórzano, & Lynn, 2009) all of which likely influence their transition to a college campus and general experiences in college. First-generation students also experience many barriers to their successful transition to college, as they enter a campus that may seem very foreign to what they knew in their families (Padgett et al., 2012; Winkle-Wagner, 2009b). We use the words "transition" and "adjustment" synonymously as pointing toward students' first experiences in acclimating to a college campus. We particularly examine the academic transition to college and issues that might affect students' adjustment processes. We start with a consideration of the way that diversity has been considered (or ignored) relative to the college transition process. The initial development for the consideration of the college transition process for underrepresented students was published in an earlier manuscript (Carter, Locks, & Winkle-Wagner, 2013).

THINKING ABOUT DIVERSITY: THEORETICAL APPROACHES TO THE TRANSITION TO COLLEGE

There are three ways to think about the college transition process theoretically:

1. Sociological perspectives that take into account students' socialization and how that influences their adjustment to college;
2. Psychological perspectives that emphasize students' cognitive processes related to their transition into college; and
3. Emergent theories that attempt to shift the direction of theories of college transition processes, highlighting underrepresented students' transitions in particular.

Sociological Perspectives on the Student Transition

The sociological approaches to college student transitions assume that as students are socialized to campus environments, they learn to adjust to campus norms, roles, opportunities, and ways of acting (Smith, Carmack, & Titsworth, 2006). For this chapter, we specifically center on Weidman's socialization model and how it relates to students' adjustment to college because this model was particularly important in theorizing about adjustment. Then, we turn attention toward an alternative advancement, a theory of validation.

Weidman's Socialization Model. Weidman's (1989) socialization model attempted to demonstrate the way that socio-structural issues influenced students' transition to college. Weidman asserted that as students transition to campus, they bring with them particular aspirations, values, and aptitudes from their previous experiences and from their family backgrounds. After arriving on campus, they are exposed to the socializing influences by faculty and peers. These socializing influences relate to normative claims for both the academic and social aspects of the campus (i.e., ways that students should behave inside and outside of the classroom). Students who are transitioning to campus are left to navigate these normative socializing influences and they must decide whether they will change their initial values, aspirations, and goals to fit into the academic and social parts of the campus. Weidman (1989) did consider the way that race or ethnicity might relate to this socialization process. He maintained that it was necessary to develop "differing patterns of socialization" for racially underrepresented groups. Weidman's (1989, 2006) notion of socialization has often been a theoretical framework to understand students' transition to college (Berger & Milem, 1999; Cruce, Wolniak, Seifert, & Pascarella, 2006).

Implied in socialization models is the idea that students are socialized into the mainstream or majority ways of a college campus. According to this idea, at predominantly White institutions (PWIs), students of color would need to adapt to White-centric ways of thinking or acting even if the campus norms were very different from their home or community backgrounds (Winkle-Wagner, 2009a). While agency or students' ability to determine their actions within their transition (Smith et al., 2006) is still possible, it might be very difficult for a student who is not in the majority group on campus.

Rendón's Theory of Validation.   Criticizing traditional socialization theories that asserted the necessity of students' adapting themselves to campus without consideration of their prior experiences, Rendón's (1994) theory of validation offered ways to connect the transition process with students' backgrounds. The theory of validation may apply more seamlessly to the transitions of underrepresented students on campus than other theories because it was crafted out of work with these populations. Initially developed in her work with nontraditional students (those students who are above the age of 22, students who are parents, returning Veterans, etc.), Rendón argued that validating students' prior knowledge and beliefs would ultimately help students to transition into a campus and also to be successful there. Rendón (1994) asserted two types of validation: academic validation that values students' innate capacity to learn and helps students to build confidence; and interpersonal validation that confirms students' backgrounds and the diversity that they bring with them to campus by nurturing students' individual development and social adjustment.

Rendón's theory of validation had important implications for diversity. Her theory presented a way to embrace diversity on campus by actively validating the prior knowledge and experiences that students bring with them to campus. Rather than encouraging students to ignore their difference as they transition to campus, Rendón (1994, 2002) argued that faculty and staff should engage in a process to enable, validate, or confirm students and their unique, diverse characteristics. This line of thinking connects to earlier empirical findings on female, first-generation, and racially underrepresented students that argues that encouragement and support significantly impact students' development in college (Belenky, Clinchy, Goldberger, & Tarule, 1986; Terenzini et al., 1994).

For faculty, staff, and peers on campus, Rendón (1994, 2002) asserted six elements that should be in place to proceed with validation of students, particularly those students who are underrepresented on campus:

1. Faculty, staff, and administrators are responsible for the initial contact with students rather than placing the onus on students to contact those within the institution;
2. Students will develop a stronger sense of self-worth when validation is present;
3. Students are more likely to become involved or integrated on campus once they are validated. Validation is a precursor to student learning;
4. The process of validation happens inside and outside of classrooms;
5. Rather than an outcome, validation is an ongoing process;
6. Validation is crucial to students' transition to college.

Rendón's theory of validation was crafted with a particular eye towards those students who may find themselves in an underrepresented group on campus: students of color, first-generation, low-income, and nontraditional students. The framework has been used to understand the college transitions of first-generation (Lundberg, Schreiner, Hovaguimian, & Miller, 2007), Latina/o (Chaves, 2006; Rendón, 2002), and African American students' (Holmes, Ebbers, Robinson, & Mugenda, 2001). While there is some evidence that validation of students' identities may help to foster successful transitions in college (Terenzini et al., 1994), more research is needed to explore how validating underrepresented students might help them to be successful while embracing the diversity that they bring to campus.

Psychological Perspectives on Student Transitions

Psychological perspectives related to the college student transition process study students' cognitive processes (i.e., mental processing), highlighting issues such as students' coping strategies, self-efficacy, or motivation. Schlossberg's transition theory (1981, 1984) is one of the primary psychological theories that connect to the initial adjustment to college. Transition theory, initiated in Schlossberg's (1981) larger counseling practice was a way to reveal individuals' unique reactions toward changes in their lives. Schlossberg (1981) was particularly interested in the way people moved from being consumed by the transition to incorporating the changes into their lives. She focused on three aspects of the transition process in particular: the influence of the transition on the self, one's individual characteristics, and the environment where a transition was happening. Transition was distinguished from the notion of adaptation, which Schlossberg (1981) framed as dependent on a person's perception of their available resources to the barriers that are present in the environment where the transition occurs.

Schlossberg applied this idea to transitions during the life course and the strategies that people employed for coping with those transitions. In her collaborative work, Schlossberg, Waters, and Goodman (1995) later adapted transition theory to contemplate students' transitions into college (e.g., changes in routines, norms, relationships, and roles during a student's adjustment within a particular campus context).

The initial three factors from Schlossberg's counseling theory, self, environment, and individual characteristics, were later expanded into what is often referred to as the Four, S's: situation, self, support, and strategies (Chickering & Schlossberg, 1995; Schlossberg et al., 1995), Chickering and Schlossberg (1995) coupled these with a student's perception of resources and barriers. Each of the S's focuses on a set of issues (Schlossberg et al., 1995):

1 Situation: (a) the catalyst for the change; (b) the timing of the change and whether the student sees the time as a good time for change; (c) the aspects of the change that are perceived to be within the student's control; (d) the changes to a student's roles and whether these are perceived as positive or negatives changes; (e) the duration of the transition (short-term change, long-term change, or permanent change); (f) the other stresses that are occurring concurrently; (g) the previous experiences that the student has had associated with the transition; and (h) who or what is seen as responsible for the transition.

2. Self: individual characteristics, demographic characteristics, and the psychological resources available (e.g., gender, socioeconomic status, state of health, and age, alongside psychological resources such as optimism, self-efficacy, and values).

3. Supports: the positive or negative way that relationships and networks influence a student's transition (e.g., family, friends, co-workers, faculty, staff, or community/groups).

4. Strategies: (a) information-seeking; (b) direct action; (c) inhibition of action; and (d) intra-psychic behavior.

While transition theory was not developed specifically for the study of students in underrepresented groups, some scholars have applied the theory to these populations. For example, transition theory has been useful in investigations into issues such as first-year academic success for women of color (Bradburn, Moen, & Dempster-McClain, 1995; Rayle, Kurpius, & Arrendondo, 2007), the college transitions of nontraditionally aged students (McAtee & Benshoff, 2006; Schaefer, 2010), or the transition of Latina/o students (Tovar & Simon, 2006).

DIVERSITY STILL MATTERS: EMPIRICAL APPROACHES TO COLLEGE STUDENT TRANSITIONS

We begin our analysis of the extant literature on college student transitions for underrepresented students with an examination of one of the primary instruments used to study this topic, the Student Adaptation to College Questionnaire (SACQ). Then, we turn our attention toward the kinds of support that the literature concludes are required for students to successfully adjust to campus. The empirical studies related to college student transitions for students of color indicate that various kinds of support are crucial to the transition process such as:

1. Academic support, particularly for those areas where students are underprepared for college;

2. Faculty and staff support in the form of educationally purposeful activities such as learning communities, orientation programs, or first-year seminars;

3. Family and peer support that can either help or hinder a student's transition to college.

The SACQ is the primary way that psychological notions of the college transition process have been empirically studied. The instrument was developed as a 67-item, self-report, Likert scale with four dimensions in order to measure difficulty or ease across four-subscales: academic, social, personal-emotional adjustment and a student's attachment to a particular institution (Baker & Siryk, 1980, 1984, 1989). The SACQ most closely relates to the psychological transition theory, and the Four S's in this theory: the academic and social adjustment scales connect to the theoretical idea of situation and support; the personal-emotional adjustment scale links to the concept of self; and the attachment to a postsecondary institution subscale relates well with the idea of strategies. The instrument, developed through data gathered at Clark University (Dahmus & Bernardin, 1992), has undergone many tests of validity and reliability (Baker, 1986; Kaase, 1994; Merker & Smith, 2001).

The SACQ has primarily been employed as either a way to identify the factors that relate to students' adjustment processes, or, to help in pinpointing students who might be "at-risk" of not adjusting well to college (Baker, 1986; Kaase, 1994; Krotseng, 1991, 1992; Schwartz & Washington, 2002). The results of studies using the SACQ to identify factors that influence students' adjustment have been used to support the development of institutional support programs for students (Dahmus & Bernardin, 1992) such as counseling support (Dahmus & Bernardin, 1992; Merker & Smith, 2001). The SACQ has also been used in studies of campus climate, or the effect of the institutional environment related to embracing racial or gender diversity (Hurtado, Carter, & Spuler, 1996). However, related to the detection of at-risk students, there are questions as to whether the SACQ is able to identify at-risk students in all institutional settings or geographic areas (Kaase, 1994).

Researchers using the SACQ to understand the college transition process for underrepresented students often offer strategies for institutional support for minority students (Gold, Burrell, Haynes, & Nardecchia, 1990; Hurtado et al., 1996). These studies reinforce the importance of in-college experiences. For example, according to the results of a study using the SACQ to explore Latina/o college students' transitions, in-college experiences might influence the transition to college more than background characteristics or experiences (Hurtado et al., 1996).

Employing the SACQ in an analysis of survey data generated from the SACQ, Schwartz and Washington (2002) found that high school rank and social adjustment predicted retention of African American men at a historically Black college. Additionally, Schwartz and Washington found that social cognitive/affective variables, such as personality, responsibility, self-concept, academic self-concept, and locus of control were useful in predicting retention, particularly for African American students. Some of the studies on students of color employ the SACQ along with other instruments such as the Multigroup Ethnic Identity Measure (Kalsner & Pistole, 2003) or the Noncognitive Questionnaire Revised (NCQ-R) (Schwartz & Washington, 2002).

In general, the SACQ has been found to be a reliable instrument to measure students' transitions to college, allowing for evaluation of cognitive and social/emotional factors related to the college experience. More work is necessary to understand the usefulness of this instrument within different kinds of institutions such as historically Black colleges and universities or Hispanic Serving Institutions (Dahmus & Bernardin, 1992). Because the SACQ questionnaire is self-reported there might be some variance in the ways in which students interpret or understand the questions. Asking the students about their interpretations of the questions, would be helpful in alleviating this limitation (also called cognitive interviews). Finally, there should be more scholarship analyzing the efficacy of using the SACQ with other instruments.

Academic Support and the College Transition Process

There are many kinds of academic support that influence students' transitions to college. First, some students are academically underprepared and are in need of remediation support or coursework to help students' gain the academic content that they need to begin transitioning into their degree program in college. Second, the way that students view their own abilities, also called academic self-efficacy, influences how students transition academically into college. Students therefore may need support in developing a positive sense of academic self-efficacy.

Lacking Academic Preparation and Remediation. Underrepresented students, such as students of color and first-generation students are at times academically underprepared for college, according to multiple empirical studies (Pascarella, Pierson, Wolniak, & Terenzini, 2004; Rendón & Hope, 1996; Terenzini, et al., 1994). A lack of academic preparation stems from many sources such as being tracked into less rigorous coursework earlier in education which then typically leads to taking less rigorous coursework in secondary education. For example, there is scholarship showing that first-generation students are less likely to take Advanced Placement courses or other college preparation classes (Reid & Moore, 2008; Warburton, Bugarin, & Nunez, 2001). Additionally, the learning environment in college can be markedly different from high schools, and some research does uncover that issues such as seeing few students of color, not being familiar with classroom technology, and different pedagogical styles can influence underrepresented students' ability to transition to the new college academic environment (Reid & Moore, 2008).

For those students who are academically underprepared, they are likely to need support in the way of coursework to help them transition into their college classes. This kind of coursework, called either developmental education or remedial coursework (also remediation) focuses on the basic skills necessary for the academic transition to college such as reading, writing, or mathematics. Developmental education is crucial to the successful college transition of many underrepresented students (Lavin & Weininger, 1998) in part, because underrepresented students comprise a large percentage of the students in remedial/developmental classes (Attewell, Lavin, Domina, & Levey, 2005).

Traditionally, nearly all kinds of institutions (both four- and two-year) offered remediation coursework (Roueche & Roueche, 1999), but, in recent years many four-year institutions have stopped offering remedial coursework, making developmental education the responsibility of two-year institutions such as community colleges (Bettinger & Long, 2004; Kozeracki, 2002; Soliday, 2002). There are a few reasons for this shift. Some people maintain that if students need remedial coursework, they should not have been admitted to college in the first place (Kozeracki, 2002; Marcus, 2000; Soliday, 2002; Trombley, 1998). There is evidence that because developmental classes do not usually count toward a degree program, students in these courses might be less likely to finish their degrees (Deil-Amen & Rosenbaum, 2002; Rosenbaum, 2001). An analysis of the High School and Beyond dataset argued that students who took many developmental classes were less likely to graduate from college (Adelman, 1999, 2004). One reason for this could be that students may not always be aware that remedial classes do not typically count toward degree programs (Deil-Amen & Rosenbaum, 2002). Yet there are many scholars who have demonstrated evidence on the contrary to this, asserting that remedial coursework might be important to helping students' transitions and ultimate completion of their degree programs (Bettinger & Long, 2009; McCabe, 2000; Merisotis & Phipps, 2000). In a study comparing students of color with White students, students of color were more likely to fail initial academic skills tests, but with remedial classes, these same students did often finish their degrees (Lavin & Weininger, 1998).

More recent research into the way that remediation might hinder or facilitate students' transitions to college stresses the idea of academic enrichment programs. The scholarship reveals that these programs, combining academic skill building and remediation with social and emotional support and attention to students' identities, may help to facilitate successful transitions for underrepresented students specifically (Colyar & Stich, 2010; Conley, 2008). Researchers have discovered that academic enrichment programs are particularly helpful in aiding the transitions of students of color into postsecondary science and mathematics coursework (Barlow & Villarejo, 2004; Villarejo, Barlow, Kogan, Veazey, & Sweeney, 2008). A partner to academic enrichment programs is co-curricular programming, targeted toward bringing together students' academic and social experiences. Scholarship on living-learning programs, for instance, maintained that first-generation students experienced a more positive transition to campus (Inkelas, Daver, Vogt, & Leonard, 2007).

Self-Efficacy and Academic Transitions. In addition to the institutional type, the students' own sense of their ability may influence their transition process. College student transitions research that is rooted in psychology explores academic self-efficacy and students' motivation to complete academic tasks. Self-efficacy allows for the consideration of a student's assessment of her/his academic ability (Bandura, 1977, 1982, 1986). This perception of academic competence leads to a set of beliefs that a student holds about his/her ability and it then effects academic achievement and motivation to complete academic tasks in the future (Bandura, 1993; Bong, 2001; Brown, Lent, & Larkin, 1989; Hackett, Betz, Casas, & Rocha-Singh, 1992; Lent, Brown, & Larkin, 1984; Martin, 2009; Multon, Brown, & Lent, 1991). For example, a study using structural equation modeling to explore the role of self-efficacy in the academic performance of students of color found that self-efficacy predicted academic performance (Zajacova, Lync, & Espenshade, 2005).

The concept of academic self-efficacy has been useful in better understanding students' transitions to college. Academic self-efficacy has been used to predict adjustment to college for underrepresented students such as students of color (Solberg, O'Brien, Villareal, Kennel, & Davis, 1993; Torres & Solberg, 2001) and first-generation students (Ramos-Sanchez & Nichols, 2007). Generally these studies report that students with higher self-efficacy will have a more successful transition process (Solberg, et al., 1993; Ramos-Sanchez & Nichols, 2007; Torres & Solberg, 2001).

One reason for the link between the college transition process and general academic success in college is that self-efficacy connects to students' academic habits and the motivation they have to attempt to master academic tasks (Zeldin & Pajares, 2000). For instance, in one study college students with a higher academic self-efficacy spent more hours studying (Torres & Solberg, 2001). In another study of women in math and science disciplines, the female students with high academic self-efficacy seemed more able to overcome academic challenges and obstacles (Zeldin & Pajares, 2000).

A student's level of motivation connects to the way in which a student perceives that she/he can (or cannot) control her or his academic environment (Pajares, 1996; Zimmerman, 1990). According to some data, students of color who perceived that they could control their academic environment (motivation, emotional, and social aspects) had a higher self-efficacy or perception of their academic ability (Zimmerman, Bandura, & Martinez-Pons, 1992). Self-efficacy also influences where students put the onus for their ability: students with high academic self-efficacy may attribute a lack of academic success to insufficient effort while students with low self-efficacy may attribute academic failure to a lack of ability (Bandura, 1993).

Ultimately, academic self-efficacy may influence whether a student persists through her/his degree program (Lent et al., 1984, 1986, 1987; Torres & Solberg, 2001). In a longitudinal study of first-year students' transitions to college, academic self-efficacy and optimism influenced academic performance, transition to college, and commitment to remain in college (Chemers, Hu, & Garcia, 2001).

There are two instruments that are commonly used to investigate self-efficacy and how it relates to the college transition process: The College Academic Self-Efficacy Scale (CASES) (Owen & Forman, 1988); and the College Self-Efficacy Inventory (Barry & Finney, 2009). The CASES instrument has demonstrated an ability to predict the way that academic self-efficacy influences college students' academic performance (Choi, 2005). The College Self-Efficacy Inventory, which some scholars assert still needs to be refined (Barry & Finney, 2009), also has been used in studies finding a connection between students' self-efficacy and college adjustment. Specifically the College Self-Efficacy Inventory has demonstrated this link between self-efficacy and successful college transitions for Latina/o students (Solberg et al., 1993; Torres & Solberg, 2001).

Educationally Purposeful Activities and Faculty-Staff Support

Students who enroll in two-year institutions may have a different academic transition than students in four-year institutions, in part because student-faculty interactions at two-year college are often very different. We state this as a way to set the stage for a potential solution to help support two-year college transitions, educationally purposeful activities. The scholarship about faculty and staff support for college student transition processes primarily explores educationally purposeful activities such as learning communities where students enroll in courses together, co-curricular learning experiences where students take learning out of the classroom, programs related to diversity, and first-year programs. These activities are typically geared toward helping students to connect students with faculty and staff, or, helping to connect students to know when and from where to seek help early in their transition to campus. Educationally purposeful activities also offer a way to bring together student affairs practitioners and faculty.

Transitions into Two-Year Institutions. One issue that can influence students' transitions to college is the type of institution in which they enroll. Students' academic transitions in two-year institutions will differ in many ways from students' transitions into four-year college. Two-year institutions have a high population of students of color, low-income students, and first-generation students (Levin, 2001; Shaw & London, 2001). With this diversity is a need for support to assure that these students transition academically. But, at these institutions, there is a very different type and level of student-faculty contact because many instructors at two-year institutions are part-time faculty who are employed on a semester-by-semester basis (Galbraith & Shedd, 1990; Jaeger & Egan, 2009; Umbach, 2007). According to Umbach (2007), part-time faculty have been demonstrated to have fewer interactions and to spend less time with students. In some cases, they do not have offices on campus, or they have to work in multiple institutions to piece together enough teaching to make an appropriate salary. For those students who take courses primarily from part-time faculty, this can have detrimental effects on their transition into and out of a two-year institution. In an advanced statistical analysis (hierarchical generalized linear modeling) of community colleges in California, results demonstrated that the more a student experiences part-time faculty, the less likely they are to actually complete an associate's degree (Jaeger & Egan, 2009). The implication of these findings at two-year institutions is that there is a greater need for supporting students' transitions into these institutions. One way that students might be supported is through educationally purposeful activities initiated by staff such as student affairs practitioners.

Educationally Purposeful Activities and College Transitions. Rendón's (1994, 2002) theory of validation has offered a fruitful way to study the role of faculty and staff support in the college transition process, particularly for underrepresented students. The theory of validation, highlighted above, has been used to explore racially underrepresented students' community college transfer (Rendón, 2002), college student transitions (Terenzini et al., 1994), and persistence in degree programs (Holmes et al., 2001). Applying the validation theory to Latina/o students through the study of a first-year experience initiative that aimed at helping students transfer from two-year to four-year colleges in California, Rendón (2002) found that a "validating team" composed of an English faculty member, a counselor, and a mentor provided information and planning help to students on how to transfer to a four-year institution, academic preparation, and encouragement regarding the benefit of getting a college degree. All of these were important aspects of supporting students in the community college transfer process. Examining the college transition process of students of color within various institutional types (community colleges, liberal arts colleges, and universities) through focus groups, Terenzini and his colleagues (1994) found that early validation from faculty and peers in particular is crucial to students' successful transition onto college campuses.

Orientation and first-year seminars are one way that campus officials have tried to foster educationally purposeful activities. These orientations and seminars may be particularly useful for students of color and first-generation students who may feel as if they are coming to a campus that is very different form their cultural or class backgrounds. First-year seminars, aimed at helping students adjust to academic coursework and campus norms, are particularly helpful to African American students' transitions and persistence from their first to their second years in college (Burgette & Magun-Jackson, 2008). Using Schlossberg's (1981) transition theory, Tovar and Simon's (2006) research on Latina/o students who were on academic probation indicated that these students were more willing to receive institutional assistance through first-year support programs than their non-Latina/o peers.

Some campus officials within particular academic disciplines or disciplinary areas (e.g., Science, technology, engineering, and mathematics or STEM) provide specific first-year seminars that help to foster transitions into that particular academic area. Freshman seminars in engineering at a predominantly White institution, for example, have been demonstrated to improve students' cognitive skills, teamwork, and self-efficacy (Sankar & Raju, 2011). In a mixed methods study of an academic support program in STEM, African American students reported that the program helped them to navigate campus climates and socialized them to seek assistance early in their transition to college (Good, Halpin, & Halpin, 2001–2002). Similarly, a study considering engineering coursework at an HBCU found that hands-on projects helped students to be more academically engaged (Halyo & Le, 2011). A program at the University of Texas at Austin, the Preview Program, encourages students of color to interact with peers from their same racial group in order to work on course content (Canagarajah, 1997). While not discipline specific, research on undergraduate research programs targeted toward women of color found these programs to be critical in aiding the students' transitions to four-year institutions (Reyes, 2011).

Educationally purposeful activities are not only important in formal learning, such as classrooms. Blending in- and out-of-class (also called co-curricular experiences) activities may also aid in students' academic transitions. For example, statistical analysis shows that first-year Latina/o students have higher academic performance (measured by GPA) and African American students are more likely to return to college for a second year when they have faculty contact outside of the classroom, and when they experience interactions about diversity and academic content with peers (Kuh, Cruce, Shoup, Kinzie, & Gonyea, 2006). Involvement in particular campus groups may also work toward offering educationally purposeful activities. The importance of educationally purposeful activities has been demonstrated in historically Black colleges and universities (HBCUs) too. For example, in a study using the National Survey for Student Engagement (NSSE) surveys at a private HBCU, students who were involved in a first-year learning community (where they enrolled in three to four courses as a cohort), were found to have higher scores on measures of active and collaborative learning, interactions between students and faculty, and enhancing educational experiences and supportive campus environment than students who were not involved in the learning community (Yancy et al., 2008).

A student's choice of where to live in the first year of college can also influence her/his transition to campus and involvement in educationally purposeful activities. Research finds that living in a residence hall during the first year is likely to increase a student's sense of belonging on campus (Locks, Hurtado, Bowman, & Oseguera, 2008). Additionally, being a student of color or living in the residence halls and being engaged in learning communities (in and out of the residence halls) may make it more likely that a student is involved in volunteer activities (Cruce & Moore, 2007). While residence-hall living may lead to a positive transition process for some students, there is contradictory evidence when it comes to students of color. While many studies do not include much analysis related to race, the research that does reveals that many students of color may experience racially hostile environments in the residence halls, particularly at predominantly White institutions (Ancis, Sedlacek, & Mohr, 2000; Yosso et al., 2009). This may be one of the reasons for a finding within a single institution study; students of color were less likely to be engaged in residence halls (Arboleda, Wang, Shelley, & Whalen, 2003).

In addition to residence halls, various student affairs units offer educationally purposeful activities. For example, in a qualitative study with first-year Cambodian American students, an Equal Opportunity Program (EOP) that provided connections to staff and membership in ethnic organizations aided in their transitions to college (Chhuon & Hudley, 2008). There is also some evidence that student-initiated retention programs may aid in students' adjustment to campus (Maldonado, Rhoads, & Beunavista, 2009).

Research about educationally purposeful activities that connect students with faculty and staff support underscores the importance of deliberately aiding students' college transitions both in and out of the classroom. Relative to underrepresented students, there is little work that specifically includes race, gender, or other issues in the analyses. Given that studies of engagement in educationally purposeful activities conclude that this aids in students successful transitions to college, specifically for students of color (Kuh et al., 2008), more research is needed on ways to foster these positive educational experiences during the first year of college. More work is needed to understand how these educational activities might uniquely influence the transitions of students who are from underrepresented groups so that these populations can be served.

Peer and Family Support and College Transitions

As students make the transition to college, they bring with them their previous relationships with families or peers. These relationships either come to college with students in explicit ways (e.g., having families visit often or continuing close family relationships, coming to college with friends from high school, fostering close friendships with high school friends, etc.) or in implicit ways (e.g., thinking about relationships, feeling obligated or responsible for families and peers who are not on campus, etc.). Regardless, it is important to consider how these earlier relationships might influence the early relationships that students create with peers, faculty, and staff on campus as they begin adjusting to campus.

Family Relationships and the College Transition Process. One of the debates in the college transitions literature is whether students should sever ties with their families in order to make a successful transition to campus (Hiester, Nordstrom, & Swenson, 2009; Winkle-Wagner, 2009b). There is also evidence, using the SACQ, that parental expectations and attachments with students might vary by racial/ethnic group (Melendez & Melendez, 2010; Yazedjian, Toews, & Navarro, 2009). In a survey study of attachments to parents among college freshman at two institutions (most of the participants were White), those students who maintained attachment with parents were associated with better adjustment to college while students whose relationships with their parents deteriorated reported more distress and lower levels of adjustment (Hiester et al., 2009). Qualitative research with Black women in college suggests that maintaining family relationships may aid in transitions to college (Winkle-Wagner, 2009b). Similarly, other researchers have found differences between racial/ethnic groups. A survey study of women's adjustment to college using the SACQ alongside the Parental Attachment Questionnaire (PAQ) revealed that for Black students, the positive relationships with family did relate to positive adjustments to college, but there were no significant relationships between parental attachment and college adjustment for Latina students (Melendez & Melendez, 2010). Examining parental attachment among women of color, Kalsner and Pistole (2003) used the SACQ along with the PAQ, the

Multigenerational Interconnectedness Scales (MIS), and the Multigroup Ethnic Identity Measure (MEIM), and discovered that female students of color (African American, Latina, and Asian American) needed to individuate from their families in order for the students' college adjustment process to be successful. The debate continues about the type of relationships with families that are helpful in college transitions, particularly for underrepresented students.

Another way that families can influence student transitions, although perhaps in a more indirect way, is through parental educational attainment levels. That is, for those students whose parents did not attend college, they may find the transition to college particularly difficult (Padgett et al., 2012; Pascarella et al., 2004; Winkle-Wagner, 2009b). Related to the successful transition into college, there is evidence that when compared to non-first-generation peers, first-generation students are more likely to live off-campus, participate in fewer co-curricular or volunteer activities, and report fewer social interactions with peers (Pascarella et al., 2004). In a study using longitudinal data from the Wabash National Study of Liberal Arts Education, first-generation students were shown to be at a significant disadvantage across cognitive (desire to seek and engage mental activities, etc.) and psychosocial (positive sense of self, positive relations with others, capacity to manage one's life, etc.) outcomes during the first year of college when compared to their non-first-generation peers (Padgett et al., 2012). However, there are fewer studies of the college transition process specifically for first-generation students. The evidence that does exist belies that more work is needed, particularly from a practical standpoint, to help first-generation students adjust to campus.

Peers, Friendships, and the College Transition Process. Families are not the only relationships that can positively and negatively influence students' transition to college, particularly for students of color. Peers and friendship groups, some of which may have initiated in primary or secondary school, also effect students' transitions. The sociological concept of "acting White" was first identified through Fordham's (Fordham & Ogbu, 1986; Ogbu, 1987) ethnographic research with African American adolescent boys in an urban high school. Through the concept of "acting White," the authors were able to explain an oppositional peer culture that occurred as African American males experienced a school culture that excluded them. Because notions of success were not embraced within the school, some of these students responded, through the peer counterculture, with disengagement in academics (Fordham, 1995). While the concept has been heavily debated as a deficit approach (i.e., an anti-intellectual peer culture, blaming African American students for choosing the peer groups that opposed academics), particularly in sociological literature, Fordham (2008) argued that the main reason for student disengagement was because the educational system was not inclusive of their needs. Many other scholars support Fordham's point (Carter, 2006; Fordham, 2008; Horvat & O'Connor, 2006; Tyson, Darity, & Castellino, 2005). While this acting White issue may have initiated in primary or secondary schooling, many students may bring these ideas or even these peer relationships with them to college (see Winkle-Wagner, 2009a, for an example).

A growing number of scholars have debated whether the idea of acting White as an anti-intellectual peer culture omits crucial analysis of what is happening within the friendship groups of students of color (Carter, 2005, 2006; Ogbu & Davis, 2003; Tyson, 2002). Carter's (2005, 2007) analysis of the concept among African American and Latina/o friendship groups in K-12 schooling, asserted that students of color value education and that "acting White" demonstrates a rejection of "White" American ways of interacting, speech patterns, dress, and musical tastes. This finding is supported by other scholarship (Ogbu & Davis, 2003; Tyson, 2002). Some of this work finds that African American students gained popularity among their peers for excelling in academics (Ogbu & Davis, 2003). The research on acting White at the primary and secondary schooling level connects to higher education by making the point that peer groups influence students' educational aspirations and ability to be prepared for college (Carter, 2007; Tyson et al., 2005). Additionally, some students may continue close relationships with their friends from high school.

Research specifically about the acting White concept connected to the college transition process has uncovered issues such as: an explanation for the Black-White achievement gap (Horvat & Lewis, 2003); the exclusivity of academic discourse (White & Lowenthal, 2011); and stressors related to minority-status (Smedley, Myers, & Harrell, 1993). Some of this work demonstrates that a manifestation of the acting White concept at the college level is an academic discourse that excludes students of color and ultimately disallows those students from making a successful transition to campus (White & Lowenthal, 2011). One of the reactions to the acting White literature has been to inquire into the other end of the spectrum, that is to examine high-achieving Black students as a way to disrupt the idea that students of color will disengage in college because of their peer groups (Fries-Britt, 1998; Fries-Britt & Griffin, 2007; Harper, 2006). For example, one longitudinal study illustrated how friendship was a *necessary* part of academic development and success (Martinez Alemàn, 2000). Similarly, other qualitative research in this area has discovered that African American students sometimes deliberately work to resist stereotypes while they pursue a high level of academic engagement (Fries-Britt & Griffin, 2007).

Another sociological line of work aimed at understanding the importance of students' peer groups in the college adjustment process has been rooted in Weidman's above-mentioned model of socialization (Attinasi, 1989; Berger & Milem, 1999; Padgett et al., 2010). In a study of students' formal and informal interactions with both peers and faculty, Berger and Milem (1999) found that those students who were more like the dominant group on campus (i.e., White students on a predominantly White campus) were more likely to have a successful transition and persist through their degree programs. Attinasi's (1989) qualitative analysis of data from first-generation, Mexican American students on an urban campus maintained that peer interactions aided students' adjustment to campus because these social interactions helped to develop cognitive maps of the environment and to assist in navigating the campus. This finding is supported by quantitative studies related to Latina/o students' transitions to college (Hurtado et al., 1996).

Peer interactions have both positive and negative influences on the college transition process. For example, an exploration of academic outcomes in the first year of college that was rooted in Schlossberg's (1981) transition theory indicated that women of color who lacked peer support had lower GPAs (Rayle et al., 2007). Student affairs practitioners could consider ways to facilitate positive peer relationships on campus through programming that builds bonds between students, for example. Additionally, as students become involved in extracurricular activities, they may begin to make more positive peer relationships.

SUMMARY: DIVERSITY AND THE COLLEGE TRANSITION PROCESS

Understanding the college transition process is crucial to a full awareness of ways to facilitate student success. This early transition process is particularly critical for students from underrepresented groups, many of whom may not experience the new campus environment as welcoming to their identities and their needs. The transition process is a time period when the action of inclusion of diversity can be manifested. Students of color and other groups of underrepresented students such as low-income or first-generation students have not been the centerpiece of most of the college transitions literature. There is work left to be done to better include these students in college transitions scholarly and practical work so that policy and practice can better suite all students' needs.

Think about Diversity

The college transitions literature began with a study of students from majority groups, both theoretically and empirically. Weidman's (1989) socialization model, one of the major sociological theories used to think about college transitions, and Schlossberg's (1981; Schlossberg et al., 1995; Chickering & Schlossberg, 1995) psychologically based transition theory were both initiated as a way of thinking about *general* transitions. While these could and have been applied to underrepresented students in some cases (e.g., Attinasi, 1989; Rayle et al., 2007), this was not the theoretical emphasis of the foundational theories. In the case of Weidman's (1989) theory of socialization, the notion that students must adapt to an institution without consideration of their past cultural experiences could actually be damaging to students' ability to fully adjust to an institutional context (Winkle-Wagner, 2009a; Yosso et al., 2009).

Schlossberg's transition theory has been applied a bit more often to understand the transition of underrepresented students (e.g., Bradburn et al., 1995; McAtee & Benshoff, 2006; Rayle et al., 2007; Schaefer, 2010; Tovar & Simon, 2006). Due to the initial focus on majority students, unexplained issues related to transitions emerge (e.g., the transition of students of color to predominantly White campuses) within these theories. Rendón's (1994) theory of validation is a contemporary answer to this issue, created out of work with nontraditional, first-generation, low-income students and students of color. Instead of assuming students should adapt to campus without consideration of their cultural pasts, the theory of validation attempts to value students' backgrounds, experiences, and the diversity that this brings to a campus. Yet more empirical work is needed on this theory to demonstrate how it might foster more successful transitions for underrepresented students.

Additionally, there is more work to do theoretically related to understanding of how students' multiple, intersecting identities connect with their transition to campus. Work on the connection between self-efficacy and racial/ethnic identity (e.g., Cano & Castillo, 2010) is promising in this regard. But, this is an area that needs further development.

Diversity Still Matters

Empirically, the research on college student transitions does not typically highlight potential differences between racial/ethnic groups or between other identity groups (e.g., first-generation status, low-income background, sexual orientations, etc.). Future scholarly work should explore differences between subgroups of students in order to best understand how to serve the plurality of students on campus. Additionally, there is a need for more nuanced empirical work related to the educational paths of students because many students are not simply progressing from high school into full-time student status in college. Thus, empirical considerations of college transitions should examine variations in enrollment patterns such as part-time enrollment, dual enrollment, or taking a few classes and then stopping out of college for a period of time (Ishitani, 2008). Students who enroll part-time, for example, might experience a different adjustment process (also dual enrollment, enrolling and then stopping out for a period of time, etc.). There is also a lack of work on the unique transitions of first-generation students, low-income students, religious minorities on campus, or non-heterosexual students (LGBTQ students). Studies about these groups would be useful to uncover unique challenges that these students might encounter.

Two final gaps in the transitions work are in the area of institutional types and understanding effective support programs. Students' transitions do differ between two-year and four-year institutions. But, there is not much work that compares transition differences between other types of institutions. For example, comparisons of transitions within minority serving institutions such as historically Black colleges and universities (HBCUs) or tribal colleges would be beneficial to the larger body of knowledge on transitions to college. If students experience different sources of support in these institutions, for example, it might be useful to explore creating that kind of support in predominantly White institutions. With regard to what programs work best to support students of color, we know very little from the broader higher education literature and more work could be done in this area.

Diversity Is Everywhere

The empirical literature claims the necessity of support programs at all levels during the transition process. Support in academics, from families and peers, and from faculty and staff are all crucial pieces to the successful transition puzzle. When students experience a lack of support in any these areas, student transitions may suffer. Practical efforts should identify ways to provide holistic and seamless support from the time of enrollment throughout the first two years (and arguably, throughout a student's time in college). One unit probably cannot provide the full support to a student, so, there is a need to communicate across units to ensure that students are receiving holistic academic, social, and emotional support during the transition. Orientations and first-year experience seminars are demonstrated to help with the initial transition. One idea might be to find ways to continue the benefits of these programs by offering mid-semester check-ins (a time to meet with faculty and staff about the transition process specifically), ongoing seminars (focused on general student skills such as studying, time management, or expectations of faculty), or orientation programs.

The college transition process differs for students from underrepresented populations. Students negotiate multiple identities (race, class, gender, sexual orientation, etc.), all of which could influence their transition to college. Student affairs practitioners and faculty would be aided by knowing the unique challenges that various groups of students may face during their college adjustment process. At least then there could be attempts to meet students where they are in order to try to help them become a part of the campus community. Additionally, this may change the campus community as staff and faculty reached out to students, reflected on ways to serve these students, and then altered institutional structures.

DISCUSSION QUESTIONS

Based on our review of the theoretical and empirical literature relative to the college student transition process for underrepresented students, we pose some questions aimed at improving practice. Additionally, we offer some questions to contemplate towards future empirical work on college student transitions.

Improving Practice

1. As a campus administrator, what programs would you want to implement to support the transition process, particularly for underrepresented students?
2. What kind of programs would offer seamless support for students as they navigate academics, families, peers, and their transition to college? Consider how you might create educationally purposeful activities in a particular unit on campus (e.g., housing, campus activities, career services, etc.).
3. As you consider the socialization theory, how might this influence the way you interact with students who are making the transition to college?
4. If you were to apply the theory of validation, what specific steps might you take as a student affairs practitioner to make your students feel validated? How would you work to creating validating teams for students?
5. How might students' relationships with their families influence their adjustment to college? As a student affairs practitioner, how might you take steps to aid students in their negotiation of these family relationships?
6. How do peer relationships and friendships influence college transitions for students? As an administrator, what steps might you take to aid in the creation of positive peer relationships for students on campus?
7. One of the major student affairs associations, Student Affairs Administrators in Higher Education (NASPA), developed a set of professional competencies that are encouraged for all student affairs professionals. How might the NASPA professional competencies inform the way you might help underrepresented students through their college transition processes as a student affairs practitioner?
   a. The NASPA Competencies are (see http://www.naspa.org/programs/profdev/default.cfm): advising and helping; assessment, evaluation, and research; equity, diversity, and inclusion; ethical professional practice; history, philosophy, and value; human organizational resources; law, policy, and governance; leadership; personal foundations; students learning and development.
8. Another national association for student affairs, College Student Educators International (ACPA) developed a Statement of Ethical Principles and Standards. How might the ACPA Ethical Principles and Standards influence the way you would help to facilitate the college adjustment process for underrepresented students in particular?
   a. The ACPA Standards are (see http://www2.myacpa.org/statement-of-ethical-principles-and-standards): professional responsibility and competence; student learning and development; responsibility to the institution; and responsibility to society.
9. The Council for the Advancement of Standards in Higher Education (CAS) developed a set of standards for student affairs. How might these CAS Standards be

applied to the college student transition process, particularly as it relates to under-represented students?

a. The domains for the CAS Standards are (see http://www.cas.edu/index.php/cas-general-standards): knowledge acquisition, integration, construction, and application; cognitive complexity; intrapersonal development; interpersonal competence; humanitarianism and civic engagement; practical competence.

Developing Future Research

1. Given that there is relatively little scholarship particularly on the transitions of underrepresented students, what study might you recommend doing? What specific methodologies might be useful to reveal more about the transitions of under-represented students?

2. How would you go about studying the socialization process as underrepresented students adjust to college?

3. If you were to conduct a study using the theory of validation, how might you proceed?

4. If you were to conduct a study about educationally purposeful activities, on what area might you focus?

5. Students' family relationships are important in their transitions to campus. How might you study these complicated family relationships related to the college transition process?

6. Relationships with peers and friendships are also important in adjustments to campus for students. What kind of study might you create to study this issue?

7. How might you take an intersectional approach (combining the study of race, class, gender, etc.) to the study of college student transitions?

========================A CASE STUDY========================

PRACTICING DIVERSITY ISSUES RELATED TO THE COLLEGE TRANSITION PROCESS

The First-Year Experience: Inclusivity for All Students

COURTNEY LUEDKE, UNIVERSITY OF WISCONSIN-MADISON

North Central University (NCU) is a mid-sized, four-year university in the Upper Midwest that primarily serves an undergraduate student population of 10,500 students with an additional 2,000 masters students enrolled in MBA programs. NCU primarily serves in-state students from low- and middle-income families. Approximately 65% of the annual freshmen classes are first-generation college students. Although the campus continues to remain predominantly White, its diversity has increased in recent years. In 2000, the campus was approximately 92% White, 3% African American, 2% Latina/o,

2% Asian American and Pacific Islander, and 1% Native American. As of 2013, the population had evolved to 84% White, 5% African American, 4% Latina/o, 5% Asian American and Pacific Islander (largely due to the state's increasing Hmong population), and 2% Native American.

The changing student demographic has brought new opportunities and challenges to the campus. Results from a recent accreditation recommended that the campus focus on improving its first-year experience programming as a proactive approach to handling the persistence problem that the institution increasingly faces. The campus reacted by hiring its first ever full-time director for the first-year experience. Previously, various actors handled programming for the first-year experience on a part-time basis across campus including academic deans, directors of residence life, and faculty members with tenure.

Six months into his position, the new director for the first-year experience established a First-year Experience Taskforce to review the current learning community practices and make recommendations for changes. The taskforce was comprised of other campus administrators such as academic deans, residence life directors and faculty members who were previously in charge of the learning communities as well as first-year academic advisors, advisors whose foci are specific racial and ethnic groups represented on campus, and upperclassman who had participated in learning communities. The new director and the taskforce took time to observe various learning communities, met with various staff members and faculty members involved with first-year programming, and held focus groups with both previous and current learning community participants. The data that were collected and analyzed found increased retention rates from the first to second semester for participants in the program. However, the increased retention rates did not continue from the first to second year. Qualitative focus group data revealed that although students acknowledged the assistance with their transition to college they felt an abrupt transition moving into their second semester of college when they no longer had courses with their cohort.

The director and his First-year Experience Taskforce made three recommendations to the curriculum planning committee. The first was that the learning community program be extended to span two semesters instead of one. The current program brings together students based on potential academic major interest areas and links three courses: one introductory major-based course, one general education literature course, and one new student seminar (already mandatory for all first-year students). The committee recommended that in the second semester of the freshman year, students be required to take one course as a cohort. The second recommendation was that the course be one that counts towards the diversity requirement. This recommendation was made as a way to alleviate some of the increasing racial tensions on campus. Moreover, while reviewing the courses offered that count towards the diversity requirement, the committee also recommended to narrow the number of courses offered that fulfill the diversity requirement, noting that a number of them did not prepare the students for collaborating with or understanding our nation's diverse composition. Examples of such courses included, Folkloric Dances of the Americas, The History of China 1600–1900, Introduction to Arabic 101 (language course), etc. The third recommendation was to increase the number of learning communities offered, including learning communities for undecided students since none are currently offered.

The director and his committee also made a fourth recommendation unrelated to

curriculum and planning. The fourth recommendation was to target both first-generation and racially/ethnically underrepresented students to increase their participation in
high impact programming, particularly the learning communities. Currently, less than
5% of participants in this high impact programming are from underrepresented groups,
and the number of first-generation students is somewhere around 40%.

The curriculum planning committee argued that it would be too difficult to coordinate the number of diversity courses offered each spring in order to meet the needs of
the extended learning communities and to allow them to be open to the small cohorts
(since they are traditionally offered in larger lecture style classrooms). They further
advised that it would take 3 to 4 years to increase the number of learning communities
offered because course planning and rotation schedules have already been planned 2
years out. Moreover, the college president felt that targeting first-generation and underrepresented students for participation in learning communities is unfairly advantaging
those groups over others.

Respond to the questions below as if you were on the First-year Experience Taskforce
as a student affairs administrator:

1. Develop a plan for targeting first-generation and racially underrepresented student participation in first-year programming such as learning communities. In
   particular, pay close attention to:
   a. How might you respond to the president's dislike of targeting these populations?
   b. What specific activities might you take to recruit and retain targeted students
      in the first-year programming?
   c. Will you develop specific programming for these underrepresented student
      populations, or, will you encourage them to be involved in the programs that
      already exist? Why?
2. How can the First-year Experience Taskforce and the Curriculum and Planning
   Office coordinate for the best interest of the students?
   a. What action steps must take place in order for this to happen?
   b. What is a realistic timeline for the lengthening of the learning community
      experience and the increase in the number of learning communities offered?
   c. Is it unfair to target underrepresented and first-generation students for partici-
      pation in learning communities? Please provide evidence for your rationale.
   d. Who should be responsible for meeting with the college president to discuss
      his concerns regarding recommended changes to the learning communities?

NOTE

1. This chapter was adapted from Carter, D. F., Locks, A. M., & Winkle-Wagner, R. (2013). From when and
   where I enter: Theoretical and empirical considerations of minority students' transition to college. In J. C.
   Smart & M. B. Paulson (Eds.), *Higher education: Handbook of theory and research* (pp. 91–149). New York,
   NY: Agathon Press.

5

THE ROLE OF MINORITY SERVING INSTITUTIONS IN SHAPING DIVERSITY IN HIGHER EDUCATION

Including Those Who Were Excluded

There is very little that is more important for any people to know than their history, culture, traditions and language; for without such knowledge, one remains naked and defenseless before the world.
—Marcus Tillus Cicero (106 BCE–43 BCE)

LeMelle wrote, "It is only through establishing Black as another legitimate point of reference that the Black American can attain first-class citizenship and the curse of racism can be neutralized" (2002, pp. 132–133). He proposed that historically Black colleges and universities (HBCUs) had a unique role in helping America make good on its promise of dream fulfillment for all of its citizens. We argue that this may be true of all minority serving institutions (MSIs), those institutions with a mission toward serving and including racially/ethnically underrepresented students. MSIs have often been leaders in empowering students to earn higher education while also valuing students' histories, cultures, traditions, and languages. An exploration of MSIs can reveal important insights as to how to better enact diversity-and-inclusion in other postsecondary institutions.

HBCUs still have a unique role to play in higher education in the United States, and the explosion of MSI designations beyond HBCUs and Tribal Colleges, is at once a reflection of the racial/ethnic demographic shifts and the countless opportunities that serving increasing numbers of people of color provides higher education institutions to re-imagine what it means to be diverse and inclusive. For example, Laden (2001) makes the case for the role of Hispanic Serving Institutions, alongside Tribal Colleges and HBCUs in facilitating access and opportunities for Hispanics or Latinas/os. Certainly, the higher education community will need to respond to Terenishi's (2010) critique of the relative exclusion of Asian American Native American Pacific Islander Serving Institutions (AANAPISIs) from the broader MSI funding, policy, and scholarly discourses. Given the long-term consequences of earning a postsecondary degree, and the rate at which MSIs confer degrees to individuals of color, MSIs play an important role in helping the United States reach its ideal of a pluralistic society. The sustainability of MSIs may well hold the key to American society "… reflecting the diversity and inclusivity of the United States of America" (LeMelle, 2002, p. 196).

This chapter initiates a two-chapter exploration of the role that postsecondary institutions play in shaping diversity-and-inclusion within higher education. We explore in these chapters the ways that institutional types and the historical missions of institutions can influence campus environments and students' experiences with inclusion during college. Chapter 6, the next chapter in this book, is an examination of the campus environment specifically in those postsecondary institutions that initially excluded many racial/ethnic populations of students. We save our exploration of those institutions, commonly called predominantly White institutions (PWIs) because of their majority White student populations, for the next chapter, after we consider a larger historical notion of racial/ethnic inclusion in this chapter.

This chapter begins the conversation with an overview of minority serving institutions, those institutions that were largely born out of exclusion within the mainstream postsecondary system in the United States. We define minority serving institutions, laying out some of the many official designations for the various types of campuses that are classified as highlighting the higher education of racially and ethnically underrepresented college students. Then, we review some of the empirical research on minority serving institutions in order to provide insight into how these campuses have influenced the diversity of students who have been included in U.S. postsecondary education.

The purpose of this chapter is not to explore the differences between PWIs and MSIs in an exhaustive manner but rather to provide a concise overview of the following areas:

1. The histories, basic mission and goals, and funding structures of MSIs;
2. The differential outcomes for students of color and unique characteristics that lend MSIs to contribute to higher education in the 21st century; and
3. Some of the challenges that MSIs may face in the future.

This overview and analysis of MSIs will be situated in the historical context of American higher education and society. We present insights into the contemporary context for MSIs with attention to practice and challenges looming on the horizon as the MSI landscape is affected by the dynamic and growing portion of college students who are steadily moving some campuses away from their predominantly or historically White campus designations. We will end this chapter with a statement of how such institutions are uniquely positioned, at the beginning of the 21st century, to meet the many challenges facing higher education and the communities of color at the core of many MSI missions.

THINKING ABOUT DIVERSITY: INSTITUTIONS THAT SERVE MINORITIZED STUDENTS

Rather than contemplating larger social theories related to minority serving institutions, we chose to reflect on historical trends and moments that shaped the need for and continued importance of these institutions. We frame this discussion as institutions whose goal is to serve populations of students who are minoritized, or made to be in the minority of the U.S. population. Then, we shift our attention toward the current designations for minority serving institutions as a way to provide some definitions for the kinds of populations that are served on these campuses. The history of U.S. higher education and the fingerprints that these eras have left on our contemporary postsecondary institutions is important to recall in providing background for the role of minority serving institutions. These historical moments can be grouped into the following five time periods, each of which is related to a period of civil unrest in the United States:

1. Colonization: 1636 to 1789;
2. American Revolution: 1790 to 1869;
3. Civil War and Reconstruction: 1870 to 1944;
4. World War II: 1945 to 1975; and
5. The end of the Vietnam War: 1976 to 1998 (Cohen, 1998).

We briefly summarize these moments to outline the ways in which some of the relevant racial/ethnic populations have been treated historically in the United States.

British colonists settled the land currently known as the United States in the 1600s and 1700s (Cohen, 1998). These colonists declared themselves independent from England and subsequently wrote a constitution for their young nation. As the nation expanded westward, Native American communities were decimated and relocated as slavery supported the agricultural economy of the Southern United States. Power and borders in the West and southwestern United States shifted. Simultaneously, immigration from Asian countries began to grow. After the Civil War, slavery ended and legislative acts affecting the status of African Americans and higher education were passed by the beginning of the 20th century, as the railroads and gold rush shaped the migration of Asian immigrants (Cohen, 1998). In the years immediately following the end of slavery, some institutions of higher learning would begin to admit African Americans in greater numbers, but certainly not relative to their numbers in the population. For the most part, African Americans (and many other racial/ethnic groups for that matter) were not a part of formal educational systems, with broader access to secondary education not occurring until the mid-20th century (Anderson, 1998). The country survived an economic crisis to engage in two world wars. In the early 1970s the U.S. military withdrew from South East Asia and the Vietnam War ended (Cohen, 1998). Each of these time periods holds significance for the current landscape of MSIs in particular, especially during the post-Civil War, post-World War II eras, and waves of immigration over time.

Minority Serving Institutional Designations

One obvious distinction between colleges and universities is their institutional type, categorized by the student populations that are primarily served: PWIs and MSIs. Minority serving institutions have grown from the two MSIs with historical designations, the Historically Black Colleges and Universities (HBCUs), and Tribal Colleges and Universities (TCUs) to include 10, according to the U.S. Department of Education (n.d.; Espino & Cheslock, 2008). Despite the variation in the U.S. system of higher education, these institutions serve a crucial role in higher education, particularly for students of color. MSIs were born out of unique historical contexts and are expanding at a time when the nation is at its most diverse with regard to racial and ethnic demographics. Each type of institution encapsulates distinct missions and distinct patterns of funding.

Given the diversity of postsecondary institutions in the United States, generalizing across higher education's institutional types presents several challenges. In the case of MSIs, the history, mission, legal status, governance and leadership, and students' and faculty experiences and outcomes are distinct from other institution types. MSIs include campuses in urban centers as well as rural areas. Their faculty and staff are distinct; they have differential effects on student outcomes and face unique challenges in the 21st century. Additionally, MSIs are diverse in their institutional scopes and sizes, including two- and four-year comprehensive instituions and research universities.

U.S. colleges and universities have evolved over time, as have the students they enroll and serve. At the beginning of the 21st century, the average college student is less likely to be 18–24 and increasingly likely to be a person of color (Ross et al., 2012). For African American, Asian American, Native American, and Latina/o students, the heterogeneity of students and their experiences varies across a number of social identities, including but not limited to socioeconomic status, ethnicity, language, and sexual orientation. As racial diversity increases in the United States, along with immigration patterns, the depth and breadth of ethnic differences within racial groups in academic and public spaces grows. So does the ever-evolving relevance of MSIs.

Minority serving institutions have always mattered in providing access to postsecondary education for people and communities of color. New and shifting designations of MSIs underscore the historical role of HBCUs and Tribal Colleges in providing access to higher education for African Americans and Native Americans. New terms like High Hispanic Enrollment, Minority Institutions, Hispanic Serving Institutions, and Asian American Native American Pacific Islander Serving Institutions, highlight the continued relevance of serving students of color within the unique context of a MSI. Moreover, many institutions meet the criteria of multiple Department of Education MSI designations, even if policy often demands that they choose an affiliation when Department of Education funds are at stake.

The discourse on institutional missions, particularly for those institutions serving large numbers of students of color has become dynamic. Institutional types like Historically Black Colleges or Universities, predominantly White institutions, and Tribal Colleges and Universities have grown to include Traditionally White Institutions, minority serving institutions, Hispanic Serving Institutions, Asian Serving Institutions, and Asian American Pacific Islander Institutions. The terms are a combination of those commonly used throughout the higher education literature and among practitioners. These terms also represent those used by the Department of Education (n.d.b) to label and categorize those institutions who serve large numbers of students of color or specific students of color subpopulations. Below, we briefly summarize the information provided by the Department of Education, Office of Civil Rights, organized by their groupings, as an introduction to MSIs.

- **Alaska Native-Serving Institutions**: This designation was authorized by the Title III of the 1965 Higher Education Act (HEA). Sixteen institutions received funding during the 2010–2014 cycle from the Department of Education, nine are located in Alaska and the others are in Hawaii. They represent a mix of private and public institutions and community colleges and four-year universities.
- **American Indian Tribally Controlled Colleges and Universities (TCUs)**: Thirty-two institutions, located in 14 mostly southwestern, midwestern, and coastal states,

have this designation. Most of the campuses are two-year institutions. Such institutions are authorized by the Department of Education via the Title III section of the Higher Education Act of 1965 and the 1978 Tribally Controlled Community College Assistance Act. However, Diné College, also grouped into this category, is unique among TCUs as it was authorized in the 1978 the Navajo Community College Assistance Act of 1978.

- **Asian American and Native American Pacific Islander-Serving Institutions (AANAPISIs):** Disproportionately, the institutions with this designation that received federal funding in 2011 are located in California and represent a combination of community colleges and four-year universities. In 2010, for example, institutions with this designation were more evenly distributed across the United States and included a greater number of community colleges.
- **High Hispanic Enrollment:** In 2011, the Department of Education designated 257 campuses, two year and four year alike, as having high Hispanic enrollment, defined as at least 25% of the student population on campus.
- **Hispanic-Serving Institutions (HSIs):** These institutions were authorized by Title V of the Higher Education Act of 1965, as amended (HEA), 20 U.S.C. §§1101-1103g. Eligibility includes at least 25% enrollment of Hispanic students, half of whom are to be from a low-income background, although campuses must apply for Title V funding in order to be considered an HSI. The Office of Postsecondary Education (OPE) within the Department of Education awards grants to HSIs and in 2012 such grants focused on the STEM pipeline at HSIs.
- **Historically Black Colleges and Universities (HBCUs):** Many of these institutions were initially started with the Morrill Act of 1890 that provided land for institutions in primarily Southern states in order to serve African Americans because state institutions were not including these students. In 1965, the definition of HBCUs was altered by the Higher Education Act. This definition designated HBCUs as those whose campuses established prior to 1964, with a mission that has consistently been the education of African Americans. HBCUs must be accredited, or articulate a clear path to accreditation.
- **Minority Institutions:** These unique institutions are clearly defined in the Minority Science and Engineering Improvement Program (MSEIP) and rely on a unique calculation of "minority" as outlined in § 365(3) the Higher Education Act (HEA) (20 U.S.C. § 1067k(3). This designation is based on a campus having more than 50% enrollment across three racial groups: African American, Native American, or Hispanic, as reported in the fall 2006 Integrated Postsecondary Education Data System (IPEDS) data. Because IPEDS does not make distinctions between Pacific Islanders and Asian Americans, Pacific Islander student enrollment is not included in the "Minority Institution" designation calculation. For-profit schools and those without accreditation are not eligible for this designation.
- **Native American-Serving, Nontribal Institutions:** Section 319 (b) (2) of the Higher Education Act of 1965, 20 U.S.C. 1059 (f) defines "Native American-Serving, Nontribal Institutions" and such institutions are eligible for Title III funding; this excludes Tribal Colleges and Universities. Institutions are eligible to receive this designation if they apply for federal funding, as with HSIs, enroll at least 10% Native American students, and emphasize serving low-income students.

- **Native Hawaiian-Serving Institutions:** As with other recognized MSI designations, these institutions must apply to the Department of Education for funding to receive this Title III, Part A, related designation, outlined in The 1965, Section 317(b)(4) of the Higher Education Act of 1965, 20 U.S.C. 1059d(b)(4). Institutions are eligible to receive this designation if they apply and enroll at least 10% Native Hawaiian students.
- **Predominantly Black Institutions (PBIs):** These institutions have some elements in common with HBCUs in regard to who they have evolved to serve and in some ways provide a pathway to a Title III association and funding that would otherwise not be available to such campuses. Section 318(b) of the Higher Education Act of 1965, 20 U.S.C. 1059e defines PBIs as those with 40% or more African American students and, as with other Title III designations, a campus must apply for support from the Department of Education in order to be considered a PBI. Further, these campuses must offer associate's degrees and/or bachelor's degrees, be accredited, and have a lower than average per undergraduate spending rate and enroll "needy" students.

Most often in the higher education literature, the above distinctions are not made, with most authors referring to minority serving institution to encapsulate HBCUs, Tribal Colleges and Hispanic Serving Institutions.

DIVERSITY STILL MATTERS: CAMPUS MISSIONS AND INSTITUTIONAL TYPES

As noted earlier in this chapter, MSIs as a collective set of institutions represent a wide array of higher education institutions; with this diversity of type, also comes diversity of missions. In this section of the chapter, we investigate research about HBCUs, Tribal colleges, and HSIs, as these three types of MSIs receive a disproportionate amount of attention in the extant higher education literature. We also call attention to the emerging work on AANAPISIs, which represents new opportunities for scholarship and practice within the MSI context. Most of the published literature on MSIs focuses on HBCUs. There may be several reasons for this, including the long history of these campuses, African Americans joining the professoriate, positioning themselves to study HBCUs, as well as a historical trend of dichotomizing our understanding of race as Black and White. Thus, as scholars who study MSIs recommend (Gasman, Baez, & Turner, 2008), we attempt to point out the interconnectedness of these institutions even though the majority of empirical literature bends toward the study of HBCUs. Below, we examine the following issues related to the diversity-and-inclusion that minority serving institutions offer the larger field of higher education:

1. Institutional missions aimed at serving minoritized populations: We explore the unique missions of HBCUS, HSIs, and Tribal Colleges, comparing and contrasting how these institutional structures may influence the way in which students of color might be included within the institutions. Then, we contemplate some of the challenges that these institutions are likely to face in the future; and
2. Student outcomes and experiences within minority serving institutions: we investigate some of the empirical literature on how these institutions influence the

experiences of racially and ethnically underrepresented students experiences in higher education.

Institutional Missions to Serve Minoritized Populations

Some MSIs have a deep, historical mission to serve and uplift the students of color who attend. Other institutions became minority serving because of demographic shifts in the student population. Regardless, MSIs do share a common ideal of striving to serve racially and ethnically underrepresented students in higher education. Many of these institutions offer important insights for diversity-and-inclusion on college campuses more generally. Below, we explore the histories of some of these institutional types, pointing out some of the differences and similarities in their missions, structures, and challenges. We focus in particular on HBCUs, tribal colleges, HSIs, and AANAPISIs. Then, we shift our attention toward some of the challenges that MSIs face as they move into the future.

Historically Black Colleges and Universities (HBCUs). Allen and Jewell (2002, p. 242) said of HBCUs "[they function] as multifaceted institutions, providing not only education, but also social, political, and religious leadership for the African American community." To say that the mission of HBCUs is grounded in the commitment to educate African Americans seems like an understatement. Allen and Jewell's point is perhaps more accurate; HBCUs not only have a mission to serve African Americans, many of these institutions aim to provide leadership to the whole community of African Americans. Many early HBCUs provided education for individuals who had been recently been freed from the bonds of slavery. These people were entering sectors of mainstream U.S. society for the first time during the Reconstruction era, the time after slavery when the country began to rebuild after the Civil War (Hill, 1994).

In 1837, the Institute for Colored Youth was established by Quakers in Philadelphia, Pennsylvania, as a teacher training college (State Library North Carolina, 2003). Lincoln University, established in 1854 and also located in Pennsylvania, is typically recognized as the first Black college to be founded in the United States (Hill, 1994). The Freedmen's Bureau also began to create Black colleges in the mid-1800s, although many of these institutions were really establishing primary and secondary education for freed Black slaves who had previously been excluded from formal education (Gasman, 2007). With the Morrill Land Grant Acts of 1862 and 1890, during the immediate years before the Civil War and the era of Reconstruction, came a tremendous growth in the number of African Americans who desired to access higher education. The Hampton Normal and Agricultural Institute, founded in 1868, and Tuskegee, founded in 1880, became the first accredited historically Black colleges (Anderson, 2002). These are just a few examples of the early HBCUs established in the United States, most of which had their start after the Civil War.

African Americans experienced backlash in the post-Reconstruction era as the country struggled to incorporate previously enslaved people into the citizenry. Jim Crow law, commonly associated with the notion of separating people across racial line (e.g., sitting separately on buses, drinking from separate fountains, etc.) and racial terrorism (e.g., public killing of Black people and other activities of terrorist organizations such as the Ku Klux Klan) flourished in the South. The North was more sophisticated at enacting quasi Jim Crow law through race neutral exclusionary policies targeting African

Americans (e.g., finding ways not to hire African Americans or admit them into college and universities; Anderson, 1998).

Prior to Reconstruction and the Great Migration after slavery (see Wilkerson, 2010), the African American population in the United States had primarily been concentrated in the South. This remains largely true today despite the Great Migration to urban industrial centers in the North and Midwest, motivated by the chance to participate in the American economy by acquiring factory jobs. The concentration of schools in a racially stratified southern context and the northern schools exclusionary admission practices excluded African Americans from PWIs (Gurin & Epps, 1975). As a result, most HBCUs are located in southern and midwestern states. Two other federal policies had a tremendous impact on African Americans' access to higher education: the G.I. Bill (1944), which afforded financial assistance for a college education to World War II veterans, and the Civil Rights Act of 1964, which outlawed explicit discrimination (e.g., Jim Crow Laws) against African Americans (Freeman & Thomas, 2002).

HBCUs do traditionally have a deep mission to give back to the African American community. Many HBCUs explicitly state a mission of uplift and empowerment for African Americans. For example, both Howard University (n.d.) and Morehouse College (n.d.) include such language in their respective mission statements posted on their websites. But, like many postsecondary institutions, they must navigate pitfalls associated with the gap between the surrounding city or town and the postsecondary institution, also called the town and gown phenomena. Some scholars assert that HBCUs could do a better job of reaching out to their communities because many of the campuses are surrounded by African American neighbors (Roebuck & Murty, 2004). Graham (2000), for example, provided some insight into the town and gown phenomena of the elitism at some HBCUs writing about deliberate exclusion of government workers, members of the clergy and teachers as not fitting the top-tier of Black society. This extreme elitism existed alongside an equally deliberate fight against racism in U.S. society. The legacy of elitism of prestigious HBCUs is lacking in those HBCUs that offer open admissions policies and serve less affluent student populations. But much more needs to be known about the differences between public and private HBCUs, despite some evidence that students at private HBCUs may have distinct pre-college experiences and thus distinct collegiate experiences as compared to their respective counterparts (Buzzetto-More, Ukoha, & Rusagi, 2010).

From their inception in the United States, most colleges and universities have relied on more than tuition to keep their doors open, and this is also the case for HBCUs (Cohen, 1998). Funding for HBCUs has rarely been stable, with many of these institutions relying heavily on federal and state support for their funding (NCES, 1996). HBCUs have had an on-going cooperative fundraising effort through the United Negro College Fund (UNCF) that was and is one of the more important players in helping to raise funds to support Black colleges and universities (see Gasman, 2007a). HBCUs also have a long history of funding through philanthropy (Gasman, 2007a; Gasman & Drezner, 2008). Among the few noteworthy individuals who helped with funding at HBCUs is Johnetta B. Cole, who raised the bar for fundraising at HBCUs during her tenure at Spelman College by raising millions of dollars, and significantly increasing Spelman's endowment (Winbush, 2007). Booker T. Washington also had tremendous success in raising funds for the Tuskegee Institute (Winbush, 2007). Despite the accomplishments of Washington and Cole, HBCU funding has yet to reach stability. Today, many HBCUs rely heavily on federal and state support for their funding and do not have access to varied funding sources such as alumni, private donors, federal and industry research dollars and endowments that can be in the millions for some PWIs. For example, in 2001, Howard had an endowment of just over $300 million and Harvard's was nearly $19 billion (Yates, 2001).

HBCUs lag behind their peer PWI institutions and evidence finds that HBCUs experience challenges maintaining funding, enrollment, and staff resources (NCES, 1994). For example, NCES (1996) reported that, private HBCUs spent 14% less per student than all private colleges and universities. The differences in funding between HBCUs and PWIs have often led HBCUs to potentially do more (or an equal amount to PWIs), even with less funding (Kim, 2002; Kim & Conrad, 2006).

Tribal Colleges and Universities (TCUs). Tribal colleges and universities are unique in that they have at their missions' center a commitment to the preservation of Native American culture and heritage. The first TCU was founded by the Navajo nation for this purpose and to provide access to college for Native American students (Guillory & Ward, 2008). All TCUs share this commitment of the preservation of culture, and this guides much of how TCUs are organized, governed, and situated in the broader higher education context. For example, TCUs often offer associate and bachelor degree programs, along with certificate programs. Such a commitment and the ability to engage the communities they serve is in contrast to the Ivy League schools' early efforts to colonize Native Americans in the 1800s (Guillory & Ward, 2008).

Tribal colleges and universities rely on funding from the federal government, most recently Executive Orders signed by Presidents Clinton and Bush, as well as the Department of Agriculture and foundations (Guillory & Ward, 2008, p. 96). Scholarship funds are raised through the American Indian College Fund and used to support students at all levels of higher education, including TCU staff that are pursuing advanced-degrees (American Indian College Fund). As with other MSIs, TCUs are frequently underfunded. This creates unique challenges for Native American students living in remote areas who are reliant on TCUs for access to postsecondary institutions (Guillory & Ward, 2008). The underfunding of TCUs is exacerbated as these campuses have grown to serve students who are not affiliated with a recognized Tribe, thereby placing greater demand on campus resources with no designated source of funding for such students (Guillory & Ward, 2008).

Hispanic Serving Institutions (HSIs). It has only been in recent years that HSIs have received recognition from the Department of Education. HSIs were designated as minority serving institutions through changes to the Higher Education Act made in 1992 (Laden, 2001). At that time, the definition of an HSI was an accredited U.S. institution with more than a quarter of full-time enrollment equivalent of Hispanic students, illustrating the role of such campuses in providing access to college and a pathway towards degree completion for Latinas/os (Laden). Since HSIs first became recognized, they have grown as a segment of higher education.

As mentioned earlier in this chapter, the HSI designation from the Department of Education is tied to Title V funding, Developing Hispanic Serving Institutions Program (U.S. Department of Education, n.d.). However, because HSIs are also often current or former PWIs (with a 25% Hispanic population) and, in some cases, they are even HBCUs (Black colleges with a 25% of more Hispanic population), Title V funds are not the only revenue stream for HSIs. HSIs are disproportionately public institutions, including both two- and four-year campuses. As such, MSIs are sensitive to the poor budget climates for higher education. Following the financial crisis of 2008, families' weathered increased constraints on their ability to pay for college. Combined with recent shifts in federal policies for financial aid (e.g. the elimination of summer Pell Grants and reductions in state aid), these shifting patterns in money available for MSI students to pay for college creates concerns for MSIs as so many of these campuses disproportionately serve first-generation, lower-income students.

Asian American and Native American Pacific Islander Serving Institutions (AANAPISIs). Campuses designated Asian American and Native American Pacific Islander Serving Institutions have more recently become a part of MSI collective. As Laanan and Starobin (2004) point out in their work proposing a definition for MSIs serving Asian American and Pacific Islander students, Asian Americans are a heterogeneous group, representing a multitude of national and ethnic backgrounds. Further, they outline how dangerous the model minority myth, the stereotype that Asian students will do well academically in comparison to their student of color peers, is to Asian American and Pacific Islander Students, as does Terenishi (2010). The myth that all Asian American and Pacific Islander students are academically successful masks the lower access and attainment that some Asian American student populations (e.g., Hmong students) have compared to their White counterparts. It further masks some of these students' experiences as English language learners, who may have spoken a language other than English in their homes growing up. These institutions have many of the same requirements as other MSIs with regard to accreditation. To be designated as an AANAPISI, these institutions must be non-profits, have lower than average per student spending (as compared to other institutions), have a portion of students be financially needy, and they must enroll at least 10% Asian American and Pacific Islander students. As these institutions are new to the MSI collective, this is an area for growth with regard to practice and research.

Future Challenges to MSIs. Moving into the future, there are a few challenges that minority serving institutions face. Community relations, faculty recruitment and retention, and student retention are all challenges facing HBCUs; yet these challenges also provide these institutions with unique opportunities to be innovative (Brown, 2001). While much of the literature highlights challenges faced by HBCUs, Tribal Colleges and Universities, other MSIs also may face similar challenges even though there is less empirical research on those institutions. Here we briefly explore issues such as inclusion of a full range of diversity within the institutions, retention of students, funding, and the accreditation of institutions so that the degrees are meaningful and useable (e.g., it is sometimes more difficult for students to gain employment with degrees from unaccredited institutions) by the students who attend.

Some scholars have argued that minority serving institutions, particularly HBCUs might be at a turning point, and in need of diversification of the faculty, curricula, and students if they are to be prepared to educate their evolving student bodies in the 21st century (Hurtado, 1999; Sims, 1994). In recent years, there have been many desegregation orders, primarily aimed at HBCUs, mandating that the campuses become more diverse to include more White, Latina/o, or Asian American students (Bridges et al., 2005; Redd, 1998). One challenge for HBCUs, and we argue that this may also be an issue in other MSIs, is to continue the empowerment of students of color without marginalizing other identities such as gender or sexual orientation (Gasman, 2007b; Patton, 2001). The mission of empowerment of African American students centers on race and ethnicity at HBCUs. Scholars have begun to contemplate the way in which other identities, such as gender or sexual orientation, might be ignored or even swept under the rug (Gasman, 2007b) by HBCUs. Gender does deserve further analysis within HBCUs and other MSIs. Additionally, some students may feel marginalized in other ways, such as through their political ideology (Harper & Gasman, 2008).

Retention, ensuring that students complete their degrees, is another issue for many MSIs (Harper & Gasman, 2008; Lundy-Wagner & Gasman, 2011; Smith & Wolf-Wendl, 2005). Because many of the students in these institutions are from underrepresented backgrounds and may be low-income or first-generation students, retention might need to be addressed in innovative ways within these institutions. For example, to foster better retention rates, some HSIs are combining student services with academic support programs as a way to help students navigate family, school, and work (Benitz & DeAro, 2004).

Funding has been and remains a significant challenge to MSIs as they prepare for the future (Bridges et al., 2005; Gasman, Baez, & Turner, 2008). Many HSIs, for example, face increased enrollments amidst severe understaffing and underfunding (Benitez, 1998). TCUs also face significant funding uncertainty as they try to upgrade facilities and retain faculty (Cunningham & Parker, 1998). These funding challenges are likely to continue into the future within many MSIs. It is likely that institutions will have to find innovative ways, such as philanthropic efforts (see Gasman & Drezner, 2008; Gasman, 2007a), to support their campuses.

Another challenge that many MSIs, particularly HBCUs and Tribal Colleges face is in their effort to either become accredited institutions or to keep the accreditation that they already have (Baylor, 2010; Gasman et al., 2007; Gasman, Baez, & Turner, 2008; Ortiz & Boyer, 2003). Much remains to be known about accreditation within these institutions (Fester, Gasman, & Nguyen, 2012). Many of them will have to create a path toward being accredited in the near future and this requires significant attention to the curriculum and how to create measurable outcomes for students (Gasman et al., 2007; Gasman et al., 2008).

Student Outcomes and Experiences within Minority Serving Institutions

The majority of the empirical research on students' experiences and outcomes (e.g., grades, graduation, etc.) at minority serving institutions centers on HBCUs. Much of this work is comparative, evaluating African American students' experiences within predominantly White institutions as compared to HBCUs, for example. There is overwhelming evidence that students within MSIs report experiencing a positive, empowering, and nurturing environment that is crucial to racially and underrepresented students' ability to succeed in higher education (Allen, 1992; Allen, Epps, & Haniff, 1991; Ortiz & Heavyrunner, 2003).

Researchers typically find that African American students attending HBCUs experience better outcomes, such as psychological adjustment, general satisfaction with their experience, and higher grade point averages (Fleming, 2002; Flowers, 2002; Jackson & Swan, 1991; LeMelle, 1969, 2002; Roebuck & Murty, 1993). HBCUs are considered more nurturing environments for African American students, in part due to their historical missions, which may help explain these positive outcomes (Key, 2003). Ortiz and Heavyrunner (2003) found similar evidence when studying TCUs, i.e., students report satisfaction with their experience in college.

In qualitative studies, Freeman (1999) and Freeman and Thomas (2002) found that just a few characteristics distinguish African Americans who choose PWIs and those who choose HBCUs. In common, PWI and HBCU students often grew up in Black environments, including their high schools, and nearly all were first-generation college students (Freeman, 2002). Janes' (1997) qualitative work echoes quantitative findings from Freeman; he found that African American students found the climate at HBCUs to be more comfortable and welcoming. Overall, the literature examining the differences between African American students' experiences at HBCUs and PWIs shows that HBCUs provide a positive social and academic atmosphere. De La Rosa (2003), however, found that African Americans at selective, liberal arts PWIs have higher levels of overall satisfaction than their HBCU counterparts.

Outcalt and Skewes-Cox (2002) used Cooperative Institutional Research Program (CIRP) data to examine engagement, interactions, and levels of satisfaction for students attending HBCUs and PWIs. They found that students attending HBCUs were twice as likely to be satisfied with the college experience as compared to their PWI counterparts because of their involvement on campus. This echoes earlier findings by Allen (1992), whose research comparing African American students' experiences within PWIs and HBCUs found that students had better cognitive outcomes at HBCUs, meaning that they may have been able to learn more and achieve more academically in the HBCU environment. Strayhorn (2011) specifically ponders involvement in the gospel choir as one way to support students' identification with their HBCU campus and found that such involvement provides an environment where students are able to further develop their ethnic identity.

With regard to cognitive ability, Kim (2002) used hierarchical linear modeling to explore potential effects of attendance at an HBCU or PWI for African American students and found no variation on any of the areas of ability examined. Kim speculates that this may be an indication that HBCUs are doing more for their African American students because, although they have far fewer resources to rely upon, their students are not suffering the effects of attending under resourced colleges and universities. Kim noted that attendance at same-sex institutions (e.g., Morehouse, Spelman, Bennett) might have confounded her findings. Contradictory to Kim, finding no differences between the cognitive abilities of African Americans attending HBCUs and PWIs, other researchers conducting quantitative analysis have found positive relationships between cognitive and academic skill development for African Americans attending HBCUs compared to their counterparts at PWIs (Pascarella, Edison, Nora, Hagedorn, & Terenzini, 1996; Watson & Kuh, 1996).

Consistent across several studies is the key finding that African American students at HBCUs are engaged in unique ways academically (Allen, 1992; Cokely, 2002; Jackson & Swan, 1991; Nettles, 1991; Rissmeyer, 1996). This finding is supported in other MSI contexts, such as TCUs and HSIs (Bridges, Cambridge, Kuh, Hawthorne, & Leegwater, 2005). An example is the research conducted by Berger and Milem (2000); they found that attendance in an HBCU was the stronger predictor of African American students' psychosocial well-being. Additionally, participants in the study self-reported higher self-ratings on academic ability. Lastly, in addition to HBCU attendance being a positive predictor of achievement orientations, four additional factors positively predicted achievement orientation: (a) faculty support, (b) effort, (c) involvement with multicultural organizations, and (d) student government involvement. It may be these factors that allow students to navigate barriers identified by Palmer, Davis, and Hilton (2009) such as finances, home and community issues and in the case of men, pride. Combined with family support (Palmer, Davis, & Maramba, 2011), the unique institutional resources may be key in helping students at HBCUs find success such that they persist through graduation. In a multi-level statistical analysis comparing the likelihood of graduation between HBCUs and PWIs, Kim and Conrad (2006) found that African American students were just as likely to complete their degrees at HBCUs as they were at PWIs.

HBCUs have been demonstrated as more successful in providing access and retaining their students through graduation when it comes to educating African Americans in certain fields. For example, in a case study of women in science, technology, engineering, and mathematics (STEM) disciplines at Spelman, the HBCU environment was found to be particularly beneficial for helping to prepare African American women for careers in the STEM fields (Perna et al., 2009).

There are also differences in outcomes for students who have attended an HBCU or a PWI. Consistently researchers have found that attending an HBCU has the following outcomes: higher GPAs, graduating with honors, intellectual self-esteem, tutoring other students, and satisfaction with overall college experiences (Astin, 1993). HBCUs, as the top producers of African Americans with baccalaureate degrees in science and engineering, have a unique role to play in meeting the training gap in U.S. science and technology fields (Perna et al., 2009). However, despite disproportionately high numbers of African Americans who received degrees from HBCUs, particularly in certain fields,[1] HBCUs are faced with challenges in helping students to persist through their degree programs. African American male students have particularly low graduation rates at HBCUs as compared to their African American female peers (Harper & Gasman, 2008; Lundy-Wagner & Gasman, 2011). In the case of HBCUs, retention challenges may be more a function of their historical commitment to access and in some cases, open access and the academic adjustment barriers faced by students entering college who received substandard, poor-quality K-12 education (Smith & Wolf-Wendl, 2005).

Given the aforementioned contradictory results, more research is needed to better understand why African Americans experience more positive outcomes at HBCUs, but such outcomes do not always translate into higher graduation rates. Additionally, given the growing racial and ethnic diversity at HBCUs, this particular institutional context provides a unique opportunity to examine cross-racial interactions (Dwyer, 2006) in the MSI context.

Beyond the growing body of research about students' experiences and outcomes at HBCUs, there is comparatively little inquiry into how students' experiences might differ at HSIs, Tribal Colleges and Universities, and AANAPISIs. This presents challenges because the student populations within these institutions may differ from students in HBCUs. For example, in their essay on student assessment in tribal colleges, Ortiz and Boyer (2003) asserted that students may need to be assessed differently than students within other MSIs. They argue that gender might be a predictor of students' ability to be successful in TCUs in a way that is unique as compared to other MSIs. They include factors such as students' goals, remedial courses taken (courses that help students prepare for more advanced courses), extracurricular involvement and course taking patterns as possible measurable areas to assess students' experiences. Some HSIs are beginning to experiment with intensive mentoring and support as way to help facilitate student success in these institutions, many of which are two-year institutions with high numbers of low-income, first-generation, and non-traditional students who are above the age of 22 (Benitez & DeAro, 2005). For example, the LifeMap approach, used in Valencia Community College in Orlando, Florida, helps students to determine how and when to take specific courses within their degree requirements, linking these requirements to the students' career and life goals. This program links academic affairs, student affairs, and even technology services as a way to support students in a seamless way, and students in the program are experiencing greater persistence rates (Benitez & DeAro, 2005).

Contreras, Malcolm, and Bensimon (2008) call deliberate attention to the easy-to-make assumption that HSIs are the corollary for their HBCU and Tribal college counterparts. In 2001, approximately 12.5% of undergraduates enrolled at Title IV institutions were attending HSIs (Mercer & Stedman, 2008). Among Title IV institutions, this is second only to those institutions that are both majority and minority with regard to undergraduate enrollment (Mercer & Stedman). While the high numbers of Latinas/os enrolled in these institutions is promising, they often have challenges in postsecondary education because many of these campuses are two-year institutions, and like many of their MSI counterparts, are inadequately funded (Contreras et al., 2008). HSIs have done much to strengthen the STEM pipeline for Latina/o students and are likely a key access point for Latina/o students in such fields (Crisp, Nora, & Taggart, 2009). But more work is needed on the experiences and outcomes that students have within these institutions.

SUMMARY: DIVERSITY AND MINORITY SERVING INSTITUTIONS

MSIs face an uncertain, yet hopeful, future with regards to funding structures, accreditation challenges, how to remain relevant amidst calls for diversification, and regarding student outcomes such as retention. How MSIs respond to these challenges will likely depend on their historical and current missions and designations as minority serving institutions. The larger project of diversity-and-inclusion in higher education is aided by the way in which MSIs have enacted the inclusion of historically underrepresented students on their campuses. With this in mind, there is significant scholarly and practical work to be done related to students' experiences of inclusion within MSIs.

Think about Diversity

There is comparatively little theoretical work that specifically focuses on MSI contexts. Rather, most scholarship on MSIs employs the theoretical models used to study higher education more broadly (e.g., predominantly White contexts, etc.). This does deserve some consideration. For example, it might be useful to contemplate unique theoretical models that *emerge* from the MSI contexts. In other words, perhaps scholars could identify theories from data collected in MSIs. In qualitative methodological traditions, grounded theory methodologies would highlight this type of emergent theory (using qualitative data such as interviews or observations as a way to develop theory). But, it may be possible to develop theories related to MSIs from quantitative data too (developing and testing hypotheses or testing theoretical models). The point is that there may be a unique opportunity to advance new theories that take into account the missions and traditions of MSIs, such as the mission to preserve cultural traditions (in the case of TCUs) or the mission to empower and serve African American students (in the case of HBCUs).

Diversity Still Matters

While a growing number of scholars are beginning to publish studies that examine college student experiences and outcomes at MSIs, there is still much that is unknown about MSIs. The previously mentioned challenges within many MSIs, of relevance amidst calls for diversification, retention, and even accreditation, could set the course for future research. Due in part to the rapid growth in institutions that have this designation from the Department of Education, there is an increasing need to understand the new and shifting designations. For example, research is needed to understand how students' experiences of inclusion might shift within various institutional types. Does a Latina/o student feel a greater sense of belonging at an HSI if that institutions simply became designated this way due to its demographic change (having 25% of more of the students self-identify as Hispanic)? Research is needed on this and other questions related to students' experiences within these institutions.

While most scholarship has been conducted on HBCUs as compared to PWIs, other comparisons would be fruitful. For instance, what might Asian American students' experiences at HSIs as compared to AANAPISIs or TCUs? There is yet to be a full exploration of students' success within MSIs aside from HBCUs. Moreover, the growth and expansion of HSIs and emergence of AANAPISIs, offers new opportunities to ask questions about student outcomes, faculty experiences, and organizational questions about MSIs.

In the study of higher education, we do not fully understand if it is possible to replicate the student success seen at some MSIs across emerging MSIs that may have other histories of exclusion at a PWI. Additionally, comparisons across institutional types within the categories of MSI are needed. For example, comparing outcomes for MSIs with historic missions to serve particular communities of color (HBCUs) with those MSIs with missions received due to meeting specific enrollment criteria would be revealing in terms of how to structure institutions that help students to be successful in the future. While MSIs do have some characteristics in common, they also have a broad spectrum of diversity across MSIs. For example, we know little about differences between two- and four-year MSIs or the differences between public and private MSIs. Palmer and Gasman (2008) offer some connections between mission and student experiences and success in a MSI context which could be used as an exemplar for future studies.

For AANAPISIs, the model minority myth will present unique challenges as new scholars and practitioners challenge our assumptions about Asian American college students. The role of the model minority myth, and the way students might grapple with it at AANAPISIs would be a useful course of study for future research. In general, greater attention must be paid to the scholarship on AANAPISIs, as well as to the nature of student affairs work and an exploration of the delivery of service to students and how these might be unique to MSI institutional contexts.

TCUs, with a mission toward preserving culture, may offer important insights into ways to include students without demanding that students' disregard their backgrounds or cultural experiences. Future research could examine how TCUs have crafted learning and development for their students as a way to reveal lessons for other types of institutions. In particular, the idea that these institutions were created with the express purpose of maintaining and celebrating cultural traditions within tribal communities might offer important insights into how to structure learning for racially and ethnically underrepresented populations more generally. For example, it might be possible to garner ideas from TCUs that could be adapted in other MSI (or even PWI) contexts.

Finally, there is a need for future inquiry related to the diversity *within* MSIs. That is, even though many of these institutions may have greater numbers of particular groups of students of color (e.g., African Americans in HBCUs), there is likely significant diversity within these groups of students. More research should be done to capture these within-group differences. One important part of this effort should be targeted toward the idea of intersectionality within MSIs. In other words, students within MSIs have multiple, complex identities related to their gender, sexual orientation, race/ethnicity, religion, and ability. One way to begin to uncover within-group differences would be to use an intersectional approach, aimed at examining multiple, overlapping, complex identities.

Diversity Is Everywhere

Allen (2004) notes that MSIs, "exist at the intersection of where the American Dream of unbridled possibilities meets the American Nightmare of persistent racial-ethnic subordination" (p. xv). This somewhat startling quote may capture some of the unique practical challenges within MSIs. While many of these institutions have a mission to empower students of color, it is important that populations of students are not essentialized, as if they are all the same. This relates to the point above, that more research taking an intersectional approach should be conducted. From a practical standpoint, this means that student affairs professionals, faculty, and other campus administrators need to think carefully about how to construct student support services on MSI campuses. Certainly, there are opportunities for the preservation of culture, the embracing of racial/ethnic identities (among other identities), and the empowerment of students of color. These opportunities should be carefully constructed so as not to stereotype, essentialize, or disempower students.

There are several areas for growth and development at MSIs. One area pertains to inclusivity along social identities that interact with students' racial and ethnic identities. For examples, LBGTQ students may face unique challenges at their HBCUs. Patton's (2011) work explores the importance of helping students navigate their social lives and coming out processes even when they find their campuses to have a supportive climate. Further, peers are an important source of support, and Patton highlights the significance of providing students with a safe space to give voice to their identities, including their sexual identity. More work on understanding the effect of the model minority myth on students of Asian descent would help practitioners better understand how best to support such students and might help us better understand the dynamics of cross-racial and cross-ethnic interactions within and across communities of color. Finally, understanding the role of the prison industrial complex and its impact on the educational experiences and trajectories of men of color, particularly those from lower income backgrounds, would push higher education scholars and practitioners to be more inclusive and innovative to serve a broader spectrum of students.

Related to student services, these efforts should be crafted with careful attention to the unique populations within each MSI. For example, in many HSIs, the campuses are two-year institutions and students might be part-time and nontraditionally aged. Campus support programs are likely to have a different approach in such contexts. In TCUs, there is often a mission of preserving American Indian cultural traditions. Student affairs practice would need to take this into account. Thus, student services face unique challenges within MSIs. However, there may also be the chance for creativity and innovation in the development of new types of services that uniquely attend the needs of students in these institutions.

DISCUSSION QUESTIONS

Based on the review above, we offer a few questions to help guide the improvement of practice and to initiate research about and for MSIs below.

Improving Practice

1. As a campus administrator, how do you leverage your MSI status to create new programs and innovate on your campus?
2. When faced with choosing what MSI designation will best serve your campus and its students, how do you make those decisions and set priorities for how students are served on your campus?
3. How are MSIs, with their specific missions, uniquely positioned to support inclusive campus communities for students of color?
4. How might student affairs practice differ within MSIs as compared to predominantly White institutions? Name some specific practices that may differ. Why might these differ?
5. What do institutions do to support marginalized populations on campus? What do they do to explore, support, and promote within group heterogeneity and cross-identity interactions?
6. Who are the institutional actors? What are the institutional actions that seem to make a difference in positive outcomes for students of color?
7. What about the institutional actors at MSIs—faculty, staff, and administrators— makes them so effective at providing access and appropriate supports to promote student success?
8. One of the major student affairs associations, Student Affairs Administrators in Higher Education (NASPA), developed a set of professional competencies that are encouraged for all student affairs professionals. How might the NASPA professional competencies be practiced in MSIs?
   a. The NASPA Competencies are (see http://www.naspa.org/programs/profdev/default.cfm): advising and helping; assessment, evaluation, and research; equity, diversity, and inclusion; ethical professional practice; history, philosophy, and value; human organizational resources; law, policy, and governance; leadership; personal foundations; students learning and development.

9. Another national association for student affairs, College Student Educators International (ACPA), developed a Statement of Ethical Principles and Standards. If you were a student affairs practitioner at an MSI, how might the ACPA Ethical Principles and Standards apply to your practice?
   a. The ACPA Standards are (see http://www2.myacpa.org/statement-of-ethical-principles-and-standards): professional responsibility and competence; student learning and development; responsibility to the institution; and responsibility to society.
10. The Council for the Advancement of Standards in Higher Education (CAS) developed a set of standards for student affairs. How might these CAS Standards be useful in your thinking about student affairs practice within an MSI?
    a. The domains for the CAS Standards are (see http://www.cas.edu/index.php/cas-general-standards/): knowledge acquisition, integration, construction, and application; cognitive complexity; intrapersonal development; interpersonal competence; humanitarianism and civic engagement; practical competence.

Developing Future Research

1. How might you go about evolving/revising theory for the study of MSIs, or, advancing new theories in MSI contexts? Describe how you might develop a project to do this kind of theoretical work.
2. In this chapter, we provided evidence of gaps in research about MSIs. What ideas to you have to future research that should be done on these institutions?
3. How might a research study of student diversity within MSIs differ from a student of student diversity within a PWI?
4. Why might it be important to compare students' experiences within different types of MSIs? Describe a comparative study that you might be able to conduct.
5. Some MSIs, such as AANAPISIs, have very little research conducted about students' experiences within them. Consider why there might be so little research. Then, describe how you might create a study to begin to provide insight into these little known institutions.

=============================A CASE STUDY=============================

PRACTICING DIVERSITY ISSUES RELATED TO THE COLLEGE TRANSITION PROCESS

Leveraging Demographic Shifts to Expand Services to Students

Gulf Region University (GRU) is a four-year, regional university of 35,000 students. Approximately 20% of students are Caucasian, another 27% are Latina/o, 23% are Asian American or Pacific Islanders and 26% are African American, and due to a transfer agreement with Tribal Colleges in your region, a growing population of students are Native American at 4%. Historically, GRU has served a large number of first-generation college students who come from poor and working-class families; recent estimates are that 55% of students are Pell-eligible. In recent years, a growing number of students who come from middle- and high-income socioeconomic backgrounds have enrolled at GRU. Unique to other campuses in the region, GRU has relative stability across racial/ethnic groups in the following student outcomes: time to degree, graduation rates, and cumulative GPA.

At GRU, students use the Academic Advising Center for support in selecting a major, choosing classes, transfer requirements, and graduation requirements. A growing number of students from middle- and high-income socioeconomic backgrounds use the center. Typically, students use the Career Center for resume help, advice on career options, job postings, and career diagnostic tests. Most of the first-generation college students who come from under-resourced pre-college environments and have fewer personal financial resources available to pay for college, use the Career Center. The Cultural Center serves as an umbrella organization for student groups with an ethnic specific foci and coordinates most events on campus that are designed to increase racial ethnic/diversity and inclusion. These events include: culturally-specific peer orientations and graduations, Hispanic History Month, Black History Month, Asian History Month, Martin Luther King, Jr., Day Celebration, the Pow Wow, the Vincent Chin Symposium on Hate Crimes, and Cinco de Mayo celebrations, to name a few.

GRU's budget is constrained due to a decrease in state revenues and overall support of higher education. Some stress on the campus budget has been ameliorated, however, because of the increased enrollment of more affluent students. However, challenges remain, and in order for the campus to maintain access for lower SES students, GRU is seeking external funds to preserve their excellent record of accomplishment with academic and social support of their racially/ethnically diverse student body.

As part of the new President's Completion Agenda, The Department of Education recently released a call for proposals to promote access and degree completion for low-income students. Minority serving institutions that have at least 50% students who are Pell eligible and have at least two MSI designations are entitled to apply. Additional criteria include:

- Demonstrated success with African American, Latina/o, Pacific Islander, and Native American students;
- Clear articulation of how multiple MSI designation allows for increased collaboration across units and cost-efficiencies on your campus; and
- Scalability, meaning that the campus has a clear plan for how to expand current successful practices.

The Provost and Vice President for Student Affairs, who enjoy a strong history of collaboration, have convened a working group to develop this proposal. They have indicated that the goal of the proposal is to streamline the multiple ways students receive support and advice while not reducing the quality of services available. They also propose to create a new Academic and Career Advising Center to be housed in the same building as the Cultural Center. This will require the academic advising staff and the career staff to collaborate but not lose sight of the goals of their individual units and figure out ways to connect with their colleagues at the Cultural Center. You currently work 50% in the Academic Advising Center and 50% in the Career Center. As the prospective assistant director of this new center, who previously worked at the Cultural Center, you have been asked to prepare a report describing the new structure and services of the new Academic and Career Advising Center. In your report, outline the proposed new structure, and explicitly delineate how the new structure of the office will combine the two centers in a collaborative manner and connect to the Cultural Center. To help construct your report, consider the following:

1. Identify the three current critical services provided by the Academic Advising Center and the three current critical services offered at the Career Center so that you have a total of six core priorities for the new center.
2. There must be a streamlining of services. Therefore, you must choose four of the six priorities to recommend to senior campus leaders as the foci of the new MSI funding opportunity from the Department of Education. You must use relevant research to support your answer. Discuss how the focus on these priorities will affect the distinct groups of students who access the Academic Advising and Career Center and allow you to respond to the call from proposals.
3. Explain how the new center will work to serve the socioeconomically and racially/ethnically diverse student body at GRU.
4. Describe and explain your plans to evaluate program effectiveness.
5. Discuss how the advising and career staff will collaborate at the new center. Give two specific examples of programs the new center will offer, clearly articulating how these services combine academic advising with career counseling.

Throughout your response, support your answer by identifying and citing sources from professional and scholarly literature.

NOTE

1. At PWIs, minority students are typically less likely to graduate in science, math, and engineering fields (Fenske, Porter, & DuBrock, 2000; Smyth & McArdle, 2004).

6

THE CAMPUS CLIMATE

Diversity on Campus Makes All the Difference

You've got to be a thermostat rather than a thermometer. A thermostat shapes the climate of opinion; a thermometer just reflects it.

—Cornel West, Professor, Princeton University

Educational researchers have repeatedly identified factors, such as the campus environment, institutional type, and organizational characteristics that affect outcomes for college students (Bean 1980, 1983; Braxton & Mundy, 2001; Pascarella & Terenzini, 1991, 2005). Organizational characteristics such as communication, fairness in the application of academic rules and grading, and involving students in decision-making are related to retention (Berger & Braxton, 1998). Students of color may be more sensitive than their White counterparts to certain aspects of their college experiences such as those relating to race or discrimination (Cabrera, Nora, Terenzini, Pascarella, & Hagedorn, 1999; Hurtado, 1992; Hurtado, Milem, Clayton-Pedersen, & Allen, 1998, 1999; Steele & Aronson, 1995). This may be because students of color possess worldviews and experiences that are likely to be different from students, staff, or peers in predominantly White institutions. Because of the historical legacy of structural racism on college campuses, conflicts between the backgrounds of students of color and the norms of some campuses may be invisible (Bensimon, 2004; Chesler, Lewis, & Crowfoot, 2005; Feagin, 2002; Hurtado et al., 1999). The study of the campus climate has become a focal area for higher education scholars and practitioners alike in an attempt to make these issues more visible. Campus climates represent a collective of actions by administrators, faculty, and peers on campus. This collective of actions is one locale where the act of inclusion is felt, or, contrarily, missed.

The campus climate refers to the campus environment and norms related to acceptance of particular issues or characteristics of the population on campus, such as general diversity, race, or gender. The campus climate allows for a metaphor of the temperature (chilly or warm) of a campus related to how accepting or welcoming that campus is toward diversity in the population of students, staff, or faculty. In the early 1990s, higher education scholars began to examine the campus climate in new ways, with an interest in experiences of racially and ethnically diverse college students (e.g., African American, Latina/o, Asian American, Native American). These studies focused on how students of color in particular perceived the campus racial climate (i.e., how welcoming was the campus towards racial diversity?), often in the context of broader studies about college student outcomes. Specifically, since the early 1990s, higher education scholars have debated the campus racial climate and how it affects students' interactions with peers who are different, grade point average (GPA), persistence through degree programs, and graduation rates. In most cases, students are asked to report on how comfortable the campus feels to them as students of color.

Over time, the campus racial climate has been expanded beyond college impact studies to examine the campus racial climate for faculty and administrators of color and Caucasian or White students. Research on the campus climate now includes examinations of college students' cross-racial interactions, also known as interactions with diverse others. This kind of work gained attention when such research was used in the Michigan affirmative action cases (see Chapter 3, this volume). As discussed in Chapter 3, the University of Michigan successfully argued before the Supreme Court that a diverse student body in the college environment was a compelling state interest (*Gratz et al., v. Bollinger et al.*, 539 U.S., 2003; *Grutter et al., v. Bollinger et al.*, 530 U.S., 2003). The campus climate research examined the impact of interactions with diverse others on college students, presenting a range of outcomes such as improved learning, for example. A portion of this research moved beyond students' experiences and examines diversity-related institutional actions and conditions that affect the experiences of students of color, all of which was used to argue cases before the Supreme Court and win.

In this chapter, we continue our institutional level examination from Chapter 5. We particularly focus on the norms and actors within institutions (how staff, students, faculty can influence diversity in higher education) and the ways that the institutions might influence students' experiences as they move through college. In Chapter 5, we contemplated how various types of institutions might influence students' outcomes in college; particularly those that serve historically underrepresented groups of students such as minority-serving institutions. Here, we explore one of the less obvious aspects of students' experiences within postsecondary institutions, the way that the general environment or climate for diversity could either facilitate or hinder students' experiences. We pay particular attention in this chapter to the experiences of underrepresented students within predominantly White institutions (PWIs) because the research and theoretical inquiry in this area centers on these institutions.

THINKING ABOUT DIVERSITY: THEORETICAL APPROACHES TO THE STUDY OF CAMPUS CLIMATES

Only a few models offer a comprehensive explanation of the campus climate for racial and ethnic diversity. These models emphasize practical examples alongside definitions or assumptions about diversity in higher education. Since the 1970s, PWIs have struggled with increasing the presence of people of color on their campuses. In their groundbreaking study, Peterson and colleagues (1978) recognized the importance of how PWIs responded to the increased presence of African Americans. They found great variability in campus case study responses, from the centrality of race-related initiatives (e.g., programs, policies, practices) to the day-to-day operations. Some campuses were reactive and others were more proactive (e.g., changing campus policies, programs, or structures to welcome new student demographics before there was a problem on campus) in relation to institutional transformation. In the 1980s, the era immediately following the *Bakke*[1] decision on the inclusion of race in admissions where quota systems (i.e., setting aside a number of spots for particular populations of students) were ruled unconstitutional, higher education research and practice focused on further refinement of racial and ethnic diversity programs, many of which primarily targeted specific racial groups (Altbach, Lomotey, & Kyle, 1999).

There are a few theoretical models for considering campus climates and institutional structures related to student diversity:

1. Richardson and Skinner's (1990) organizational framework outlining how institutions might adapt to increased diversity;
2. A four-dimensional framework for ways that campuses can support diversity by Hurtado, Milem, Clayton-Pederson, and Allen (1999);
3. An expansion of the four dimensional framework to include organizational diversity by Milem, Antonio, and Chang (2005);
4. The Diversity Scorecard by Bensimon (2004), a framework for creating more inclusive environments that lead to diverse students' success; and
5. An Inclusive Excellence Change Model by Williams, Berger, and McClendon (2005) that emphasizes diversity as part of excellence within higher education institutions.

Richardson and Skinner's Model of Organizational Adaptation to Diversity

There are a few models that offer an organizational framework to explain the linkages between an institution's commitment to policies and practices that support racial and ethnic diversity and related student outcomes. One model by Richardson and Skinner (1990) hypothesized how institutions adapt to increased racial and ethnic diversity in the student body. Richardson and Skinner argued that the policy environment and institutional mission shape higher education organizational culture, which in turn affects institutional outcomes such as equity in enrollment and graduation rates. In their model of institutional adaptation to student diversity, the legal context, funding priorities, access initiatives, and information and communication of the state policy environment are considered important. They argued that the policy environment and institutional mission dictate selectivity (e.g., making it more difficult to merit admission) and this might lower expectations for racially diverse students (i.e., make it seem too difficult to get into that institution), which leads to lower enrollments for students of color. In other words, students of color may perceive highly selective admissions as unavailable to them, even if they are eligible. Open access policies have the opposite effect where students of color may see the institution as open to their presence. Ultimately, their view was that institutional actions such as setting clear goals and priorities, allocating resources, coordinating holistic student affairs practices, and involving faculty in initiatives can resolve tensions between quality and diversity.

Finally, Richardson and Skinner (1990) investigated the sensitivity of institutions to state policies. Some states' policies call for the increased representation of students of color on college campuses. Thus, institutions may follow the lead of their states in some cases. Or, on the contrary, in states where there is no policy discussion about diversity, institutional actors may also follow that lead and opt not to take much deliberate action to diversify statewide campuses.

A Four Dimensional Diversity Framework by Hurtado, Milem, Clayton-Pederson, and Allen

Hurtado et al. (1999) proposed a four-dimensional framework to explain the context in which campuses could create and support diverse learning environments. Each of these dimensions shapes the campus climate for race and ethnicity in distinct ways. The four dimensions are:

1. Historical Legacy of Inclusion/Exclusion: This dimension allows for an examination of the way that the particular campuses have treated racial/ethnic diversity in the past. For example, were some students (e.g., African Americans and women) disallowed from being admitted? For students of color or women who were eventually admitted to the institution, how were they treated? How have various groups been treated on the campus historically? Have there been negative racial or gender incidents on campus?

2. Structural Diversity: In this dimension, the demographics of the campus are considered. Questions might include: What percentage of the campus self-identifies as White (or male, heterosexual, Christian, etc.)? What percentage of the campus is comprised of racially underrepresented students, staff, or faculty? Within particular disciplines, campus organizations or groups, what is the demographic composition?

3. Psychological: This dimension offers a way to investigate how the campus environment shapes perceptions of experience and mental processes for students, faculty, and staff. Some questions to ponder might be: Are some students supported in ways that other students are not? Are some students experiencing psychological distress on campus? Are students able to develop cognitively and psychosocially in the campus environment? Or, are there barriers to development for some students?

4. Behavioral: Focusing on the way that people within the institution act, this dimension allows for reflection on the way that diversity is (or is not) enacted in the institution. Some of the questions to contemplate could be: If diversity is part of the mission on campus, is this enacted within daily interactions between faculty, staff, and students? How do students act toward one another? How do faculty or staff act toward various groups of students? How do students behave toward faculty or staff? Are there trends in behavior based on race, gender, or other categories?

Milem, Chang, and Antonio's Organizational Dimension of Diversity

Institutions create, support, and enact policies to increase racial/ethnic diversity in higher education institutions. Milem et al. (2005) provided a framework to evaluate institutional commitments to racial/ethnic diversity, expanding on the four-dimensional framework. Their expanded *five*-dimensional conceptual framework (including Historical Legacy of Inclusion/Exclusion, Compositional Diversity, Psychological, Behavioral) added an Organizational/Structural Dimension to the Hurtado et al. (1999) model. Milem and his colleagues used the work completed by Milem, Dey, and White (2004) to add this Organizational/Structural Dimension to the Hurtado et al. (1999)

framework. In doing so, they named actionable areas on which institutions could consider working to create better campus climates—diversity of the curriculum, tenure policies, organizational decision-making policies, and budget allocations and policies. They further changed the language used to refer to the number of people of color on a campus from Structural Diversity (percentages and numbers) to Compositional Diversity (inclusion of new groups).

This organizational dimension of diversity was designed to capture the institutional policies and practices that support racial and ethnic diversity and was a way to deliberately connect the theoretical ideas of accepting campus climates with practical applications. The organizational/structural dimension by Milem et al. (2005) provided a missing piece of the puzzle to help explain why PWIs continue to struggle with how they respond to, manage, and value the presence of racially and ethnically diverse students on their campuses. More importantly, it spotlights institutional accountability for the campus climate as it relates to racial and ethnic diversity in a distinct way.

Institutions are responsible for the quality and context of their undergraduate academic programs. What institutions articulate as their values, along with their policies and actions at the organizational/structural level, are key to realizing student-related outcomes in the psychological and behavioral dimensions. For example, a campus whose mission espouses a commitment to diversity might have explicit programs designed to increase the compositional diversity of their faculty and students. Williams et al. (2005) underscored that institutions must deliberately institute policies and practices if they are to create a campus climate that will become more inclusive. This responsibility begins with recruiting a diverse group of students and extends to the curriculum, hiring of diverse faculty and staff, and fostering opportunities for cross-racial interactions in formal (e.g., classrooms) and informal (e.g., cafeterias, unions, residence halls, etc.) settings. The documented educational value of a diverse student body makes colleges and universities (and the actors within them such as administrators, faculty, staff) increasingly culpable when a diverse student body is not maintained. Despite the importance of understanding the connection between diversity-related institutional actions and student outcomes, there is relatively little research on this topic.

The new organizational/structural dimension also offers a reframing to the previous historical dimension because many predominantly White institutions have exclusionary legacies they must confront as they enact their commitment to racial/ethnic diversity and inclusion. Historically, many institutions that are now considered predominantly White purposely excluded students based on gender, race/ethnicity, and religious affiliation. The history of how institutions transformed exclusionary policies and practices to inclusive ones illuminates the challenge of how institutions manage race/ethnicity in the current context of higher education. Institutional commitments to racial/ethnic diversity in many cases may be a preemptive remedy for past discriminatory policies and practices. As institutions first began to increase the numbers of racially/ethnically diverse students on their campuses, many students of color had a token presence on those campuses and were often isolated among their predominantly White peers (Cabrera et al., 1999; Davis et al., 2004). Understanding this history of institutional movement from deliberate exclusion of particular racial groups, to token inclusion (trying to have numbers of students of color to appear more inclusive without making changes to the institution to welcome these groups), to an eventual commitment to opening the institution to new groups of student is crucial. Once this history is understood, an institution can begin crafting new policies and practices to respond to and heal from that history.

There are implications for student learning and a host of additional college outcomes related to the campus climate. The organizational structures and practices of an institution dictate whether those within the institution create and maintain an environment where students benefit from diversity. These institutional practices include the inclusion of diversity in the curriculum, tenure policies, organizational decision-making policies, and budget allocations. For example, instituting a diversity course as a graduation requirement is a specific curricular initiative that helps to foster a racially and ethnically inclusive environment if the class is done well (students feel accepted, empowered to speak their views, and challenged to grow). Co-curricular initiatives may include living-learning programs or an intergroup relations program (IGR) where students come together to talk about differences and diversity. Institutions that value students' tolerance of diverse others and want students to work cooperatively and develop empathy with diverse others may be more likely to articulate a commitment to giving undergraduates the opportunity to develop democratic skills during college. Decisions that support IGR programs, culturally themed residence halls, and other diversity-centered co-curricular activities (e.g., diversity retreats) demonstrate this commitment in concrete ways.

The aforementioned institutional policies and practices shape the psychological climate of a campus and have the potential to affect student behaviors in and out of the classroom (Hurtado et al., 1999; Milem et al., 2005). Given the challenges associated with responding to histories of exclusion and the dynamic sociopolitical context outlined by Hurtado et al. (1999), institutional action becomes even more crucial. If institutions do not have clearly defined policies and practices that support racial and ethnic diversity on their campuses, they will likely be unsuccessful with creating inclusive environments.

The Elements Influencing the Climate for Racial/Ethnic Diversity framework provided by Hurtado et al. (1999) and, more recently, the Campus Climate Framework by Milem et al. (2005) represent two of the more comprehensive conceptualizations of the campus climate for racial/ethnic diversity. Both frameworks account for the governmental and political contexts and forces that influence higher education institutions, as well as the sociohistorical context and forces that shape institutional policies for racial and ethnic diversity.

Bensimon's Diversity Scorecard

The work of Bensimon and colleagues in the Equity Scorecard presents opportunities to consider best practices to improve the campus climate from organizational leadership perspectives in ways that cultivate the implementation of evidence-based best practices and promotes culture change to address racial and ethnic inequity on campuses. While the work of Milem et al. (2005) provides a broader theoretical framework that links the organizational context of the campus climate to best-practices, Bensimon's Scorecard, highlighted in the first 2004 issues of *Change* and initially termed the Diversity Scorecard, provides a clearly delineated process for campuses to self-assess their climates through the use of institutional data. Specifically, the Equity Scorecard focuses on four areas: (a) access, (b) excellence, (c) institutional receptivity, and (d) retention, each of which calls for an examination of data by race and ethnicity, identification of specific targets that indicate improvement, and a clear definition of equity. The core concept of this scorecard is to create actionable diversity goals and ways to measure those goals and gives institutions a tool to evaluate their goals and progress relative to eliminating educational inequities across racial and ethnic groups.

Bensimon's most recent work with Bensimon and Malcolm (2012), represents a significant contribution toward praxis in that it explores the application of the theory undergirding Bensimon's Equity Scorecard. This edited volume of work truly blends theory, practice, and research, the latter of which we include later in this chapter. In many ways, this edited volume argues that diversity work, particularly, the portion of this work in post-secondary education that has as its core the amelioration of racial and ethnic inequity, is a theoretically grounded, tightly bound practice, and worthy of the time and investment as an area of study in the field of higher education and beyond. This volume gives greater understanding of the theoretical foundation of the Equity Scorecard, how to use it effectively, and concludes with evidence of how the scorecard is effective at moving campuses towards greater racial and ethnic parity in outcomes and experiences.

The Inclusive Excellence Change Model by Williams, Berger, and McClendon

Williams et al. (2005) proposed an Inclusive Excellence Change Model designed to assess institutional change for diversity in a 21st-century context. They claimed that diversity is a vital part of excellence within postsecondary institutions more generally. They included students' academic excellence alongside helping students to develop skills that can be applied in an intercultural society. They argued that such an approach to diversity allows higher education institutions to stay relevant by positioning themselves to be responsive to 21st-century challenges. Williams and colleagues argued that institutions must use diversity to maintain and increase the relevancy of higher education as well to promote sustainable change. They based their conceptualization on earlier work toward institutional accountability for diversity (e.g., Bensimon, 2004; Hurtado, et al., 1999; Smith et al., 1997).

Drawing on the work of Bensimon's Scorecard, they proposed an Inclusive Excellence Scorecard to evaluate institutional change with regard to diversity and recommended the following four areas be evaluated to embrace diversity within institutions:

1. Access and equity: Focusing on the area of admissions to the institution and in how students are treated once they enroll;
2. Diversity in formal and informal contexts: Centering on the compositional diversity both in and out of classrooms on campuses (e.g., in student organizations, on committees, in informal spaces such as unions, etc.);
3. Campus climate: Stressing the importance of students, staff, and faculty perceptions of the racial and gender experience on campus; and
4. Student learning and development: Considering how diversity at the institution can affect how students engage in their education and develop in their identities.

Further, they recommended that the objective of each area be developed along with goals and strategies so that the ideas move from theoretical conceptions toward actionable tasks. As part of the ability to assess institutional diversity change and excellence, they also called for measures to capture baselines and identify targets, which would then be used as a ratio to form an "equity score" in the assessment and evaluation of institutional change.

Building on this idea, Williams and Clowney (2007) recommended that a diversity approach should simultaneously address the following three rationales for diversity in higher education: educational value, business case, and social justice. This extension of the Inclusive Excellence Change model makes a case for how diversity can be part of the core educational values of an institution. Additionally, Williams and Clowney saw diversity as part of the business side of campus (e.g., that there can be an economic incentive to diversifying institutions as new populations enroll and graduate). Finally, by relating diversity to social justice, they made the point that campus diversity is something that can transcend into larger societal approaches and perspectives on diversity.

DIVERSITY STILL MATTERS: EMPIRICAL APPROACHES TO CAMPUS CLIMATES

Hurtado's (1992) national survey research that examined students' openness and interactions related to diversity on college campuses launched the campus climate scholarship. Responding to numerous instances of racial tension on college campuses during the 1980s, Hurtado was primarily concerned with the way that students from different racial/ethnic backgrounds experienced campuses and the racial climate. This initial line of work initiated a series of surveys and projects through the Higher Education Research Institute housed at the University of California, Los Angeles. The series of surveys, Cooperative Institutional Research Program (CIRP), has resulted in numerous studies of campus racial climates (Harper & Hurtado, 2007; Hurtado et al., 1998; Milem et al., 2005). Subsequently, the campus racial climate has been explained quantitatively and qualitatively and in mixed methods studies.

After our review of the extant literature in the area, we separated the campus climate research into four categories:

1. Students and the campus racial climate: This area of research demonstrates students' perceptions of campus climates within their college institutions;
2. Faculty and the campus racial climate: These studies focus on either faculty perspectives of the campus climate, or, on issues related to the campus that faculty might influence (e.g., curriculum, classroom experiences, student-faculty interactions);
3. The educative value of diversity: This line of scholarship maintains that diversity on college campuses aids in warmer campus climates. One way that this diversity is fostered is through students' interactions with others who are not like them (i.e., interactions with diverse others);
4. Institutions and the campus climate: This smaller body of work highlights the role of institutional policies, practices, and actors (e.g., administrators, etc.) in helping to foster a particular climate on college campuses.

Students and the Campus Racial Climate

A number of studies published in the 1990s examined the climate for racial and ethnic diversity in U.S. colleges and universities. This may have been partially in response to a number of incidents occurring on college campus where students of color were the targets of racially motivated incidents (Gerstenfeld, 2011). Many students report tense racial climates during college (Gusa, 2010; Miller, Anderson, Cannon, Perez, &

Moore, 1998; Solórzano, Ceja, & Yosso, 2000). The way that students describe the campus climate differs by racial/ethnic background (Harper & Hurtado, 2007; Kalof, Eby, Matheson, & Kroska, 2001; Rankin & Reason, 2005). For example, while there have been contradictory examples (Nora & Cabrera, 1996), in general, students of color consistently report a more hostile racial climate within predominantly White campuses than do their White peers (Ancis, Sedlacek, & Mohr, 2000; Hurtado, Carter, & Spuler, 1996; Rankin & Reason, 2005).

Campus racial climates scholarship often connects students' perceptions of the climate with academic outcomes (Cabrera et al., 1999; Chang, Astin, & Kim, 2004; Gurin, Dey, Hurtado, & Gurin, 2002). Research has demonstrated the importance of campus climates and concerted institutional efforts toward improving the experiences and outcomes for students of color in particular (Cabrera et al., 1999; Hurtado, 1992; Hurtado & Carter, 1997; Hurtado et al., 1998, 1999). Mechanisms for academic, social, and financial support (e.g., campus financial aid programs that offer academic and social support) provided within institutions can help institutional actors, such as campus administrators or faculty, to demonstrate a campus commitment to people of color, thus improving the campus climate for racial and ethnic diversity (Freeman, 1997; Green, 2001; Hurtado et al., 1998, 1999).

Given the continuing significance of race in education and college experiences, due in part to structural and interpersonal racism, students of color often navigate their institutions, professors, and peers in ways that are distinct from those of White students. For students of color, race is a salient factor during their undergraduate years and as such must be central to examining their college experiences and the institutional actions and climates that promote positive outcomes in college. The campus climate for racial and ethnic diversity merits attention in understanding specific experiences that lead to success in college for historically underrepresented students of color. One reason for the importance of investigations into students' experiences with campus climates is that this places the responsibility on the institution, and not just on the student. For example, a student of color might have negative racial experiences on campus (e.g., racist comments from peers), and the campus climate framework would contemplate how to help students institutionally (e.g., programs that allow students to uncover their stereotypes of racial groups) instead of simply assuming that the student of color should alter his or her actions.

Faculty and the Campus Racial Climate

Faculty play a key role in shaping the climate at their institutions, yet most research relevant to understanding the institutional context for diversity has been inquiry into student experiences. Studies have examined faculty only in rare cases. One such study found that faculty of color are more likely to be hired when institutions mention diversity in the job description, have hiring programs to diversify the campus, and are often hired into or affiliated with ethnic studies programs (Smith, Turner, Osei-Kofi, & Richards, 2004). One of the few studies that included staff found that social identity characteristics are important in how staff view the climate for diversity, but so is the individual's own work environment (Mayhew, Grunwald, & Dey, 2006). Beyond the inclusion of racial diversity in the faculty and staff of an institution, studies that connect the faculty and campus climates primarily focus on curriculum and student-faculty initiatives.

The curricula at colleges and universities, largely faculty driven, provide campuses with ways to affect the climate for students (Hurtado et al., 1998, 1999; Milem et al., 2005). Yet institutional policies and procedures play a role in how supported faculty feel in fostering diversity in their teaching. Colbeck (2002) found that institutions where engineering faculty perceived support for their teaching (e.g., faculty development offices, support for high teaching evaluations in tenure and promotion, etc.) were more likely to be attuned to the needs of underrepresented students of color. In another study, Mayhew and Grunwald (2006) found that faculty members who perceive their campus to be more committed to inclusion are more likely to incorporate diversity into their courses. Flowers (2003) found that the racial composition of campus has an effect on African American students' interactions with faculty, and that African American students at PWIs report fewer interactions with faculty. From this research, it is clear that faculty play a large role in fostering a warm climate for diversity within their classrooms and on campus more generally. The research on the roles of faculty and staff relative to campus climate connects well to the idea below, that diversity plays a role in education more generally.

The Educative Value of Diversity

Twenty-first-century college student diversity outcomes is a term used to describe the skills necessary for college graduates to function in an increasingly diverse U.S. society and an interdependent global community, which includes the ability to interact with diverse others and demonstrate democratic and civil engagement (Chang et al., 2004; Chang, Denson, Saenz, & Misa, 2006; Gurin et al., 2002, 2003; Hurtado, 2003). In recent years, research on the campus climate has expanded to include empirical investigations centered on how diversity affects college students.

Gurin et al. (2002) used theoretical frameworks grounded in psychology to shape their explanation of the process by which college students from racially and socially homogenous pre-college environments (e.g., racially segregated high schools) interact with diverse others in ways that challenge their notions of their diverse peers. Gurin and her colleagues (2002), Chang (1996), and others (e.g., Nelson-Laird, Engberg, & Hurtado, 2005; Saenz, Ngai, Hurtado, 2007) have documented the educational value of diversity for both cognitive and social outcomes. Not fully explored in the literature are the relationships between institutional policies and practices that support racial and ethnic diversity and 21st-century college student diversity outcomes. Further insight into the educative value of diversity is needed, given predictions about the changing demographics in higher education and the increasing restrictions on the use of race by colleges and universities. This is no small task, as research on campus climate and the educational value of diversity must be context specific, including but not limited to institutional type, state, and region. For example, private institutions often have a degree of freedom in recruiting and retaining students of color that public institutions do not. As such, assessment of issues related to racial and ethnic diversity need to account for these and other types of differences. The impetus to better understand how institutions manage, respond to, and benefit from racial/ethnic diversity is evidenced both by the growing number of diversity offices on campus and the plethora of research on racial/ethnic diversity in the higher education context that focuses specifically on students (Williams & Clowney, 2007). One line of research that has centered on students' experiences contemplates the way students interact across racial/ethnic groups.

Interactions with Diverse Others. One of the ways that education through diversity can be fostered is to provide opportunities for students to engage with people who are not like them. Interactions across difference have been shown to effect learning in positive ways (Gurin et al., 2002). Terenzini, Cabrera, Colbeck, Bjorland, and Parente (2001) found that diversity in the classroom positively related to student problem solving and ability to work in groups, even when controlling for other student attributes. Additionally, there is evidence that when students interact with students who are not like them (e.g., from a different racial/ethnic background), all students are more likely to feel a sense of belonging on campus (Hurtado et al., 2007; Locks, Hurtado, Bowman, & Oseguera, 2008). A sense of belonging may go a long way toward making a campus feel welcoming to students.

Institutions do play a role in fostering these interactions. The notion of a critical mass, where there is a focus on recruiting and retaining a group of students of color, began to influence institutional policies in the late 1980s and early 1990s as some institutions purposefully started to align their commitments to racial/ethnic diversity with admission policies and practices. Increasing the critical mass was a useful strategy for promoting eventual diversity and it shifted the campus climates to make them more welcoming to students of color in many cases (Hurtado et al., 1999; Williams & Clowney, 2007). A critical mass of students of color also aids in the possibilities for interactions across racial groups, which can help students to be more accepting of diversity in general. For example, research by Pike, Kuh, and Gonyea (2007) has shown that at private institutions a positive relationship between the quality of students' interactions with diverse peers and other student outcomes exists in the first year as well as in the senior year of college. They found that compositional diversity (e.g., the number of people of color) on a campus had a statistically significant positive indirect relationship to gains in understanding racially and ethnically diverse others. This indirect relationship, mediated by the amount of interaction with diverse others, held true for the first year of college and in the senior year of college.

Despite the many benefits of interactions with diverse others, cross-racial interactions in particular do not necessarily happen easily on campus. There is research finding that students are more likely to continue to interact in ways that they previously did; if students were used to interacting with students who were like them, for instance, they would be more likely to continue this pattern (Sáenz, 2005; Sáenz et al., 2007). Deliberate programmatic efforts, such as the previously mentioned intergroup dialogues where the purpose is for students to have an opportunity to learn to interact with people who are unlike them, may help students to shift their habits in this regard (Zúñiga, Nagda, Chesler, & Cytron-Walker, 2007). In addition, some students who report high levels of interaction with diverse others, also report a more acute awareness of racial hostilities on campus, according to a study of Latina/o educational outcomes by Hurtado and Ponjuan (2005). This finding is one reason why the notion of interactions with diverse others should not be divorced from the larger campus climate discussion. As campuses become more supportive of creating opportunities for students to interact across difference, there should also be attention to the larger campus climate especially whether the campus offers a warm environment for diversity where all students, staff, and faculty feel welcome.

Institution Focused Studies

Despite increased calls for institutional accountability for student outcomes, there is little literature featuring institutions as the focal point of empirical investigations into racial and ethnic diversity. This is particularly true of quantitative studies. Among studies published in a 10-year period, where a derivative of the word *race*, *ethnic*, or *diverse* appeared in the abstract, only seven had a campus or institution as the unit of analysis.[2] Of the seven articles, Meredith (2004) is the only one not directly studying student outcomes or behaviors. The others studied outcomes such as college students' engagement, academic development, critical thinking, cognitive outcomes, social and personal competence, and leaving college. Meredith examined the effects of the *U.S. News and World Report* annual college rankings on institutions' admissions practices and found that an improvement in ranking lowered public institutions' acceptance rates by 4% while private institutions had a decrease of 1%.

In their case study of 10 campuses, Richardson and Skinner (1990) found that the complexity of institutional responses to increases in racial and ethnic diversity has particular relevance for institutional studies. For example, several of the less selective campuses had high enrollment rates but low graduation rates for students of color; the converse was true for selective institutions. Many studies have found this same positive relationship between selectivity and graduation rates. A more recent quantitative investigation, completed by Rowley, Hurtado, and Ponjuan (2005) argued for diversity to be studied as an organizational issue. They examined institutional diversity and found a positive relationship between central administrative/organizational structures and the presence of racially and ethnically diverse faculty. They also found that institutions that focus on prestige had more faculty of color. Based on these findings, they argue that diversity and excellence are closely linked. Their study supports Milem et al.'s (2005) assertions about the influence of institutional core values and practices on the climate of racial and ethnic diversity.

A new, more complex approach to diversity is necessary if U.S. higher education is to respond to changing demographics and increased dependency on globalized economies and cultures. The need to respond to the current and future demands on higher education is underscored by Williams and Clowney's (2007) synopsis of organization models that have evolved over time. There was an initial emphasis on equity through affirmative action policies in the 1950s and 1960s. This ushered in the beginning of inclusion with the advent of multiculturalism in the Civil Rights era in the 1970s and the consideration of academic diversity in the 1990s and 2000s. Williams and Clowney note that each movement produced small, incremental changes that were key to the educative benefits of diversity arguments made in the Supreme Court cases such as *Grutter* and *Gratz*. The *Fisher v. University of Texas* case, involving a White student who claimed she was denied admission to the university because of her race was heard at the U.S. Supreme Court in the 2012–2013 term, and is likely to shape the next wave of diversity practices in the 21st century. For example, the ruling dictates that campuses may need to demonstrate that all neutral alternatives were used before using race in admission decisions. This would influence institutional policies relates to recruitment and retention of students of color in particular.

Campus self-studies occur regularly but are rarely published (Hurtado, Carter, & Kardia, 1998). There are a few notable exceptions. For example, Bauman, Bustillos, Bensimon, Brown, and Bartee (2005) examined how organizations can engage in self-study to ensure outcomes that are more equitable for students across racial and ethnic groups; the result of their study was the development of the Diversity Scorecard covered earlier in this chapter, now called the Equity Scorecard.

If the health of regional economies and the overall U.S. economy rest on a workforce with the skills and training to function and fully participate in a global, knowledge-based context, higher education administrators and practitioners have much to change about their campuses. Principal among these tasks is addressing and encouraging the inclusion of peoples and practices that reflect the reality of a racially and ethnically diverse U.S. population. Bensimon's Equity Scorecard (Bensimon 2004; Bensimon & Malcolm, 2012) gives institutions a tool to evaluate their goals and progress relative to eliminating educational inequities across racial and ethnic groups. Williams and colleagues (2005) call for ways to assess an institution's ability to effect change, stressing the need for baseline indicators of success. Milem et al.'s (2005) campus climate framework includes many of these same areas for assessment using the Inclusive Excellence Scorecard and therefore provides a way to begin to quantify baseline measures of an institution's commitment to racial/ethnic diversity. Other campuses could adopt similar efforts in order to pursue institutional-level campus climate evaluations.

SUMMARY: DIVERSITY AND THE CAMPUS CLIMATE

Supreme Court Justice O'Connor recommended a 2028 deadline to end affirmative action in higher education in her opinion during the 2003 Michigan Supreme Courts cases (*Gratz* and *Grutter*). As that deadline draws nearer and the U.S. Supreme Court ruling on the case of Abigail Fisher, the legality of admissions policies may be under fire. The ruling could eventually restrict public institutions' ability to admit a diverse student body and in turn this could influence campus climates. The Supreme Court case of *Fisher vs. The University of Texas* precipitates an urgent need to better explicate and quantify the affect that the campus racial climate has on college students' academic outcomes, as well as their development over time. Students may perceive the campus climate as a collective of actions toward inclusion or exclusion of diversity on campus. This means that the campus climate is one area where energy could be placed toward enacting diversity in higher education. With this goal, there remains work to be done on campus climates.

Think about Diversity

The theoretical models used to explore the campus climate emphasize practical applications. For example, Richardson and Skinner's (1990) organizational framework is specifically geared to institutional work toward adapting to diversity on campus. The four-dimensional framework by Hurtado and her colleagues (1999), and the expansion of that framework to include organizational diversity (Milem, et al., 2005) provided a guide to institutions that could be employed to create a supportive environment for diversity. The Equity Scorecard (Bensimon, 2004; Bensimon & Malcolm, 2012) and the Inclusive Excellence Change Model followed this line of theoretical work, offering ways to highlight diversity as an integral aspect of excellence (Williams at el., 2005). These links between theoretical models and practical applications on college campuses are useful because they can provide institutional actors with direct ideas for how to better deal with diversity. But, more theoretical work would be beneficial in this area. For example, theoretical work that ponders at what point a campus shifts from being perceived as a chilly climate toward being a warm climate would be useful. Additionally, finding ways to link campus climate theory with larger social theories (e.g., Bourdieu's social reproduction theory) might be helpful at making the campus climate connect with larger structural issues of inequality.

Diversity Still Matters

To date, most national studies on the campus climate have been limited particularly to the Cooperative Institutional Research Program out of University of California, Los Angeles. It may help to include campus climate questions on national datasets like the federally supported data collection initiatives such as the Integrated Postsecondary Education Data System (IPEDS) or National Center for Education Statistics (NCES) postsecondary data collection efforts. Early studies on the campus racial climate focused on the perceived discrimination of African America, Latina/o, and/or Native American students, often asking about their college experience, and then linking these perceptions of campus experiences with persistence rates. These early studies most often used students' experiences with race as a predictive variable in regression models or in structural equation models (SEM) used to calculate persistence rates. While persistence is an important outcome of campus climates, more insight is needed as to what happens before a student makes a decision to leave or stay on campus, meaning that more work is needed on the many potential outcomes of campus climates (e.g., learning outcomes, identity development outcomes, etc.).

There remains minimal research that connects the campus racial climate to issues of gender (Lundy-Wagner & Winkle-Wagner, 2013) or other categories such as sexual orientation, religion, or socioeconomic background. While some work has been done on the campus gender climate (Morris & Daneil, 2008; Whitt et al., 1999), research on campus climates has primarily centered on race and ethnicity. Future research should begin to consider the intersections of categories, connecting campus climates as they relate to race, gender, class, sexual orientation, and religion simultaneously. For instance, it might be the case that a campus climate is warm relative to religion, but chilly relative to gender or race.

In addition to understanding campus climates from multiple vantage points, there is a need for within-group difference studies. Data and methods need to allow scholars to ask questions about heterogeneity among racially and ethnically diverse students. In other words, because a significant portion of the research on campus climates is rooted in large-scale survey studies, the goal of these studies is often to be able to generalize as to how the campus climate influences particular groups (e.g., African American students vs. White students vs. Latina/o students). Yet there could be significant differences among students within a single racial/ethnic group. For instance, among Latina/o students, there may be multiple national identities (e.g., Mexican, Puerto Rican, Dominican) that could greatly influence how they experience the campus climate. Even within single ethnic groups (e.g., Mexican), students may vary in their experience depending on their socioeconomic background. Future research should contemplate how students in a particular racial/ethnic group vary and contemplate ways to study this variance because this could influence the general understanding of how the campus climate is perceived by students.

Since the onset of campus climate studies, there has been a need to better understand students' subjective experiences of their experiences with race, class, or gender during college (Hurtado & Carter, 1997). While there has been some scholarship that takes a qualitative approach, attempting to explore how students make sense of their daily experiences in college, more work is needed. Qualitative research could help to fill in the gaps as to why some students may report positive interactions with diverse others, while still reporting a great deal of racial hostility on campus (see Hurtado & Ponjuan, 2005), for instance. Additionally, qualitative approaches may help to reveal the ways in which students' experiences with race may not be disconnected from their experiences with other identity categories such as gender, class, sexual orientation, and religion.

Diversity is Everywhere

The campus climate is the responsibility of everyone on the campus, from the top administrators to the students to the custodial staff. An effective approach to take in attempting to alter campus climates so that they are more welcoming and inclusive is to involve people at all levels of the campus. However, in many ways, the initiative for a positive shift in campus climates begins at the top. Chief academic officers, presidents, provosts, and other central administrators, have key roles in establishing policies and supporting practices that cultivate a campus climate that is responsive to and inclusive of racial and ethnic diversity. Such individuals may encourage racial and ethnic diversity by aligning institutional values and commitments to diversity through budget allocations, instituting supportive programs and structures that support diversity, overseeing the Deans' responsible for the curriculum, and rewarding campus community members for a commitment to diversity.

The growing number of chief diversity officers on college campuses signals a new way for institutions to manage and respond to diversity related matters, and these officers may have a permanent role in the post-affirmative action era. Williams and Wade-Golden (2006, 2007) assert that chief diversity officers may serve as change agents, responsible for new diversity-related initiatives. They also may be the point leaders on issues of diversity. Such individuals may be situated in the institutions' human resources unit, responsible for serving the entire campus community. Lastly, chief diversity officers may develop relationships across their campuses and units, developing coalitions to better support the development of inclusive spaces on campus. In summary, the growing number of chief diversity officers may potentially act as coordinators of campus initiatives, priorities, and policies reflected in Milem et al.'s (2005) Organizational/Structural dimension. Additionally, at some colleges and universities, a chief diversity officer may be responsible for creating infrastructures to support diversity.

Student affairs administrators have an important role to play in fostering a positive campus climate because of their close contact with students. In many ways, student affairs administrators can serve as a bridge between students, faculty, and upper administrators. It is important that student affairs professionals take an assessment of their own perspectives on diversity, examining closely the areas in which they are or are not as open to students from various populations. Then, they can play a leading role in creating campus programs that help students to engage with diverse others. Additionally, student affairs practitioners can report instances of racial hostility or discrimination when they hear of it or see it.

DISCUSSION QUESTIONS

There are many ways that scholars and practitioners can contribute to the improvement of campus climates. We provide some questions to stimulate thinking about future practice and research below.

Improving Practice

1. As a professional in student affairs, what role do you have in fostering a warm campus racial climate?
2. Describe some specific practices that you could implement to help create a warmer campus climate (e.g., reporting hostile or discriminatory acts on campus, creating opportunities for students to learn about diversity, treating students in a manner that respects their individuality, etc.).
3. How might a campus with which you are familiar go about a self-study to evaluate the campus climate? What role could you play in that effort?
4. One of the major student affairs associations, Student Affairs Administrators in Higher Education (NASPA), developed a set of professional competencies that are encouraged for all student affairs professionals. How might the NASPA professional competencies inform the way you think about your role in fostering a positive campus climate?
    a. The NASPA Competencies are (see http://www.naspa.org/programs/profdev/ default.cfm): advising and helping; assessment, evaluation, and research; equity, diversity, and inclusion; ethical professional practice; history, philosophy, and value; human organizational resources; law, policy, and governance; leadership; personal foundations; students learning and development.
5. Another national association for student affairs, College Student Educators International (ACPA) developed a Statement of Ethical Principles and Standards. How might the ACPA Ethical Principles and Standards influence your approach to the campus climate?
    a. The ACPA Standards are (see http://www2.myacpa.org/statement-of-ethical-principles-and-standards): professional responsibility and competence; student learning and development; responsibility to the institution; and responsibility to society.
6. The Council for the Advancement of Standards in Higher Education (CAS) developed a set of standards for student affairs. How might these CAS Standards be applied in practice related to the campus climate?
    a. The domains for the CAS Standards are (see http://www.cas.edu/index.php/ cas-general-standards/): knowledge acquisition, integration, construction, and application; cognitive complexity; intrapersonal development; interpersonal competence; humanitarianism and civic engagement; practical competence.

Developing Future Research

1. Given the research presented here, what trends do you see in the work that has been conducted about campus climates?
2. What are some limitations or gaps that you see in the research on campus climates?

3. How might you construct a research study that considers the varied areas of campus climates such as the climate related to race, gender, sexual orientation, or religion?

4. One issue that we recommend for future research is for campus climate studies to contemplate students' multiple identities (race, class, gender, sexual orientation, religion, ability). How might you develop a study about campus climates that would allow for these various identities to be represented?

5. Describe a methodology for a study that might allow for an opportunity to understand within-group differences (i.e., the differences that may exist within a particular racial/ethnic group).

========================A CASE STUDY========================

PRACTICING DIVERSITY ISSUES RELATED TO THE CAMPUS CLIMATE

Dealing with Hate: Responding to Hostility on Campus

Regional State University (RSU) is a four-year, master's comprehensive institution that serves 25,000 students. For many decades, RSU served college students who came from middle- and high-income socioeconomic backgrounds. Over the past 10 years, racial, ethnic, and socioeconomic diversity has increased significantly. Currently approximately 45% of students are Caucasian, another 25% are Latina/o, 20% are African American, 10% are Asian American or Pacific Islanders, and just under 1/2% are Native American.

At RSU, you work as the vice-president for the Division of Student Affairs and report directly to the president. This division funds both the Multicultural Center, which serves students of color, and the LBGTQ Center, which serves lesbian, bisexual, gay, transgendered, and queer students at RSU.

Last Friday evening, two incidents occurred that increased tensions among various groups of students at RSU. A noose was found on the steps of the Multicultural Center and there were racial epithets and anti-immigration slurs spray-painted on the front door. The front door to the LGBTQ center had homophobic, derogatory terms spray-painted on the front door.

Monday evening, the campus and local police investigators identified perpetrators and released this information to local news outlets, including the local television stations. The two students who committed the acts at the Multicultural Center are alleged to be Caucasian. Of the two students who committed the acts at the LGBTQ center, one is alleged to be African American and the other is alleged to be Latina/o.

It is now Tuesday. At 8:00 a.m., your campus president announced that the university's response to recent incidents is to create a new center called the Intercultural Center (ICC) within the next month that will house both the Multicultural Center and the LGBTQ Center—without consultation with your division.

You arrive to campus at 9:00 a.m. Tuesday morning to find hundreds of students outside your building. They are protesting the hate crimes, the president's announcement, and challenging the need for the new ICC, which your office is expected to implement.

You are working with your staff in the Division of Student Affairs to develop a response plan to the incidents and the president's mandate to create a new ICC. You have been asked to prepare a report, including (a) key points that must be addressed by the president, (b) a plan to address the student perpetrators' behavior, and (c) short- and long-term plans to gain support for the new ICC in the next week and month.

To help construct your response, respond to each of the following:

1. Describe and discuss the two key points the president must address in his next public speech on campus that will help ease tensions on campus.
2. Describe and discuss two key issues that must be addressed when you and your staff meet with the alleged student perpetrators. You must do this for the two Caucasian students who allegedly committed the acts at the Multicultural Center and you must do this for the African American and the Latina/o students who allegedly committed the acts at the LGBTQ Center.
3. Develop an outline for a comprehensive plan to address the key steps the Division of Student Affairs must take within the next week to gain campus support for the new ICC.
4. Discuss two long-term goals that will be implemented in the next four weeks to open the ICC within the time frame mandated by the president, as well as likely challenges or obstacles to achieving these goals.
5. How might your response fit with the culture and values of the institutions?
6. How do you/can you affect the climate for diversity at the institution/school?
7. How can stakeholders and decision-makers affect the institutional climate for diversity?

NOTES

1. In the Supreme Court case, *Regents of California v. Bakke*, Allan Bakke, a White man who had been denied admission to the University of California-Davis medical school two times, claimed that his denied admission was because of his race, taking issue with the quota system (setting aside a particular number of spots for people from particular groups) used in the admissions process. The ruling determined that the use of quotas in admissions processes was unconstitutional.
2. Based on a review of 51 articles from the Review of Higher Education and 69 articles from Research in Higher Education published between January 1998 and June 2008.

7

IDENTITY AND GETTING THROUGH COLLEGE

What Do "I" Have To Do With Inclusion-and-Diversity?

> *Our task is that of making ourselves individuals. The conscience of a race is the gift of its individuals who see, evaluate, record ... We create the race by creating ourselves and then to our great astonishment we will have created something far more important: We will have created a culture.*

—Ralph Ellison (1952/1995, p. 8)

A college student is likely to encounter many instances that will influence his or her thoughts, feelings, and actions. The study of how college affects students often connects with who the student is, or, with a student's identity (Evans, Forney, Guido, Patton, & Renn, 2010). There is vast evidence that the college experience often acts as a catalyst for numerous developmental processes and growth for students (Evans et al., 2010). The action of including a full range of diversity in the student population on campuses is at least in part an act of incorporating students' many identities into colleges and universities.

The notion of identity can refer to many aspects of the way one views oneself: the way a student negotiates the college environment in relation to him- or herself, personality characteristics, the way his or her thinking or moral reasoning develops, and the way in which a student might see herself/himself in relation to others. In college student development theory, not all areas of development are classified as "identity" development (Evans et al., 2010). However, to remain consistent with other disciplines, such as sociology, for example (Winkle-Wagner, 2012b), we chose to use the word "identity" here as a way to encompass multiple branches of work on development. We shift back and forth in the chapter with the word "identity" and the phrase "college student development" as a way to be inclusive to the many lines of thinking on the topic.

Sometimes this process of development in college can be positive and satisfying students as they experience support on their journey toward who they are becoming. Or, on the contrary, the process of development can be hindered by negative experiences in college, particularly for students of color who are in the minority on many college campuses. For example, experiences with racism, hostility, or not feeling like who a student is (one's racial group, gender, sexual orientation, class, background) is the norm or standard on campus can create tensions and dissonance in students' attempt to develop themselves during college. Student affairs professionals have a big role to play in students' development during the college years. Most master's programs in student affairs require some type of student development theory course for this reason; it is crucial to prepare for ways to work with students during their journey to self. Some would argue that student development theory, knowing how students grow and change during college, is the centerpiece of the student affairs profession. Thus, it is important that we pay due attention to this topic in a book on diversity and inclusion. It is our view that students cannot be fully included on college campuses unless they feel safe and free to develop during the process. In this spirit, it is vital to have some understanding of the large body of scholarship that has offered ideas as to various processes, statuses, stages, or issues that students may experience during this process of development in order to know how to best work with and for students.

In this chapter, we explore the field of college student development theory, and particularly the work that explores the way students see themselves, or their identity. We first explore the foundations of theories of identity before presenting some of the more recent advances in thinking about students' identity in college (the longer reflection on foundations and advances in college student identity development can be seen and was rooted in Winkle-Wagner, 2012b). Then, we turn attention toward some of the empirical literature that has been published on college students' identity. Identity work for college students is a vast body of scholarship and theory; for this chapter we pay particular attention to theories and empirical studies that centered on identity issues related to students' experiences with being in an underrepresented group (race, gender, sexual orientation) in certain college settings. Given the depth and breadth of this area, we did have to makes some choices regarding what to present here. We opted for studies and theories that were foundational or path breaking, creating a branch of scholarship on identity or development. Then, we decided to present some examples of alternative approaches to propose some ideas as to where this field of research might be headed in the future.

THINKING ABOUT DIVERSITY: THEORETICAL IDEAS ABOUT COLLEGE STUDENT IDENTITY DEVELOPMENT

There is a large body of theoretical work that contemplates the ways in which college influences students' development, much of which is summarized well in the multiple editions of the volume on the topic, *Student Development in College: Theory, Research, and Practice* (Evans et al., 2010). We offer a brief synopsis of a burgeoning field of work below, but, we do encourage readers who desire to deepen their knowledge on this topic, and the Evans et al. volume is an excellent guide.

Foundational Theories of College Student Development

College student development theory primarily initiated from psychological notions of development, through the psychological practice of scholars like Erikson, Piaget, and Jung (Evans et al., 2010; Winkle-Wagner, 2012b). The foundational theories are typically separated into the following categories:

1. Psychosocial theories that highlight students' personal and interpersonal lives, the ways that students change as they encounter new experiences, are rooted in the clinical work of Erik Erikson (1959/1980), who investigated human development from adolescence through adulthood.

2. Cognitive-structural theories were initiated with Piaget's (1952) psychological work, focusing on the way that students' thinking changes in college. Piaget was interested in life stages and how what he called cognitive dissonance created opportunities for growth and change.

3. Typological theories, with origins in the psychology of Carl Jung, explore mental processing and how people relate to their world.

4. Person-environment interaction theories are based on the psychological practice of Kurt Lewin (1935). Karl Rodgers (1990) adapted this line of thinking to understand how students interact with their college environment.

Each of the foundational areas has led to a line of research and theory related to college students' development so large that an entire volume could be dedicated just to tracking the branches of scholarship related to each of the foundational areas. Here, we give a few examples that could serve as starting points to further study.

Psychosocial theories most often relate to a set of stages or a process through which a student progresses. College student development theory was work initially based on the premise that students must experience a series of "crises" in order to progress to the next stage of development (Erikson, 1959/1980; Marcia, 1966). Chickering and Reisser (1993; Chickering, 1969) advanced this theoretical work in their crafting of seven "vectors" of development that included students' progression during college. The vectors symbolized areas that students needed to master in their personal and social lives such as developing competence, managing emotions, moving through autonomy to interdependence, developing maturity in interpersonal relationships, establishing identity, developing purpose, and developing integrity.

The vectors have provided student affairs staff with ways to assess areas in which students need to be encouraged to develop. For example, many students may need encouragement to develop maturity in interpersonal relationships and student affairs staff could create programming that centers on those issues (e.g., dating issues, friendships, etc.). Or, in one-on-one advising of students, the vectors could be useful as a way to understand the challenges that students might be having as they move through college. For instance, perhaps a student is exhibiting challenges with being more autonomous. A student affairs practitioner could help advise that student on ways to practice being more interdependent, to be able to think independently and also understand how to think within a group (e.g., this experience of interdependence could occur through students' involvement and decision-making on an athletic team, in student government, within Greek life, or other campus areas).

The typological theories extended to a set of appraisals that were meant to be non-evaluative. These appraisals attempted to offer insight into issues such as the way students learn (Kolb, 1984) or personality types such as the Myers-Briggs inventory (Myers, 1980). With college students, these typologies have insight into how to better teach students so that they learn, understand the manner in which students' preferences or personalities may influence their behaviors and choices, and counsel students into particular fields or careers. In student affairs, the Myers-Briggs inventory has been particularly helpful in the areas of career services and for staff relations in other areas (e.g., resident assistants in housing, student involvement staff, etc.).

Cognitive-structural theories have been applied to college students' moral reasoning development (Kohlberg, 1969) and to students' progression in thinking (King & Kitchner, 1994; Perry, 1970). Similar to the idea of crises in psychosocial theories, many of these theories assume that students must undergo "cognitive dissonance" where a particular way of thinking no longer works in a certain setting and the student must then develop new ways of thinking (King, 2009). Cognitive development theories have been particularly valuable to understand changes in students' thinking that could be a result of what they are learning both inside and outside of the classroom. Student affairs practitioners (and faculty, for that matter) can use these theories to understand how students might process some of the challenges that they encounter during college. Additionally, faculty or student affairs staff could use these theories as a way to reach students where they currently are with their thinking and then challenge them to move toward new ways of knowing and thinking.

Person-environment theories place particular emphasis on the way that students interact with the college environment and how this shapes their subsequent development. For example, Holland's (1992) vocational development model, used often in career services units of student affairs, has offered a way to consider how the college environment influenced students' decision-making about their long-term careers. Bronfenbrenner's ecological systems theory has been applied to the study of college students (e.g., Renn, 2003, 2007) in order to better understand the way that students' interactions within a particular environment influence the way they see particular aspects of their identity (race, sexual orientation, etc.).

A major criticism of many of the foundational theories of college student development has been that these theories may not be as relevant to underrepresented populations such as students of color, gay, bisexual, or transgender students, or women (Torres, Howard-Hamilton, & Cooper, 2003). One reason for this criticism stems from the initial development of these theories, out of the psychological practice of Erikson, Piaget, Jung, and Lewin. The clinical observations and experiences in these cases were primarily with White, heterosexual men, and therefore, the theories were not initially related to or tested on other populations (Evans et al., 2010; Torres et al., 2003).

Advances and Alternatives in College Student Development Theory

While college student development theory primarily grew out of psychological approaches in the field of social psychology, there are both sociological and psychological approaches to identity which has been a growing area of discussion among scholars of student development theory (Torres, Jones, & Renn, 2009; Winkle-Wagner, 2012b). As a way to make student development theory more relevant to increasingly diverse student populations, theory development in the past few decades has focused on students from underrepresented groups such as women (Gilligan, 1982/1993; Josselson, 1987), students of color (Cross, 1995), and gay, lesbian, transgender, and bisexual students (Cass, 1984).

Other advances in college student development theory have contemplated issues such as:

1. Identities such as those associated with race (Cross, 1995; Robinson & Howard-Hamilton, 1994) or sexual orientation (Cass, 1984);

2. Holistic approaches to identity that identified multiple, intersecting identities or dimensions of identity (Abes, Jones, & McEwen, 2007; Baxter Magolda, 2009b; King, 2009; Taylor, 2008; Torres & Hernandez, 2007; Winkle-Wagner 2009a); and
3. Sociological notions of identity (Stryker, 1980, 1997; Thoits, 2003; Winkle-Wagner, 2009a, 2009b).

Some of the more recent advances in college student development theory and identity use different theoretical foundations. For example, some scholars use sociological notions of identity that are more fluid, dynamic, and not dependent on progress through stages, statuses, or phases (Torres et al., 2009; Winkle-Wagner, 2009a, 2012b). Others pull from human ecology, the analysis of the environment in which students are situated and how students respond to or alter that environment (Renn, 2003, 2007).

Many of the advances in identity development theories have adapted previous theories to groups that were initially left out of consideration. Some of this work started with the inclusion of women, who were often excluded from many of the original theories of development. For example, Gilligan's (1982/1993) research extended previous cognitive-structural theories of development to understand how women develop their way of thinking because Perry's (1970) initial cognitive development theory only aimed at understanding White male development. Josselson (1987) reflected on the seven vectors of development originated by Chickering's (1969) psychosocial theory for women, finding that women progress through the vectors in a slightly different way than men. These advances and more were an important part of creating a field on college student development that was inclusive of shifting demographics in higher education.

Racial and Ethnic Identity Development Models.   One of the major ways that scholars and practitioners in higher education have addressed the limitation of a lack of attention toward underrepresented students within the foundational theories of college student development is through the crafting of theories that relate to particular identities or aspects of identity. While a longer explanation of the many theories in this area is not well suited for this particular venue, an excellent resource that we utilized in our consideration of this topic is the ASHE-ERIC Higher Education Report on *Identity Development of Diverse Populations* authored by Torres et al. (2003). Additionally, Jackson and Wijeyesinghe (2012) compiled a useful volume that examines advances in racial identity development called, *New Perspectives on Racial Identity Development: Integrating Emerging Frameworks.* We do recommend these volumes as resources for those who wish to delve deeper into these particular models of identity development.

Similar to the scholarship that began the deliberate inclusion of women into college student development theory, researchers became concerned that race and ethnicity were not yet given in-depth consideration in students' development in college. Helms (1990) combined racial and gender identity to contemplate a womanist identity for Black women in particular, outlining the progression from considering maleness as central to women's conceptions of themselves toward a positive identity as both a woman and a woman of color. There are a handful of models of identity development that have been particularly applied to students of color (men and/or women). The minority identity development model (Atkinson, Morten, & Sue, 1989), later called the racial/cultural identity development model, presented a five-stage mode where a student progresses from conformity, at which point they may devalue their own racial/ethnic identity and value majority group identity instead, to integrative awareness where a student develops a strong sense of self. Phinney (1992) extended Marcia's (1966) model where students experience a series of crises that help them progress from an ethnic identity that is unexamined to an achieved ethnic identity.

Alongside the models of development that feature how students of color more generally might be influenced by their experience in college, there are a series of theoretical models aimed at particular racial/ethnic groups. For example, Cross' (1995) five-stage psychology of nigrescence, or the way that an African American or Black individual comes to identify with being Black, has been used pretty extensively to understand how African American college students develop their identity (also see Baldwin, Duncan, & Bell, 1992; Jackson, 2001). Taking a slightly different approach, Robinson and Howard-Hamilton (1994) crafted an Afrocentric resistance model of development, aiming to understand the development of psychological health and well-being rather than progression toward an achieved identity.

There are also models of identity development geared toward understanding the development of identity among Native American or American Indian[1] students. These theories often consider how an American Indian is adapting, acculturating, or assimilating into non-tribal culture and the factors that influence this process (Horse, 2001). For instance, one model classifies Native Americans by their level of "Indianness" or their association with their tribal background, based in research with the Menomini tribe of Wisconsin (Spindler & Spindler, 1958). This model progressed from a person being native-oriented (associated deeply with the tribe) to acculturated (accepted by mainstream, non-tribal society; Spindler & Spindler, 1958). The initial model was later revised in an unpublished manuscript, presenting a progression from traditional (completely engaged in the tribe) to assimilated (accepted by mainstream, non-tribal society) and then to bicultural (able to engage in the tribe and mainstream society; Ryan & Ryan, 1982). The models were adapted with an eye toward how to better serve American Indian people in counseling settings, using traditional healing perspectives (in place of a clinical model, looking for pathologies) that might be more relevant to this population (LaFromboise, Trimball, & Mohatt, 1990). Noticeably, there are not identity development models for each Native American tribe or geographic clusters of tribes even though there are likely to be significant differences in tribal culture, depending on the location or background of that tribe.

For Latina/o students, there are a few models of identity development that primarily inquire into Latinas/os' awareness of an association with Latina/o or Hispanic heritage and culture (Ferdman & Gallegos, 2001; Keefe & Padilla, 1987). Torres' (2003) development model examined the ways that students' changed in their association with being Latina/o based on conflicts with their culture and changes in their environment. These models appear to be more open to the many nuances in Latina/o or Hispanic heritage as compared to the models for Native American students, calling out ways that students might define their heritage or culture and then how they associate with it in the college environment.

Asian American identity development models have typically been geared toward particular ethnic groups within this large, diverse population although some models do group all Asian Americans together (e.g., Maekawa Kodama, McEwen, Liang, & Lee, 2002). Kim's (2001) Asian American identity development model primarily focused on Japanese women's progression through five stages of development from childhood through adulthood. Kim's model demonstrated a student's progress from the beginning of ethnic awareness (in childhood), to identification with being White, to seeing oneself as a minority in society, to Asian American consciousness and incorporation of that identity. The model proposed by Ibrahim, Ohnishi, and Sandhu (1997) investigated the development of South Asian American immigrant populations and reconceptualized the minority identity development (Atkinson et al., 1989). The biggest difference in this model was that it attempted to inquire into the way in which South Asian Americans may not go through an early stage of pre-encounter or conformity because their immigrant status may already be a signal that they have accepted cultural differences. But similar to other theoretical conceptions of racial/ethnic identity development, this model demonstrates progression into a secure sense of self within one's ethnic and racial identity. Nadal (2004) concentrated his theoretical efforts on Filipino identity development, with a particular eye towards ways to better serving Filipino people in counseling situations. Nadal's model offered a five stage non-linear process of development from awareness of Filipino ethnicity over the life course from assimilation to dominant culture, toward beginning to incorporate Asian American identity, to acceptance of one's own ethnic heritage alongside those of others.

White racial identity development has been linked to issues of privilege or the systematic advantages that White people have been given in society (Helms, 1992; McIntosh, 1998). Helm's (1992) White racial identity development model outlines six statuses through which a White student might progress from contact (initial consideration of race) to beginning to see racial injustice, to removing oneself from White people who are racist or insensitive to race, to eventual autonomy where a White student could notice racial inequality and also have a strong sense of self-worth. Hardiman's (2001) White racial identity development model is similar to some of the other racially specific models in that there are five stages through which a person progresses. The model differs in that the model attempts to identify a White student's progression from naivety about race and racial identity toward acceptance that White people have been differentially treated and privileged, and eventual internalization of racial injustices. Another difference in Hardiman's model is that the focus is on actions for White people to take in their development of understanding ways in which they may have been advantaged.

Sexual Orientation Identity Development.   While there has been significant theoretical work on racial identities, there are also some theories that particularly explore identity related to one's sexual orientation or gender. For example, Cass (1984) developed a gay/lesbian identity development model that, similar to the racial/ethnic identity models, has stages through which a gay or lesbian student might progress from beginning to have same sex thoughts or attractions toward pride in one's gay or lesbian identity and eventual incorporation of that identity within a society that is often more accepting of heterosexuals. Another model, developed by D'Augelli (1994), described the processes (rather than stages) through which a person might progress from understanding that one is not heterosexual toward eventually entering a gay, lesbian, or bisexual community and incorporating one of these identities.

Summary of Racial/Ethnic and Sexual Orientation Theories.   There are a few common characteristics of the racial/ethnic and sexual orientation identity development theories. First, these theories primarily demonstrate a progression (although sexual orientation models frame this as a process) through which students move from a rejection of or ignorance about their racial/ethnic or sexual orientation identity, toward a disassociation with identities that are different from their own (e.g., disassociating from Whiteness if they are students of color), toward a general level of acceptance of themselves and others (e.g., accepting one's identity as a student of color or lesbian/gay/bisexual/transgender/ queer or questioning (LGBTQ) student and accepting White or straight students). These models are aimed at reflecting the way a person begins to grapple with being in a minoritized (Gillborn, 2005) or marginalized group (i.e., the student is put in a position of being in a minority group and did not choose this position). Second, these theories assume a linear progression in most cases (Winkle-Wagner, 2012b) where a student moves from less developed (or knowing less about their racial/ethnic or sexual orientation identity) toward being more developed and self-actualized (knowing oneself, knowing one's background and identity). There is some valuing in this process where it seems as if it is better to be further along in the process of development because there is an endpoint or goal of accepting oneself alongside differences in other people (Winkle-Wagner, 2012b).

These theories aim at generalizations in order to understand subpopulations. That is, they are useful in identifying ways that African American students may differ in their development from Latina/o or White students. Along with this generalization does come the potential to put students into identity boxes or categories (e.g., this student is Native American so she must be dealing with particular issues as identified in those theories). Those who use these theories, and we do recommend their use, should be aware of the potential for stereotyping or essentializing students (Winkle-Wagner, 2012b). In other words, although these theories are useful to get at potential issues that subgroups of students may experience, all students should still be seen as individuals who may differ from these trends.

Most of the theories that involve identity development among underrepresented or diverse (Torres et al., 2003) populations, parse out identity by race, gender, or sexual orientation. Very few of the theories that are rooted in a psychological approach include overlapping racial, gendered, or sexual orientation identities (but see Helms, 1990). There is a particular gap relative to considerations of the way that class influences identity in the theories that are connected to foundational psychological identity models.

In spite of some limitations, that all theories are likely to have, there are some important implications from these theories for student affairs professionals. The general racial/ethnic and sexual orientation identity theories offer some insight into ways to structure diversity training, for example. Students could be encouraged to begin to gain knowledge about their own background or identity. Then, student affairs professionals or faculty could facilitate the process of helping students to associate with their racial/ ethnic or sexual orientation identity. Finally, an important part of the process of diversity training would be to foster a movement towards accepting oneself and others. Additionally, student affairs practitioners could use these models as a way to gain insight into where students might be in their development. Having a sense of this would help practitioners or faculty to better advise, supervise, or support students in their learning and development during college.

Holistic Identity Development Models. Recently, theorists of college student identity development have discussed integration, nuance, and holism in their approaches to developmental theory (Abes & Kasch, 2007; Baxter Magolda, 2009b; Jones, 2009a, 2009b; King, 2009; Taylor, 2008; Torres, et al., 2009; Winkle-Wagner, 2012b). These holistic approaches of studying students' development offer alternative theoretical frameworks, contemplating multiple *components, dimensions,* or *categories* of identity (Baxter Magolda, 2001, 2009a; Jones 1997; Jones & McEwen, 2000; Reynolds & Pope, 1991; Torres & Hernandez, 2007; Torres et al., 2009). This scholarship and thinking frames identity categories as connected or as multiple identities (Stewart, 2008, 2009) instead of parsing out characteristics of identity (Abes, 2012; Jones, 1997; Jones, 2009a, 2009b; Jones & McEwen, 2000; McEwen, 1996).

Others have advocated for a more holistic approach through the use of multiple theoretical frameworks within their studies of identity (Abes et al., 2007; Taylor, 2008). Baxter Magolda's (2001) self-authorship theory considers the idea of meaning-making connecting together cognitive, interpersonal, and intrapersonal development. Her work shifts student development theory toward a more holistic approach of studying students' social interactions. In another example, Torres and Hernandez (2007) contemplate cognitive and affective (emotional) aspects of multiple dimensions of identity and this helps to remedy some of the limitations of both psychological and sociological frames (also see, Abes et al., 2007; Torres & Hernandez, 2007). Renn (2003) uses an ecological approach that provides a perspective blending environmental, social, and cognitive aspects of development.

The holistic perspectives on college student development attempt to solve some of the potential limitations of the linear progression that is assumed by many of the initial racial/ethnic identity models in particular. The idea is that students might experience multiple aspects of identity concurrently, and this may occur as a process that is more fluid and dynamic. Additionally, these approaches begin to fill a gap in earlier models that parsed out identity characteristics, moving toward a more intersectional approach that explores identity aspects like race, gender, and class simultaneously. This would call for student affairs professionals and faculty to view students as whole people, taking into account a variety of racial, socioeconomic, gender, sexual orientation and religious characteristics, all of which could influence the students' interactions and behaviors. It could be more difficult to generalize to subgroups of students with holistic approaches because of the variations within groups (e.g., an Asian American woman may have a different experience from an Asian American man, etc.). Still, these holistic approaches are likely to be more realistic to the way students might actually encounter their identities on campus.

Sociological Identity Development Models. The sociological perspective of identity called, identity theory, stems from the philosophical work of pragmatist thinkers such as William James, Charles Cooley, and George Herbert Mead. Their models consider identity as an ongoing process and interaction. For example, Mead (1934/1967) asserted that there was a purely subjective aspect of self called the "I" which can be likened to the part of one's identities that are beyond objectification (one's ability to reflect, for example). He identified the "me" aspect of self as the socialized part of self that is an accumulation of cultural norms, values, and attitudes. This "me" part of the self branched into the sociological study of identity. Stryker (1980, 2000) adapted Mead's "me" and expanded it into the study of an individual's roles (e.g., as a student, parent, son/daughter, etc.), how committed a person is to those roles, and how salient that role is in a particular setting. For example, if a student is particularly committed to the role of being a student, she might exhibit behaviors on campus such as using particular terms or studying in a particular setting that she may not exhibit with her family. Scholars have adapted Stryker's identity theory to examine the way in which college experiences influence identity for students (Burke & Reitzes, 1991; Owens & Serpe, 2003; Thoits, 2003; Winkle-Wagner, 2009a, 2009b).

Similar to the holistic approaches to college student development, the sociological notions of identity allow for a great deal of nuance and dynamism in identity. Students could have as many "me" identities as there are roles available to them (Winkle-Wagner, 2012b). For example, a student could have roles as a daughter/son, student, employee, research assistant, aunt/uncle, or parent. All of these roles would exist simultaneously, but the student may find some of these roles to be particularly salient (i.e., obvious) on campus. As a faculty member or student affairs practitioner, one could begin to understand students' identities by asking about these various roles. There could be conflicts in one's roles as a parent and a student, for example. Or, perhaps a student feels conflict between an identity as an African American man, a Christian, and a gay man. Once potential conflicting roles are established, it could be easier to find ways to help the student to navigate challenges. This line of thinking about identity calls for those working with students to be highly attuned to students' unique configurations of identities. This approach does create a way toward a more nuanced, intersectional understanding of identity. But, it also means that it would be highly individualized and could take more time on the part of student affairs professionals or faculty to figure out. Understanding students' identity sociologically would be dependent on creating a relationship with the student to be able to get to know how the student viewed his or her roles (e.g., what roles does the student seem to have as part of her/his identities?), how committed she or he was to those roles in the campus setting (e.g., she or he may not feel as committed to the role of being an athlete if he or she no longer plays a sport in college), and how those roles might influence his/her behavior. One of the benefits of this sociological approach is that is does offer a way to avoid putting students into particular identity categories or boxes (e.g., this is a Latina student, so she must be dealing with her Latina identity).

DIVERSITY STILL MATTERS: LITERATURE ON COLLEGE STUDENT IDENTITY DEVELOPMENT

The empirical work on college student development has often mirrored the theoretical contributions in that many of the studies focus on particular aspects of identity such as race, gender, or sexual orientation. We chose to present larger trends in this line of work, giving examples that appeared to shift the research in college student development. Additionally, we present brief examples from the research studies that specifically applied to students from underrepresented groups. Much of this work has its roots in the foundational psychological theories above, particularly psychosocial theories. Rather than reviewing the research that has been done on each of the foundational areas, we emphasize the scholarship that specifically studies students of color, female students, and LGBTQ students.

The literature on identity development related to gender, race, and sexual orientation for students reports that:

1. White students often experience privileges in the larger social structure that influences the way they think about their racial identity. White students may move from a position of not knowing or thinking about their racial identity toward thinking about their race in relation to people of color with the hope of moving toward multicultural acceptance where White students accept their own racial identity and history, and those of others.
2. Students of color often start by denying their racial identity and eventually move toward accepting it and also accepting those around them (e.g., White students).
3. Women tend to develop their identity differently (in a different order, taking a different path in stage theories) than men.
4. Students who are lesbian, gay, bisexual, transgender, or queer (LGBTQ) may develop this identity through a process where they view the world as primarily heterosexual and then eventually are able to incorporate, accept, and embrace their LGBTQ identity.
5. More recent literature maintains that identities may be overlapping, experienced as multi-faceted, intersecting, or fluid and dynamic.

White Racial Identity Development

The development of identity among White students has primarily been linked to the ways in which that population grapples with a national social history that has been oppressive to people who are not White (Feagin, 2000; Goodman, 2001; Hardiman, 2001; Helms & Cook, 1999; McIntosh, 1998). Taken together, the research on White racial identity development focuses on:

1. Historical and current privileges that are afforded to White people and White students;
2. The process that White students experience in moving from not thinking that racial identity pertains to them toward understanding their racial history and accepting their identity alongside the identity of those who are not White;
3. Autobiographical essays of White people discussing their experiences of coming to know their racial identity or their White privilege; and
4. Teaching or training practice to help students learn about diversity issues and race.

This line of research initiated at least in part in Hardiman's (2001) White racial identity development model that outlined how people dealt with being part of a group that had oppressed others. Helms (1992) developed a scale (survey instrument) to identify White racial identity development. While some scholars have raised concerns about the instrument (Rowe & Atkinson, 1995), Helms' scale is one of the few tools used to study White racial identity development (Hardiman, 2001). Taking another approach, Frankenberg (1993) examined the feminist movement, considering invisible privileges associated with being White (her later work rejected the simple understanding of invisible privilege).

McIntosh's (1998) self study of her racial identity, which initiated out of her teaching and thinking about gender, led to a list of privileges that she identified in her daily life as a White woman. While this idea has not been well tested empirically, the concepts have been very popular in teaching White students about their racial positioning and identities. There are similar autobiographical accounts of White privilege where White people outline their path toward realizing their privilege and identity that have become standard literature in this area (Stalvey, 1989).

Rooted in the models and thinking of Hardiman, Helms and McIntosh, Ortiz and Rhoads (2000) created an actionable framework for teaching multicultural education wherein teachers create opportunities for understanding and learning about culture in general, recognizing White culture and privilege as well as the legitimacy of cultures that are unfamiliar to their own, and then develop a multicultural outlook. This framework is primarily aimed at teaching White students to understand racial issues and their own identity. There are others who have primarily concentrated on the teaching aspect of White identity, teaching educators or students about their White identity as a way to begin diversity conversations and efforts (e.g., Gillespie, Ashbaugh, & DeFiore, 2002; McIntyre, 1997).

Scholarship on White racial identity development is generally lacking (McDermott & Samson, 2005). While there are theoretical examinations or self-studies of what it means to be White in the United States, there are much fewer empirical investigations into the topic, and even fewer instruments or formal measures to measure White students' development, aside from Helms' (1992) instrument which is decades old. While autobiographical reflection (McDermott & Samson, 2005; Stalvey, 1989) has at least worked to put White racial identity development on the radar, this work does not offer a rigorous examination of the way that social structures may continually advantage or disadvantage particular racial groups. For college students' development, the lack of empirical work is a concern because these autobiographical essays are not generalizable to the larger White population of students and yet they are still at the root of training and teaching about race. Without better evidence as to whether these autobiographical accounts are empirically accurate or generalizable in some way, the training and teaching on the topic may also be seriously lacking in terms of their ability to help students develop and think about race more generally.

Identity Development among Students of Color

There are a few important general findings about the work on racial/ethnic identity development as it relates to students of color:

1. The empirical research on identity is often separated into discrete categories separated by racial/ethnic group, mirroring the theoretical models of racial/ethnic identity development;
2. Involvement in activities or sub-groups during college can facilitate or hinder racial/ethnic identity development;
3. Institutional and personal pressures or the internalization of negative stereotypes about one's racial/ethnic group can influence a student's ability to develop identity.

Racial/Ethnic Identity as Discrete Categories Separated by Subgroups. Identity development among students of color has primarily been studied using separate models and measures based on each particular racial/ethnic group. Many of these studies are quantitative, survey methodologies. For instance, Cross and his colleagues developed the Cross Racial Identity Scale (CRIS) to study his theory of nigrescence (Vandiver, Fhagen-Smith, Cokley, Cross, & Worrell, 2001). The Black Racial Identity Attitude Scale (RIAS-B) was developed subsequently and used to delve deeper into Black racial identity (Parham & Helms, 1981; Worrell, Cross, & Vandiver, 2001). Scholars have used these scales to explore the ways that college influences African American students' racial identity development. Racial identity development has often been linked with other aspects of the college experience, such as engagement on or the connection that students have to campus (Harper & Quaye, 2007; Mitchell & Dell, 1992; Taylor & Howard-Hamilton, 19958). Additionally, some scholars have expanded their research with African American college students to develop other instruments, such as the Multidimensional Inventory of Black Identity (MIBI; Sellers, Rowley, Chavous, Shelton, & Smith, 1997).

Alternatively, some of the models were created from earlier studies or from empirical measurement tools. Keefe and Padilla (1987) developed an instrument to understand Mexican students' development, and they subsequently created a Typology of Mexican American Ethnic Orientation from the results of the studies that used this instrument. Torres' (2003) longitudinal, qualitative, grounded theory research with Latina/o college students led to findings related to conditions that influence Latina/o students' identity development (environment where they grew up, family influences, and ideas about society). Torres' work with Latina/o students who identified as either Anglo, Latina/o, or marginally oriented (e.g., feeling as if they were not the norm on campus) led to a bicultural model of identity development (Torres, 1999; Torres et al., 2003).

There is a comparatively limited amount of scholarship regarding Asian American, Pacific Islander, and Native American students' identities. While we are grouping these populations together here because of the limited scholarship in the area and because this is commonly done in the empirical literature, we want to underscore the many ways in which students from these groups differ. One review of the literature on Asian American students found that only 1% of the studies in major higher education journals in recent years were centered on these populations (Museus, 2009). This is troubling because there is so much within-group diversity among these populations, meaning that there are so many ethnic and cultural differences within this group (e.g., Filipino, Japanese, Chinese, Hawaiian, American Indian tribes are numerous, etc.).

The gap in literature on Asian and indigenous populations may encourage stereotypes and misunderstanding. For example, among Asian American students, one line of research grapples with how students negotiate academics alongside the model minority myth, or the idea that all Asian students will do well academically (Lee, 2009; Museus, 2009; Museus & Kiang, 2009). Asian American students may experience various aspects of the campus quite differently from their student of color peers such as the campus climate related to the acceptance of diversity on campus (Maramba, 2008). In a quantitative questionnaire study with Filipino students at a public research university, findings argued that students were more likely to feel that they belonged on campus if they had opportunities to deepen their understanding of their cultural background; students appeared to be more successful if they could reflect on their culture (Museus & Maramba, 2011). Fostering chances for students to reflect on their racial/ethnic identity may influence their ability to be successful in college. Some scholarship maintains that Asian American students may exhibit a collectivist orientation toward identity, meaning that they might be more likely to see their identity as integrally linked to their ethnic group (Yeh, & Huang, 1996). While this study was not specifically about identity development, the idea that Asian American students, and specifically Filipino students in this case, needed chances to explore their cultural background relates well to an understanding of better ways to support racial/ethnic identity development for students of color.

While there is a reported gap in research on Asian American and Pacific Islander students (Museus, 2009), the lacuna may be even deeper for research about American Indian students, although the empirical analysis remains to be done. The lack of study of this population could have serious consequences relative to their success in college. American Indian students have one of the highest rates of attrition of any other racial group (Shotton, Oosahwe, & Cintròn, 2007). One way that American Indian identity has been studied is through recording how many people self-identify as American Indian on U.S. Census data. For example, in Nagel's (1995) analysis of federal policy, she asserted that some Native populations might be experiencing what she called "ethnic renewal" where they are reclaiming a previously discarded identity (also see, Nagel, 1997). While this work does not examine American Indian students' identity processes per se, there may be implications for Native students in college too. In a comparison between White and American Indian students, Okagaki, Helling, and Bingham (2009) found that mother's socialization influenced American Indian students' association with their ethnic identity in college and that a belief that the students could be bicultural on campus was associated with a stronger sense of academic identity. Additionally, similar to studies with Asian American students that indicate the importance of a collective identity, there is evidence that when American Indian students find ways to create collective relationships (e.g., peer mentoring in this case), they may be more likely to be successful in college (Shotton et al., 2007).

While the majority of the research on racial identity development focuses on singular racial identities (e.g., African American, Native American, etc.), there are a few scholars who have advanced inquiry related to multiracial students or for students of color as a larger group. For example, Phinney (1992) created an instrument for measuring the racial identity of students of color more generally, the multigroup ethnic identity measure (MEIM). However, more research using this instrument is needed in order to strengthen the instrument (Ponterotto, Casas, Suzuki, & Alexander, 2001).

There are a few models and research projects aimed at understanding the racial identity development for students who identify with more than one racial/ethnic group (Kerwin & Ponterotto, 1995; Poston, 1990; Renn, 2004; Rockquemore, Brunsma, & Delgado, 2009; Shih & Sanchez, 2005). Renn's (2000) grounded theory study of multiracial students at a predominantly White institution offered five multiracial identity patterns: a monoracial identity, multiple monoracial identities dependent on the situation in which a student finds him/herself, multiracial identity (Renn, 2008), extraracial identity opting out of racial categories, or situation identity where a student identifies differently in various contexts. Other scholars have adapted Renn's multiracial identity model to understand the way that students from multiple racial or ethnic backgrounds may shift their identities in different situations (Aspinall, 2003; Chaudhari & Pizzolato, 2008; Jourdan, 2006; King, 2008; Shih & Sanchez, 2005). For example, in one qualitative study of multiethnic students using Renn's framework, family members were found to be important to students' ability to develop a positive multiethnic identity (Jourdan, 2006).

The Influence of Involvement in Activities and Sub-Groups on Racial/Ethnic Identity Development. Campus involvement may influence identity development for students of color across racial/ethnic groups. Using an ecological model of human development, Guardia and Evans (2008) found that fraternity membership for Latina/o students in a Hispanic Serving Institution (HSI) enhanced their ethnic identity development. In a study of the relationship between student engagement on campus and racial identity attitudes, Taylor and Howard-Hamilton (1995) discovered that involvement in activities outside of class may lead to stronger racial identity attitudes (also see, Harper & Quaye, 2007). Museus' (2008) interview study with African American and Asian American students' cultural adjustment concurred that involvement in co-curricular activities (e.g., clubs, organizations) might facilitate students' development. There is evidence that involvement, particularly in spaces that allow for students to define their own identities (racial/ethnic organizations, etc.) may facilitate multiracial student development too (King, 2008). Renn's (2000) qualitative research with multiracial students found that sometimes students found a place to deal with their racial/ethnic identity in organizations on campuses, and in some cases, students created private spaces with peers where they could grapple with their multiracial identity. Additionally, being a part of particular subgroups may influence the development of racial or ethnic identity in positive ways. According to the findings of a conceptual study on Black females' involvement with hip-hop culture, the women may be able to question stereotypical views of Black women through their involvement in this subgroup during college (Henry, West, & Jackson, 2010).

Institutional and Personal Pressures on Identity Development. There are many institutional and personal factors such as experiences with racism (Hipolito-Delgado, 2010; Kellogg & Liddell, 2012) that can hinder the identity development of students of color in college. Through a qualitative exploration of critical incidents for multiracial students' identity development (e.g., confronting racism, responding to external definitions of self, affirming one's racial identity), Kellogg and Liddell (2012) learned that these incidents did appear to facilitate the students' identity development. In a multiple regression dissertation study of internalized racism (the internalization of negative stereotypes about one's racial/ethnic group), Hipolito-Delgado (2007) found that internalized racism was inversely related to racial/ethnic identity development, that internalized racism does impede students' ability to develop identity. Among Latina/o and Chicana/o students, Hipolito-Delgado (2010) found that perceived interpersonal racism predicted internalized racism that could influence a student's ability to develop identity. Winkle-Wagner's (2009a) ethnographic study of African American women's identity development in a predominantly White institution asserted that pressures to acclimate to the institution from the institution, peers, faculty, and administrators were experienced as impositions on the women's identity that often hindered the women's ability to develop their own sense of self.

It is worth noting that most of the research on ways that students of color develop their identity related to race/ethnicity in college underlines students' individual responsibility and choice rather than studying the role of the college environment (i.e., the institution and institutional actors) in hindering or facilitating identity development. This line of scholarship that stresses the importance of the institution in shaping racial and ethnic identities for students of color is not vast. In Chapter 6, we reviewed research on campus climates and that inquiry does relate. But, the campus climate research generally does not underscore identity as a key variable or concept of study.

Gender and Sexual Orientation Identity Development

Another area of scholarship on college student identity argues for the importance of thinking about the development of gender identity (Edward & Jones, 2009; O'Neil, Egan, Owen, & Murry, 1993; Ossana, Helms, & Leonard, 1992) and sexual orientation identity (Abes, 2012; Cass, 1979; McCarn & Fassinger, 1996; Mueller & Cole, 2009; Renn, 2010; Rhoads, 1994). Scholarship on gender identity developed as a reflection of foundational theories of college student development that largely excluded consideration of women, or assumed a male population (Gilligan, 1982/1993; Josselson, 1987, 1996a, 1996b). For example, Gilligan's (1982) qualitative inquiry, *In a Different Voice,* examined the moral development of women finding that women place more attention on care and responsibility when making moral decisions and that this differed from previous models of moral development for men that emphasized rules and regulations (also see Gilligan & Attanucci, 1988). Her work led to decades-long debates about moral reasoning in the field of psychology (Jaffee & Hyde, 2000). Gilligan's work has influenced the way that counseling practice, residence life, and career development practices have been structured in student affairs in particular (Enns, 1991; Picard & Guido-DiBrito, 1993; Stonewater, 1989).

Jones and McEwen's (2000) work on multiple dimensions of identity (considered in more detail below) also has contributed to empirical work on gender development in college because they studied female students. While much of the work on gender identity has attempted to better include women in student development theory models, there is some research indicating that male gender identity is a necessary topic of study too. Edward and Jones' (2009) grounded theory study with men found that these students often felt as if they had to perform in a particular way to demonstrate their gender identity. However, in the area of gender identity, there is currently more work on women than there is on male identity development, specifically for men who identify as heterosexual.

Research on sexual identity began with Cass' (1979) Homosexual Identity Model. McCarn and Fassinger (1996) extended the model to explain how a student might develop a gay identity as part of a community. Subsequent research has explored LGBTQ identity development and how this identity might influence behavior (Wilkerson, Brooks, & Ross, 2010). Other studies investigated sexual identity among particular racial or ethnic groups asserting that many students struggle with integrating sexual identities into other aspects of their identities such as race (Chan, 1989; Garcia, 1998). Jones and Abes (2004) expanded the multiple dimensions of identity idea in their narrative study of lesbian college students finding that the participants described their identity in a cognitively complex manner in that their position as non-heterosexual students may have facilitated their development of thinking in more complex ways. Similarly, Stevens' (2004) grounded theory study with gay men in college suggested that sexual identity might be at odds with other aspects of their identities. Abes' (2012) qualitative work with lesbian identity development uncovered an approach toward embracing multiple, intersecting identities that might be more useful in understanding how LGBTQ students experience their identity development in college. While there is less research on heterosexual sexual identity development, Mueller and Cole's (2009) qualitative inquiry into the topic posed that perhaps this line of research would be beneficial. Participants discussed the way that they developed their identity as heterosexuals and their attempt to distance themselves from homophobia (Mueller & Cole). Future research could benefit from a queer theoretical approach, according to a review of the scholarship in this area (Renn, 2010).

Multiple, Overlapping, and Intersecting Identities

In contrast to the research that envisages student identity as fitting into discrete categories such as race, sexual orientation, or gender, some of the more recent work reveals that identity might be more multifaceted and dynamic than some of the psychosocial models might suggest (Torres et al., 2009; Stewart, 2008, 2009; Winkle-Wagner, 2012b). Jones and McEwen (2000) led the charge in a grounded theory study with female college students, arguing that there were multiple dimensions of identity with intersecting circles surrounding a core central identity (also see, Jones & Abes, 2004).

Scholars considering identity in this manner have noted that identity is multifaceted or overlapping, fluid or dynamic rather than an endpoint (Deaux, 1993), and multiple rather than singular (Robinson, 1993; Stewart, 2008, 2009; Winkle-Wagner, 2009a, 2012b). For example, evidence from studies using this approach shows that students of color often report multiple identities whereby they act one way with their ethnic group and another way when they are the minority (Arroyo & Zigler, 1995; Stewart, 2008, 2009), the pressure of which can result in academic disengagement, influencing academic achievement (Brewer & Silver, 2000; Oyersman, Kemmelmeier, Fryberg, Brosh, & Hart-Johnson, 2003). Winkle-Wagner's (2009a, 2009b) ethnographic study with African American women in a predominantly White institution indicated that the women experienced multiple identities in various contexts; their identities changed depending on the people they were around or the social context in which they found themselves. The African American women in this study described significant pressures on their identities, the need to act, think, or speak in particular ways in order to be successful on campus. Stewart's (2008) portraiture methodology with Black college students found that the students were able to name and use multiple identities in settings where they felt nurtured and supported. The implication of that study could be that students need more spaces on college campuses where they feel supported in pursuing multiple identities.

SUMMARY: DIVERSITY AND COLLEGE STUDENT IDENTITY DEVELOPMENT

There is much to be garnered about how to better serve underrepresented students in college from the vast area of inquiry on college student development theory. Taken together, the identity theory and research that is related to underrepresented college students can be summarized as making a strong argument that identity development can either be facilitated and enacted in college, or, the college experience can become a barrier to students' development. The inclusion of space for students' many identities is in itself an act of inclusion of diversity. Most scholars who study postsecondary education and administrators who work on college campuses would prefer that the college experience were beneficial, offering a catalyst toward positive identity development for students. In our hope of positive identity development for students, we summarize this work and contemplate what remains to be done on the topic of college student identity development for underrepresented populations.

Think about Diversity

The foundational theories of college student development, many of which grew out of clinical observations in psychology, often lacked applicability to students of color and students from other underrepresented groups (e.g., LGBTQ, women, first-generation, or low-income students) because they were typically initiated among White male clients (Evans et al., 2010; Torres et al., 2003). Psychosocial theories in particular were subsequently expanded to be more inclusive to particular components of identity such as racial/ethnic identity, sexual identity, or gender identity. These theories, initiated principally as stage theories where students would progress in a linear manner from one stage or level to the next, as a way to examine how a student's progression through the college environment, might help or hinder progress through these various stages, phases, or levels (e.g., racial or ethnic identity development theories where students progress toward acceptance of their own racial/ethnic identity and that of others). While these theories were a shift toward being more inclusive of underrepresented students, scholars subsequently challenged them as being too linear, value-laden (that there was an assumption of it being better to be at a higher stage), or potentially too essentializing (Torres et al., 2009; Winkle-Wagner, 2012b).

Newer advances and alternatives in college student development theory have presented identity as multi-dimensional, nuanced, or situational where a student might shift identity in different contexts (Abes & Jones, 2004; Jones & McEwen, 2000; Renn, 2004). Sociological approaches that contemplate multiple identities and roles associated with these identities have also started to be used more in discussions about college students (Torres et al., 2009; Winkle-Wagner, 2009a, 2009b, 2012b). Some scholars in higher education have started to use the concept of intersectionality to highlight the way that students' various categories of their identities such as race, class, or gender are linked (Abes, 2012; Abes et al., 2007; Gonzalez, 1998; Jones, 2009). Settles (2006) employed an intersectional framework to understand Black women's race and gender identities simultaneously. Other scholars have begun to compile volumes to use as exemplars for intersectional approaches toward studying identity. For example, Strayhorn's (2013) edited book about African American students' experiences in college presents various studies using intersectional approaches throughout the book. Another example of multiple scholars beginning to employ an intersection approach is Chambers' (2011) book on support systems for Black female students.

Among the numerous theories of college student development, both the foundational theories and the recent advances, there is very little work that contemplates the role of class or socioeconomic status relative to identity development. This is a huge limitation, particularly given the increasing number of first-generation and/or low-income students who are attending college. Social theories, such as cultural capital or social reproduction theory, might offer insight into ways that class status could influence identity development (Winkle-Wagner, 2010). However, these theories do not specifically examine the way that one sees oneself in the way that work specific to identity does. Future theoretical work on college student identity should work to better include this important social category of class status.

In addition to an absence of the study of class location in many of the college student development theories, there is also very little attention being given to religious diversity and how this might influence identity. Bowman and Small's (2010, 2012) research on spiritual development among students from religious majority (Lutheran, Methodist, etc.) and minority (Muslim, Seventh Day Adventist, etc.) groups is a step in this direction. But, more work is needed (also see, Bryant & Astin, 2008). Cole and Ahmadi's (2010) research with Muslim students found that these students were less satisfied with their college experience than were those in other religious groups. Future research and theoretical work that contemplated how religious identity connects with other aspects of identity would be particularly useful to understand students' complex identity experiences in college.

Diversity Still Matters

The college experience influences identity development according to the empirical literature. For students of color, women, and LGBTQ students the college experience may hinder or facilitate the development of identity (Abes & Jones, 2004; Arroyo & Zigler, 1995; Brewer & Silver, 2000; Oyersman et al., 2003; Stevens, 2004; Torres et al., 2003; Winkle-Wagner, 2009a). The campus environment matters greatly not only to students' academic success, but, also in terms of their personal development. Ultimately, a student's position as being in a minority group on campus *does* influence the student's experience in positive or negative ways. A student could experience the freedom to explore his or her identity as someone who is in the position of being minoritized (Gillborn, 2005, put into a minority position regardless of whether this was necessarily a choice) within a particular campus setting. Or, the student can feel pressured to acclimate in a way that could be detrimental to the development of identity (Winkle-Wagner, 2009a).

While we alluded to this earlier, there is a significant weight given to individual identity development and students' choices, responsibilities, or role in crafting identity in the literature. We question whether all students feel as if they have a full buffet of choices when it comes to identity in college. For example, some students who experience marginalization or the feeling of being minoritized (Gillborn, 2005) may not see many viable options for their identity development (also see Winkle-Wagner, 2009a). Postsecondary institutions and the actors within them (students, staff, faculty) may play a prominent role in how students are allowed (or feel compelled) to develop in their identity, particularly if those students are from underrepresented populations in the campus context. Many of the theories of college student development do allow some consideration of the institution because the purpose is to explore identity construction within the college context (i.e., how college affects students' development). Yet, aside from a few examples (Renn, 2000) there is little research that accentuates the institutional role in potentially shaping identity construction for college students. We recommend that future researchers find ways to stress the importance of the institution and institutional actors in potentially shaping and guiding identity, particularly among underrepresented student populations.

There is growing evidence that parsing out identity by particular categories or characteristics such as race, sexual orientation, or gender may not be accurate to the way that students actually experience their identity on campus (Abes & Jones, 2004; Jones & McEwen, 2000; Renn, 2004; Winkle-Wagner, 2009a). Rather, students are much more likely to experience their identities as multi-dimensional (Jones & McEwen, 2000), dependent on the situation or context (Renn, 2004), or as multiple identities that are fluid, and dynamic (Winkle-Wagner, 2009a). Sociological approaches may be useful in helping to tease out the complex and nuanced experience of identity (Winkle-Wagner, 2012b).

Finally, as we described previously, intersectional approaches are useful in helping to reconsider ways to study identity so that categories such as race, class, gender, and sexual orientation can be considered as simultaneously occurring and influencing factors in identity development (Abes, 2012; Abes et al., 2007; Gonzaelez, 1998; Jones, 2009a, 2009b; Settles, 2006). In other words, a student is much more likely to experience his/her race, class, gender, and sexual orientation *together* without necessarily being able to parse them out as separate categories. For example, a White female from a low-income background is going to have a different identity development experience than a White female from a high-income background. Or, a Black woman may have a different identity experience from a Black man. Intersectional approaches embrace the complexity of identities (Jones, 2009a, 2009b).

Diversity is Everywhere

Student affairs practitioners and faculty have a major role to play in students' identity development. Who students are matters in their campus experience, particularly when students are from underrepresented populations. In many ways, the field of student affairs emerged side-by-side with student development theory (Hamrick, Evans, & Schuh, 2002). For this reason, it would seem that these theories would be easily applied to practice. However, the application of college student development and/or identity theories primarily lies in the hands of practitioners themselves. Student affairs practitioners must be deliberate about learning theories and then finding ways that these theories can be applied for practice. For example, when a student comes to a student affairs administrator for advice on a challenging situation, having an understanding of identity theory can be useful for the student affairs practitioner to consider how to best advise the student. These moments can lead to hindering or helping students to continue in their development of self. Additionally, there is some research offering that one way to approach work on identity from a practical standpoint is to use identity development as a way to learn about difference. In a qualitative study, Bergerson and Huftalin (2011) found that institutional and personal factors support a shift in their openness to identity-based difference. This type of work recommends that student affairs practitioners use students' differences in identity as one way to learn about diversity issues more generally (also see, Bergerson & Huftalin, 2011; Bowman & Small, 2010, 2012; Patton, 2011). Future research should pick up where these scholars leave off, examining how the facilitation of students' identity development in college could actually shift campus culture or climates.

DISCUSSION QUESTIONS

Based on the conclusions made from theory and empirical research in this chapter, we have a few remaining questions. Below are questions aimed at both those who might be interested in serving as student affairs professionals or administrators, or, for those who desire to do research in the area of identity development for underrepresented students in college.

Improving Practice

1. Why should student affairs professionals continue to review foundational theories of college student development?

2. What is the role of identity development theory in student affairs practices? Think of an area of student affairs and describe how you might use foundational theories of student identity development in daily interactions with students.

3. Now, consider some of the more recent advances in student development theory that contemplate identity as multifaceted or multi-dimensional. How might the use of these theories shift the use of theory in the practical example you just considered?

4. What are some of the challenges to using identity development theories in student affairs practice? Think in particular about what might be challenging in the application of these theories in your everyday interactions with students.

5. What are the benefits of creating student affairs practice from an approach that focuses on particular aspects of identity such as race, gender, or sexual orientation? Describe a particular area of student affairs practice and how a theory (e.g., racial identity development theory) might apply towards practice.

6. What are some of the benefits of creating student affairs practice from an approach toward consideration of multiple, overlapping or situational identities? Consider a particular area of student affairs practice and describe how you might apply some of these approaches in that practice.

7. What might be some of the benefits and challenges to adopting sociological approaches to identity development in student affairs practice?

8. One of the major student affairs associations, NASPA (Student Affairs Administrators in Higher Education), developed a set of professional competencies that are encouraged for all student affairs professionals. How might the NASPA professional competencies relate to college student development theories, particularly for work with underrepresented students?

    a. The NASPA Competencies are (see http://www.naspa.org/programs/profdev/default.cfm): advising and helping; assessment, evaluation, and research; equity, diversity, and inclusion; ethical professional practice; history, philosophy, and value; human organizational resources; law, policy, and governance; leadership; personal foundations; students learning and development.

9. Another national association for student affairs, College Student Educators International, developed a Statement of Ethical Principles and Standards. How might the ACPA Ethical Principles and Standards influence your thinking about college student identity development for underrepresented students?

    a. The ACPA Standards are (see http://www2.myacpa.org/statement-of-ethical-principles-and-standards): professional responsibility and competence; student learning and development; responsibility to the institution; and responsibility to society.

10. The Council for the Advancement of Standards in Higher Education (CAS) developed a set of standards for student affairs. How might these CAS Standards relate to the college student development theories that were reviewed in this chapter?

    a. The domains for the CAS Standards are (see http://www.cas.edu/index.php/cas-general-standards/): knowledge acquisition, integration, construction, and application; cognitive complexity; intrapersonal development; interpersonal competence; humanitarianism and civic engagement; practical competence.

Developing Future Research

1. What are some of the strengths and limitations to identity development models that contemplate separate identity categories such as race, gender, or sexual identity?

2. How might you construct a theoretical model that would consider class or religion more centrally?

3. What are some of the strengths and limitations to the approaches toward identity development that contemplate overlapping, multiple dimensions of identity, situational identities, or multiple identities?

4. What remains to be done related to theories of identity development as they apply to underrepresented students? Describe a particular research study that you could do to address these gaps in the current theoretical work.

5. Describe a study that you might be interested in pursuing that takes an intersectional approach toward the study of college students' identity development.

6. If you were to think of an empirical research study that still needs to be done on identity development for underrepresented students, what might that study look like?

═══════════════════════════════=A CASE STUDY═══════════════════════════════

PRACTICING DIVERSITY ISSUES RELATED TO COLLEGE STUDENT IDENTITY DEVELOPMENT

Exploring Cultural Climate and Identity at MidState University

TASHA WILLIS, CALIFORNIA STATE UNIVERSITY, LOS ANGELES

RASHIDA CRUTCHFIELD, CALIFORNIA STATE UNIVERSITY, LONG BEACH

MidState is a suburban, public institution in the midwestern United States situated in a college town. It is attended by 12,000 undergraduate and 3,000 graduate students, 85% of whom are White, 24% of whom are students of color (12% Asian Pacific Islander, 8% African American, 3% Latina/o, 07% Native American), and 1% who are undeclared. Sixty-eight percent of all students live in campus housing and the remaining 32% are commuter students. The faculty and staff are 94% White. Other than the university, which is the town's predominant employer, the automotive technological industry and several factories spur the local economy.

Stephen, a White male who has been supervising the resident advisor (RA) program for 3 years, is leading the annual resident advisor orientation and training. Participation is required for all 25 RAs, all of whom are returning students, ranging from sophomores through seniors. Demographically, the group is made up of 16 White, 3 African American, 2 Latina/o, 2 Asian Pacific Islander, 1 Native American student; there are 15 women and 9 men. Data on sexual orientation is not collected, but at least one student has come out to the group as a gay man.

After participating in a day of team building activities and dialogue, the students are expressing feelings of safety and cohesion as a group. Stephen is pleased and eager to find a way to bridge their experiences to influence the wider campus climate. For their final activity, Stephen suggests that the group explore ways to create and/or maintain this kind of safety for all students in the residence halls. He invites the participants to share how they have felt as part of the retreat in relation to how they feel on campus day-to-day. He then encourages them to discuss ideas for future activities that might promote this cohesion and safe climate on campus.

Lysa, a junior who has become an informal leader in the group, jumps into the discussion passionately:

> I feel really safe in this space and even on campus, actually. Sure, as a Philipina, I know some folks are surprised that I don't fit their stereotype of the quiet, "don't rock the boat" Asian woman. But generally, I'm affirmed for being a student leader from staff and faculty and even some of my peers. I do feel pulled though, because people ask me to be on all these campus committees and leadership stuff, which I love. But my family doesn't really get it. They want me to focus just on academics, graduate, and get on with having a career but more importantly, a family. So even taking a day for this retreat was tricky with the pressure I feel from home. I pointed out that this is required for my job and that helped, but I'm not sure I'll even tell them I'm involved if we do volunteer activities after this.

Noemi, a sophomore, relates to that and is also aware of assumptions about her identity as a dark skinned woman:

> People look at me and think I'm African American because of my dark skin, but I'm not. My parents emigrated from Honduras. It's hard because I really am starting to see that my dark skin makes me different from most of the Latinos on campus. They don't really see me as a member of the community, and I'm not really Black so I don't belong with the Black students either. I'm starting to embrace that my dark skin is a reflection of our indigenous and African roots and I really want to honor that *mestizo* (mixed) heritage. I feel split, loving who I am, but not rooted in the community on campus. I am also the first person in my family to attend college. So, while I live in the residence hall with all of you, my family needs me to help with my brothers and sisters at home on the weekends and I'm working lots of extra hours to help support myself and the family bills.

Richard, a senior, is surprised that Noemi isn't feeling accepted in the community because he is happy to embrace her racially. He responded:

> I love to hear you're identifying with your Black roots—you should absolutely join us in the Black Student Union. And I will educate you about some crucial Black history you should know. I also belong to a Black male group where we talk about the importance of supporting our families and education. So, I'm sure

your father and brother can handle it if you give yourself the chance to focus on school. Also, don't forget to use financial aid. That's what it's for.

Richard minimizes Noemi's struggles around ethnicity, immigration, and financial realities, and is focused on the racism and stereotypes he experiences on campus. He continued:

I get these looks on campus like I'm going to be a problem. I don't get the benefit of the doubt. People assume I'm going to flunk out. I mean, my parents worked hard to be an engineer and a lawyer and they sent me to private schools. I get great grades, and I am the President of the BSU. I should be the mentor, not automatically tapped to be in some endangered Black male mentoring program!

Joe, a junior, changes the subject a bit and shares his perspective:

As a gay man, I really feel like I identify with what you're all saying about being stereotyped on campus. People perceive me as this really privileged guy, as "the White man," but I've had to deal with hate coming at me ever since I came out in high school. Plus, I come from a working class family like Noemi so I'm on financial aid too. But everyone just assumes I've got it made because I'm a White male.

Farrah, a junior, points out that, while she feels really comfortable in the group, she feels largely isolated on campus:

My mother is Lakota and my father is White, but since I grew up on the res, I really identify with my Native heritage. I was really recruited by the school to be here, but I feel like the token Indian on campus to just add to the numbers on campus to represent diversity. I've met this really amazing professor who is mentoring me, but I feel generally so isolated because there's no one like me here. I have the full support of my tribe financially, and they are all behind me. That's great, but also adds a lot of pressure because I think about all their hopes for me. I'm supposed to be the one who "makes it," but it also makes me feel disconnected from them as different when I go home. They have high expectations for me. I'm the only one, both on campus and at home.

Stephen is left wondering how to maintain the unity that the students have developed while also addressing the divergent concerns they have raised about feeling safe on campus. Aware that each student is exploring various aspects of their social identities, Stephen wonders how he can best support them. He begins to consider how he can utilize various identity development theories as a basis for creating some action steps in support of these students and the larger campus climate issues that their concerns raise.

Imagine yourself in Stephen's role as staff supervisor of the resident advisors. How would you proceed during and after the orientation and training? Consider the following questions:

1. How do you proceed with the students so that they feel like their stories are validated?
2. What racial issues did the students identify in this case? Which theories would you draw upon to help yourself understand their development?

3. Consider some of the gender issues that might be important to explore.
4. What role might sexual orientation play for the students in this case and how might Cass (1984) support your understanding?
5. What class or socioeconomic issues might have been raised in this case?
6. What other identity theories might you use to help you think about where the students are in their development?
   a. For example, how might using Chickering and Reisser's (1993) framework help you understand the developmental stages of the various students?
   b. What are the limitations to this framework in understanding these particular students?
   c. Or, consider using some of the racial/ethnic identity theories. How might those theories apply to these students?
   d. Would a multiple identities perspective or sociological approach be useful in helping to work with these students? Why or why not?
7. How could the use of a holistic and/or intersectional approach in understanding the students' experiences and their social identities aid you in supporting them as resident advisors?

NOTE

1. We use both terms in the text as some members of this community self-identify as American Indian and the literature more commonly uses Native American.

Section III

Getting Out

8

DIVERSITY-AND-INCLUSION TOWARD PERSISTENCE

Crossing to the Other Side

The paradox of education is precisely this—that as one begins to become conscious, one begins to examine the society in which he is being educated.

—James A. Baldwin, Author

The culmination of a student's college experience is the completion of a degree program, persistence, and graduation. Perhaps one way to evaluate whether the inclusion of diversity has really been enacted on college campuses is to examine whether students are able to get to the end of their degree, to the other side. After doing this examination, we argue that there is work to be done.

Despite numerous studies and practical efforts to increase college completion rates, college completion or persistence rates have not changed all that much in the past 20 years (Radford, Berkner, Wheeless, & Shepherd, 2010; Tinto, 2012). At four-year institutions, approximately 63% of students will complete their degrees while approximately 40% of students at two-year colleges will graduate (Radford et al., 2010; Tinto, 2012). But, when looking at students in all kinds of institutions including community colleges, for example, only about 40% of students graduate within a six-year time period (Tinto, 2012).

There are huge disparities between demographic groups. Students of color and women have a higher probability of leaving postsecondary education than do White students and men (Bowen, Chingos, & McPherson, 2009; DesJardins, Stephen, & McCall, 2002; Hatch & Mommsen, 1984; Mehan, Hubbard, & Villanueva, 1994; Melguizo, 2008; Myers, 2003; Oseguera, 2006; Pathways to College Network, 2003; Ross et al., 2012; Snyder & Dillow, 2011). Students from high-income families are approximately three times more likely to complete a college degree than are students from low-income backgrounds (Bowen, Chingos, & McPherson, 2009; Tinto, 2012).

Clearly, college student persistence remains a huge issue. Researchers are challenged with better ways to study persistence so that this information can inform policy and program development. Administrators and practitioners are tasked with better ways of serving students to foster college completion through policies and programs. This chapter investigates what has been done on the topic of persistence, both theoretically and empirically, to shed light on what needs to be done in the future to help students complete their degrees after they gain access to college. We use the terms "persistence," "college completion," and "retention" synonymously, all to refer to the completion of students' degree programs.

THINKING ABOUT DIVERSITY: THEORETICAL IDEAS ABOUT COLLEGE STUDENT PERSISTENCE

There are a variety of approaches and theoretical models regarding the study of college student persistence such as:

1. Tinto's (1975, 1993) social and academic integration model that asserts that as students become part of the campus community, they are more likely to persist;
2. Astin's (1984, 1985) student involvement model, which initiated the importance of becoming involved, particularly in co-curricular or extra-curricular activities during college as a way to increase the chance that a student is retained; and
3. Bean and Eaton's (2001) psychological models investigating individual cognitive processes that might influence degree completion.

We pay close attention here to Tinto's (1975, 1993) academic-social integration model (also known as the Tinto model, or Tinto's socialization model) and to Astin's (1984, 1985) involvement model because these theoretical models have arguably influenced the greatest portion of the thinking and work on college student persistence. Practitioners often use these models as a way to think about retention in terms of developing student support or success programs. For example, many of the persistence programs on college campuses encourage involvement in co-curricular activities, as recommended by the Astin and Tinto models, as a way for students to attach to the campus and subsequently persist through their degree programs.

One of the most influential theories regarding student retention, Tinto's student departure model (1975, 1993), was based on earlier research by Spady (1971), which employed Durkheim's sociological discussion of suicide. Durkheim's (1951) research into suicide for Protestants and Catholics demonstrated that suicide is more likely to occur when a person is not integrated into society. Spady (1971) adapted Durkheim's notion of suicide and related it to college student attrition. Tinto (1975, 1993) built on Spady's use of Durkheim, coupled with Van Gennep's anthropological rites of passage, stressing the importance of students' academic and institutional commitment and fit. Later discussion amended the original model, weaving together academics and social life (Tinto, 1997). Essentially, this model assumes that a student must become a part of the campus community. For example, the more invested a student is in the classroom (e.g., speaking up during class, meeting with faculty outside of class, creating study groups with peers, etc.), the more academically integrated a student will become, and subsequently, the more likely a student is to persist. Social integration refers to a student's participation in co-curricular activities (e.g., organizations, clubs) or investment in informal friendship groups. The more socially involved a student becomes on campus, the more integrated he or she will be, and this will lead to persistence.

Tinto's work, asserting the importance of academic and social integration, has provided the backdrop to a vast amount of the scholarly work in higher education in many areas. For example, Bean and Eaton (2001; Bean, 1980, 1985) developed a psychological model claiming that individual psychological processes involved in developing academic and social integration may affect students' ability to persist through degree programs. Within this model, issues such as institutional fit, students' academic performance, and institutional commitment are key. Practical applications to foster positive individual psychological processes might include programs like learning communities, freshman interest groups, tutoring, mentoring, and student orientation (Myers, 2003).

A plethora of research validates Tinto's (1975, 1993) model, maintaining that the social and academic integration of students is correlated to student persistence (Astin, 1996; Beil, Reisen, Zea, & Caplan, 1999; Guifridda, 2003; Kuh, Hu, & Vesper, 2000; Schwartz & Washington, 2002; Tinto, 1997, 2000; Titus, 2006). Tinto's academic-social integration model has greatly influenced the way scholars and practitioners think about how to foster students' successful access to and persistence through degree programs, effecting research and practice on everything from the fostering of students' identity development to college choice, to support programs in college (Christie & Dinham, 1991; Stage & Rushin, 1993; Terenzini & Wright, 1987). Much of student affairs practice, for example, is connected to Tinto's academic-social integration model. Everything from academic support programs (e.g., academic enrichment programs, tutoring, summer programs) to student activities (e.g., student government, live-learning communities, Greek life, other organizations or clubs) rests on the assumption of the importance of helping students to integrate into college campuses as a way to be successful (i.e., persist).

It is not surprising that such an influential theoretical model of student persistence might also be the topic of criticism. Many scholars have criticized Tinto's model for lacking diversity in the empirical work that supports it. For example, issues facing students of color were not the point of the original analysis. Thus, many scholars assert that the academic-social integration model may not work in quite the same way, or might be completely inappropriate for students of color or those from other underrepresented groups like part-time students, religious minorities, female, and lesbian/gay/bisexual/transgender/queer or questioning (LGBTQ) students (Howard-Hamilton, 1997; Jones, 2010; Rendón, Jalomo, & Nora 2000; Taylor & Miller, 2002; Torres, 2003). Some scholars have claimed Tinto's model assumes the assimilation of minority students; students must deny their own cultural background to fit into campus (Tierney, 1992, 1999, 2000). Others have taken a softer approach, claiming that the academic-social integration model is in need of revision (Braxton, 2000; Padilla, Trevino, Gonzalez, & Trevino, 1997), particularly when it comes to the experiences of students of color (Guiffrida, 2004, 2005; Hausmann, Ye, Schofield, & Wood, 2009; Lee & Donlan, 2011). Jones (2010) studied the social integration aspect of Tinto's theory, finding that social integration has a stronger, more positive impact on institutional commitment and persistence for female students than for male students. More research is needed to demonstrate how academic-social integration may vary among various student subpopulations (e.g., LGBTQ students, religious minority students, etc.).

Astin's (1985, 1993, 1996) student involvement model provides another approach to considerations of student persistence, studying in-class and co-curricular learning in college and ways that these experiences might encourage students to persist through degree programs. Astin offered a way to view the college experience in terms of inputs (a student's background, earlier educational experiences), experiences (a student's experiences in college), and outputs (how a student does during the college experience). This linear approach assumes that if particular experiences could be fostered in college, certain outputs (i.e., persistence) could be achieved. In other words, the idea is that if only students would become more involved in campus, they would be more likely to persist through degree programs. Not unlike Tinto's model, Astin's model is the basis for a great deal of student affairs practice. The idea that it is necessary to help students become involved in a variety of ways during their time in college is connected to the student involvement model.

DIVERSITY STILL MATTERS:
LITERATURE ON COLLEGE STUDENT PERSISTENCE

The empirical work on college student persistence can be separated into three groups:

1. Students' backgrounds influence persistence in college: This scholarship considers the ways that family backgrounds might relate to students' likelihood of persistence.
2. Students' adjustment, integration, or engagement as factors facilitating persistence: This research emphasizes students' processes or the outcomes of their integration and socialization on college campuses.
3. Institutional and structural influences on persistence: Scholarship in this area focuses on institutional or larger socio-structural influences and actions on students' retention.

These three lines of inquiry have divergent underlying assumptions. The first, highlighting students' backgrounds, presents research on the way that families, cultural, and class backgrounds influence students' ability to persist through college. The second explores integration/engagement, and this work often rests on the idea of some level of individual responsibility on the part of the students to connect to campus. The assumption is that students are always able to decide to take actions that allow them to connect, integrate, or become socialized into the existing institutional structures and norms on a college campus. The third body of research assumes that institutions and those within them (e.g., faculty, staff) play an integral role in creating an environment that fosters student success. The institutional considerations include the effect of campus race or gender climates or institutional types (e.g., predominantly White, historically Black, etc.) on students' persistence and the outcomes of institutional programs particularly targeted toward the retention of students who are underrepresented within that environment.

Student Backgrounds and Persistence

Students' families often play a crucial role in persistence in college. Some of the theoretical work related to college student persistence initially claimed that it was important for students to begin to disassociate with families in order to develop independence in college and to integrate into postsecondary institutions (Tinto, 1990). But, there is conflicting evidence for some populations of students such as African American (Winkle-Wagner, 2009b) and Native American students (Jackson, Smith, & Hill, 2003; Guillory

& Wolverton, 2008). Numerous scholars have asserted that continuing connections with families may be important to racially or ethnically underrepresented students' desire to stay in college and complete their degrees (Astin, 1982; Barnhardt, 1994; Guillory & Wolverton, 2008; Jackson et al., 2003; Lin, 1990; Winkle-Wagner, 2009b). In a qualitative study of Native American students' persistence in three institutions, family was the most frequently mentioned factor that students perceived as vital to their persistence through college (Guillory & Wolverton, 2008). An ethnographic study of African American women on a predominantly White campus came to a similar conclusion; while family relationships are sometimes complicated, these relationships are an integral part of students' success in college (Winkle-Wagner, 2009b).

Student Adjustment, Integration, or Engagement

Tinto's model, and the subsequent scholarship rooted in this model can be described as a socialization model, implying that as students enter the college environment, they need to take steps to adjust to that environment in order to be successful. For example, using this model, a student would be more likely to graduate college if she joined a few organizations. She would also be more likely to persist if she went to all of her classes, talked to her professors, and spoke up during class meetings. Many retention programs often gear a component of their mission toward aiding this type of socialization by teaching students campus norms while offering them academic support (e.g., tutoring, study sessions, etc.) and social support (e.g., encouragement to get involved, social activities, etc.).

Building on Astin's assertion that student involvement greatly influences student success (i.e., persistence in this case), C. Robert Pace (1984) created the College Student Experiences Questionnaire (CSEQ) to examine the various factors that facilitate or impede students' successful persistence through college. The CSEQ launched a huge body of scholarship that laid the groundwork for the National Survey of Student Engagement (NSSE). The NSSE, developed by George Kuh and launched in 2000, is second only to the U.S. Census in its breadth and sample size and is comprised of a group of surveys, many of which are focused on particular populations. As an example of the widespread usage of these surveys, over 1,400 colleges and universities (and growing) have participated in one of the NSSE surveys since 2000 (see http://nsse.iub.edu/html/about.cfm). The NSSE's set of surveys has been expanded to specific aspects of students' engagement in particular kinds of academic programs or postsecondary institutions. These surveys explore students' engagement in high school as a way to prepare for college (High School Survey of Student Engagement, HSSSE); the college adjustment process for first-year students (Beginning College Survey of Student Engagement, BCSSE); students' experiences in classes or their academic engagement (Classroom Survey of Student Engagement, CSSE); faculty perceptions of student involvement (Faculty Survey of Student Engagement, FSSE); students' experiences in law school (Law School Survey of Student Engagement, LSSE); and students' experiences in community colleges (Community College Survey of Student Engagement, CCSSE).

The NSSE surveys emphasize the campus experience (Kuh, 1993). Through his notion of college student engagement, Kuh (1993, 2009; Kuh, Kinzie, Schuh, & Whitt, 2011) claims that students are more likely to be retained in college if they "engage" academically and socially. The general tenor of the engagement scholarship is similar to Tinto and Astin, that students must somehow connect academically and socially in order to get the most out of college, and ultimately, to persist through their degree programs.

For student affairs units, the outcomes of the NSSE surveys have been monumental in making a case for the importance of these divisions in facilitating students' successful progression through college. Within institutions deemed effective at facilitating educational success for students, the collaboration between student affairs and academic affairs units has been highlighted as one of the most important factors (Kuh, Kinzie, Buckley, Bridges, & Hayek, 2007; Kuh, Kinzie, Schuh, Whitt, and associates, 2010). Student affairs units such as service learning offices, residence halls, or Greek life (fraternity and sorority membership) are often demonstrated to be key components in students' experiences while in college and in students' persistence within degree programs. For instance, service-learning experiences have been shown to encourage deeper connections to faculty and peers while also maintaining a link to communities outside of college campuses (Bringle & Hatcher, 2009). Living in the residence halls has been associated with higher levels of student engagement and openness to diversity (Pascarella & Terenzini, 2005). Greek life has been shown to positively connect with student engagement however; some of the risky behaviors that often are associated with participation in sororities and fraternities may at times reduce these positive outcomes (Hayek, Carini, O'Day, & Kuh, 2002).

Similar to Tinto, the NSSE surveys have been criticized as poorly representing, or even ignoring, underrepresented students' experiences, particularly students of color, low-income, and first-generation college students (Dowd, Sawatzky, & Korn, 2011; Olivas, 2011). The primary concern is that the notion of "student effort" relative to student engagement or involvement in college might omit intercultural effort. Also, students from underrepresented populations might experience a campus differently and therefore put their efforts into negotiating the campus in different ways than students from majority groups (Dowd et al., 2011). In other words, students might be putting in a significant amount of effort into "countering" categories relative to race on campus (Dowd et al., 2011, p. 27). For instance, an African American student attending college at a predominantly White university might spend significant energy and time navigating feelings of isolation, alienation, or differences between his or her background and the norms of campus (Winkle-Wagner, 2009b). If intercultural effort is not accounted for, students from underrepresented populations may be misrepresented as having a low "student effort," implying that they are less likely to succeed on campus, when in actuality, these students may be putting in their efforts differently. Additionally, there may be limitations regarding students from lower socioeconomic backgrounds. Some students who are from low-income backgrounds, for example, may not be able to engage on campus in the same way because of financial constraints. Students from low-income backgrounds may have to work a significant number of hours outside of their campus responsibilities. From a practical standpoint, resituating the idea of engagement to be more inclusive of the way that underrepresented students might have to negotiate campuses could inform programs. Perhaps programs could assist in students finding ways to not have to expend so much "intercultural effort" (or inter-class effort for that matter) while helping them to feel that their experiences are valid on these campuses.

Institutional or Structural Issues and Persistence

The institution in which a student is enrolled plays a big role in students' persistence in college. These institutional or structural issues can explore programmatic efforts (e.g., academic support programs), campus actors such as administrators, faculty, or staff in addition to institutional norms and environments. We considered such institutional factors to include issues such as:

1. The type of institution that a student attends, highlighting differences in missions between predominantly White institutions and historically Black colleges or universities in addition to four-year versus two-year institutions;
2. The campus climate or environment, inquiring into how students experience the campus environment related to race or gender;
3. Campus support programs including both academic and social programs that are targeted toward facilitating students' persistence in college; and
4. College affordability or financial aid contemplating how students' financial need and the available financial support may influence students' retention.

Institutional Types and Persistence.   The type of institution in which a student enrolls can have a large influence on students' ability to persist through their degree. This research contemplates the mission, size, or scope of postsecondary institutions relative to students' chances of completing their degree programs.

There is a growing population of students who begin (and some who end) their college careers within two-year institutions such as community colleges. This is particularly the case for some populations of students including the majority of Hispanic or Latina/o students (Fry, 2004; Snyder, Tan, & Hoffman, 2006). The concept of persistence in two-year institutions such as community colleges is complicated because many students are of non-traditional age, attend part-time, or they may have other plans for continuing their postsecondary education beyond the two-year institution (Marti, 2008). For example, many of the students who enter community colleges intend to transfer to a four-year institution to complete their degrees (Hoachlander, Sikora, & Horn, 2003; Marti, 2008; Rendón & Nora, 1997). Yet the likelihood of completing a two-year degree and transferring is very low, particularly for Hispanic or Latina/o students and other racially underrepresented students (Alexander, Garcia, Gonzalez, Grimes, & O'Brien, 2007; Bailey & Weininger, 2002). Students' persistence at community colleges is influenced by numerous factors such as English proficiency (Rendón & Hope, 1996), academic preparation in high school (Arbona & Nora, 2007; Castellanos & Jones, 2004), or financial background; students from low-income background are less likely to persist (Crisp & Nora, 2010; Nora, 1990). Students of color may have to overcome many barriers in order to complete a two-year degree and/or transfer to a four-year institution to complete a bachelor's degree. In a study examining educational outcomes at community colleges, Greene, Marti, and McClenney (2008) asserted that African American students demonstrated an effort-to-outcome gap in which they may have to expend more effort overcoming barriers to academic success.

For students of color attending predominantly White institutions (PWIs), the campus environment may have a serious bearing on their persistence. There is a long line of research indicating that students of color often have dramatically different experiences than White students at PWIs (Allen, 1992), experiencing alienation or isolation (Davis et al., 2004; Loo & Rolison, 1986; Nilsson, Paul, Lupini, & Tatem, 1999; Winkle-Wagner, 2009a). For example, in interviews of 11 students conducted by Davis et al. (2004), one student reported feeling like a "fly in the buttermilk" (p. 420). This alienation, taking both subtle and overt forms, can be manifested in many ways. For example, there may be a general sense that students of color are not integrated in the main life of the campus at PWIs (Branch Douglas, 1998). Beyond inclusiveness, many students who are in the minority on PWI campuses report experiences with racism or discrimination, as that reported by African American students in a daily diary mixed methods study (Swim, Hyers, Cohen, Fitzgerald, & Bylsma, 2003; Winkle-Wagner, 2009a). According to the findings of some studies, this alienation, racism, and discrimination have negative consequences for many students, potentially leading to academic disengagement (Cureton, 2003; Oyserman, Kemmelmeier, Fryberg, Brosh, & Hart-Johnson, 2003), marginal academic performance (Benson, 2000; Cureton, 2003), and a "dual identity" where students feel that they have to act differently in different contexts (Oyserman et al., 2003; Winkle-Wagner, 2009a).

On the contrary, research about minority-serving institutions such as historically Black colleges and universities (HBCUs) tells a slightly different story (see Chapter 5, this volume). According to multiple studies, African American students are more socially and academically integrated at HBCUs than at PWIs (Fries-Britt & Turner, 2002; Freeman & Cohen, 2001). Allen's (1992) path-breaking study, comparing questionnaires completed by African American students at HBCUs and PWIs, found that students attending HBCUs reported better psychological adjustment, higher academic gains, and greater cultural awareness than African American students at PWIs. Subsequent research corroborated these findings that HBCUs may promote general empowerment and uplift for African American students (Bridges, Kinzie, Nelson Laird, & Kuh, 2008; Freeman & Cohen, 2001; Hale, 2006; Palmer, Davis, & Maramba, 2010; Perna et al., 2009). These positive outcomes at HBCUs may have important implications for persistence.

The Campus Climate and Persistence. In addition to the type of institution in which a student is enrolled, the particular environment of each campus is crucial to students' experiences and ultimately, to persistence. Research underscores the need for institutions and those within them, to be more culturally responsive to the diverse needs of students from various groups. One way that this has been framed in the literature is through the study of the campus climate or the campus environment related to students' perceptions of the ways that race or gender are treated by peers, faculty, staff, or others on campus. The campus climate literature offers a national, multi-institutional perspective (through the Cooperative Institutional Research Project or CIRP data) on ways that campus environments influence students' experiences, finds that students' experiences in college can have a greater impact on adjustment and retention than their background (Hurtado, Carter, & Spuler, 1996). As discussed in Chapter 6, some of the scholarship illustrates the role of positive campus climates or campus cultures that are welcoming to students, fostering students' desire to persist through college (Braxton & Mundy, 2001; Hurtado & Carter, 1997; Hurtado et al., 1996; Hurtado, Carter, & Kardia, 1998; Hurtado, Milem, Clayton-Pederson, & Allen, 1998; Kuh, 2001). The campus racial or gender climate can conceivably create barriers for students in underrepresented populations. For instance, in a landmark study using the CIRP data, results indicated that the cognitive effects of a chilly climate for women lasted throughout the participants' degree programs, affecting students' cognitive outcomes (Whitt, Edison, Pascarella, Nora, & Terenzini, 1999). This is consistent with Jacobs' (1996) review of women's experiences in higher education finding that women encounter unequal treatment in college experiences. Generally, however, there are few campus climate studies that specifically examine gender.

Students of color report experiences with stereotyping and discrimination more often than their White peers (Ancis, Sedlacek, & Mohr, 2000). For example, students of color may have to negotiate stereotypes or negative perceptions of their academic ability during college (McGee & Martin, 2011). In a qualitative study of Black math and engineering students, many students were acutely aware that their racial identities were not valued on campus, leading the students to spend considerable time trying to manage stereotypes even though the students were academically successful (McGee & Martin, 2011). There is a growing body of evidence that stereotype threat (Steele & Aronson, 1995, 1998; Steele, Spencer, & Aronson, 2002), or the idea that students have to manage negative perceptions of their racial groups' abilities, can negatively impact academic performance (Oyserman, Brickman, & Rhodes, 2007; Taylor & Antony, 2000). These negative experiences do have an adverse consequence when it comes to student persistence in college. Discriminatory or hostile campus environments have been shown to have a detrimental effect on intellectual development, social experiences, and academic outcomes such as grades or retention in degree programs (Cabrera, Nora, Terenzini, Pascarella, & Hagedorn, 1999; Love, 1993; Prillerman, Myers, & Smedley, 1989; Smedley, Myers, & Harrell, 1993; Solórzano, Ceja, & Yosso, 2000).

Students cope with negative racial experiences or hostile racial climates in various ways. One way is to deal with negative perceptions of one's racial group through stereotype management (McGee & Martin, 2011). Other students might deal with negative experiences by changing their behaviors. Winkle-Wagner's (2009a) ethnographic research with Black undergraduate women in a predominantly White university found that the women often felt as if they had to alter their thinking, appearance, and behavior to be successful on campus.

Support Programs and Student Persistence. Also considering the role of institutional responsibility in facilitating students' persistence is research on campus programs and services that help support students during their time in college. This work presents ideas for support structures such as advising, counseling, or mentoring (Braxton & McClendon, 2001; Eby, Allen, Evans, Ng, & DuBois, 2008; Freeman, 1999; Hu & Ma, 2010; Shultz, Colton, & Colton, 2001; Torres & Hernandez, 2009; Turner & Berry, 2000). Tinto's more recent work (2012) is an attempt to synthesize decades of work on student persistence and has focused more on institutional action and accountability for retention efforts. Through practical case studies, providing exemplars of programs and policies that have fostered students' persistence, this new work provides insight into ways to take persistence theory and findings and apply them to real work with students. Tinto maintained that the following conditions can help to foster persistence: upholding high expectations for students and encouraging students to hold high expectations for themselves; academic, social, and financial support; assessment of performance and feedback on these assessments; and involvement on campus. These conditions could be particularly helpful in aiding practitioners in the development of programmatic efforts for students. For example, academic support programs could aim at encouraging high academic expectations while offering tutoring (academic support), social programming (social support), and scholarships (financial support).

There is a growing body of scholarship that examines the link between students' persistence in college and involvement in academic support programs. These programs may be particularly important for underrepresented students in some disciplines such as science, technology, engineering, or mathematics (STEM). Research shows that involvement in undergraduate research programs, for instance, may foster students' ability and desire to complete their degrees and enter careers in STEM fields (Kinkead, 2003; Lopatto, 2004). For example, in a qualitative study of science research programs for undergraduates in four institutions, students developed confidence in their scientific abilities and an identity as scientists during these programs and this ultimately was likely to foster their persistence through their degree programs in these fields (Hurtado, Cabrera, Lin, Arellano, & Espinosa, 2009). Other studies of discipline-based support programs that offer insight into the norms of particular academic disciplines (e.g., biology, mathematics, etc.) have aided in persistence of students (Barlow & Villarejo, 2004; Villarejo & Barlow, 2007). A case study of an intervention program aimed at helping the retention of students of color in the life sciences concluded that the program offered students the skills that they needed to be academically successful in science-related majors (Ovink & Veazey, 2011).

One reason for the success of discipline specific academic support programs might be that these programs foster closer connections and engagement with faculty. Students' positive mentoring connections to faculty have been evidenced as an important factor in persistence, specifically for students of color (Anaya & Cole, 2001; Cole, 2007; Cole & Espinoza, 2008; Hurtado & Carter, 1997; Schreiner, Noel, Anderson, & Cantwell, 2011). In a qualitative study with students at nine institutions who were labeled as high-risk for leaving college, faculty and staff were cited by students as very important to their ability to persist (Schreiner et al., 2011). But, the quality of the interaction between students and faculty or staff also matters. For example, African Americans in one large-scale study interacted more frequently with faculty, but these students were still dissatisfied with the quality of those interactions (Lundberg & Schreiner, 2004). Yet other research argues that low socioeconomic status (SES) African American students in particular often experience fewer interactions with faculty than do their White and high SES peers (Walpole, 2008). More research is needed about the ways that students' relationships with staff may differ from their relationships with faculty. Aside from a few outliers (Shreiner et al., 2011), the research on student-staff interactions is particularly sparse (Bensimon, 2007).

In addition to support in the form of advising or mentoring, some students may garner campus support from racially or ethnically based centers or programs on campus. For example, for American Indian students, there are links between students' involvement in American Indian student centers (culture centers) and the likelihood that such students will persist through their degree programs (Brown & Robinson Kurpius, 1997; Carney, 1999; Cibik & Chambers, 1991; Jenkins, 1999; Pavel & Padilla, 1993). A similar finding has been reported for the importance of culture centers for African American students (Patton, 2006).

Financial Aid and Persistence. Financial barriers may hinder students' persistence in college. Utilizing data from the Cooperative Institutional Research Project (CIRP), one study found that low SES students had less contact with faculty during college, studied less, worked more, were less involved in campus organizations, and had lower grades than their higher SES peers (Walpole, 2008). Financial assistance is crucial to attempt to mitigate the potentially negative consequences of coming from a lower income background. We discussed financial aid in greater detail in Chapter 2, but it is worth noting a few of the trends related to financial aid and persistence. While financial barriers are often considered a crucial consideration in fostering access to college, there are some studies that indicate that financial aid, both the type and the availability of it, may influence students' ability to persist through college (Baum, 2003; Chen & DesJardins, 2010; Hu & St. John, 2001; St. John, Cabrera, Nora, & Asker, 2000). For example, there is evidence that working part- or full time during college, particularly off campus, can impede students' ability to persist through degree programs (McSwain & Davis, 2007). Additionally, the *type* of financial aid matters. Financial assistance in the form of grants or scholarships that do not need to be paid back has been linked to a higher likelihood of retention in college than loans or forms of financial aid that must be paid back, often with interest (Alon, 2007; Bettinger, 2004; Hu & St. John, 2001). This is particularly important for some underrepresented student populations. For example, there are findings that show that African American, Latina/o, and low-income students may be particularly resistant to taking on student debt, potentially hindering persistence (Alon, 2007; Hu & St. John, 2001; Kim, 2007; St. John et al., 2000). For example, in a study using national longitudinal datasets (the Beginning Postsecondary Students, BPS, and the National Postsecondary Student Aid Study, NPSAS), the results revealed that students of color who receive Pell grants have a lower risk of leaving college (Chen & DesJardins, 2010). Other research concurred with this finding. A study of need-based financial aid (that is aimed at the most financially needy students) found that state need-based funding was positively associated with students' chances of persistence in college (Chen & St. John, 2011).

SUMMARY: DIVERSITY AND COLLEGE STUDENT PERSISTENCE

The culmination of a student's degree program, persistence, represents the accumulation of many moments where diversity-and-inclusion could be enacted. On the contrary, when students do not persist through their degree programs, particularly when those students are from historically underrepresented groups, this can be indicative of missed opportunities and missteps in the full inclusion of those students on college campuses. Given that there are continued racial and socioeconomic disparities in persistence, we argue that much work remains to be done in this area.

Think about Diversity

The foundational theories of college student persistence do not actively consider the unique experiences of underrepresented student populations. On the contrary, the foundational theories primarily focused on majority students (White, male, heterosexual, Christian) on college campuses. While the lack of consideration toward students of color and other underrepresented students has been heavily criticized, there have been relatively few theoretical updates and revisions to these foundational theories. Those theoretical ideas that *have* centrally contemplated the role of underrepresentation in college student persistence (e.g., Perna & Thomas, 2008) have not been canonized, or as widely applied, in the same way as the foundational theories. Additionally, the tendency toward generalization about persistence has affected the way that the persistence needs of students of color in particular are considered (or not considered) in models and theories aimed at aiding in the retention of students. Additionally, among non-traditionally aged students, involvement and integration could vary dramatically. For students from low-income backgrounds, involvement might appear different because of a need to work full- or part-time to be able to pay for tuition. Finally, for students who are nonheterosexual, there is very little theoretical work about persistence.

Future theoretical work should contemplate persistence for underrepresented students in a way that can then be applied to empirical research, practice, and policy. Or, perhaps there are different theoretical models for student persistence and success that could be more easily applied to students of color and other underrepresented groups of students. Contemplating multiple models for and approaches to student success and persistence, Perna and Thomas (2008) considered a model that might be more adaptable to underrepresented students in their monograph. For example, Conrad and Dunek (2012) assert that student success should be reframed toward inquiry (asking burning questions, engaging in critical dialogue, etc.), encouraging students to develop ways of thinking and approaching ideas so that they can engage academically and in the public sphere. This is a step in a new direction and it would be useful to pursue practical implications of this for practitioners too. For instance, student affairs practice might shift if inquiry (framing important questions and then working toward answers to those questions) was at the center of the practice. What if programming fostered students' development of questions or inquiry? What if involvement on campus was geared toward helping students to engage in inquiry? These ideas could help to connect student affairs and academic affairs in more meaningful ways.

Diversity Still Matters

Diversity is a huge part of the persistence equation. There continue to be racial disparities in persistence rates. The empirical research on college student retention often analyzes large, national datasets through the National Center for Education Statistics (Tinto, 1993). While some of the more recent work has taken a qualitative approach, particularly related to the retention of students of color, more work that uncovers students' subjective experiences of persisting through college is needed. In particular, research into the strategies that underrepresented students have self-identified as helping them to persist through degree programs would help to reveal whether the traditional approaches to retention need to be altered. Much more work is needed on the unique persistence issues for women, lesbian, gay, bisexual, transgender, or queer students, religious minority students, and low-income students. All of these groups may vary in the ways that they find to be successful in persisting through degree programs. Future research should work toward more understanding of these groups.

Diversity Is Everywhere

Intersectional approaches that take into account students' multiple race, class, gender, or sexual orientation identities have been rarely used in the study of college student retention. In part because of the data and modeling used in quantitative studies, the findings often point to particular categories of inequality. For instance, the point that there are racial or socioeconomic disparities in student persistence is important but it still parses out students' experiences into discrete categories when their experiences are likely connected to race and class simultaneously. To think in more intersecting ways about disparities in persistence might reveal different solutions for how to help students be successful in college. For example, how might students' race and class categories combine to increase or decrease their likelihood of remaining in college? There is evidence, for instance, that African American *women* are more likely to persist through college than African American *men* (NCES, 2006). In this case, it is not just race, but the combination of race and gender that appears to lead to differential retention outcomes. Considerations of students' multiple identities and categories (race, class, gender, sexual orientation, religion, etc.) might lead to a more meaningful approach toward meeting students' multifaceted needs.

DISCUSSION QUESTIONS

Based on the research and theory presented in this chapter, we provide some questions aimed at improving practice and contributing toward advancements in research.

Improving Practice

1. Given the information in this chapter, are there challenges to good practices in college student persistence for underrepresented students? What role might practitioners play in helping to remedy these challenges?
2. If time and money were not issues, what kind of program might you create to help retention efforts for underrepresented students?
3. Given that there is research suggesting that students of color might engage differently than White students, how might you help to foster engagement in college for students of color?
4. If families are crucial to persistence for many underrepresented students, how might you work as a student affairs administrator to better connect with students' families during college?
5. What is the role of student affairs practitioners in helping to create a positive campus climate that facilitates persistence for all students? What are some practical ways this can be achieved?
6. How could student affairs practitioners help students in the area of financial barriers?
7. What ideas do you have for connecting student affairs and academic affairs around efforts to help students persist through their degree programs?
8. One of the major student affairs associations, Student Affairs Administrators in Higher Education (NASPA), developed a set of professional competencies that are encouraged for all student affairs professionals. How might the NASPA professional competencies affect how student affairs practitioners work to foster student persistence?
   a. The NASPA Competencies are (see http://www.naspa.org/programs/profdev/default.cfm): advising and helping; assessment, evaluation, and research; equity, diversity, and inclusion; ethical professional practice; history, philosophy, and value; human organizational resources; law, policy, and governance; leadership; personal foundations; students learning and development.
9. Another national association for student affairs, College Student Educators International (CAS) developed a Statement of Ethical Principles and Standards. How

might the ACPA Ethical Principles and Standards relate to the issues on student persistence that were presented in this chapter?

a. The ACPA Standards are (see http://www2.myacpa.org/statement-of-ethical-principles-and-standards): professional responsibility and competence; student learning and development; responsibility to the institution; and responsibility to society.

10. The Council for the Advancement of Standards in Higher Education (CAS) developed a set of standards for student affairs. How might these CAS Standards be applied to college student persistence challenges?

a. The domains for the CAS Standards are (see http://www.cas.edu/index.php/cas-general-standards/): knowledge acquisition, integration, construction, and application; cognitive complexity; intrapersonal development; interpersonal competence; humanitarianism and civic engagement; practical competence.

Developing Future Research

1. What research is lacking in the area of college student persistence as it relates to underrepresented students?
2. If time and money were not issues, what kind of research project might you develop to study this issue?
3. Much of the research in college student persistence uses the foundational theories. What ideas do you have for moving the scholarship forward?
4. There is some scholarship finding that students of color might engage in different ways than White students in college. How might you develop a research project that takes this into account?
5. What kinds of quantitative projects need to be done in this area?
6. What kinds of qualitative projects should be done on this topic?
7. How might you construct a mixed method, historical, or other methodological approach to studying this topic?

==========================A CASE STUDY==========================

PRACTICING DIVERSITY ISSUES RELATED TO PERSISTENCE

A Will to Succeed

AUNDRIA GREEN, UNIVERSITY OF NEBRASKA - LINCOLN

Green University (GU) is a large, public university in the southwestern region of the United States. GU is a beautiful campus that is located in the heart of a small college town with a population of 12,000 people. Palm trees and green grass surround the university; it is easy to forget that GU is in the desert. The Fighting Iguanas reign supreme in the arid lands.

Roughly 30,000 students attend Green University. The population consists of 60% commuter students and 40% of the students reside on campus. Since its inception in 1900, GU has been a predominantly White institution. However, in the last 15 to 20 years, the Latina/o population at GU has increased to 35%, the Native American population has increased to 10%, the African American population is currently 3%, and the last 2% is comprised of Asian/Pacific Islander and Multiracial students.

Jasara McMercer is a fun, energetic student affairs professional. She coordinates a First-Year Experience Program at Green University. The program offers free tutoring; each student is assigned a peer mentor, and has a one-on-one meeting with Jasara. The students in the program also attend a weekly seminar on a variety of topics ranging from how to work out roommate problems to how to pay for college. The goal of the program is to help the students get acclimated to college life. This is Jasara's fifth year coordinating the program. In preparation for the school year, she sends each student in the program an email introducing herself and giving them the schedule for the fall semester.

A month into the school year she gets a call from Emilia González, one of her new students, who asks to come meet with her. They schedule a meeting for early the next week. Tuesday morning comes and Jasara hears a knock on her door. Emilia comes in. She is a caramel colored young woman with long black hair. She stands about five feet one inch tall. She has a huge smile and pleasant demeanor. Jasara stands, and they shake hands. As the meeting begins, Emilia tells her story. She originally came to Green in 1992 when she graduated from high school. She had a blast in college but she was not focused. She ended up getting all Ds and Fs and did not return after that first semester.

She tells Jasara that she recently learned that the school policy is that a student will have the same grades/academic status they had when they last attended. This is alarming to her because it means she will begin her new college career on academic probation. Emilia admits that she feels stressed out by this especially as she anticipates that school might be difficult due to being away from it for so long. She is determined to do well in school and believes that she can even with this minor setback.

Emilia tells Jasara that she works a split shift at Gallup (a public opinion polling center) off-campus to be able to afford to be a full-time student. She works from 7 a.m. to 9 a.m. then goes to class. She returns to work from 12 noon to 6 p.m. a few days a week and on the weekend in order to complete 40 hours each week. Emilia states that the real reason she requested the meeting is because she has two assignments that she does not know how she will complete. In her English class, she has a group project in which her group needs to physically get together in order to conduct an activity and answer questions. This is problematic for Emilia because of her work schedule and because she has a 9-year-old son, Jeremiah, at home. Almost in tears, she confesses that she cannot possibly spend any more time away from him than she already does.

She tells Jasara that her group members are very friendly. She told them about her work schedule, and they have been trying to accommodate her. One group member, a man named Seth, suggested that they meet on Sunday evening so that Emilia can come to the session. He has been saving her a seat if she comes to class a little late and collecting the handouts if she misses them. She says that she finds him attractive but that is all. She does not want to get too involved with her classmates because she is so much older than they are. She hesitates to tell them that she has a 9-year-old son for the same reason.

Emilia continues to explain that she is one of the only people of color in most of her courses. She says that it does not bother her too much, but she does notice it. Emilia shares an example of a time where her English class was discussing Latina/o authors. The professor was well versed about the book being discussed but wanted Emilia to share her experience because he "wasn't a Mexican." This upset her and she told her professor that she was not Mexican but Peruvian. She still feels offended that the professor assumed her nationality and requested that she speak on behalf of all Latinas/os.

The second assignment is for this same English course. She has been tasked with identifying a piece of literature to recite in class that relates to her personal experience. The assignment indicates that the each student will be given 7 minutes to perform their piece and then explain why it is important to them. Emilia is deathly afraid of public speaking. She tells Jasara when she gave a speech for a high school class she was so nervous that she began to stutter and sweat profusely. The teacher allowed her an opportunity to get a drink of water to collect herself. However, when she started her speech again, the nervousness overcame her and she passed out. She was so embarrassed that she vowed to never participate in any activity that involved public speaking. She states that she is so frazzled about the two assignments that she does not even know where to start.

Please answer the questions below as if you were Jasara and your goal was to try to help Emilia as much as possible:

1. Identify a minimum of five on-campus services to assist Emilia with her challenges in college.
2. Discuss your position on academic return policies (the necessary steps a student needs to take in order to return to an college or university when they are on academic probation). Consider the current practices in place your institution.
   a. Would these policies help a student like Emilia?
   b. What issues might need to be specifically considered for students like Emilia?
3. Describe steps that can be taken to eliminate some of Emilia's anxiety about college.
4. Discuss the role that race plays in the case. Explain alternative techniques to address Emilia's concerns.
5. Discuss the role of socioeconomic status in Emilia's issues. What are some ways that you might be able to offer help if you were in an administrative position.
6. Create a plan(s) for a non-traditional student like Emilia. Think about the services offered at your institution. How will you proceed to support her?

9

ACCESS TO GRADUATE AND PROFESSIONAL PROGRAMS
Climbing Up the Tower

We have learned to say that the good must be extended to all of society before it can be held secure by any one person or any one class. But we have not yet learned to add to that statement, that unless all [people] and all classes contribute to a good, we cannot even be sure that it is worth having.

—Jane Addams, Women's Suffrage Leader, Author, Activist

After a student successfully persists through a degree program in college, attention turns toward the student's next steps. While many students have traditionally aspired to seek gainful employment directly after college, a growing number of them make the decision to attend graduate school. Scholars have hypothesized a few reasons for this. Perhaps one of the most compelling reasons to attend graduate school is that advanced-degrees are now expected for an increasing number of positions that used to only require a bachelor's degree (Eide, Brewer, & Ehrenberg, 1998). Graduate degrees offer a way for many to advance professionally in their field (Anderson & Swazey, 1998; Cottrell & Hayden, 2007; King & Chepyator-Thomson, 1996; Padula & Miller, 1999; Poock, 2000; Schwartz, Bower, Rice, & Washington, 2003). Additionally, an advanced-degree often comes with the potential for earning more money (Anderson & Swazey, 1998; James & Alsalam, 1993). We explore access to graduate and professional programs as a way to think about the larger picture of diversity-and-inclusion. As historically underrepresented students make their way through college and into advanced-degree programs, this represents an opportunity to deeply enact the inclusion of diversity into higher education; those earning advanced-degrees could become the next leaders, faculty members, and policymakers influencing college campuses.

Likely due in part to the increase in students who decide to attend graduate programs, there has been growing attention toward students' experiences in graduate programs in the past 20 years (e.g., Bowen & Rudenstine, 1992). An examination of who attends and completes advanced-degree programs reveals a persistent racial disparity in graduate degree earning (Almanac of Higher Education, 2012; Thomas, 1992). For example, in 2009–2010, White people held more than 74% of the doctoral degrees while Black people held only 6% of the doctorates in the United States (Almanac of Higher Education, 2012).[1]

Research about advanced-degree programs has reported the ways in which students are socialized into graduate programs (Antony, 2002; Austin, 2002; Austin & McDaniels, 2006; Ellis, 2001) or differences between academic disciplinary foci and norms (Gardner, 2007; Golde, 2005; Walker, Golde, Jones, Bueschel, & Hutchings, 2009). Other research centers on the process of finishing an advanced-degree such as issues related to dissertation writing or students' experiences with their academic advisors (Boote & Beile, 2005; Nettles & Millet, 2006), or students' persistence through their graduate programs (Bowen & Rudenstine, 1992; Golde, 2005; Lovitts, 2001). However, aside from a few examples (Griffin & Muniz, 2011), much of this work does not refer to the experiences of underrepresented students such as students of color in advanced-degree programs (Howard-Hamilton, Morelon-Quainoo, Johnson, Winkle-Wagner, & Santiague, 2009).

We turn our attention in this chapter toward diversity issues in graduate and professional programs. We use the terms graduate school, graduate and professional education, and advanced-degree programs synonymously in this chapter to refer to those degree programs that students may enter after they complete a bachelor's degree. This discussion of graduate education can contribute to the conversation about the educational and life trajectory of underrepresented students more generally. For those students who successfully complete bachelor's degrees, graduate education may be the next step in attaining greater career opportunities or occupational attainment.

THINKING ABOUT DIVERSITY: THEORETICAL APPROACHES TO GRADUATE SCHOOL ACCESS

There are two major theories that have been applied to students' experiences in gaining access to and finding success in graduate programs:

1. Socialization models aimed at describing the process of students' adjustment to being graduate students and eventually, professionals in their fields; and
2. A model of doctoral student persistence focused on the decisions students make to persist through their programs.

Socialization Models of Graduate Education

Much thinking related to graduate education has been about the way students are socialized as scholars and professionals into the norms of their programs, departments, institutions, or academic disciplines. Weidman's (1989) model of undergraduate socialization, for example, has been used to contemplate graduate students' socialization into their programs. The undergraduate socialization model allowed for consideration of students' interpersonal (interactions with others), intrapersonal (students' ideas about themselves), and integration (how connected students felt to an institution) experiences. Weidman collaborated with colleagues to adapt his socialization model for the graduate level through a peer reviewed paper presentation (Stein & Weidman, 1989). This was primarily a structural-functional approach (assuming that all roles in society serve to help society function) where socialization was connected with students' adaptation as professionals in their fields. The socialization at the graduate level, according to Stein and Weidman (1989), was particularly centered on knowledge acquisition where a student develops knowledge and skills in his or her discipline.

This socialization model emphasized the following aspects of a student's adaptation to being a graduate student (Weidman, Twale, & Stein, 2001, p. 36): (a) A student enters a graduate program with values about oneself and anticipated career; (b) A student is exposed to socializing influences including normative practices as expressed by faculty, peers, and professional associations; (c) A student assesses the salience of the various normative influences for his or her goals; and (d) A student assumes, changes, or maintains those values, aspirations, identity, and personal commitment that were held at the outset of the program. Weidman and his colleagues advanced four stages of socialization: anticipatory, formal, informal, and personal. The anticipatory stage refers to a student's socialization before she or he becomes an academic or a scholar. Formal socialization occurs through interactions with faculty and institutional agents, and also those in a student's academic discipline (e.g., peers and colleagues in the field). Informal socialization can occur through faculty or peers in a student's program. Personal socialization refers to a student's sense of his/her beliefs and knowledge coming into the program and the way that this changes (or does not change) during the program. For instance, a student might begin to see herself or himself as a scholar during graduate school. Weidman and his colleagues (2001) provided three major components of socialization processes: knowledge acquisition, investment, and involvement. This is the time when a graduate student begins to feel like she or he is part of the academic discipline and has become a member of that discipline (e.g., I am a scholar in education). The student may begin to think, write, or ask questions that connect with that academic discipline or subfield.

The model presented by Weidman et al. (2001) initiated a line of work that explored doctoral student socialization more generally (Boden, Borrego, & Newswander, 2011; Gardner, 2010; O'Meara, 2008). Subsequently, much of the scholarship on graduate students has studied socialization as a crucial element of students' success in advanced-degree programs (Antony, 2002; Austin, 2002; Ellis, 2001; Gardner, 2007, 2009a).

While the socialization model has been particularly influential in the study of students' adaptation to and success in graduate and professional programs, some areas remain for future theorizing. Little attention has been paid to the way that students' experiences in graduate degree programs might influence their identities more generally (but see Neumann, 2006, 2009). For instance, students' various identities (race, class, gender, identity as scholars, or combinations of these) might shift as they begin to see themselves as scholars (for many doctoral students) or professionals (for professional degree-seeking students such as those in law or medical school) in their field of study.

Although socialization is a crucial part of students' adjustment to graduate degree programs, it is also important to contemplate the general persistence and success of students in these programs. The model of doctoral student persistence that we present next offers a theory as to how students might successfully complete their degree programs. This model also points to the importance of socialization, but, the key difference is that the focus is on the outcome of persistence.

A Model of Doctoral Student Persistence

At the end of Tinto's (1993) book that introduces his theory for college student persistence (see Chapter 8 for a more detailed description), there is an appendix that extends this persistence model into doctoral education. Similar to the undergraduate academic-social integration model, Tinto's discussion of doctoral student persistence centers on an argument that students must be socialized into their programs and disciplines, integrating academically and socially, in order to successfully persist through their programs. Tinto (1993) asserted that while he was extending his theory to graduate education, it is important to note that the referent groups for doctoral students differ from undergraduates. In particular, at the graduate level, students may be much more influenced by their disciplinary faculty and peers (p. 232). Additionally, persistence at the graduate level is much more localized and dependent on the cultural norms of the particular school or department in which a student is situated. That is, the academic and social integration required in this model of persistence is integration into the field of study (i.e., academic discipline) or the department, not necessarily the larger university (as is the case for the undergraduate model). Tinto corroborated earlier findings (e.g., Thomas, Clewell, & Pearson, 1988) that interactions between faculty and students are paramount in fostering persistence through doctoral programs.

Describing the process of earning a doctoral degree that occurs in a number of departments in many institutions nationally, Tinto (1993) presents the three stages of doctoral student persistence: the transition into doctoral study, the candidacy stage, and the dissertation stage. The transition stage typically covers the first year of study in a doctoral program. In this stage, a student makes a series of judgments about how much he or she desires to be a member of the department and academic discipline. This is the stage in which the academic and social integration into the discipline must occur. After the student transitions into doctoral study, she or he progresses through coursework and then moves into the candidacy stage. At the candidacy stage, a student acquires the knowledge and skills necessary to complete doctoral level research. In Tinto's model, academic and social integration leads directly to this candidacy stage and are set up as a prerequisite for entering the stage. In other words, a student must be academically and socially integrated into doctoral study, and into his/her discipline, to move toward the candidacy stage. This stage culminates in the doctoral comprehensive examination process. Academic and social integration become blurred at this stage in a way that they do not at the undergraduate level (see Chapter 8 for a deeper discussion on integration at the undergraduate level). For instance, students' academic and social activities may connect (e.g., reading groups, study groups, social activities where students discuss research, etc.). Finally, a student enters the dissertation stage encompassing the time from early candidacy through the doctoral dissertation proposal, up until the student defends her/his dissertation. This stage reflects the nature of a student's abilities, according to Tinto, meaning that this final stage is connected to how well prepared and tenacious a student is in terms of finishing the program. Persistence may be idiosyncratic because it is often partially connected to the relationship between a student's advisor and the student.

Tinto's (1993) model of doctoral student persistence is one of the underlying theories framing much of the scholarship on doctoral student persistence (e.g., Gardner, 2009b; Gardner & Barnes, 2007; Golde, 2005). For example, in a national study of doctoral education, Golde (2005) maintained that the department was the primary locale of control for doctoral students, similar to Tinto's point that doctoral persistence is more localized. Studies of student-faculty interaction argue for the importance of this relationship that Tinto initially asserted (e.g., Herzig, 2006; Milner, Husband, & Jackson, 2002; Patton & Harper, 2003; Sallee, 2011; Winkle-Wagner, Johnson, Morelon-Quainoo, & Santiague,

2010). Much of the research on graduate students' social integration and involvement is also often rooted in, extending, or critiquing Tinto's model too (Gardner, 2008, 2009b; Gardner & Barnes, 2007; Golde, 2000).

Tinto's (1993) theory of doctoral persistence itself has not been expanded or revised all that much since its inception as an appendix to a book about undergraduate student persistence. Additionally, as reviewed in Chapter 8, Tinto's theory of undergraduate persistence has been criticized as being less relevant for students of color and other underrepresented students (Guiffrida, 2004, 2005; Hausmann, Ye, Schofield, & Wood, 2009; Lee & Donlan, 2011; Tierney, 1992, 1999, 2000). The same critique could be made of the doctoral student persistence model because it was an extension of the initial work for undergraduate persistence on Tinto's part and therefore did not give much attention towards students from underrepresented groups.

DIVERSITY STILL MATTERS: EMPIRICAL APPROACHES TO GRADUATE SCHOOL ACCESS

After reviewing the literature on the graduate educational pipeline, we categorized the scholarship into two areas:

1. Access to advanced-degree programs: this research focuses on the process of learning about, deciding to attend, and then gaining access to advanced-degree programs; and
2. Socialization within advanced-degree programs, which generally considers the period of time after a student enrolls in graduate or professional degree programs and then learns the norms for that particular discipline.

Access to Advanced-Degree Programs

There is relatively little empirical research on access to graduate education, particularly for students from underrepresented groups (Howard-Hamilton et al., 2009). The scholarship that does link to gaining access to graduate programs identifies the following issues:

1. The way that undergraduate experiences influence the likelihood of graduate school enrollment; and
2. How socialization into graduate education and academic disciplines influences students' ability to gain access to advanced-degree programs.

UNDERGRADUATE PREPARATION AND THE DECISION TO ATTEND GRADUATE EDUCATION

Preparation for graduate education is dependent on students' experiences at the undergraduate level. There are a few factors that predict whether a college student will attend graduate school, such as attending a four-year postsecondary institution rather than a two-year institution (Eide et al., 1998; Mullen, Goyette, & Soares, 2003; Walpole, 2003). Additionally, a student is more likely to earn an advanced-degree if she or he attended a more selective institution (Mullen et al., 2003; Schapiro, O'Malley, & Litten, 1999; Walpole, 2003). African American students are more likely to attend graduate school if they attended a historically Black college or university (HBCU) over a predominantly White institution (PWI) for their undergraduate degree (Barnes, 2010; Gasman et al., 2011; Tudico & Schmid, 2007). HBCUs offer unmatched preparation for advanced-degree programs (Barnes, 2010), and eventually, for students to enter the professoriate (Perna, 2001; Perna et al., 2009). Part of the preparation process at HBCUs might be connected to the support structures facilitated within those institutions (Thompson, 2009). Students have reported receiving more support from faculty and staff at HBCUs than they report receiving in PWIs (Palmer & Gasman, 2008). In a case study of Black women's undergraduate experiences in science, technology, engineering, and mathematics at Spelman College, students reported that the HBCU environment offered a supportive environment in which to pursue a STEM degree, opportunities for undergraduate research, and ultimately supported high academic achievement and preparation for graduate programs for the women (Perna et al., 2009).

Beyond institutional type, student involvement in organizations at the undergraduate level has been linked to graduate school enrollment (Patton & Bonner, 2001; Schuh, Triponey, Heim, & Nishimura, 1992; Harper, Byars, & Jelke, 2005). The type of involvement may be important to consider. For example, in a study of undergraduate women's plans to attend graduate school in the STEM disciplines, findings suggested that involvement in a STEM living-learning community was positively related to women's aspirations to earn advanced-degrees in STEM fields. In addition to involvement, students with higher grade point averages have been demonstrated to be more likely to earn graduate degrees (Zhang, 2005). Finally, scholars have linked graduate school preparation to programs aimed deliberately at graduate school preparation (Ishiyama & Hopkins, 2003) such as involvement in undergraduate research projects (Barlow & Villarejo, 2004; Hathaway, Nagda, & Gregerman, 2002; Huss, Randall, Davis, & Hansen, 2002; Jones, Barlow, & Villarejo, 2010; Lammers, 2001; Ridgewell & Creamer, 2003). Hathaway, Nagda and Gregerman (2002) found that an undergraduate research experience, whether through a formal, structured program or through less formal opportunities, leads to enrollment in graduate education. Not only is undergraduate research linked to enrollment in graduate school, these opportunities may influence students' success in undergraduate education too. In an analysis of the association between participation in undergraduate research and college success in biology (using transcripts and admissions data), Jones, Barlow, and Villarejo (2010) found that undergraduate research participation was significantly associated with persisting through an undergraduate degree, particularly for students of color. It may be that undergraduate research serves as an early opportunity for students to learn about the research process and become excited about continuing their involvement in it, therefore they finish their degrees and look toward pursuing a graduate degree. Further, undergraduate research affords students the opportunity to become socialized to the research process and the academic enterprise.

Faculty and staff have been shown to influence students' likelihood of attending graduate programs. Those students who interact more with faculty are more likely to attend graduate programs (Hathaway et al., 2002; Lammers, 2001; Peppas, 1981). Additionally, there is some evidence that when undergraduate students are exposed to graduate school, they may be more likely to contemplate earning an advanced-degree (Uloa & Herrera, 2006), although more empirical work is needed. Once students enter graduate programs, they may be more successful if they have positive experiences with faculty (Griffin, Pèrez, Holmes, & Mayo, 2010).

Alternatively, if students have negative experiences with advising, they may be less likely to earn a graduate degree. Some research shows that African American students have more experiences with discrimination in college and that these negative experiences have been shown to deter them from attending graduate school (Harper & Davis, 2012; McCallum, in press; Williams, Brewley, Reed, White, Davis-Haley, 2005). For instance, one study examined students in science and engineering and found that some students of color with high GPAs who may have been good candidates for graduate school did not enroll because their undergraduate advisors did not tell them about graduate programs as much as they did White students (Brazziel & Brazziel, 2001). Coordinators of graduate programs are also crucial players in facilitating access to graduate programs. According to some evidence, students of color have been considered unqualified by graduate coordinators, and then they are discouraged from applying to advanced-degrees programs through a lack of engagement by the graduate coordinator (e.g., not answering calls, unfriendly treatment during the application process, etc.). For instance, there is evidence that some coordinators of graduate programs who deem students to be unqualified based on non-academic criteria (e.g., race) often discourage students from engaging in the application process (Anchor & Morales, 1990; Johnson-Bailey, 2004). Johnson-Bailey's (2004) qualitative study of Black women documents incidents of graduate coordinators denying students applications and refusing to return phone calls based on their beliefs that the student was unqualified or somehow not graduate school material (see Fries-Britt & Griffin, 2007, for a study on resisting stereotypes about Black women).

Students have identified a few of their own reasons for choosing to pursue graduate education such as a desire to advance in their current jobs (Cottrell & Hayden, 2007; King & Chepyator-Thomson, 1996; Padula & Miller, 1999; Poock, 2000; Schwartz et al., 2003). Other students report a desire to learn to conduct research so as to advance in their careers more generally (Belcastro & Koeske, 1996; Cottrell & Hayden, 2007; Padula & Miller, 1999; Patchner, 1982; Stoecker, 1991), or a hope to make more money (Anderson & Swazey, 1999; Eide et al., 1998; James & Alsalam, 1993). However, there is evidence that some underrepresented groups may have a slightly different rationale for earning an advanced-degree. Studies including African American students uncover that many of these students choose to earn a graduate-level degree as a way to uplift their racial group or communities (Howard-Hamilton et al., 2009; Robinson, 2012; Williams et al., 2005). Research into this motivating factor for earning an advanced-degree might be particularly helpful in determining ways to help students link their advanced-degrees to their backgrounds.

Socialization within Graduate Programs

After a student is admitted to a graduate program, he or she begins the "entering phase" and begins to adjust and become socialized to what it means to be a graduate student (Brailsford, 2010; Gardner, 2009) and, eventually, to what it means to be a professional (Renn & Jessup-Anger, 2008). Most of the work on the pipeline to graduate programs explores students' socialization into a particular academic discipline, program, or into graduate education more generally (Gardner, 2007). Socialization has been defined by Austin (2002, p. 96) as a multi-step process whereby a student becomes a part of a particular "group, organization, or community." The first step in the process of being socialized into academia is usually referred to as anticipatory socialization, beginning at the time of admissions to an advanced-degree program when a student begins to understand the culture, norms, and expectations of graduate school or of their academic programs more generally (Austin, 2002; Gardner, 2009; McCoy, 2007).

Relationships with faculty and peers are crucial to the socialization process, particularly for students of color (Herzig, 2006). Socialization for students occurs through interacting with and modeling faculty, particularly their advisors (Gardner, 2007; Sallee, 2011). Faculty advisors or mentors are particularly important to the success of students of color in graduate programs, especially for African American students (Herzig, 2006; Milner, Husband, & Jackson, 2002; Patton & Harper, 2003; Winkle-Wagner et al., 2010).

Within predominantly White environments, faculty mentoring may be vital to reframing negative institutional messages related to race and gender, as one reflection asserted (Hinton, Grim, & Howard-Hamilton, 2009). While it is not always possible for students of color to find a faculty mentor of color, it is necessary that faculty mentoring be culturally sensitive, meaning that it must deliberately attempt to offer a counter-space or alternative to negative images or perspectives of racially underrepresented students (Hinton et al., 2009; Milner et al., 2002). According to Barnes' (2010) study of Black women in graduate programs, faculty mentors should hold high expectations as one of the most important factors influencing doctoral student persistence. Brown, Davis, and McClendon (1999) argue that faculty mentoring of students of color must be institutionalized so that the mentoring and support of underrepresented students transcends a single relationship and becomes a programmatic or institutional goal. One such example is the Peabody Mentoring Program where the focus is on mentoring underrepresented students through their doctoral programs and into faculty careers (Brown et al., 1999). In the HBCU context, research finds that faculty members are particularly supportive of Black students, making the environment more welcoming (Hirt, Strayhorn, Amelink, & Bennett, 2006). There may be useful lessons from some of these departments within HBCUs that predominantly White institutions could use to better serve students of color.

While socialization has been connected to interactions with faculty and staff, there is some evidence that students of color may not have access to the same level of socialization as their White peers. Students of color, particularly African American students, often receive less support in the form of opportunities to engage with faculty, and graduate assistantships which offer money alongside formal socialization into teaching and research (Howard-Hamilton et al., 2009; McCoy, 2007; Nettles, 1990; Noy & Ray, 2012). If faculty mentoring is such a crucial part of success in graduate school for students of color, more attention is needed to explore whether underrepresented students have the same access to both informal (e.g., going for coffee, informal conversations) or formal (e.g., assistantships, working on research together) faculty interactions.

In addition to faculty, peers provide another set of relationships that facilitate graduate student socialization. Peers who are more advanced in their particular degree program have been evidenced to be important in the socialization process (Austin, 2002). These peer relationships should be fostered early in a graduate program so that peers can help a student adjust to campus and to graduate school more generally (Gardner, 2008). Mentoring, networking, or collaborative peer relationships have been demonstrated as vital aspects of the socialization process, and also the general success of students of color and African American graduate students specifically (Milner et al., 2002; Milner, 2004; Winkle-Wagner et al., 2010). Peer relationships, and socialization more generally, can be facilitated through students' involvement in activities such as graduate student councils, departmental councils or organizations, or professional associations (Barnes, 2009). In Gardner and Barnes' (2007) study about involvement in graduate programs (half of the participants were African American), becoming involved fostered peer networking that later could influence students' general success in graduate programs.

Faculty and peers are not the only socializing agents for graduate students. Families can also play an important role in helping to support students. For example, in a study of Black women in doctoral programs, Sulè (2009) found that the women's mothers were crucial in supporting the women's educational pursuits. Patton's (2009) qualitative study of African American women's experiences with mentoring in graduate and professional programs presented evidence of an even broader support network of women; mothers, grandmothers, aunts, sisters, and friends were all crucial to the success of these women in their advanced-degree programs.

In addition to relationships with peers, faculty, and families, students must have financial support to be successful in graduate education. High amounts of loan debt from undergraduate education can be a detriment to graduate school enrollment, according to some inquiry (Nettles & Millett, 2006). Financial support, typically in the form of fellowships or assistantships (McWade, 1995) has been shown to be a crucial factor in creating access to graduate school, particularly for students of color, first-generation, and low-income students (Ethington & Smart, 1986; Winkle-Wagner et al., 2010). Assistantships and fellowships also relate to the completion of graduate programs, likely because of the faculty mentoring and socialization that often occurs during these experiences (Cardon & Rogers, 2002; Ethington & Smart, 1986; Gardner, 2009; Kallio, 1995; Winkle-Wagner et al., 2010). Johnson, Kuykendall, and Winkle-Wagner's (2009) qualitative analysis of racially underrepresented doctoral students reported that research and teaching assistantships were the primary factors that students named as crucial to their access to and eventual success in graduate school.

As students become socialized into their roles as graduate or professional students, they may begin to see themselves differently. Part of this socialization process is about beginning to see oneself as a scholar or professional in a chosen field. Neumann's (2006, 2009) qualitative work with recently tenured faculty uncovers that a critical component of being in the professoriate is identification of a substantive area about which one is passionate and development of a scholarly identity. More inquiry is needed to understand the full transition and scholarly trajectory for underrepresented students in particular.

SUMMARY: DIVERSITY AND ACCESS TO ADVANCED-DEGREE PROGRAMS

In climbing the proverbial tower to advanced-degree programs, students, and the diversity they bring with them, are able to be more fully included in higher education. These advanced-degree holders could later lead our colleges and universities through their scholarship and practice. Though experiences and socialization in graduate education is a growing body of inquiry in higher education, there remains a gap in this line of research. Specifically, there is not that much research on the way that students gain access to these programs. Additionally, very little research includes students of color or other underrepresented students (e.g., religious minorities, first-generation students, low-income students, LGBTQ students, etc.). As undergraduate education continues to diversify, it can be expected that graduate and professional programs should also see increases in student diversity related to race, ethnicity, socioeconomic background, religion, or sexual orientation. Thus, there remains much scholarly and practical work to do in order to better understand, include, and serve new populations of graduate students in advanced-degree programs.

Think About Diversity

There is much room for advancement in theory relative to the pathway toward graduate and professional education. As compared to other areas of diversity in higher education, the theoretical ideas on advanced-degree programs are in their infancy. The primary socialization model, from Weidman et al. (2001), has helped to guide thinking about how graduate and professional students begin to become socialized into their programs, disciplines, and as professionals in their fields. Yet, because there are not conflicting or alternative models, thinking in this area may be limited. Future theoretical work should ponder if there might be alternative socialization models or issues that could be tested in empirical research.

Tinto's (1993) model of graduate student persistence was quite literally just an appendix to his work on undergraduate persistence through college. It would be a large contribution to the thinking about graduate and professional students' persistence in their degree programs if new theories of graduate student retention were contemplated. One of the major differences in Tinto's representation of graduate and professional student persistence is his emphasis on the local department; he maintains that in advanced-degree programs, much of the persistence equation is likely related to the department. Thus, theories that consider how persistence might play out within academic departments would be beneficial to understand how retention in graduate school differs from that of undergraduate education.

Diversity Still Matters

While there is a growing body of scholarship related to the socialization of graduate students (Austin, 2002; Gardner, 2007, 2009), there remains relatively little inquiry into the process of gaining access to graduate programs. The research that does exist on the topic of graduate school access suggests that the undergraduate experience, and particularly the type of institution that was attended, is crucial in the pipeline to graduate school. Rising college seniors are more likely to gain access to graduate programs if they attended a four-year institution (Eide et al., 1998; Mullen et al., 2003; Walpole, 2003) and if that institution was more selective during the admissions process (Mullen et al., 2003; Schapiro et al., 1999; Walpole, 2003). African American students in particular are more likely to enroll in graduate programs if they attended an HBCU for their undergraduate degree (Barnes, 2010; Gasman et al., 2007). Additionally, there is evidence that being more involved and participating in undergraduate research increases the chances that a student might attend graduate school (Hathaway et al., 2002; Pascarella & Terenzini, 2005).

The body of inquiry on graduate school enrollment largely jumps from the predictors of that enrollment to students' experiences in the programs in which they enroll. There is limited work on the process of deciding to attend a particular program or on the process of actually gaining financial or academic access to these programs. This gap, related to accessibility of graduate education, is particularly important for underrepresented students because the scholarship that does exist on graduate school access demonstrates that the reasons that students of color attend graduate programs may differ from their White peers (Howard-Hamilton et al., 2009; Williams et al., 2005). Additionally, there is research finding that students of color in particular may experience differential treatment from advisors in some programs (Howard-Hamilton et al., 2009; Nettles, 1990). It is necessary to reveal these discrepancies in treatment so that they can be remedied.

Future research should contemplate the issue of access to graduate programs. More insight into students' decision-making processes for choosing a particular discipline and also particular programs or institutions would be useful for understanding how to better recruit a diverse graduate student population. For example, little is known about how students, particularly those students who are the most financially needy, are paying for their graduate or professional degrees. While there is clear evidence that financial assistance is important for many graduate students to enroll in and graduate from their programs (Cardon & Rogers, 2002; Ethington & Smart, 1986; Winkle-Wagner et al., 2010), there has been little to no national-level research examining trends in financial assistance (e.g., the kinds of financial assistance that are particularly beneficial or detrimental to success in these programs, etc.). Such an inquiry would aid in knowing what kinds of assistance seem to increase the likelihood of enrollment and persistence in graduate programs, particularly for underrepresented students who might need this assistance the most.

Additionally, there is little information on how students prepare academically for advanced-degree programs. It would be useful to uncover whether particular college courses were helpful in preparations for graduate education. Or, if students attend graduate school in fields that they did not study as undergraduates, how is the transition to a new academic area experienced? Finally, more research is needed on the Graduate Records Examination (GRE), the Law School Admissions Test (LSAT), and the Medical College Admissions Test (MCAT) and their usefulness in graduate school admissions processes.

Research clearly shows that involvement in particular undergraduate co-curricular activities or in undergraduate research opportunities supports access to graduate school and encourages graduate school enrollment (Barlow & Villarejo, 2004; Hathaway et al., 2002; Huss, Randall, Davis, & Hansen, 2002; Jones et al., 2010; Lammers, 2001; Ridgewell & Creamer, 2003). But there is still not as much work on programs that are geared toward facilitating access to graduate and professional programs. For example, studies on summer bridge programs or federally funded programs such as the McNair Scholars Program[2] would be particularly useful to reveal ways to better prepare students for graduate study. These programs, aimed at deliberately preparing racially or socio-economically underrepresented students for graduate study, may provide important insights into issues of accessibility for graduate education more generally. For example, there might be aspects of those programs (e.g., workshops on financial aid, preparation for graduate school, undergraduate researcher opportunities, internships, etc.) that could be transferred into academic departments to help these departments reach out to different populations of prospective graduate students.

There are some privately funded or not-for-profit programs and organizations aimed at helping to socialize students of color into life as scholars[3] (e.g., Sisters of the Academy, Brothers of the Academy). But there is not much empirical work on how these programs help participants to be successful in graduate and professional programs. This kind of research would be very beneficial to reveal better ways of supporting students within academic departments. An examination of programs specifically targeted toward scholars of color may also offer a way to connect students' aspirations to give back to their community with ways to provide better access and socialization to these groups of students.

Finally, while much of the work on graduate education is centered in socialization processes that do or do not work in fostering student success in graduate school, there is not much research on the way that graduate school participation influences students' identities or sense of self (but see Neumann, 2006, 2009). This kind of inquiry would be helpful for understanding how the socialization process interacts with a students' prior sense of self, and how students, particularly underrepresented students, begin to see themselves as central actors in academia. It may be that some students experience conflicts with their previous sense of who they were before graduate study, and who they are becoming as scholars. If these conflicts do exist, it would be important to find ways for students to navigate these complex identity issues. Additionally, a study of identity relative to advanced-degree experiences might reveal important insights about intersectionality, or, the way that students' perceive their identities (race, class, gender, sexual orientation) to be complexly connected.

Diversity Is Everywhere

The research on graduate education indicates that advising, mentoring, and general support are critical to the success of graduate students. Graduate coordinators and administrators who work with graduate students could learn from the research concluding that sometimes students of color and other underrepresented students such as low-income or first-generation students are treated differently than White or high-income students (Anchor & Morales, 1990; Johnson-Bailey, 2004). Administrators should use this work as a lesson in how to act in more equitable ways. Some students may not have as much training in their undergraduate education related to how to communicate about graduate programs, or, the questions to ask. The creation of orientation programs where they do not already exist, or, sessions on graduate school norms (e.g., how to talk to an advisor, what is expected of graduate students and how it differs from undergraduate education) might be particularly useful to support particularly underrepresented students. Additionally, for those students who are less familiar with graduate education processes (see Tinto's 2003 model of persistence), it might be very helpful to create timelines or workshops to walk students through the procedures and stages of their programs very early in their careers, or, even before they enroll in those programs.

Once students enroll, they need continued support. Often this support falls primarily on the shoulders of the academic advisor. However, students might benefit from more formalized institutional support. For example, if students had a central location within an academic unit such as a school or college where they could go to discuss problems that they are having in their coursework, or issues that they are having with their advisors, this might help them feel more supported. Student may be able to get some help from graduate student associations or graduate student governments. But, the influence of graduate student governments may vary depending on the campus. Aside from a few campuses,[4] there are not all that many exemplars of Graduate Student Affairs programs that are centralized. Many students may attempt to visit undergraduate student services units (e.g., career services, writing or academic tutoring centers, etc.) and be turned away because they are not undergraduates. We encourage campuses to pursue the idea of creating units or subunits for student affairs issues that graduate and professional students may uniquely encounter during their programs.

Faculty advisors, while experts in their academic areas, may not have much advising experience, particularly when they begin their careers. It is likely that many use a model of advising that stems from the way that they were guided in their own graduate programs. Additionally, unless the faculty member's research agenda is already centered on issues related to diversity, or unless the faculty member is from an underrepresented group, it is likely that he or she may not have much experience in working with diverse populations. The creation of faculty advising workshops might be very helpful at the college or school level. It would be important to discuss more than the nuts and bolts of how to help a student progress through coursework and useful for faculty to have a place to learn how to best interact with various populations of students and ways that they might make their advising style culturally sensitive for those students.

DISCUSSION QUESTIONS

There are many directions that future practical work or research could take relative to access into advanced-degree programs. Below we offer some questions related to improvements in practice and to guide the creation of ideas for future research.

Improving Practice

1. Given the barriers to access to advanced-degree programs for students of color, what ideas do you have for ways to help students gain access to graduate programs?
2. What are some of the unique needs of students of color in graduate programs? How do these needs differ from undergraduate students?
3. What programs, events, or workshops might you be able to facilitate as a student affairs practitioner that could help undergraduate students to think about graduate or professional programs?
4. Why is socialization a particularly important part of graduate school?
5. For graduate students who are enrolled at your institution, what might you be able to do to support them in a practical way (e.g., providing programs or other forms of support)?
6. What is Graduate Student Affairs? How might it differ from student affairs units that focus more on undergraduate students?
7. One of the major student affairs associations, Student Affairs Administrators in Higher Education (NASPA), developed a set of professional competencies that are encouraged for all student affairs professionals. How might the NASPA professional competencies affect how graduate students should be served?
    a. The NASPA Competencies are (see http://www.naspa.org/programs/profdev/default.cfm): advising and helping; assessment, evaluation, and research; equity, diversity, and inclusion; ethical professional practice; history, philosophy, and value; human organizational resources; law, policy, and governance; leadership; personal foundations; students learning and development.
8. Another national association for student affairs, College Student Educators International, developed a Statement of Ethical Principles and Standards. How might

the ACPA Ethical Principles and Standards influence how graduate students should be served?

a. The ACPA Standards are (see http://www2.myacpa.org/statement-of-ethical-principles-and-standards): professional responsibility and competence; student learning and development; responsibility to the institution; and responsibility to society.

9. The Council for the Advancement of Standards in Higher Education (CAS) developed a set of standards for student affairs. How might these CAS Standards be applied to graduate education?

a. The domains for the CAS Standards are (see http://www.cas.edu/index.php/cas-general-standards/): knowledge acquisition, integration, construction, and application; cognitive complexity; intrapersonal development; interpersonal competence; humanitarianism and civic engagement; practical competence.

10. Who is responsible for serving graduate students (e.g., graduate schools, departments, divisions of graduate studies)? What partnerships between student affairs and academic affairs might help to better serve graduate students?

Developing Future Research

1. In what ways might the socialization models used to understand graduate students' experiences be further developed?

2. If you were to develop a study using Tinto's theoretical framework, what questions might this study be able to answer? How might you construct this study?

3. What research still needs to be done on the topic of accessing graduate and professional programs for underrepresented students?

4. How might you construct a study to explore the topic of the graduate student access?

5. What research study still needs to be done on students' experiences transitioning into graduate education, or being socialized into their programs?

═══════════════════════════════ A CASE STUDY ═══════════════════════════════

PRACTICING DIVERSITY ISSUES RELATED TO THE GRADUATE STUDENT PIPELINE

First Things First: Gaining Access to Graduate School

CARMEN MCCALLUM, BUFFALO STATE, STATE UNIVERSITY OF NEW YORK

Butter University (BU) is a large public research institution located in the midwestern United States. BU attracts students from around the world. Last year students from over 50 states and 100 different countries were enrolled. BU describes itself as a diverse university where every individual has an opportunity to succeed.

Ninety percent of the approximately 10,000 students that attend BU are proud to call themselves Vikings. In recent years, the school changed its mascot to a Viking after students protested against the controversial previous mascot. The majority of the students who attend BU are White, however, over the last 10 years enrollment of racially and ethnically underrepresented students has significantly increased at the undergraduate and graduate levels. Currently, 60% of the students are White, 13% Asian, 11% African American, 9% Latina/o, 5% Hawaiian/Pacific Islander, and the last 2% is comprised of Native Americans and multi-racial students.

Jacob Miller, a 25-year-old, single, White male, has been working for the School of Education as an academic advisor for the last 5 years. In addition to advising, he is responsible for recruiting graduate students for BU's Educational Leadership and Higher Education program. Jacob is extremely proud that during his tenure, graduate enrollment has significantly increased, especially for racially and ethnically underrepresented students. He attributes the increase to his creativity in programming and recruitment strategies. Jacob is the first advisor in his role to hold night advising sessions and to attend recruitment affairs out-of-state. Although he likes to think that he is mainly responsible for enrollment increases, he acknowledges that the change in policies regarding incoming students funding packages has also had a great impact. Nevertheless, Jacob loves his position and has been known to go above and beyond his job description to help diverse graduate students gain enrollment and succeed.

After several days at recruitment fairs, Jacob has returned to his office to meet with students interested in applying. Jacob is tired from being on the road and breathes a sigh of relief when he realizes he only has one student on his schedule. The student, Jazzmine Sloan, is a university employee. It is common for university employees, especially administrators, to apply. However, Jacob is a little surprised that someone at Jazzmine's level is coming to see him.

Jazzmine arrives to Jacob's office right on time. She is a 5 feet 7 inches, 36-year-old, African American women who carries herself with confidence and grace. She has a pleasant demeanor and greets the office staff as well as students in the lobby with a charming nod and a smile. Hearing this, Jacob warmly greets Jazzmine and escorts her back to his office. It is less than 5 minutes into the conversation that Jazzmine's demeanor changes, and she can no longer hold back the tears.

In order to provide Jacob a complete picture of her situation, Jazzmine starts from the beginning. She explains that she has never been a great student. During high school and in her early college years her grades were average at best. However, after sophomore year things began to change. She met a counselor who diagnosed her with a learning disability. Once diagnosed, the counselor shared with Jazzmine various studying techniques that allowed her to become academically successful. As she became more confident in her abilities, she joined various student organizations on campus. She regrets that she did not take advantage of the opportunity to participate in a research project with her favorite professor, but with her current involvement she didn't want to risk jeopardizing her grades. However, the idea of conducting research stuck with her. Those early experiences of overcoming adversity inspired Jazzmine to pursue her PhD.

Jazzmine explained that it was always her intention to earn her PhD, but, after obtaining a job at BU, getting married, and having a child, she decided to put her dream aside and focus on her career and family. Over the last 12 years Jazzmine has been extremely successful. She has received several promotions and is now an executive working in the provost's office. But despite all of her employment success, she has not been able to achieve the personal goal that mattered the most to her: earning her PhD.

Jazzmine informed Jacob that she was aware that various things influence admission decisions. However, after significantly improving her GRE scores, demonstrating her ability to write and analyze factual information through public policy briefs, and successfully completing courses in the Educational Leadership and Higher Education program as a non-degree student, she was still unable to obtain admission after applying three times. Jazzmine mentioned that she was concerned that her lack of interactions with students outside the classroom while taking classes may have influenced the committee's decision. As the only older student of color in the class, her classmates often did not invite her to outside events, but it was Jazzmine's hope that once she gained admissions she could work harder to fit in. She also mentioned that she had not reached out to faculty in the program, but, she wanted to do so after she was admitted. In addition to not getting along with fellow students, Jazzmine stated that she realized the program admitted few part-time, working students and in her application materials, she explicitly stated that she did not intend to quit her job. Still, Jazzmine was puzzled as to why the program did not see her as a good fit.

In closing, Jazzmine informed Jacob that she was coming to him just as any other student would because she did not want to use her status in the institution to elicit special treatment. As the recruitment specialist, Jazzmine asked Jacob for advice about gaining enrollment to the PhD program in Educational Leadership and Higher Education at Butter University.

Please answer the questions below as if you were Jacob and your goal was to try to provide the most effective advising:

1. Identify five questions Jacob could ask Jazzmine to obtain a better understanding of her situation.
    a. Are there any questions that Jacob may feel uncomfortable asking because of their racial/ethnic and age differences? How can he overcome this feeling of discomfort?
2. What are some of the socialization issues that Jazzmine might be facing (e.g., what graduate school norms such as interacting with faculty might she not know about)?
3. Identify five strategies Jacob might suggest for Jazzmine in her quest to earn her PhD.
4. Discuss whether you believe race, age, ability, and/or gender may play a role in this scenario.
    a. Could these identities play a role in how Jacob responds to Jazzmine and how Jazzmine receives Jacob's advice?
5. Jazzmine has applied to the PhD program three times. Discuss whether or not you believe it is ethical to advise Jazzmine to pursue an alternative path?
6. What other individuals should Jacob suggest that Jazzmine speak with as she makes her decision to pursue a PhD?
7. What kinds of suggestions can Jacob offer in order to help Jazzmine manage her full time employment and familial responsibilities while she applies to graduate school?

8. Identify services on your campus for students with disabilities. With those services in mind, create a plan for Jazzmine.

NOTES

1. During the same year, Whites comprised 60% and Blacks 12% of the total U.S. population. Doctoral degrees earned by other racial/ethnic groups in 2009–2010 were: American Indian, 0.4%; Asian, 9.0%; Hispanic, 5.9%; More than 1 race, 2.1%; Other, 1.9%. For more information see: http://chronicle.com. ezproxy.library.wisc.edu/article/Characteristics-of-Recipients-of-Doctorates/133407/

2. The McNair Program is designed to prepare undergraduate, low-income students, first-generation students, or students of color for graduate education through research and involvement in scholarly activities. For more information see: http://mcnairscholars.com/about/

3. For more information on Sisters of the Academy, see http://www.sistersoftheacademy.org. For information on Brothers of the Academy, see http://www.brothersoftheacademy.org

4. For examples of private institutions with a Graduate Student Affairs office, see the University of Chicago (http://grad-affairs.uchicago.edu/page/about-gsa) or Drake University (http://gradschool.duke.edu/gsa/index.php).

EPILOGUE

For now decisions are upon us and we cannot afford delay. We must act, knowing that our work will be imperfect. We must act, knowing that today's victories will be only partial and that it will be up to those who stand here in 4 years and 40 years and 400 years hence to advance the timeless spirit ...

—President Barack Obama (2013)

In higher education institutions, and more accurately, in our nation, we stand poised at a time when diversity-and-inclusion must be partnered. The idea of diversity as an adjective, a describer of the differences that have and will continue to exist between us, should be left behind. Rather, diversity must be joined together with action, specifically, the act of inclusion. Our aim in this book was to offer a synthesis of the thinking and research on the topic of inclusion in higher education as a way to provide a glimpse into how racial/ethnic diversity in the student population in particular can be enacted within the ivory towers and bustling sidewalks of college campuses. We emphasized race and ethnicity. This choice was not to disregard other aspects of diversity such as ability, gender, socioeconomic status, or sexual orientation; we tried whenever possible to bring those concepts into the discussion knowing that the task of fully representing the plurality of diversity is enormous, and at best, imperfect. We concentrated on race and ethnicity here because *Race [still] Matters* (West, 1993/2001).

We framed our discussion of diversity in higher education as a process of getting into college, getting through the experience, and getting out. This approach was a way to demonstrate how diversity-and-inclusion must be enacted not only when students attempt to enter college, but throughout their entire experience. Diversity-and-inclusion is a continual process, an action, and a commitment to beginning and then continuing to work toward full inclusion and participation for all students in higher education.

It is simply not good enough, nor is it accurate, to claim that prospective college students all have equal opportunities to compete to go to college. Access to college is predicated on experiences in schooling, families, and neighborhoods that happen at least a decade before a student stands at the gate to a college or university, trying to be admitted. As the theory and research in this book stress, we have a larger social obligation to ensure that students have the opportunity to prepare for college at the earlier levels of education, starting in primary, middle-level, and secondary schooling. Students must have access to college preparatory coursework at the earliest levels of education, access to knowledge about processes like applying for financial aid or applying to colleges, access to people who know about college and can help these students navigate the long and winding road to the college gate.

It is simply not enough to admit students into college under the ideal of diversifying higher education institutions, only to let these students wander without direction through hallways, classrooms, residence halls, cafeterias, libraries, quads, and campus green spaces as if they are visiting a foreign land. Nor is it acceptable to admit students without addressing the institutionalized policies and practices that promote their marginalization on our campuses. Students' adjustments, transitions, and eventual persistence in college are dependent on deliberate acts of inclusion for the duration of their time in college. For some postsecondary institutions, campus missions need to evolve and shift to include new populations of students. For other campuses whose missions espouse inclusion and serving diverse students, the call to action is centered on enacting their missions in ways that promote true inclusion and therefore student success. Institutions, policies, and programs need to change. People within postsecondary institutions need to change to make space for these new students. This change requires action, the action of inclusion.

Inclusion can come in many forms. Transitions into college are aided by deliberate acts of support (e.g., formal and informal support programs, tutoring, etc.). The ability of students to develop their identity is fostered through support of who they are when they come to college, including race/ethnicity, gender, socioeconomic background, sexual orientation, religious affiliation, or ability. There must be room for students to express their backgrounds, their roles, and their complex identities inside and outside of college classrooms in order for all of them to be empowered to continue in their identity development during college. Finally, there are numerous issues that students must navigate to finish their degrees: families, friends, finances, academics, among many others. Students need multiple levels of support to navigate them all, and this support must be more than encouragement for them to become involved on campus, as if the campus is stagnate and students of color are simply pieces of the puzzle to fit into the existing picture. Instead, those who have power and leadership roles at institutions (faculty, staff, student affairs professionals, administrators) should be trying to arrange the picture of the campus to fit these new students into it, and thereby create a whole new campus portrait. This means that we must be open to change, to the idea that what we thought was useful and beneficial to students may be different for some populations.

There are economic and moral imperatives for enacting diversity-and-inclusion on college campuses, ensuring that all students can gain access to, navigate through, and graduate from college. While it was beyond the task of this book to provide a detailed examination of the economic imperative of diversity-and-inclusion, we end with this idea as a way to harken our call to action. These ideas can be a way to stimulate some potential pathways for scholars, practitioners, and policymakers to take toward enacting better inclusion of students of color into higher education.

The economic incentives of earning a college degree are well documented, particularly for individuals (Blau & Duncan, 1967; Kane & Rouse, 1995; Sewell & Hauser, 1975). According to recent U.S. Census data (2012b), the median household income of a person who holds only a high school diploma was $25,604 per year while the median household income for those with a bachelor's degree was $75,518. Income levels are perhaps one of the more tangible economic incentives of earning a college degree. But, there is evidence that median incomes might tell only part of the story.

Sociologists have been able to statistically model the long-term benefits of a college education, finding that the people in society who are most likely to be disadvantaged (i.e., those from low-income backgrounds, students of color, first-generation students) would reap the biggest benefits of a college degree in terms of social mobility (Brand & Xie, 2010). These economic benefits connect with the accumulation of wealth over the life course. Some sociologists have initiated an examination of intergenerational wealth and assets (e.g., studying the accumulation of inheritance, assets that families have through home ownership, stocks, bonds, etc.), demonstrating that wealth disparities have potential long-term effects across generations (Conley, 1999; Shapiro, 2004). The economic imperative of going to college, and including all groups of people in college, is compelling from the vantage point of returns on incomes (one will make more money), but, the idea that one's economic advantage could lead to intergenerational wealth means that entire groups of people could be uplifted. Or, on the contrary, if particular groups are left out of college, the result is likely to be longstanding negative effects on the life chances of those groups across generations. The notion that one's life, and perhaps the lives of whole groups of people, could be made better, economically and in other ways, through the earning of a college degree is one path toward action that we encourage as we conclude this book.

In addition to an economic argument for diversity-and-inclusion, there is a moral imperative. The moral argument of relevance here is that by taking action toward including all groups in higher education, there is more likely to be an engaged, educated citizenry to participate in our democratic nation. Democracy is predicated on representation and participation. For democracy to exist, people must participate (Verba & Nie, 1972). But, first, people must know how to participate and this is the task of education (Callan, 1997). Diversity-and-inclusion in higher education will manifest in society as engaged, educated citizens.

Our undertaking in this book was not to analyze moral philosophy and discourse and we will not attempt that in this brief space here. But, we also feel compelled to underscore, at least in part, some of the moral arguments for inclusion that have been the topic of epic scholarly debates and political battles. One example of this type of moral imperative for inclusion can be traced back to Rawls' (1999) argument (which is part of a tradition in political philosophy called liberalism that can be connected with thinkers like John Locke or moral philosophers like Immanual Kant) that society might be structured differently if it were to be done again and no one would know in what position he or she would be placed. Rawls' (1999) "veil of ignorance" wherein people would choose social positions or statuses without knowing where they would be in the hierarchy assumes that society might be more equitable. The point here is that there is a long debate as to how society should be structured so that it not only functions well, but, so that most people can successfully participate in it.

In education in the United States, the idea of inclusion and participation has mani-fested in arguments that the purpose of education is to create citizens who can par-ticipate in our democracy (Furhman & Lazerson, 2005). In higher education, many institutions were created with a civic mission, to educate the citizenry of their states (Checkoway, 2001; Ehrlich, 2000). This civic mission can also be linked to diversity in that part of this mission is to create opportunities for civic participation for all citizens (Hurtado, 2007). This is the place from which we hope others can launch actions toward diversity-and-inclusion. There is a moral imperative to create a whole citizenry that is educated and able to participate. Without that ability to participate, and if some groups are excluded from participation, we risk our future, our democracy (West, 2005).

Diversity is an action. The action requires inclusion. We cannot let the fear of our imperfection to persuade us to remain stagnant. With the marriage of diversity-and-inclusion, there will be missteps, mistakes, and missed opportunities. But, we must act, if not for ourselves, for the prosperity and participation of our future generations. Diversity-and-inclusion can help to set our course, and now the time has arrived for us to determine our actions.

REFERENCES

Aberson, C. L. (2007). Diversity, merit, fairness, and discrimination beliefs as predictors of support for affirmative-action policy actions. *Journal of Applied Social Psychology, 37*(10), 2451–2474.

Abes, E. S. (2012). Constructivist and intersectional interpretations of a lesbian college student's multiple social identities. *The Journal of Higher Education, 83*(2), 186–216.

Abes, E. S., & Jones, S. R. (2004). Meaning-making capacity and the dynamics of lesbian college students' multiple dimensions of identity. *Journal of College Student Development, 45*(6), 612–632.

Abes, E. S., Jones, S. R., & McEwen, M. K. (2007). Reconceptualizing the model of multiple dimensions of identity: The role of meaning-making capacity in the construction of multiple identities. *Journal of College Student Development, 48*(1), 1–22

Abes, E. S., & Kasch, D. (2007). Using queer theory to explore lesbian college students' multiple dimensions of identity. *Journal of College Student Development, 48*(6), 619–636.

Adams, M., Hackman, H. W., Peters, M. L., & Zúñiga, X. (2000). *Readings for diversity and social justice.* In W. J. Blumenfeld & R. Castañeda (Eds.), *Readings for diversity and social justice* (pp. 382–391). New York, NY: Routledge.

Adelman, C. (1999). *Answers in the tool box: Academic intensity, attendance patterns, and bachelor's degree attainment.* Washington, DC: U.S. Department of Education, Office of Educational Research and Development.

Adelman, C. (2004). *Principal indicators of student academic histories in postsecondary education, 1972–2000.* Washington, DC: U.S. Department of Education, Institute of Education Sciences.

Alexander, B. C., Garcia, V., Gonzalez, L., Grimes, G., & O'Brien, D. (2007). Barriers in the transfer process for Hispanic and Hispanic immigrant students. *Journal of Hispanic Higher Education, 6*(2), 174–184.

Allen, W. R. (1992). The color of success: African-American college student outcomes at predominantly White and historically Black public colleges and universities. *Harvard Educational Review, 62*(1), 26–45.

Allen, W. R. (2008). Forward. In M. Gasman, B. Baez, & C. S. V. Turner (Eds.), *Understanding minority serving institutions* (pp. 71–90). New York, NY: State University of New York Press.

Allen, W. R., Epps, E. G., & Haniff, N. Z. (Eds.). (1991). *College in Black and White: African American students in predominantly White and in historically Black public universities.* Albany: State University of New York Press.

Allen, W. R., & Jewell, J. O. (2002). A backward glance forward: Past, present, and future perspectives on historically Black colleges and universities. *The Review of Higher Education, 25*(3), 241–261.

Allensworth, E., Nomi, T., Montgomery, N., & Lee, V. E. (2009). College preparatory curriculum for all: Academic consequences of requiring algebra and English I for ninth graders in Chicago. *Educational Evaluation and Policy Analysis, 31*(4), 367–391.

Almanac of Higher Education. (2012). Characteristics of recipients of research doctorates, 2009–10. *The Chronicle of Higher Education.*

Alon, S. (2007). The influence of financial aid in leveling group differences in graduating from elite institutions. *Economics of Education Review, 26*(3), 296–311.

Alon, S., & Tienda, M. (2007). Diversity, opportunity, and the shifting meritocracy in higher education. *The American Sociological Reviews, 72*(4), 487–511.

Altbach, P. G., Lomotey, K., & Kyle, S. R. (1999). Race in higher education: The continuing crisis. In P. G. Altbach, R. O. Berhahl, & P. J. Gumport (Eds.), *American higher education in the twenty-first century: Social, political, and economic challenges* (pp. 448–466). Baltimore, MD: John Hopkins University Press.

Anaya, G., & Cole, D. (2001). Latina/o student achievement: Exploring the influence of student-faculty interaction on college grades. *Journal of College Student Development, 42*(1), 3–14.

Anchor, S., & Morales, A. (1990). Chicanas holding doctoral degrees: Social reproduction and cultural ecological approaches. *Anthropology and Education Quarterly, 21*(3), 269–287.

Ancis, J. R., Sedlacek, W. E., & Mohr, J. J. (2000). Student perceptions of campus cultural climate by race. *Journal of Counseling and Development, 78*(2), 180–185.

Anderson, E. (2002). Integration, affirmative action, and strict scrutiny. *New York University Law Review, 77*, 1195–1271.

Anderson, J. D. (1998). *The education of Blacks in the south, 1860-1935.* Chapel Hill: University of North Carolina Press.

Anderson, J. D. (2002a). Race in American higher education: Historical perspectives on current conditions. In W. A. Smith, P. G. Altbach, & K. Lomotey (Eds.), *The racial crisis in American higher education* (pp. 3–21). Albany, NY: State University of New York.

Anderson, J. D. (2002b). Race, meritocracy, and the American academy during the immediate post-World War II era. In C. S. Turner, A. L. Antonio, M. Garcia, B. V. Laden, A. Nora, & C. L. Presley (Eds.), *Racial and ethnic diversity in higher education* (pp. 3–17). Boston, MA: Pearson Custom Publishing.

Anderson, M. S., & Swazey, J. P. (1998). Reflections on the graduate student experience: An overview. *New Directions for Higher Education, 101*, 3–13.

Antonio, A. L., Chang, M. J., Hakuta, K., Kenny, D. A., Levin, S., & Milem, J. F. (2004). Effects of racial diversity on complex thinking in college students. *Psychological Science, 15*(8), 507–510.

Antony, J. S. (2002). Reexamining doctoral student socialization and professional development: Moving beyond the congruence and assimilation orientation. In J. S. Smart & W. G. Tierney (Eds.), *Higher education: Handbook of theory and research* (pp. 349–380). Dordrecht, The Netherlands: Kluwer.

Arboleda, A., Wang, Y., Shelley, M. C., & Whalen, D. F. (2003). Predictors of residence hall involvement. *Journal of College Student Development, 44*(4), 517–531.

Arbona, C., & Nora, A. (2007). Predicting college attainment of Hispanic students: Individual, institutional, and environmental factors. *The Review of Higher Education, 30*(3), 247–270.

Arcidiacono, P., & Vigdor, J. L. (2009). Does the river spill over? Estimating the economic returns to attending a racially diverse college. *Economic Inquiry, 48*(3), 537–557.

Arroyo, C. G., & Zigler, E. (1995). Racial identity, academic achievement and the psychological well-being of economically disadvantaged adolescents. *Journal of Personality and Social Psychology, 69*(5), 903–914.

Aspinall, P. J. (2003). The conceptualization and categorization of mixed race/ethnicity in Britain and North America: identity options and the role of the state. *International Journal of Intercultural Relations, 27*(3), 269–296.

Astin, A. W. (1982). *Minorities in American higher education.* San Francisco, CA: Jossey-Bass.

Astin, A. W. (1984). Student involvement: A developmental theory for higher education. *Journal of College Student Personnel, 25*(4), 297–308.

Astin, A. W. (1985). *Achieving educational excellence: A critical assessment of priorities and practices in higher education.* San Francisco, CA: Jossey-Bass.

Astin, A.W. (1993). *What matters in college: Four critical years revisited.* San Francisco, CA: Jossey-Bass.

Astin, A. W. (1996). Involvement in learning revisited: Lessons we have learned. *Journal of College Student Development, 37*(2), 123–134.

Atkinson, D. R., Morten, G., & Sue, D. W. (1989). Proposed minority identity development model. In D. R. Atkinson, G. Morten, & D. W. Sue (Eds.), *Counseling American minorities: A cross-cultural perspective* (pp. 35–52). Dubuque, IA: William C. Brown.

Attewell, P. (2001). The winner-take-all high school: Organizational adaptations to educational stratification. *Sociology of Education, 74*(4), 267–295.

Attewell, P., Lavin, D., Domina, T., & Levey, T. (2005). New evidence on college remediation. *Journal of Higher Education, 77*(5), 886–924.

Attinasi,Jr., L. C. (1989). Getting in: Mexican Americans' perceptions of university attendance and the implications for freshman year persistence. *Journal of Higher Education, 60*(3), 247–277.

Attiyeh, G., & Attiyeh, R. (1997). Testing for bias in graduate school admissions. *Journal of Human Resources, 32*(3), 524–548.

Aud, S., Hussar, W., Johnson, F., Kena, G., Roth, E., Manning, E., … Zhang, J. (2012). *The condition of education 2012 (NCES 2012-045).* U.S. Department of Education, National Center for Education Statistics. Washington, DC. Retrieved June 30, 2012, from http://nces.ed.gov/pubsearch

Austin, A. E. (2002). Preparing the next generation of faculty: Graduate school as socialization to the academic career. *The Journal of Higher Education, 73*(1), 94–122.

Austin, A. E., & McDaniels, M. (2006). Using doctoral education to prepare faculty to work within Boyer's four domains of scholarship. *New Directions for Institutional Research, 129,* 51–65.

Backes, B. (2012). Do affirmative action bans lower minority college enrollment and attainment?: Evidence from state-wide bans. *Journal of Human Resources, 47*(2), 435–455.

Baez, B. (2006). Merit and difference. *Teachers College Record, 108*(6), 996–1016.

Bailey, T., & Weininger, E. B. (2002). Performance, graduation, and transfer of immigrants and natives in City University of New York community colleges. *Educational Evaluation and Policy Analysis, 24*(4), 359–377.

Baldwin, J. A., Duncan, J. A., & Bell, Y. R. (1992). Assessment of African self-consciousness among Black students from two college environments. In A. K. H. Burlew, W. C. Banks, H. P. McAdoo, & D. A. Azibo (Eds.), *African American psychology: Theory, research and practice* (pp. 283–299). Newbury Park, CA: Sage.

Baker, R. W., & Siryk, B. (1980). Alienation and freshman transition to college. *Journal of College Student Personnel, 21*(5), 437–442.

Baker, R. W., & Siryk, B. (1984). Measuring adjustment to college. *Journal of Counseling Psychology, 31*(2), 179–189.

Baker, R. W., & Siryk, B. (1989). *Student adaptation to college questionnaire manual.* Los Angeles: Western Psychological Services.

Bandura, A. (1977). Self-efficacy: Toward a unifying theory of behavioral change. *Psychological Review, 84*(2), 191–215.

Bandura, A. (1982). Self-efficacy mechanism in human agency. *American Psychologist, 37*(2), 122–147.

Bandura, A. (1986). *Social foundations of thought and action: A social cognitive theory.* Englewood Cliffs, NJ: Prentice-Hall.

Bandura, A. (1993). Perceived self-efficacy in cognitive development and functioning. *Educational Psychologist, 28*(2), 117–148.

Banks, R. (2001). Meritocratic values and racial outcomes: Defending class-based college admissions. *North Carolina Law Review, 79,* 1029. Retrieved from http://dx.doi.org/10.2139/ssrn.283711

Barlow, A. E. L., & Villarejo, M. (2004). Making a difference for minorities: Evaluation of an educational enrichment program. *Journal of Research in Science Teaching, 41*(9), 861–881. doi:10.1002/tea.20029

Barnes, B. J. (2009). A look back and a look ahead: How to navigate the doctoral degree process successfully. In V. B. Bush, C. R. Chambers, & M. Walpole (Eds.), *From diplomas to doctorates: The success of Black women in higher education and its implications for equal education for all* (pp. 161–182). Sterling, VA: Stylus Publishing.

Barnes, B. J. (2010). The nature of exemplary adviser's expectations and the ways they may influence doctoral persistence. *Journal of College Student Retention: Research, Theory, and Practice, 11*(3), 323–343.

Barnhardt, C. (1994). Life on the other side: Native student survival in a university world. *Peabody Journal of Education, 69,* 115–139. doi:10.1080/01619569409538768

Barry, C. L., & Finney, S. J. (2009). Can we feel confident in how we measure college confidence? A psychometric investigation of the college self-efficacy inventory. *Measurement and Evaluation in Counseling and Development, 42*(3), 197–222. doi:10.1177/0748175609344095/

Baum, S. (2003). *The role of student loans in college access.* National Dialogue on Student Financial Aid. New York, NY: College Board.

Baum, S., & Flores, S. M. (2011). Higher education and children in immigrant families. *The Future of Children, 21*(1), 171–193.

Bauman, G., Bustillos, L., Bensimon, E., Brown, M. C., & Bartee, R. (2005). *Achieving equitable educational outcomes with all students: The institution's role and responsibilities.* Retrieved April 23, 2007, from http//:www.aacu.org/inclusive_excellence/

Baxter Magolda, M. B. (2001). *Making their own way: Narratives for transforming higher education to promote self-development.* Sterling, VA: Stylus Publishing.

Baxter Magolda, M. B. (2009a). *Authoring your life: Developing an internal voice to meet life's challenges.* Sterling, VA: Stylus Publishing.

Baxter Magolda, M. B. (2009b). The activity of meaning making: A holistic perspective on college student development. *Journal of College Student Development, 50,* 621–639. doi:10.1353/csd.0.0106

Baylor, R. E. (2010). Loss of accreditation at historically Black colleges and universities. *New Directions for Higher Education, 151,* 29–38.

Bean, J. P. (1980). Dropouts and turnover: The synthesis and test of a causal model of student attrition. *Research in Higher Education, 12*(2), 155–187.

Bean, J. P. (1983). The application of a model of turnover in work organizations to the student attrition process. *Review of Higher Education, 6*(2), 129–148.

Bean, J. P. (1985). Interaction effects based on class level in an explanatory model of college student dropout syndrome. *American Educational Research Journal, 22,* 35–64. doi:10.3102/00028312022001035

Bean, J. P., & Eaton, S. B. (2001). The psychology underlying successful retention practices. *Journal of College Student Retention, 3*, 73–89. doi:10.2190/6R55-4B30-28XG-L8U0

Becker, G. (1964). *Human capital*. New York, NY: National Bureau of Economic Research.

Beil, C., Reisen, C.A., Zea, M.C., & Caplan, R.C. (1999). A longitudinal study of the effects of academic and social integration and commitment on retention. *NASPA Journal, 37*(1), 376–385.

Belcastro, B. R., & Koeske, G. F. (1996). Job satisfaction an intention to seek graduate education. *Journal of Social Work Education, 32*(3), 315–327.

Belenky, M., Clinchy, B., Goldberger, N., & Tarule, J. (1986). *Women's ways of knowing: The development of self, voice, and mind*. New York, NY: Basic Books.

Bell, A. D., Rowan-Kenyon, H. T., & Perna, L. W. (2009). College knowledge of 9th and 11th grade students: Variation by school and state context. *The Journal of Higher Education, 80*(6), 663–685.

Bell, D. A. (2003). Diversity's distractions. *Columbia Law Review, 103*, 1622.

Bell, D. A. (2004). *Silent covenants*. New York, NY: Oxford University Press.

Benitez, M. (1998). Hispanic-serving institutions: Challenges and opportunities. In J. P. Merisotis & C. T. O'Brien (Eds.), *Minority-serving institutions: Distinct purposes, common goals*. New Directions in Higher Education, no. 102. San Francisco, CA: Jossey-Bass.

Bensimon, E. B., & Malcolm, L. (Eds.). (2012). *Confronting equity issues on campus: Implementing the Equity Scorecard in theory and practice*. Sterling, VA: Stylus Publishing

Bensimon, E. M. (2004). The diversity scorecard: A learning approach to institutional change. *Change, 36*(1), 45–52.

Bensimon, E. M. (2007). The underestimated significance of practitioner knowledge in the scholarship on student success. *Review of Higher Education, 30*(4), 441–469.

Benson, K. F. (2000). Constructing academic inadequacy: African American athletes' stories of schooling. *The Journal of Higher Education, 71*(2), 223–246.

Berger, J. B., & Braxton, J. M. (1998). Revising Tinto's interactionalist theory of student departure through theory elaboration: Examining the role of organizational attributes in the persistence process. *Research in Higher Education, 39*(2), 103–119.

Berger, J. B., & Milem, J. F. (1999). The role of student involvement and perceptions of integration in a causal model of student persistence. *Research in Higher Education, 40*(6), 641–664.

Bergerson, A. A., & Huftalin, D. (2011). Becoming more open to social identity-based difference: Understanding the meaning college students make of this movement. *Journal of College Student Development, 52*(4), 377–395.

Bettinger, E. (2004). How financial aid affects persistence. In C. M. Hoxby (Ed.), *College choices: The economics of where to go, when to go and how to pay for it* (pp. 207-238). National Bureau of Economic Research. Chicago, IL: University of Chicago Press.

Bettinger, E. P., & Long, B. T. (2004). *Shape up or ship out: The effects of remediation on students at four-year colleges*. (Working Paper no. w10369). Cambridge, MA: National Bureau of Economic Research.

Bettinger, E. P., & Long, B, T. (2009). Addressing the needs of underprepared students in higher education: Does college remediation work? *Journal of Human Resources, 44*(3), 736–771.

Black, D. A., & Smith, J. A. (2004). How robust is the evidence on the effects of college quality? Evidence from matching. *Journal of Econometrics, 121*(1), 99–124.

Blau, P. M., & Duncan. O. D. (1967). *The American occupational structure*. New York, NY: Wiley.

Boden, D., Borrego, M., & Newswander, L. K. (2011). Student socialization in interdisciplinary doctoral education. *Higher Education, 62*(6), 741–755.

Boisjoly, J., Duncan, G. J., Kremer, M., Levy, D. M., & Eccles, J. (2006). Empathy or antipathy? The impact of diversity. *The American Economic Review, 96*(5), 1890–1905.

Bong, M. (2001). Role of self-efficacy and task-value in predicting college students' course performance and future enrollment intentions. *Contemporary Educational Psychology, 26*(4), 553–570.

Bonner, F. A., Marbley, A. F., & Howard-Hamilton, M. F. (2011). *Diverse millennial students in college: Implications for faculty and student affairs*. Sterling, VA: Stylus Publishing.

Boote, D. N., & Beile, P. (2005). Centrality of the dissertation literature review in research preparation. *Educational Researcher, 34*(6), 3–15.

Bourdieu, P. (1984). *Distinction: A social critique of the judgment of taste* (R. Nice, Trans.). Cambridge, MA: Harvard University Press. (Originally published in 1979)

Bourdieu, P., & Passeron, J. C. (1979). *The inheritors: French students and their relation to culture* (R. Nice, Trans.). Chicago, IL: University of Chicago Press. (Original work published in 1964)

Bourdieu, P., & Passeron, J. C. (1990). *Reproduction in education, society and culture* (Vol. 4). Thousand Oaks, CA: Sage.

Bowen, W., & Bok, D. (1998). *Shape of the river: Long term consequences of considering race in college and university admissions*. Princeton, NJ: Princeton University Press.

Bowen, W. G., Chingos, M. M., & McPherson, M. S. (2009). *Crossing the finish line: Completing college at America's public universities.* Princeton, NJ: Princeton University Press.

Bowen, W. G., Kurzweil, M. A., & Tobin, E. M. (2005). *Equity and excellence in American higher education.* Charlottesville: University of Virginia Press.

Bowen, W. G., & Rudenstine, N. (1992). *In pursuit of the PhD.* Princeton, NJ: Princeton University Press.

Bowman, N. A. (2010). Can 1st-year college students accurately report their learning and development?. *American Educational Research Journal, 47*(2), 466–496.

Bowman, N. A., & Small, J. L. (2010). Do college students who identify with a privileged religion experience greater spiritual development? Exploring individual and institutional dynamics. *Research in Higher Education, 51*(7), 595–614.

Bowman, N. A., & Small, J. L. (2012). Exploring a hidden form of minority status: College students' religious affiliation and well-being. *Journal of College Student Development, 53*(4), 491–509.

Bozick, R. (2007). Making it through the first year of college: The role of students' economic resources, employment, and living arrangements. *Sociology of Education, 80*(3), 261–285.

Bradburn, E. M., Moen, P., & Dempster-McClain, D. (1995). Women's return to school following the transition to motherhood. *Social Forces, 73*(4), 1517–1551.

Brailsford, I. (2010). Motives and aspirations for doctoral study: Career, personal, and inter-personal factors in the decision to embark on a history PhD. *International Journal of Doctoral Studies, 5,* 15–27.

Branch Douglas, K. (1998). Impressions: African American first-year students' perceptions of a predominantly white university. *The Journal of Negro Education, 67*(4), 416–31.

Brand, J. E., & Xie, Y. (2010). Who benefits most from college? Evidence for negative selection in heterogeneous economic returns to higher education. *American Sociological Review, 75*(2), 273–302.

Braxton, J. M. (2000). Reinvigorating theory and research on the departure puzzle. In J. M. Braxton (Ed.), *Reworking the student departure puzzle* (pp. 257-274). Nashville, TN: Vanderbilt University Press.

Braxton, J. M., & McClendon, S. A. (2001). The fostering of social integration and retention through institutional practice. *Journal of College Student Retention, 3*(1), 57–71.

Braxton, J. M., & Mundy, M. E. (2001/2002). Powerful institutional levers to reduce college student departure. *Journal of College Student Retention, 3*(1), 91–118.

Brazziel, M. E., & Brazziel, W. F. (2001). Factors in decisions of underrepresented minorities to forego science and engineering doctoral study: A pilot study. *Journal of Science Education and Technology, 10*(3), 273–281.

Brewer, M. B., & Silver, M. D. (2000). Group distinctiveness, social identification, and collective mobilization. In S. Stryker, T. Owens, & R. White (Eds.), *Self, identity and social movements* (pp. 157-171). Minneapolis: University of Minnesota Press.

Bridges, B. K., Cambridge, B., Kuh, G. D., & Leegwater, L. H. (2005). Student engagement at minority-serving institutions: Emerging lessons from the BEAMS project. *New Directions for Institutional Research, 125,* 25–43

Bridges, B., K., Kinzie, J., Nelson Laird, T. F., & Kuh, G. D. (2008). Student engagement and student success at historically Black and Hispanic-serving institutions. In M. Gasman, B. Baez, & C. S. V. Turner (Eds.), *Understanding minority-serving institutions* (pp. 217–236). Albany: State University of New York Press.

Bringle, R. G., & Hatcher, J. A. (2009). Innovative practices in service-learning and curriculum engagement. *New Directions for Higher Education, 147,* 37–46. doi:10.1002/he.356

Brown v. The Board of Education, 347 U.S. 483 (1954).

Brown, C. M., Davis, G. L., & McClendon, S. A. (1999). Mentoring graduate students of color: Myths, models, and modes. *Peabody Journal of Education, 74*(2), 105–119.

Brown, L. L., & Robinson Kurpius, S. E. (1997). Psychosocial factors influencing academic persistence of American Indian college students. *Journal of College Student Development, 38*(1), 3–12.

Brown, M. C. (2002). Good intentions: Collegiate desegregation and transdemographic enrollments. *The Review of Higher Education, 25*(3), 263–280.

Brown, S. D., Lent, R. W., & Larkin, K. C. (1989). Self-efficacy as a moderator of scholastic aptitude-academic performance relationships. *Journal of Vocational Behavior, 75*(1), 64–75.

Brown-Glaude, W. (Ed.). (2008). *Doing diversity in higher education: Faculty leaders share challenges and strategies.* Piscataway, NJ: Rutgers University Press.

Bryant, A. N., & Astin, H. S. (2008). The correlates of spiritual struggle during the college years. *The Journal of Higher Education, 79*(1), 1–27.

Burdman, P. (2005). *The student debt dilemma: Debt aversion as a barrier to college access* (Research and Occasional Paper Series, CSHE.13.05). Berkeley: University of California, Berkeley, Center for Studies in Higher Education.

Burgette, J. E., & Magun-Jackson, S. (2008). Freshman orientation, persistence, and achievement: A longitudinal analysis. *Journal of College Student Retention: Research, Theory and Practice, 10*(3), 235–263.

Burke, P. J., & Reitzes, D. (1991). An identity theory approach to commitment. *Social Psychology Quarterly, 54,* 239–251.

Burris, C. C., Heubert, J., & Levin, H. (2006). Accelerating mathematics achievement using heterogeneous grouping. *American Educational Research Journal, 43*(1), 103–134.

Buzzetto-More, N., Ukoha, O., & Rustagi, N. (2010). Unlocking the barriers to women and minorities in computer science and information systems studies: Results from a multi-methodological study conducted at two minority serving institutions. *Journal of Information Technology Education, 9*, 115–131.

Cabrera, A. F., & La Nasa, S. M. (2001). On the path to college: Three critical tasks facing American's disadvantaged. *Research in Higher Education, 42*(2), 119–149.

Cabrera, A. F., Nora, A., & Castaneda, M. B. (1992). The role of finances in the persistence process: A structural model. *Research in Higher Education, 33*(5), 571–593.

Cabrera, A. F., Nora, A., Terenzini, P. T., Pascarella, E. T., & Hagedorn, L. S. (1999). Campus racial climate and the adjustment of students to college: A comparison between White students and African-American students. *Journal of Higher Education, 70*(2), 134–160.

Callan, E. (1997). *Creating citizens: Political education and liberal democracy.* New York, NY: Oxford University Press.

Canagarajah, A. S. (1997). Safe houses in the contact zone: Coping strategies of African-American students in the academy. *College Composition and Communication, 48*(2), 173–196.

Cancian, M. (1998). Race-based versus class-based affirmative action in college admissions. *Journal of Policy Analysis and Management, 17*(1), 94–105.

Cancio, A. S., Evans, T. D., & Maume Jr, D. J. (1996). Reconsidering the declining significance of race: Racial differences in early career wages. *American Sociological Review, 61*(4), 541 556.

Cano, M. A., & Castillo, L. G. (2010). The role of enculturation and acculturation on Latina college student distress. *Journal of Hispanics in Higher Education, 9*, 221–231. doi:10.1177/1538192710370899

Cardon, P. L., & Rogers, G. E. (2002). *Technology education graduate education: Factors influencing participation.* East Lansing, MI: National Center for Research on Teaching Learning. (ERIC Document Reproduction Service No. ED462615).

Carney, C. M. (1999). *Native American higher education in the United States.* New Brunswick, NJ: Transaction.

Carter, D. F., Locks, A. M., & Winkle-Wagner, R. (2013). From when and where I enter: Theoretical and empirical considerations of minority students' transition to college. In J. C. Smart & M. B. Paulson (Eds.), *Higher education: Handbook of theory and research* (pp. 91–149). New York, NY: Agathon Press.

Carter, P. (2005). *Keepin' it real: School success beyond Black and White.* Oxford, England: Oxford University Press.

Carter, P. (2006). Straddling boundaries: Identity, culture, and school. *Sociology of Education, 79*(3), 304–328.

Cass, V. C. (1979). Homosexuality identity formation: A theoretical model. *Journal of Homosexuality, 4*(3), 219–235.

Cass, V. C. (1984). Homosexual identity formation: Testing a theoretical model. *Journal of Sex Research, 20*(2), 143–167.

Castellanos, J., & Jones, L. (2004). Latino/a undergraduate experiences in American higher education. In J. Castellanos & L. Jones (Eds.), *The majority in the minority* (pp. 111–125). Sterling, VA: Stylus Publishing.

Ceja, M. (2006). Understanding the role of parents and siblings as information sources in the college choice process of Chicana students. *Journal of College Student Development, 47*(1), 87–104.

Chambers, C. R. (2011). *Support systems and services for diverse populations: Considering the intersection of race, gender, and the needs of Black female undergraduates* (Vol. 8). Bingley, England: Emerald Group.

Chambers, D. L., Clydesdale, T. T., Kidder, W. C., & Lempert, R. O. (2005). The real impact of eliminating affirmative action in American law schools: An empirical critique of Richard Sander's study. *University of Michigan Program in Law and Economics Archive: 2003–2009.* [Working Paper 50]. Retrieved from http://law.bepress.com/umichlwps-olin/art50

Chan, C. S. (1989). Issues of identity development among Asian-American lesbians and gay men. *Journal of Counseling and Development, 68*, 16–20. doi:10.1002/j.1556-6676.1989.tb02485

Chang, M. J. (1996). *Racial diversity in higher education: Does a racially mixed student population affect educational outcomes?* (Unpublished doctoral dissertation). University of California, Los Angeles, CA.

Chang, M. J. (1999). Does racial diversity matter? The educational impact of a racially diverse undergraduate population. *Journal of College Student Development, 40*(4), 377–395.

Chang, M. J. (2001). The positive educational effects of racial diversity on campus. In G. Orfield (with M. Kurlaender) (Ed.), *Diversity challenged: Evidence on the impact of affirmative action* (pp. 175–186). Cambridge, MA: Civil Rights Project and Harvard Education Publishing.

Chang, M. J., Astin, A. W., & Kim, D. (2004). Cross-racial interaction among undergraduates: Some consequences, causes, and patterns. *Research in Higher Education, 45*(5), 529–553.

Chang, M. J., Denson, N., Saenz, V., & Misa, K. (2006). The educational benefits of sustaining cross-racial interaction among undergraduates. *The Journal of Higher Education, 77*(3), 430–455.

Chang, M., Witt, D., Jones, J., & Hakuta, K. (2003). *Compelling interest: Examining the evidence on racial dynamics in colleges and universities.* Stanford, CA: Stanford Education.

Chaudhari, P., & Pizzolato, J. E. (2008). Understanding the epistemology of ethnic identity development in multiethnic college students. *Journal of College Student Development, 49*(5), 443–458.

Chaves, C. (2006). Involvement, development, and retention theoretical foundations and potential extensions for adult community college students. *Community College Review, 34*(2), 139–152.

Cheadle, J. E. (2008). Educational investment, family context, and children's math and reading growth from kindergarten through the third grade. *Sociology of Education, 81*(1), 1–31.

Checkoway, B. (2001). Renewing the civic mission of the American research university. *Journal of Higher Education, 72*(2), 125–147.

Chemers, M. M., Hu, L., & Garcia, B. F. (2001). Academic self-efficacy and first year college student performance and adjustment. *Journal of Educational Psychology, 93*(1), 55–64. doi:10.1037/0022-0663.93.1.55

Chen, R., & DesJardins, S. L. (2010). Investigating the impact of financial aid on student dropout risks: Racial and ethnic differences. *The Journal of Higher Education, 81*(2), 179–208.

Chen, R., & St. John, E. P. (2011). State financial policies and college student persistence: A national study. *The Journal of Higher Education, 82*(5), 629–660.

Chen, X. (2005). *First-generation students in postsecondary education: A look at their college transcripts* (NCES 205-171). U.S. Department of Education, National Center for Education Statistics. Washington, DC: U.S. Government Printing Office.

Chesler, M. A., Lewis, A. E., & Crowfoot, J. E. (2005). *Challenging racism in higher education: Promoting justice.* Lanham, MD: Rowman & Littlefield.

Chhuon, V., & Hudley, C. (2008). Factors supporting Cambodian American students' successful adjustment into the university. *Journal of College Student Development, 49*(1), 15–30.

Chickering, A. W. (1969). *Education and Identity.* San Francisco, CA: Jossey-Bass.

Chickering, A. W., & Reisser, L. (1993). *Education and identity (2nd ed.).* San Francisco, CA: Jossey-Bass.

Chickering, A. W., & Schlossberg, N. K. (1995). *Getting the most out of college.* Needham Heights, MA: Allyn and Bacon.

Chickering, A. W., & Schlossberg, N. K. (2002). *Getting the most out of college.* New York, NY: Prentice Hall.

Choi, N. (2005). Self-efficacy and self-concept as predictors of college students' academic performance. *Psychology in the Schools, 42*(2), 197–205. doi:10.1002/pits.20048

Christie, N. G., & Dinham, S. M. (1991). Institutional and external influences on social integration in the freshman year. *Journal of Higher Education, 62*(4), 412–436.

Cibik, M. A., & Chambers, S. L. (1991). Similarities and differences among Native Americans, Hispanics, Blacks, and Anglos. *NASPA Journal, 28*(2), 129–139.

Cohen, A. M. (1998). *The shaping of American higher education: Emergence and growth of the contemporary system.* San Francisco, CA: Jossey Bass.

Colbeck, C. L. (2002). Assessing institutionalization of curricular and pedagogical reforms. *Research in Higher Education, 43*(4), 397–421.

Colburn, D. R., Young, C. E., & Yellen, V. M. (2008). Admissions and public higher education in California, Texas, and Florida: The post-affirmative action era, *UCLA Journal of Education and Information Studies, 4*(1). Article 2. Retrieved from http://repositories.cdlib.org/gseis/interactions/vol4/iss1/art2

Cole, D. (2007). Do interracial interactions matter? An examination of student-faculty contact and intellectual self-concept. *Journal of Higher Education, 78*(3), 248–272.

Cole, D., & Ahmadi, S. (2010). Reconsidering campus diversity: An examination of Muslim students' experiences. *The Journal of Higher Education, 81*(2), 121–139.

Cole, D., & Espinoza, A. (2008). Examining the academic success of Latino students in science, technology, engineering, and mathematics (STEM) majors. *Journal of College Student Development, 49*(4), 285–300.

Coleman, J. S. (1988). Social capital in the creation of human capital. *American Journal of Sociology, 94*, S95–S120.

Collins, P. H. (2000). *Black feminist though: Knowledge, consciousness, and the politics of empowerment.* New York, NY: Routledge.

Colyar, J. E., & Stich, A. E. (2011). Discourses of remediation: Low-income students and academic identities. *American Behavioral Scientist, 55*(2), 121–141. doi:10.1177/0002764210381870

Conley, D. (1999). *Being black, living in the red: Race, wealth, and social policy in America.* Berkeley: University of California Press.

Conrad, C., & Dunek, L. (2012). *Cultivating inquiry-driven learners: A College education for the twenty-first century.* Baltimore, MD: Johns Hopkins University Press.

Connerly, W. (2000). *Creating equal: My fight against race preferences.* San Francisco, CA: Encounter Books.

Connerly, W. (2009, Winter). Achieving equal treatment through the ballot box. *Harvard Journal of Law and Public Policy, 32*(1), 105–112.

Contreras, F. E., Malcolm, L. E., & Bensimon, E. M. (2008). Hispanic-serving institutions: Closeted identity and the production of equitable outcomes for Latino/a students. In M. Gasman, B. Baez, & C. S. V. Turner (Eds.), *Understanding minority-serving institutions*. Albany, NY: State University of New York.

Corrigan, M. E. (2003). Beyond access: Persistence challenges and the diversity of low-income students. *New Directions for Higher Education, 121,* 25–34.

Cottrell, R. R., & Hayden, J. (2007). The why, when, what, where, and how of graduate school. *Health Promotion Practice, 8*(1), 16–21.

Crenshaw, K., Gotanta, N., Peller, G., & Thomas, K. (Eds.). (1996). *Critical race theory: The key writings that formed the movement.* New York, NY: The New Press.

Crenshaw, K. W. (1991). Mapping the margins: Intersectionality, identity, politics, and violence against women of color. *Stanford Law Review, 43*(6), 1241–1299.

Crisp, G., & Nora, A. (2010). Hispanic student success: Factors influencing the persistence and transfer decisions of Latino community college students enrolled in developmental education. *Research in Higher Education, 51*(2), 175–194.

Crisp, G., Nora, A., & Taggart, A. (2009). Student characteristics, pre-college, college, and environmental factors as predictors of majoring in and earning a STEM degree: An analysis of students attending a Hispanic serving institution. *American Educational Research Journal, 46*(4), 924–942.

Cross, T., & Slater, R. B. (1997). Special report: Why the end of affirmative action would exclude all but a very few Blacks from America's leading universities and graduate schools. *Journal of Blacks in Higher Education, 17,* 8–17.

Cross, W. E. Jr. (1995). *The psychology of Nigrescence: Revising the Cross model.* In J. G. Ponterotto, J. M. Casas, L. A. Suzuki, & C. M Alexander (Eds.), *Handbook of multicultural counseling* (pp. 93–122). Thousand Oaks, CA: Sage.

Cruce, T. M., & Moore, J. V. III. (2007). First-year students' plans to volunteer: An examination of the predictors of community service participation. *Journal of College Student Development, 48*(6), 655–673.

Cruce, T., Wolniak, G. C., Seifert, T. A., & Pascarella, E. T. (2006). Impacts of good practices on cognitive development, learning orientations, and graduate degree plans during the first year of college. *Journal of College Student Development, 47*(4), 365–383.

Cunningham, A. F., & Parker, C. (1998). Tribal colleges as community institutions and resources. In J. P. Merisotis & C. T. O'Brien (Eds.), *Minority-serving institutions: Distinct purposes, common goals.* New directions in higher rducation, no. 102. San Francisco, CA: Jossey-Bass.

Cureton, S. R. (2003). Race-specific college student experiences on a predominantly white campus. *Journal of Black Studies, 33*(3), 295–311.

Cuyjet, M. J., Howard-Hamilton, M. F., & Cooper, D. L. (Eds.). (2011). *Multiculturalism on campus: Theory, models, and practices for understanding diversity and creating inclusion.* Sterling, VA: Stylus Publishing.

D'Augelli, A. R. (1994). Identity development and sexual orientation: Toward a model of lesbian, gay, and bisexual development In E. J. Trickett, R. J. Watts, & D. Birman (Eds.), *Human diversity: Perspectives on people in context. The Jossey-Bass social and behavioral science series* (pp. 312–333). San Francisco, CA: Jossey-Bass.

Dahmus, S., Bernardin, H. J., & Bernardin, K. (1992). Student adaptation to college questionnaire. *Measurement and Evaluation in Counseling and Development, 25*(3), 139–142.

Darity, W., Deshpande, A., & Weisskopf, T. (2011). Who is eligible? Should affirmative action be group- or class-based? *American Journal of Economics and Sociology, 70*(1), 238–268.

Davis, M., Dias-Bowie, Y., Greenberg, K., Klukken, G., Pollio, H. R., Thomas, S. P., & Thompson, C. L. (2004). "A fly in the buttermilk": Descriptions of university life by successful black undergraduate students at a predominately white southeastern university. *Journal of Higher Education, 75*(4), 420–445.

Deaux, K. (1993). Reconstructing social identity. *Personality and Social Psychology Bulletin, 19*(1), 4–12.

Deil-Amen, R., & Rosenbaum, J. E. (2002). The unintended consequences of stigma-free remediation. *Sociology of Education, 75*(3), 249–268.

DesJardins, S. L., McCall, B. P., Ott, M., & Kim, J. (2010). A quasi-experimental investigation of how the Gates Millennium Scholars Program is related to college students' time use and activities. *Educational Evaluation and Policy Analysis, 32*(4), 456–475.

DesJardins, S. L., & Toutkoushian, R. K. (2005). Are students really rational? The development of rational thought and its application to student choice. In J. C. Smart (Ed.), *Higher education: Handbook of theory and research* (Vol. 20, pp. 191–240). Dordrecht, The Netherlands: Springer.

Diaz-Strong, D., Gómez, C., Luna-Duarte, M. E., & Meiners, E. R. (2011). Purged: Undocumented students, financial aid policies, and access to higher education. *Journal of Hispanic Higher Education, 10*(2), 107–119.

Dickson, L. (2004). Does ending affirmative action in college admissions lower the percent of minority students applying to college? *Economics of Education Review, 25,* 109–119. http://dx.doi.org/10.1016/j.econedurev.2004.11.005

Dowd, A. C., & Coury, T. (2006). The effects of loans on the persistence and attainment of community college students. *Research in Higher Education, 46*(1), 33–62.

Dowd, A. C., Sawatzky, M., & Korn, R. (2011). Theoretical foundations and a research agenda to validate measure of intercultural effort. *The Review of Higher Education, 35*(1), 17–45.

Doyle, W. R. (2010). Changes in institutional aid, 1992–2003: The evolving role of merit aid. *Research in Higher Education, 51*(8), 789–810.

Durkheim, E. (1951). *Suicide: A study in sociology* (Trans. J. A. Spaulding & G. Simpson). New York, NY: Free Press.

Dworkin, R. (2000). *Sovereign virtue: The theory and practice of equality*. Cambridge, MA: Harvard University Press.

Dwyer, B. D. (2006). Framing the effect of multiculturalism on diversity outcomes among students at historically black colleges and universities. *Educational Foundations, 20*(1-2), 37–59.

Eby, L. T., Allen, T. D., Evans, S. C., Ng, T., & DuBois, D. L. (2008). Does mentoring matter? A multidisciplinary meta-analysis comparing mentored and non-mentored individuals. *Journal of Vocational Behavior, 72*(2), 254-267.

Edwards, K. E., & Jones, S. R. (2009). "Putting my man face on": A grounded theory of college men's gender identity development. *Journal of College Student Development, 50*(2), 210–228.

Ehrlich, T. (2000). *Civic responsibility and higher education*. Lanham, MD: Rowman & Littlefield.

Eide, E., Brewer, D., & Ehrenberg, R. G. (1998). Does it pay to attend an elite private college? Evidence on the effects of undergraduate college quality on graduate school attendance. *Economics of Education Review, 17*(4), 371–376.

Ellis, E. M. (2001). The impact of race and gender on graduate school socialization, satisfaction with doctoral study, and commitment to degree completion. *Western Journal of Black Studies, 25*(1), 30–45.

Ellison, R. (1995). *Invisible man*. New York, NY: Vintage. (Original work published in 1952)

Engberg, M., & Wolniak, G. (2010). Examining the effects of high school contexts on postsecondary enrollment. *Research in Higher Education, 51*(2), 132–153.

Engberg, M. E. (2007). Educating the workforce for the 21st century: A cross-disciplinary analysis of the impact of the undergraduate experience on students' development of a pluralistic orientation. *Research in Higher Education, 48*(3), 283–317.

England-Siegerdt, C. (2011). Do loans really expand opportunities for community college students? *Community College Journal of Research and Practice, 35*(1), 88–98.

Enns, C. Z. (1991). The new relationship models of women's identity: A review and critique for counselors. *Journal of Counseling Development, 69*, 209–217. doi:10.1002/j.1556-6676.1991.tb01489.x

Erikson, E. (1980). *Identity and the life cycle*. New York, NY: Norton. (Original work published 1959)

Espino, M. M., & Cheslock, J. J. (2008). Considering the federal classification of Hispanic-Serving Institutions and Historically Black Colleges and Universities. In M. Gasman, B. Baez, & C. S. V. Turner (Eds.), *Understanding Minority serving institutions* (pp. 257–268). Albany, NY: State University of New York Press.

Ethington, C. A., & Smart, J. C. (1986). Persistence to graduate education. *Research in Higher Education, 24*(35), 287–303.

Evans, N. J., Forney, D. S., Guido, F. M., Patton, L, D., & Renn, K, A. (2010). *Student development in college: Theory, research, and practice*. San Francisco, CA: Jossey-Bass.

Falick, M. (2009, May 25). Senate bill 175 gets watered down in the house: Minimal reform yields top 10% light [Web log message]. Retrieved from http://mikefalick.blogs.com/my_blog/2009/05/senate-bill-175-gets-watered-down-in-the-house-minimal-reform-yields-top-10-light.html

Feagin, J. R. (2000). *Racist America: roots, current realities, and future reparations*. New York, NY: Routledge.

Feagin, J. R. (2002). *The continuing significance of racism: US colleges and universities*. Washington, DC: American Council on Education.

Feinberg, W. (1998). *On higher ground: Education and the case for affirmative action*. Williston, VT: Teachers College Press.

Fenske, R. H., Porter, J. D., & DuBrock, C. P. (2000). Tracking financial aid and persistence of women, minority, and needy students in science, engineering, and mathematics. *Research in Higher Education, 41*(1), 67–94.

Ferdman, B. M., & Gallegos, P. I. (2001). Racial identity development and Latinos in the United States. In C. L. Wijeyesinghe & B. W. Jackson III (Eds.), *New perspectives on racial identity development* (pp. 32–66). New York, NY: New York University Press.

Fester, R., Gasman, M., & Nguyen, T. H. (2012). We know very little accreditation and historically Black colleges and universities. *Journal of Black Studies, 43*(7), 806–819.

Ficklen, E., & Stone, J. E. (Eds.). (2002). *Empty promises: The myth of college access in America. A report of the Advisory Committee on Student Financial Assistance*. Washington, D.C.: Advisory Committee on Student Financial Assistance.

Finnell, S. (1998). The *Hopwood* chill: How the court derailed diversity efforts at Texas A&M. In G. Orfield & E. Miller (Eds.), *Chilling admissions: The affirmative action crisis and the search for alternatives* (pp. 71–82). Cambridge, MA: Harvard Education Publishing Group.

Fleming, J. (2002). Who will succeed in college? When the SAT predicts Black students' performance. *The Review of Higher Education, 25*(3), 281–296.

Flores, S. M. (2010). The first state dream act in-state resident tuition and Immigration in Texas. *Educational Evaluation and Policy Analysis, 32*(4), 435–455.

Flowers, L. A. (2002). The impact of college racial composition on African American students' academic and social gains: Additional evidence. *Journal of College Student Development, 43*(3), 403–410.

Flowers, L. A. (2003). Effects of college racial composition on African American students' interactions with faculty. *College Student Affairs Journal, 23*(1), 54–63.

Fordham, S. (1995). *Blacked out: Dilemmas of race, identity and success at Capital High.* Chicago, IL: University of Chicago Press.

Fordham, S., & Ogbu, J. U. (1986). Black students' school success: Coping with the "burden of 'acting white.'" *The Urban Review, 18*(3), 176–206.

Frankenberg, R. (1993). *White women, race matter: The social construction of Whiteness.* Minneapolis: University of Minnesota Press.

Freeman, K. (1997). Increasing African Americans' participation in higher education: African American high-school students' perspectives. *The Journal of Higher Education, 68*(5), 523–550.

Freeman, K. (1999a). HBCUs or PWIs: African American high school students' consideration of higher education institution types. *Review of Higher Education, 23*(1), 91–106.

Freeman, K. (1999b). No services needed? The case for mentoring high-achieving African American students. *Peabody Journal of Education, 74*(2), 15–27.

Freeman, K. & Cohen, R. T. (2001). Bridging the gap between economic development and cultural empowerment: HBCUs challenges for the future. *Urban Education, 36*(5), 585–506.

Freeman, K., & Thomas, G. E. (2002). Black college and college choice: Characteristics of students who choose HBCUs. *The Review of Higher Education, 25*(3), 349–358.

Fries-Britt, S. (1998). Moving beyond Black achiever isolation: Experiences of gifted Black collegians. *The Journal of Higher Education, 69*(5), 556–576.

Fries-Britt, S., & Griffin, K. (2007). The Black box: How high-achieving Black resist stereotypes about Black Americans. *Journal of College Student Development, 48*(5), 509–524.

Fry, R. (2004). *Latino youth finishing college: The role of selective pathways.* Pew Hispanic Center. Retrieved June 24, 2012, from http://www.pewhispanic.org

Fuhrman, S., & Lazerson, M. (Eds.). (2005). *The institutions of American democracy: The public schools.* New York, NY: Oxford University Press.

Furr, S. R., & Elling, T. W. (2000). The influence of work on college student development. *NASPA Journal, 37*(2), 454–470.

Galbraith, M. W., & Shedd, P. E. (1990). Building skills and proficiencies of the community college instructor of adult learners. *Community College Review, 18*(2), 6–14.

Gandara, P. (2001). *Paving the way to postsecondary education: K-12 intervention programs for underrepresented youth.* Washington, DC: National Center for Education Statistics, Office of Educational Research and Improvement, US Department of Education.

Garces, L. M. (2012a). Necessary but not sufficient: The impact of Grutter v. Bollinger on student of color enrollment in graduate and professional schools in Texas. *The Journal of Higher Education, 83*(4), 497–534.

Garces, L. M. (2012b). Racial diversity, legitimacy, and the citizenry: The impact of affirmative action bans on graduate school enrollment. *The Review of Higher Education, 36*(1), 93–132.

Garciá, B. (1998). *The development of a Latino gay identity.* New York, NY: Garland.

Gardner, S. K. (2007). I heard it through the grapevine: Doctoral student socialization in chemistry and history. *Higher Education, 54*(5), 723–740.

Gardner, S. K. (2008). Fitting the mold of graduate school: A qualitative study of socialization in doctoral education. *Innovative Higher Education, 33,* 125–138.

Gardner, S. K. (2009a). Conceptualizing success in doctoral education: perspectives of faculty in seven disciplines. *The Review of Higher Education, 32*(3), 383–406.

Gardner, S. K. (2009b). The development of doctoral students: Phases of challenge and support. *ASHE Higher Education Report: 1551–6970.*

Gardner, S. K. (2010). Faculty perspectives on doctoral student socialization in five disciplines. *International Journal of Doctoral Studies, 5,* 39–53.

Gardner, S. K., & Barnes, B. J. (2007). Graduate student involvement: Socialization from the professional role. *Journal of College Student Development, 48*(4), 1–19.

Gasman, M. (2007a). *Envisioning Black colleges: A history of the United Negro College Fund.* Baltimore, MD: Johns Hopkins University Press.

Gasman, M. (2007b). Swept under the rug? A historiography of gender and Black colleges. *American Educational Research Journal, 44*(4), 760–805.

Gasman, M., Baez, B., Drezner, N .D., Sedgwick, K., Tudico, C., & Schmid, J. M. (2007). Historically Black college and universities: Recent trends. *Academe, 93*(1), 69–78.

Gasman, M., Baez, B., & Turner, C. S. V. (2008). *Understanding minority-serving institutions.* Albany: State University of New York Press.

Gasman, M., & Drezner, N. (2008). White corporate philanthropy and its support of private Black colleges in the 1960s and 70s. *International Journal of Educational Advancement, 8*(2), 79–92.

Geiser, S. (2008). *Back to the basics: In defense of achievement (and achievement tests) in college admissions.* Research and Occasional Papers Series, Center for Studies in Higher Education, University of California, Berkeley.

Geiser, S. (2009). Back to the basics: In defense of achievement (and achievement tests) in college admissions. *Change, 41*(1), 16–23.

Geiser, S., & Caspary, K. (2005). "No show" study: College destinations of University of California applicants and admits who did not enroll, 1997–2002. *Educational Policy, 19*(2), 396–417.

Gerstenfeld, P. B. (2011). *Hate crimes: Causes, controls, and controversies* (2nd ed.). Thousand Oaks, CA: Sage.

Gillborn, D. (2005). Education policy as an act of white supremacy: Whiteness, critical race theory and education reform. *Journal of Education Policy, 20*(4), 485–505.

Gillespie, D., Ashbaugh, L., & DeFiore, J. (2002). White women teaching white women about white privilege, race cognizance and social action: Toward a pedagogical pragmatics. *Race, Ethnicity and Education, 5*(3), 237–253.

Gilligan, C. (1993). *In a different voice: Psychological theory and women's development.* Cambridge, MA: Harvard University Press. (Original work published in 1982)

Gilligan, C., & Attanucci, J. (1988). Two moral orientations: Gender differences and similarities. *Merrill-Palmer Quarterly, 34*(3), 223–237.

Gilligan, H. (2012). *An examination of the financial literacy of California college students* (Unpublished doctoral dissertation). Long Beach: California State University, Long Beach.

Gladieux, L. E., Hauptman, A.M., & Knap, G.L. (1997). The federal government and higher education. In L. F. Goodchild, C. D. Lovell, E. R. Hines, & J. I. Gill (Eds.), *Public policy and higher education* (pp. 103–124). *ASHE Reader Series.* Needham Heights, MA: Simon and Schuster.

Gladieux, L. E., & Swail, W. S. (2000). Beyond access: Improving the odds of college success. *Phi Delta Kappan, 81(9),* 688–692.

Goggin, W. J., & Virginia, A. (1999). A "merit-aware" model for college admissions and affirmative action. *Postsecondary Education Opportunity, 83,* 1–8. Retrieved from http://www.postsecondary.org/last12/83599Goggin.pdf

Gold, J., Burrell, S., Haynes, C., & Nardecchia, D. (1990). Student adaptation to college as a predictor of academic success: An exploratory study of Black undergraduate education students. (Research Report 143). (ERIC Document Reproduction Service No. ED 331 946)

Golde, C. M. (2000). Should I stay or should I go? Student descriptions of the doctoral attrition process. *The Review of Higher Education, 23*(2), 199–227.

Golde, C. M. (2005). The role of the department and discipline in doctoral student attrition: Lessons from four departments. *Journal of Higher Education, 76,* 669–700. doi:10.1353/jhe.2005.0039

Goldrick-Rab, S. (2006). Following their every move: How social class shapes postsecondary pathways. *Sociology of Education, 79*(1), 61–79.

Goldrick-Rab, S., & Han, S. W. (2011). The "class gap" in "The Gap Year": Academic coursetaking, family formation, and the socioeconomic transition to college. *Review of Higher Education, 34*(3), 423–445.

Good, J., Halpin, G., & Halpin, G. (2001–2002). Retaining black students in engineering: Do minority programs have a longitudinal impact? *Journal of College Student Retention: Research, Theory & Practice, 3*(4), 351–364.

Goodman, D. J. (2001). *Promoting diversity and social justice: Educating people from privileged groups.* Thousand Oaks, CA: Sage.

Gorman, T. J. (1998). Social class and parental attitudes toward education-Resistance and conformity to schooling in the family. *Journal of Contemporary Ethnography, 27*(1), 10–44.

Goyette, K. A. (2008). College for some to college for all: Social background, occupational expectations, and educational expectations over time. *Social Science Research, 37*(2), 461–484.

Grace, S., & Gravestock, P. (2009). *Inclusion and diversity: Meeting the needs of all students.* New York, NY: Routledge.

Graham, H. D. (1990). *The civil rights era: Origins and development of national policy 1960–1972.* New York, NY: Oxford University Press.

Graham, H. D., & Diamond, N. (1997). *The rise of American research universities: Elites and challengers in the postwar era.* Baltimore, MD: John Hopkins University Press.

Graham, L. O. (2000). *Our kind of people: Inside Americas' Black upper class.* New York, NY: First Harper Perennial.

Gratz et al. v. Bollinger et al., 539 U.S. (2003).

Green, P. E. (2001). The policies and politics of retention and access of African American students in public White institutions. In L. Jones (Ed.), *Retaining African Americans in higher education: Challenging paradigms for retaining students, faculty and administrators* (pp. 45–58). Sterling, VA: Stylus Publishing.

Greene, T. G., Marti, C. N., & McClenney, K. (2008). The effort–outcome gap: Differences for African American and Hispanic community college students in student engagement and academic achievement. *The Journal of Higher Education, 79*(5), 513–539.

Griffin, K. A., & Muniz, M. M. (2011). The strategies and struggles of graduate diversity officers in the recruitment of doctoral students of color. *Equity and Excellence in Education, 44*(1), 57–76.

Griffin, K. A., Pèrez, D., Holmes, A. P. E., & Mayo, C. E. P. (2010). Investing in the future: The importance of faculty mentoring in the development of students of color in STEM. *New Directions for Institutional Research, 48,* 95–103.

Griffith, A. L. (2011). Keeping up with the Joneses: Institutional changes following the adoption of a merit aid policy. *Economics of Education Review, 30*(5), 1022–1033.

Grodsky, E., & Jones, M. T. (2007). Real and imagined barriers to college entry: Perceptions of cost. *Social Science Research, 36*(2), 745–766.

Grodsky, E., & Kalogrides, D. (2008). The declining significance of race in college admissions decisions. *American Journal of Education, 115*(1), 1–33.

Grutter et al. v. Bollinger et al., 530 U.S. (2003).

Guardia, J. R., & Evans, N. J. (2008). Factors influencing the ethnic identity development of Latino fraternity members at a Hispanic Serving Institution. *Journal of College Student Development, 49*(3), 163–181.

Guiffrida, D. A. (2003). African American student organizations as agents of social integration. *Journal of College Student Development, 44*(3), 304–319.

Guiffrida, D. A. (2004). Friends from home: Asset and liability to African American students attending a predominantly white institution. *NASPA Journal, 41*(4), 693–708.

Guiffrida, D. A. (2005). To break away or strengthen ties to home: A complex issue for African American college students attending predominantly white institutions. *Equity and Excellence in Education, 38*(1), 49–60.

Guillory, J. P., & Ward, K. (2008). Tribal colleges and universities: Identity, invisibility, and current issues. In M. Gasman, B. Baez, & C. S. V. Turner (Eds.), *Understanding minority serving institutions* (pp. 91–110). Albany, NY: State University of New York Press.

Guillory, R. M., & Wolverton, M. (2008). It's about family: Native American student persistence in higher education. *The Journal of Higher Education, 79*(1), 58–87.

Guinier, L., & Sturm, S. (2001). *Who's qualified.* Boston, MA: Beacon Press.

Gurin, P. (1999a). New research on the benefits of diversity in college and beyond: An empirical analysis. *Diversity Digest, 3*(3), 5–15.

Gurin, P. (1999b). Selections from the compelling need for diversity in higher education: Expert report of Patricia Gurin. *Equity and Excellence in Education, 32*(2), 36–62.

Gurin, P. Y., Dey, E. L., Hurtado, S., & Gurin, G. (2002). Diversity and higher education: Theory and impact on educational outcomes. *Harvard Educational Review, 72*(3), 330–366.

Gurin, P. Y., Dey, E. L., Gurin, G., & Hurtado, S. (2003). How does racial/ethnic diversity promote education? *Western Journal of Black Studies, 27*(1), 20–29.

Gurin, P., & Epps, E. G. (1975). *Black consciousness, identity, and achievement: A study of students in historically Black colleges.* New York, NY: Wiley.

Gurin, P., Nagda, B. R. A., & Lopez, G. E. (2004). The benefits of diversity in education for democratic citizenship. *Journal of Social Issues, 60*(1), 17–34.

Gusa, D. L. (2010). White institutional presence: The impact of Whiteness on campus climate. *Harvard Educational Review, 80*(4), 464–490.

Hackett, G., Betz, N. E., Casas, J. M., & Rocha-Singh, I. A. (1992). Gender, ethnicity, and social cognitive factors predicting the academic achievement of students in engineering. *Journal of Counseling Psychology, 39*(4), 527–538.

Hale, F. W. (2006). *How Black colleges empower Black students: Lessons for higher education.* Sterling, VA: Stylus Publishing.

Hallinan, M. T. (1994a). Tracking: From theory to practice. *Sociology of Education, 67*(2), 79–83.

Hallinan, M. T. (1994b). School differences in tracking effects on achievement. *Social Forces, 72*(3), 5–16.

Hallinan, M. T., & Williams, R. A. (1990). Students' characteristics and the peer-influence process. *Sociology of Education, 63,* 122–132.

Hamrick, F. A., Evans, N. J., & Schuh, J. H. (2002). *Foundations of student affairs practice: How philosophy, theory and research strengthen educational outcomes.* San Francisco, CA: Jossey-Bass.

Hannah, S. B. (1996). The Higher Education Act of 1992: Skills, constraints, and the politics of higher education. *The Journal of Higher Education, 67,* 498–527.

Hardiman, R. (2001). Reflection on White identity development theory. In C. L. Wijeyesinghe & B. W. Jackson (Eds.), *New perspectives on racial identity development* (pp. 108–128). New York, NY: New York University Press.

Harkreader, S., Hughes, J., Tozzi, M. H., & Vanlandingham, G. (2008). The impact of Florida's bright futures scholarship program on high school performance and college enrollment. *Journal of Student Financial Aid, 38*(1), 5–16.

Harper, S. R. (2006). Peer support for African American male college achievement: Beyond internalized racism and the burden of 'acting White.' *Journal of Men's Studies, 14*(3), 337–358.

Harper, S. R., Byars, L. F., & Jelke, T. B. (2005). How membership affects college adjustment and African American undergraduate student outcomes. In T. L. Brown, G. S. Parks, & C. M. Phillips (Eds.), *African American fraternities and sororities: The legacy and the vision* (pp. 393–416). Lexington: University Press of Kentucky.

Harper, S. R., & Davis III, C. H. F. (2012). They (don't) care about education: A counternarrative on Black male students' responses to inequitable schooling. *Educational Foundations, 26*(1), 103–120.

Harper, S. R., & Gasman, M. (2008). Consequences of conservatism: Black male students and the politics of historically Black colleges and universities. *Journal of Negro Education, 77*(4), 336–351.

Harper, S. R., & Hurtado, S. (2007). Nine themes in campus racial climates and implications for institutional transformation. In S. R. Harper & L. D. Patton (Eds.), *Responding to the realities of race on campus: New directions for student services* (No. 120, pp. 7–24). San Francisco, CA: Jossey-Bass.

Harper, S. R.. & Quaye, S. J. (2007). Student organizations as venues for Black identity expression and development among African American male student leaders. *Journal of College Student Development, 48*(2), 127–144.

Harris, A., & Tienda, M. (2010). Minority higher education pipeline: Consequences of changes in college admissions policy in Texas. *The ANNALS of the Academy of Policy and Social Science, 672*(1), 60–81.

Hart, N. K., & Mustafa, S. (2008). What determines the amount students borrow? Revisiting the crisis-convenience debate. *Journal of Student Financial Aid, 38*(1), 17–39.

Hathaway, R. S., Nagda, B. R., & Gregerman, S. R. (2002). The relationship of undergraduate research participation to graduate and professional education pursuit: An empirical study. *Journal of College Student Development, 43*(5), 614–631.

Hatch, L. R., & Mommsen, K. (1984). The widening racial gap in American higher education. *Journal of Black Studies, 14*(4), 457–476.

Hausmann, L. R. M., Ye, F., Schofield, J. W., & Woods, R. L. (2009). Sense of belonging and persistence in White and African American first-year students. *Research in Higher Education, 50*(7), 649–669.

Hawley, T. H., & Harris, T. A. (2005). Student characteristics related to persistence for first-year community college students. *Journal of College Student Retention: Research, Theory and Practice, 7*(1), 117–142.

Hayek, J. C., Carini, R. M., O'Day, P. T., & Kuh, G. D. (2002). Triumph or Tragedy: Comparing student engagement levels of members of Greek-letter organizations and other students. *Journal of College Student Development, 43*(5), 643–663.

Haylo, N., & Le, Q. (2011). Results of using multimedia case studies and openended hands-on design projects in an 'introduction to engineering' course at Hampton University. *Journal of STEM Education, 12*(7 & 8), 32–35.

Hearn, J. C., & Holdsworth, J. M. (2004). Federal student aid. In E. P. St. John & M. P. Parsons (Eds.), *Public funding of higher education: Changing contexts and new rationales* (pp. 40–59). Baltimore, MD: John Hopkins University Press.

Heller, D. E. (1997). Student price response in higher education: An update to Leslie and Brinkman. *The Journal of Higher Education, 68*(6), 624–659.

Heller, D. E. (1999). The effects of tuition and state financial aid on public college enrollment. *Review of Higher Education, 23*(1), 65–89.

Heller, D. E. (2004). State merit scholarship programs. In E. P. St. John (Ed.), *Readings on equal education, 19, public policy and college access: Investigating the federal and state roles in equalizing postsecondary opportunity* (pp. 99–108). New York, NY: AMS Press.

Helms, J. E. (1990). *Black and White racial identity: Theory, research, and practice. Contributions in Afro-American and African studies, No. 129.* New York, NY: Greenwood Press.

Helms, J. E. (1992). Why is there no study of cultural equivalence in standardized cognitive ability testing? *American Psychologist, 47*(9), 1083–1101.

Helms, J., & Cook, D. A. (1999). *Using race and culture in counseling and psychotherapy: Theory and process.* Needham Heights, MA: Allyn & Bacon.

Henry, W. J., West, N. M., & Jackson, A. (2010). Hip-Hop's influence on the identity development of Black female college students: A literature review. *Journal of College Student Development, 51*(3), 237–251.

Herzig, A. H. (2006). How can women and students of color come to belong in graduate mathematics? In J. M. Bystydzienski (Ed.), *Removing barriers: Women in academic science, technology, engineering, and mathematics* (pp. 254–270). Bloomington: Indiana University Press.

Hicklin, A. (2007). The effects of race-based admissions in public universities: Debunking the myths about Hopwood and proposition 209. *Public Administration Review, 67*(2), 331–340.

Hiester, M., Nordstrom, A., & Swenson, L. M. (2009). Stability and change in parental attachment and adjustment outcomes during the first semester transition to college life. *Journal of College Student Development, 50*(5), 521–538.

Hill, S. T. (1994). *The traditionally Black institutions of higher education (1860 to 1982).* Washington, DC: National Center for Education Statistics.

Hilmer, M. J. (2001). Redistributive fee increases, net attendance costs, and the distribution of students at the public university. *Economics of Education Review, 20*(6), 551–562.

Hinricks, P. (2012). The effects of affirmative action bans on college enrollment, educational attainment, and the demographic composition of universities. *Review of Economics and Statistics, 94*(3), 712–722. doi: 10.1162/REST_a_00170

Hinton, K. G., Grim, V., & Howard-Hamilton, M. F. (2009). Our stories of mentoring and guidance in a higher education and student affairs program. In M. F. Howard-Hamilton, C. L. Morelon-Quainoo, S.D. Johnson, R. Winkle-Wagner, & L. Santiague (Eds.), *Standing on the outside looking in: Underrepresented students' experiences in advanced degree programs* (pp. 184–202). Sterling, VA: Stylus Publishing.

Hipolito-Delgado, C. P. (2007). *Internalized racism and ethnic identity in Chicana/o and Latina/o college students* (Unpublished doctoral dissertation). University of Maryland College Park.

Hipolito-Delgado, C. P. (2010). Exploring the etiology of ethnic self-hatred: Internalized racism in Chicana/o and Latina/o college students. *Journal of College Student Development, 51*(3), 319–331.

Hirt, J. B., Strayhorn, T. L., Amelink, C. T., & Bennett, B. R. (2006). The nature of student affairs work at historically Black colleges and universities. *Journal of College Student Development, 47*(6), 661–676.

Hoachlander, G., Sikora, A. C., & Horn, L. (2003). *Community college students: Goals, academic preparation, and outcomes.* Washington, DC: U.S. Department of Education, National Center for Education Statistics.

Holdsworth, J.M. (2004). Federal student aid: The shift from grants to loans. In E. P. St. John (Ed.), *Readings on equal education, 19, Public policy and college access: Investigating the federal and state roles in equalizing postsecondary opportunity* (pp. 40–59). New York, NY: AMS Press.

Holland, J. L. (1992). *Making vocational choices: A theory of vocational personalities and work environments* (2nd ed.). Odessa, FL: Psychological Assessment Resources. (Original work published in 1985)

Holmes, L. S., Ebbers, L. H., Robinson, D. C., & Mugenda, A. B. (2001). Validating African-American students at predominantly white institutions. *Journal of College Student Retention, 2*(1), 41–58.

hooks, B. (1981). *Ain't I a woman: Black women and feminism* (Vol. 3). Boston, MA: South End Press.

hooks, B. (2000). *Feminist theory: From margin to center.* London, England: Pluto Press.

hooks, B. (2003). *Teaching community: A pedagogy of hope.* New York, NY: Routledge.

Hopwood v. Texas. (1996). U.S. Court of Appeals. Case Number 94-50569.

Horn, C. L., & Flores, S. M. (2003). *Percent plans in college admissions: A comparative analysis of three states' experiences.* Cambridge, MA: The Civil Rights Project at Harvard University.

Horn, C., & Flores, S. M. (2012). When policy opportunity is not enough: College access and enrollment patterns among Texas percent plan eligible students. *Journal of Applied Research on Children, 3*(2), Article 9, 1–26.

Horn, L., Chen, X., & Chapman, C. (2003). *Getting ready to pay for college.* Washington, DC: U.S. Department of Education/Institute of Education Sciences: NCES #2003-030.

Horse, P. G. (2001). Reflections on American Indian identity. In C. L. Wijeyesinghe & B. W. Jackson III (Eds.), *New perspectives on racial identity development: A theoretical and practical anthology* (pp. 91–107). New York, NY: New York University Press.

Horvat, E., & O'Connor, C. (Eds.). (2006). *Beyond acting White: Reframing the debate on Black student achievement.* Lanham, MD: Rowman and Littlefield.

Horvat, E. M., & Lewis, K. (2003). Reassessing the 'burden of acting White': The importance of peer groups in managing academic success. *Sociology of Education, 76,* 265–280

Hossler, D., Braxton, J., & Coopersmith, G. (1989). Understanding student college choice. In J. C. Smart (Ed.), *Higher education: Handbook of theory and research, Vol. 5* (pp. 231–288). New York, NY: Agathon Press.

Hossler, D., & Gallagher, K. S. (1987). Study student college choice: A three-phase model and the implications for policymakers. *College and University, 2*(3), 207–221.

Hossler, D., & Stage, F. K. (1992). Family and high school experience influences on the postsecondary educational plans of ninth-grade students. *American Educational Research Journal, 29*(2), 425–451.

Howard-Hamilton, M. F. (1997). Theory to practice: Applying development theories relevant to African American men. *New Directions for Student Services, 80,* 17–30.

Howard-Hamilton, M. F., Morelon-Quainoo, C., Winkle-Wagner, R., Johnson, S. D., & Santiague, L. (2009). *Standing on the outside looking in: Multiple causes, implications, and potential remedies to address under-representation among minorities in graduate programs.* Sterling, VA: Stylus Publishing.

Howard University. (n.d.). Mission statement. Retrieved from http://www.howard.edu/president/vision.htm

Howell, J. S. (2010). Assessing the impact of eliminating affirmative action in higher education. *Journal of Labor Economics, 28*(1), 113–166.

Hu, S. (2010). Scholarship awards, college choice, and student engagement in college activities: A study of high-achieving low-income students of color. *Journal of College Student Development, 51*(2), 150–161.

Hu, S. (2011). Scholarship awards, student engagement, and leadership capacity of high-achieving low-income students of color. *The Journal of Higher Education, 82*(5), 511–534.

Hu, S., & Ma, Y. (2010). Mentoring and student persistence in college: A study of the Washington state achievers program. *Innovative Higher Education, 35*(5), 329–341.

Hu, S., & St. John, E. P. (2001). Student persistence in a public higher education system: Understanding racial and ethnic differences. *Journal of Higher Education, 72*(3), 265–286.

Hurtado, A. (1996). *The color of privilege: Three blasphemies on race and feminism.* Ann Arbor: University of Michigan Press.

Hurtado, S. (1992). The campus racial climate: Contexts of conflict. *The Journal of Higher Education, 63*(5), 539–569.

Hurtado, S. (2003). *Preparing college students for a diverse democracy: Final report to the U.S. Department of Education, OERI, Field Initiated Studies Program.* Ann Arbor, MI: Center for the Study of Higher and Postsecondary Education.

Hurtado, S. (2007). Linking diversity with the educational and civic missions of higher education. *The Review of Higher Education, 30*(2), 185–196.

Hurtado, S., Cabrera, N. L., Lin, M. H., Arellano, L., & Espinosa, L. L. (2009). Diversifying science: Underrepresented student experiences in structured research programs. *Research in Higher Education, 50*(2), 189–214.

Hurtado, S., & Carter, D. F. (1997). Effects of college transition and perceptions of the campus racial climate on Latino college students' sense of belonging. *Sociology of Education, 70,* 324–345.

Hurtado, S., Carter, D. F., & Kardia, D. (1998). The climate for diversity: Key issues for institutional self-study. *New Directions for Institutional Research, 25*(2), 53–63.

Hurtado, S., Carter, D. F., & Spuler, A. J. (1996). Latino student transition to college: Assessing Difficulties and factors in successful adjustment. *Research in Higher Education, 37*(2), 135–157.

Hurtado, S., Eagan, M. K., Cabrera, N. L., Lin, M. H., Park, J., & Lopez, M. (2008). Training future scientists: Predicting first-year minority student participation in health science research. *Research in Higher Education, 49*(2), 126–152.

Hurtado, S., Han, J. C., Sáenz, V. B., Espinosa, L. L., Cabrera, N. L., & Cerna, O. S. (2007). Predicting transition and adjustment to college: Biomedical and behavioral science aspirants' and minority students' first year of college. *Research in Higher Education, 48*(7), 841–887.

Hurtado, S., Milem, J. F., Clayton-Pedersen, A. R., & Allen, W. R. (1998). Enhancing campus climates for racial/ethnic diversity: Educational policy and practice. *The Review of Higher Education, 21*(3), 279–302.

Hurtado, S., Milem, J. F., Clayton-Pedersen, A., & Allen, W. A. (1999). Enacting diverse learning environments: Improving the climate for racial/ethnic diversity in higher education. *ASHE-ERIC Higher Education Reports, 26*(8).

Hurtado, S., & Ponjuan, L. (2005). Latino educational outcomes and the campus climate. *Journal of Hispanic Higher Education, 4*(3), 235–251.

Hurwitz, M. (2011). The impact of legacy status on undergraduate admissions at elite colleges and universities. *Economics of Education Review, 30,* 480–492.

Huss, M. T., Randall, B.A., Davis, S. F., & Hansen, D. J. (2002). Factors influencing self-rated preparedness for graduate school: A survey of graduate students. *Teaching of Psychology, 29*(4), 275–281.

Ibrahim, F., Ohnishi, H., & Sandhu, D. S. (1997). Asian American identity development: A culture specific model for South Asian Americans. *Journal of Multicultural Counseling and Development, 25,* 34–50. doi:10.1002/j.2161-1912.1997.tb00314.x

Inkelas, K. K. (2003). Caught in the middle: Understanding Asian Pacific American perspectives on affirmative action through Blumer's group position theory. *Journal of College Student Development, 44*(5), 625–643.

Inkelas, K. K., Daver, Z. E., Vogt, K. E., & Leonard, J. B. (2007). Living-learning programs and first-generation college students' academic and social transition to college. *Research in Higher Education, 48*(4), 403–434. doi:10.1007/s11162-006-9031-6

Inkelas, K. K., & Soldner, M. (2011). Undergraduate living-learning programs and student outcomes. In J. Smart & M. Paulsen (Eds.), *Handbook of theory and research* (Vol. 26, pp. 1–56). New York, NY: Springer.

Ishitani, T. T. (2003). A longitudinal approach to assessing attrition behavior among first-generation students: Time-varying effects of pre-college characteristics. *Research in Higher Education, 44*(4), 433–449.

Ishitani, T. T. (2006). Studying attrition and degree completion behavior among first-generation college students in the United States. *Journal of Higher Education, 77*(5), 861–885.

Ishiyama, J. T., & Hopkins, V. M. (2003). Assessing the impact of a graduate school preparation program on first-generation, low-income college students at a public liberal arts university. *Journal of College Student Retention: Research, Theory and Practice, 4*(4), 393–405.

Jackson, A. P., Smith, S. A., & Hill, C. L. (2003). Academic persistence among Native American college students. *Journal of College Student Development, 44*(4), 548–565.

Jackson, B. W. (2001). Black identity development: Further analysis and elaboration. In C. L. Wijeyesinghe & B. W. Jackson (Eds.), *New perspectives on racial identity development: A theoretical and practical anthology* (pp. 8–31). New York, NY: New York University Press.

Jackson, B. W., & Wijeyesinghe, C. L. (2012). *New perspectives on racial identity development: Integrating emerging frameworks, second edition.* New York, NY: New York University Press.

Jackson, K., & Swan, L. (1991). Institutional and individual factors affecting African American undergraduate student performance: Campus race and student gender. In W. R. Allen, E. G. Epps, & N. Z. Haniff (Ed.), *College in Black and White: African American students in predominantly White and in historically Black public universities* (pp. 127–141). Albany: State University of New York Press.

Jacobs, J. A. (1996). Gender inequality and higher education. *Annual Review of Sociology, 22,* 153–185.

Jaeger, A. J., & Eagan, M. K., Jr. (2009). Unintended consequences: Examining the effect of part-time faculty members on associate's degrees completion. *Community College Review, 36*(3), 167–194.

Jaffee, S., & Hyde, J. S. (2000). Gender differences in moral orientation: a meta-analysis. *Psychological Bulletin, 126*(5), 703.

James, E., & Alsalam, N. (1993). College choice, academic achievement, and future earnings. In E. P. Hoffman (Ed.), *Essays on the economics of education* (pp. 11–138). Kalamazoo, MI: W.E. Upjohn Institute for Employment Research.

Jayakumar, U. (2008). Can higher education meet the needs of an increasingly diverse and global society? Campus diversity and cross-cultural workforce competencies. *Harvard Educational Review, 78*(4), 615–651.

Jenkins, M. (1999). Factors which influence the success or failure of American Indian/Native American college students. *Research and Teaching in Developmental Education, 15*(20), 49–52.

Johnson, A. (2006). The destruction of the holistic approach to admissions: The pernicious effects of rankings. *Indiana Law Journal, 81,* 309–358.

Johnson, S. D., Kuykendall, J. A., & Winkle-Wagner, R. (2009). Financing the dream: The impact of financial aid on graduate education for underrepresented minority students. In M. F. Howard-Hamilton, C. Morelon-Quainoo, R. Winkle-Wagner, S. D. Johnson, & L. Santiague (Eds.), *Standing on the outside looking in: Multiple causes, implications, and potential remedies to address under-representation among minorities in graduate programs* (pp. 45–52). Sterling, VA: Stylus Publishing.

Johnson-Bailey, J. (2004). Hitting and climbing the proverbial wall: participation and retention issues for Black graduate women. *Race Ethnicity and Education, 7*(4), 331–349.

Jones, M. T., Barlow, A. E., & Villarejo, M. (2010). Importance of undergraduate research for minority persistence and achievement in biology. *The Journal of Higher Education, 81*(1), 82–115.

Jones, S. R. (1997). Voices of identity and difference: A qualitative exploration of the multiple dimensions of identity development in women college students. *Journal of College Student Development, 38*(4), 376–386.

Jones, S. R. (2009a). Exploration of multiple dimensions of identity. *Journal of College Student Development, 50,* 287–304. doi 10.1353/csd.0.0070

Jones, S. R. (2009b). Constructing identities at the intersections: An autoethnographic exploration of multiple dimensions of identity. *Journal of College Student Development, 50*(3), 287–304.

Jones, S. R., & Abes, E. S. (2004). Meaning-making capacity and the dynamics of lesbian college students' multiple dimensions of identity. *Journal of College Student Development, 45*(6), 612–632.

Jones, S. R., & McEwen, M. K. (2000). A conceptual model of multiple dimensions of identity. *Journal of College Student Development, 41*(4), 405–414.

Jones, W. A. (2010). The impact of social integration on subsequent institutional commitment conditional on gender. *Research in Higher Education, 51*(7), 687–700.

Josselson, R. (1987). *Finding herself: Pathways to identity development in women.* San Francisco, CA: Jossey-Bass.

Josselson, R. (1996a). *Revising herself: The story of women's identity from college to midlife.* New York, NY: Oxford University Press.

Josselson, R. (1996b). *The space between us: Exploring the dimensions of human relationships.* Thousand Oaks, CA: Sage.

Jourdan, A. (2006). The impact of the family environment on the ethnic identity development of multiethnic college students. *Journal of Counseling & Development, 84*(3), 328–340.

Kaase, K. J. (1994, May). *Testing the limits of student adaptation to college questionnaire.* Paper presented at the Annual Forum of the Association for Institutional Research, New Orleans, LA. (ERIC Document Reproduction Service No. 373619).

Kahlenberg, R. D. (1997). *The remedy: Class, race, and affirmative action.* New York, NY: Basic Books.

Kallio, R. E. (1995). Factors influencing the college choice decisions of graduate students. *Research in Higher Education, 36*(1), 109–124.

Kalof, L., Eby, K. K., Matheson, J. L., & Kroska, R. J. (2001). The influence of race and gender on student self-reports of sexual harassment by college professors. *Gender & Society, 15*(2), 282–302.

Kalsner, L., & Pistole, M. C. (2003). College adjustment in a multiethnic sample: Attachment, separation-individuation, and ethnic identity. *Journal of College Student Development, 44*(1), 92–109.

Kane, T. J. (1998). Racial and ethnic preferences in college admissions. *Ohio St. LJ, 59,* 971.

Kane, T. J. (2006). Public intervention in post-secondary education. In E. Hanushek & F. Welch (Eds.), *Handbook of the economics of education* (Vol. 2, pp. 1369–1401). Amsterdam, The Netherlands: Elsevier.

Kane, T. J., & Rouse, C.-E. (1995). Labor market returns to two-year and four-year college. *The American Economic Review, 85*(3), 600–614.

Karabel, J. (2005). *The chosen: The hidden history of admission and exclusion at Harvard, Yale and Princeton.* New York, NY: Houghton Mifflin.

Kash, J. P., & Lasley, S. (2009). Defining merit: The impact of award structure on the distribution of merit aid. *Journal of Student Financial Aid, 39*(1), 30–40.

Keefe, S. E., & Padilla, A. M. (1987). *Chicano ethnicity.* Albuquerque: University of New Mexico Press.

Kellogg, A. H., & Liddell, D. L. (2012). "Not half but double": Exploring critical incidents in the racial identity of multiracial college students. *Journal of College Student Development, 53*(4), 524–541.

Keppel, F. (1987/1997). The higher education acts contrasted, 1965–1986: Has federal policy come of age? In L. F. Goodchild, C. D. Lovell, E. R. Hines, & J. I. Gill (Eds.), *Public policy and higher education: ASHE reader series,* 189–205.

Kerwin, C., & Ponterotto, J. G. (1995). Biracial identity development: Theory and research. In J. G. Ponterotto, J. M. Casas, L. A. Suzuki, & C. M. Alexander (Eds.), *Handbook of multicultural counseling* (pp. 199–217). Thousand Oaks, CA: Sage.

Killgore, L. (2009). Merit and competition in selective college admissions. *The Review of Higher Education, 32*(4), 469–488.

Kim, D. (2007). The effect of loans on students' degree attainment: Differences by student and institutional characteristics. *Harvard Educational Review, 77*(1), 64–100.

Kim, J. (2001). Asian American identity development theory. In C. Wijeyesinghe & B. W. Jackson (Eds.), *New perspectives on racial identity development: A theoretical and practical anthology* (pp. 67–90). New York, NY: NYU Press.

Kim, J. (2012). Exploring the relationship between state financial aid policy and postsecondary enrollment choices: A focus on income and race differences. *Research in Higher Education, 53,* 1–29. doi: 10.1007/s11162-011-9244-1

Kim, J., DesJardins, S. L., & McCall, B. P. (2009). Exploring the effects of student expectations about financial aid on postsecondary choice: A focus on income and racial/ethnic differences. *Research in Higher Education, 50*(8), 741–774.

Kim, J., & Gasman, M. (2011). In search of a "good" school: First and second generation Asian American students describe their college choice process. *Journal of College Student Development, 52*(6), 706–728.

Kim, M. M. (2002). Historically Black vs. White institutions: Academic development among Black students. *The Review of Higher Education, 25*(4), 385–407.

Kim, M. M., & Conrad, C. F. (2006). The impact of historically Black colleges and universities on the academic success of African-American students. *Research in Higher Education, 47*(4), 399–427.

King, A. R. (2008). Student perspectives on multiracial identity. *New Directions for Student Services, 2008*(123), 33–41.

King, J. E. (Ed.). (2005). *Black education: A transformative research and action agenda for the new century.* Mahwah, NJ: Erlbaum.

King, J. E. (2006). Working their way through college: Student employment and its impact on the college experience. *ACE Issue Brief.* Washington, DC: American Council on Education.

King, P. M. (2009). Principles of development and developmental change underlying theories of cognitive and moral development. *Journal of College Student Development, 50*(6), 597–620.

King, P. M., & Kitchener, K. S. (1994). *Developing reflective judgment: Understanding and promoting intellectual growth and critical thinking in adolescents and adults.* San Francisco, CA: Jossey-Bass.

King, S. E., & Chepyator-Thomson. (1996). Factors affecting the enrollment and persistence of African-American doctoral students. *The Physical Educator, 53*(4), 170–180.

King, T., & Bannon, E. (2002). At what cost?: *The price that working students pay for a college education.* Washington, DC: The State PIRGs' Higher Education Project. .

Kinkead, J. (2003). Learning through inquiry: An overview of undergraduate research. *New Directions for Teaching and Learning, 93,* 5–17.

Kiyama, J. M. (2010). College aspirations and limitations: The role of educational ideologies and funds of knowledge in Mexican American families. *American Educational Research Journal, 47*(2), 330–356.

Kohlberg, L. (1969). Stage and sequence: the cognitive developmental approach to socialization. In D. A. Gosling (Ed.), *Handbook of socialization theory and research* (pp. 347–480). Chicago, IL: Rand McNally.

Kolb, D. A. (1984). *Experiential learning: Experience as the source of learning and development.* Englewood Cliffs, NJ: Prentice Hall.

Konrad, A. M., & Linehan, F. (1995). Race and sex differences in line manager's reactions to equal employment opportunity and affirmative action interventions. *Groups Organization Management, 20*(4), 409–439.

Kozeracki, C. (2002). Issues in developmental education. *Community College Review, 29*(4), 83–100.

Krosteng, M. V. (1992). Predicting persistence from the student adaptation to college questionnaire: Early warning or siren song? *Research in Higher Education, 33*(1), 99–111.

Kuh, G. D. (1993). In their own words: What students learn outside the classroom. *American Educational Research Journal, 30*(2), 277–304.

Kuh, G. D. (2009). What student affairs professional needs to know about student engagement. *Journal of College Student Development, 50*(6), 683–706.

Kuh, G. D., Cruce, T. M., Shoup, R., Kinzie, J., & Gonyea, R. M. (2008). Unmasking the effects of student engagement on first-year college grades and persistence. *The Journal of Higher Education, 79*(5), 540–563.

Kuh, G. D., Hu, S., & Vesper, N. (2000). They shall be known by what they do: An activities-based typology of college students. *Journal of College Student Development, 41*(2), 228–244.

Kuh, G. D., Kinzie, J., Buckley, J. A., Bridges, B. K., & Hayek, J. C. (2006, July). What matters to student success: A review of the literature. *Commissioned report for the National Symposium on Postsecondary Student Success: Spearheading a dialog on student success.* Unpublished white paper.

Kuh, G. D., Kinzie, J., Buckley, J. A., Bridges, B. K., & Hayek, J. C. (2007). Piecing together the student success puzzle: Research, propositions, and recommendations. *ASHE Higher Education Report, 32*(5).

Kuh, G. D., Kinzie, J., Cruce, T., Shoup, R., & Gonyea, R. M. (2006). *Connecting the dots: Multi-faceted analyses of the relationships between student engagement results from the NSSE, and the institutional practices and conditions that foster student success.* Bloomington: Center for Postsecondary Research, Indiana University.

Kuh, G. D., Kinzie, J., Schuh, J. H., Whitt, E., & Associates. (2010). *Creating conditions that matter.* San Francisco, CA: Jossey-Bass.

Laanan, F. S., & Starobin, S. S. (2004). Defining Asian American and Pacific Islander-Serving Institutions. *New Directions for Community College, 127,* 49–59.

Laden, B. V. (2001). Hispanic-serving institutions: Myth and realities. *Peabody Journal of Education, 76*(1), 73–92.

LaFromboise, T. D., Trimble, J. E., & Mohatt, G. V. (1990). Counseling intervention and American Indian tradition: An integrative approach. *The Counseling Psychologist, 18*(4), 628–654.

Lammers, W. J. (2001). An informal seminar to prepare the best undergraduates for doctoral programs in psychology. *Teaching of Psychology, 28*(1), 58–59.

Lareau, A. (1987). Social class difference in family-school relationships: The importance of cultural capital. *Sociology of Education, 60*(2), 73–85.

Lareau, A. (2003). *Unequal childhoods: Class, race, and family life.* Berkeley: University of California Press.

Lavin, D. E., & Weininger, E. (1998, March 19). *New admissions criteria at the City University of New York: Ethnic and enrollment consequences and Addendum: Their impact on women.* Report prepared for hearings of the New York City Council, Committee on Higher Education. Unpublished white paper.

Lawrence, C. R. (2001). Two views of the river: A critique of the liberal defense of affirmative action. *Columbia Law Review, 101*(4), 928–976.

Law-Sander, R. H. (2004). A systematic analysis of affirmative action in American law schools. *Standard Law Review, 57*(2), 367–483.

Lee, J., & Donlan, W. (2011). American Indian/Alaskan Native undergraduate retention at predominantly White institutions: An elaboration of Tinto's theory of college student departure. *Journal of College Student Retention: Research, Theory & Practice, 12*(3), 257–276.

Lee, S. J. (2009). Behind the model minority stereotype: Voices of high and low achieving Asian American students. *Anthropology & Education Quarterly, 25*(4), 413–429.

Lemann, N. (1999). *The big test.* New York, NY: Farrar, Straus & Giroux.

LeMelle, T. T. (2002). The HBCU: Yesterday, today and tomorrow. *Education, 123*(1), 190–196.

LeMelle, T. T., & LeMelle, W. J. (1969). *The Black college: A strategy for relevancy.* New York, NY: Praeger.

Lent, R. W., Brown, S. D., & Larkin, K. C. (1984). Relation of self-efficacy expectations to academic achievement and persistence. *Journal of Counseling Psychology, 31*(3), 356–362.

Lent, R. W., Brown, S. D., & Larkin, K. C. (1986). Self-efficacy in the prediction of academic performance and perceived career options. *Journal of Counseling Psychology, 33*(3), 265–269.

Lent, R. W., Brown, S. D., & Larkin, K. C. (1987). Comparison of three theoretically derived variables in predicting career and academic behavior: Self-efficacy, interest congruence, and consequence thinking. *Journal of Counseling Psychology, 34*(3), 293–298.

Leslie, L. L., & Brinkman, P. T. (1987). Student price response in higher education: The student demand studies. *The Journal of Higher Education, 58*(2), 181–204.

Levey, C. A. (2004). Troubled waters ahead for race-based admissions. *Texas Review of Law & Politics, 9,* 63–103.

Levin, J. S. (2001). *Globalizing the community college: Strategies for change in the twenty first century.* New York, NY: Palgrave.

Lewin, K. (1935). *A dynamic theory of personality.* New York, NY: McGraw-Hill.

Lewin, T. (2007, January 26). Colleges regroup after voters ban race preferences. *New York Times.* Retrieved December 1, 2007, from http://www.nytimes.com/2007/01/26/education/26affirm.html?n=Top/Reference/Times%20Topics/People/L/Lewin,%20Tamar.

Lewis, E. (2003, October). *Affirmative action court decisions: Q & A with Dean Lewis*. A Rackham workshop. University of Michigan, Ann Arbor.

Li, Y., McCoy, E., Shelley, M. C., & Whalen, D. F. (2005). Contributors to student satisfaction with special program (fresh start) residence halls. *Journal of College Student Development, 46*(2), 176–192.

Light, A., & Strayer, W. (2000). Determinants of college completion: School quality or student ability? *Journal of Human Resources, 35*(2), 299–332.

Lin, N. (1999). Building a network theory of social capital. *Connections, 22*(1), 28–51.

Lin, R.-L. (1990). Perceptions of family background and personal characteristics among Indian college students. *Journal of American Indian Education, 29*(3), 19–26.

Locks, A. M., Hurtado, S., Bowman, N. A., & Oseguera, L. (2008). Extending notions of campus climate and diversity to students' transition to college. *The Review of Higher Education, 31*(3), 257–285.

Lohfink, M., & Paulsen, M. B. (2005). Comparing the determinants of persistence for first-generation and continuing-generation students. *Journal of College Student Development, 46*(4), 409–428.

Long, B. T., & Riley, E. (2007). Financial aid: A broken bridge to college access? *Harvard Educational Review, 77*(1), 39–63.

Long, M. C. (2004a). College applications and the effect of affirmative actions. *Journal of Econometrics, 121*, 319–342.

Long, M. C. (2004b). Race and college admissions: An alternative to affirmative action? *The Review of Economics and Statistics, 86*(4), 1020–1033. doi:10.1162/0034653043125211

Long, M. C. (2007). Affirmative action and its alternatives in public universities: What do we know? *Public Administration Review, 67*, 315–330. doi:10.1111/j.1540-6210.2007.00715.x

Long, M.C., Sáenz, V., & Tienda, M. (2006). Policy transparency and college enrollment: Did the Texas Top Ten Percent Law broaden access to the public flagships? *Economics of Education Reviews, 25*(1), 109–119.

Long, M. C., & Tienda, M. (2008). Winners and losers: Changes in Texas university admissions Post-Hopwood. *Educational Evaluation and Policy Analysis, 30*(3), 255–280.

Loo, C. M., & Rolison, G. (1986). Alienation of ethnic minority students at a predominantly white university. *The Journal of Higher Education,57*(1), 58-77.

Lopatto, D. (2003). The essential features of undergraduate research. *Council on Undergraduate Research Quarterly, 23*, 139–142.

Love, B. J. (1993). Issues and problems in the retention of Black students in predominantly White institutions of higher education. *Equity and Excellence in Education, 26*, 27–33. doi:10.1080/1066568930260105

Lovitts, B. E. (2001). *Leaving the ivory tower: The causes and consequences of departure from doctoral study*. Lanham, MD: Rowman & Littlefield .

Lundberg, C. A., Schreiner, L. A., Hovaguimian, K. D., & Miller, S. S. (2007). First-generation status and student race/ ethnicity as distinct predictors of student involvement and learning. *NASPA Journal, 44*(1), 57–83.

Lundy-Wagner, V., & Gasman, M. (2011). When gender issues are not just about women: Reconsidering male students at historically Black colleges and universities. *Teachers College Record, 113*(5), 934–968.

Lundy-Wagner, V., & Winkle-Wagner, R. (2013). A harassing climate? The implications of sexual harassment for campus climate. *Journal of Diversity in Higher Education, 6*(1), 51–68.

MacCallum, M. (2008). Effect of financial aid processing policies on student enrollment, retention and success. *Journal of Student Financial Aid, 37*(2), 17–32.

Maekawa Kodama, C., McEwen, M. K., Liang, C. T., & Lee, S. (2002). An Asian American perspective on psychosocial student development theory. In M. K. McEwen, C. M. Kodoma, A. N. Alvarez, S. Lee, & C. T. H. Liang (Eds.), *Working with Asian American college students* (pp. 45–59; New Directions for Student Services, no. 97). San Francisco, CA: Jossey-Bass.

Maher, F. A., & Tetreault, M. K. T. (2007). *Privilege and diversity in the academy*. New York, NY: Routledge.

Maldonado, D. E. Z., Rhoads, R. & Buenavista, T. L. (2009). The student-initiated retention project: theoretical contributions and the role of self-empowerment. *American Educational Research Journal, 42*(4), 605–638.

Maralani, V. (2011). From GED to college age trajectories of nontraditional educational paths. *American Educational Research Journal, 48*(5), 1058–1090.

Maramba, D. C. (2008). Understanding campus climate through the voices of Filipina/o American college students. *College Student Journal, 42*(4), 1045–1060.

Marcia, J. (1966). Development and validation of ego-identity status. *Journal of Personality and Social Psychology, 3*, 551–588. doi:10.1037/h0023281

Marcus, J. (2000). Revamping remedial education. *National CrossTalk, 8*(1). Retrieved from http://www.highereducation.org/crosstalk/ct0100/news0100-revamp.shtml

Marin, P., & Horn, C. L. (Eds.). (2008). *Realizing Bakke's legacy: Affirmative action, equal opportunity, and access to higher education*. Sterling, VA: Stylus.

Marks , H. M., & Robb, S. R. (2004). Community service in the transition: Shifts and continuities in participation from high school to college. *Journal of Higher Education, 75*(3), 307–339.

Marti, C. N. (2008). Latent postsecondary persistence pathways: Educational pathways in American two-year colleges. *Research in Higher Education, 49*(4), 317–336.

Martin, A. J. (2009). Motivation and engagement across the academic life span: A developmental construct validity study of elementary school, high school, and university/college students. *Educational and Psychological Measurement, 69*(5), 794–782.

Martinez, M., & Klopott, S. (2005). *The link between high school reform and college access and success for low-income and minority youth.* Washington, DC: American Youth Policy Forum.

Martínez Alemán, A. M. (2000). Race talks: Undergraduate women of color and female friendships. *The Review of Higher Education, 23*(2), 133–152.

Mayhew, M. J. (2012). A multilevel examination of the influence of institutional type on the moral reasoning development of first-year students. *The Journal of Higher Education, 83*(3), 367–388.

Mayhew, M. J., & Grunwald, H. E. (2006). Factors contributing to faculty incorporation of diversity-related course content. *Journal of Higher Education, 77*(1), 148–168.

Mayhew, M. J., Grunwald, H. E., & Dey, E. L. (2006). Breaking the silence: Achieving a positive campus climate for diversity from the staff perspective. *Research in Higher Education, 41*(1), 63–88.

McAtee, A. B., & Benschoff, J. M. (2006). Rural dislocated women in career transition: The importance of support and strategies. *Community College Journal of Research and Practice, 30,* 697–714. doi: 10.1080/10668920500207858

McCabe, R. (2000). *No one to waste: A report to public decision-makers and community college leaders.* Washington, DC: American Association of Community Colleges, Community College Press.

McCallister, L., Evans, J., & Illich, P. (2010). Perceptions about higher education among parents of Hispanic students in middle school: Implications for community colleges. *Community College Journal of Research and Practice, 34*(10), 784–796.

McCallum, C. M. (in press). Examining first-generation doctoral students' decision to pursue the doctorate. In E. M. Zamani-Gallaher & V. C. Polite (Eds.), *Pride, pain, and promise: Addressing challenges and nurturing the future of African American females.* Lansing: Michigan State University Press.

McCarn, S. R., & Fassinger, R. E. (1996). Revisioning sexual minority identity formation: A new model of lesbian identity and its implications for counseling and research. *The Counseling Psychologist, 24,* 508–534. doi:10.1177/0011000096243011

McCoy, D. L. (2007). Entering the academy: Exploring the socialization of African American male faculty at HBCUs and PWIs. *Journal of the Professoriate, 2*(2), 75–91.

McDermott, M., & Samson F.L. (2005). White racial and ethnic identity in the United States. *Annual Review of Sociology, 31,* 245–261. doi:10.1146/annurev.soc.31.041304.122322

McDonough, P. M. (1997). *Choosing colleges: How social class and schools structure opportunity.* Albany, NY: State University of New York Press.

McDonough, P. M. (2005). Counseling and college counseling in America's high schools. In D. Hawkins (Ed.), *The 2004–2005 state of college admission* (pp. 102–127). Washington, DC: National Association for College Admission Counseling.

McDonough, P. M., & Calderone, S. (2006). The meaning of money perceptual differences between college counselors and low-income families about college costs and financial aid. *American Behavioral Scientist, 49*(12), 1703–1718.

McDonough, P. M., & Fann, A. J. (2007). The study of inequality. In P. J. Gumport (Ed.), *Sociology of higher education: Contributions and their contexts* (pp. 53–93). Baltimore, MD: John Hopkins University Press.

McDonough, P. M., Lising, A., Walpole, A. M., & Perez, L. X. (1998). College rankings: democratized college knowledge for whom? *Research in Higher Education, 39*(5), 513–537.

McDonough, P. M., McClafferty, K. A., & Fann, A. J. (2002, April). *Rural college opportunity: Issues and challenges.* Paper presented at the 2002 annual meeting of the American Educational Research Association, New Orleans.

McEwen, M. K. (1996). New perspectives on identity development. In S. R. Komives & D. B. Woodard Jr. (Eds.), *Student services: A handbook for the profession* (3rd ed., pp. 188–217). San Francisco, CA: Jossey-Bass.

McGee, E. O., & Martin, D. B. (2011). "You would not believe what I have to go through to prove my intellectual value!" Stereotype management among academically successful black Mathematics and engineering students. *American Educational Research Journal, 48*(6), 1347–1389.

McIntosh, P. (1998). White privilege, color, and crime: A personal account. In C. R. Mann & M. S. Katz (Eds.), *Images of color and images of crime: Readings* (pp. 207–216). Los Angeles, CA: Roxbury.

McIntyre, A. (1997). *Making meaning of whiteness: Exploring racial identity with White teachers.* Albany, NY: SUNY Press.

McPherson, M. S., & Shapiro, M. O. (1999). *The student aid game: Meeting need and rewarding talent in American higher education.* Princeton, NJ: Princeton University Press.

McSwain, C., & Davis, R. (2007). *College access for the working poor: Overcoming burdens to succeed in higher education.* Washington, DC: Institute for Higher Education Policy.

McWade, P. (1995). Financial aid for graduate study. *New Directions for Student Services, 72,* 51–57.

Mead, G. H. (1967). *Mind, self, and society: From the standpoint of a social behaviorist* (Vol. 1). Chicago. IL: University of Chicago Press. (Original work published in 1934)

Mehan, H., Hubbard, L., & Villanueva, I. (1994). Forming academic identities: Accommodation without assimilation among involuntary minorities. *Anthropology and Education Quarterly, 25*(2), 91–117.

Melendez, M. C., & Melendez, N. B. (2010). The influence of parental attachment on the college adjustment of White, Black, and Latina/Hispanic women: A cross-cultural investigation. *Journal of College Student Development, 51*(4), 419–435.

Melguizo, T. (2008). Quality matters: Assessing the impact of attending more selective institutions on college completion rates of minorities. *Research in Higher Education, 49*(3), 214–236.

Melguizo, T. (2009). Are community colleges an alternative path for Hispanic students to attain a bachelor's degree?. *The Teachers College Record, 111*(1), 90–123.

Mendoza, P., Mendez, J. P., & Malcolm, Z. (2009). Financial aid and persistence in community colleges: Assessing the effectiveness of federal and state financial aid programs in Oklahoma. *Community College Review, 37*(2), 112–135.

Mercer, C. J., & Stedman, J. B. (2008). Minority-serving institutions: Selected institutional and student characteristics. In M. Gasman, B. Baez, & C. S. V. Turner (Eds.), *Understanding minority-serving institutions* (pp. 28–42). Albany: State University of New York Press.

Meredith, M. (2004). Why do universities compete in the ratings game? An empirical analysis of the effects of the US News and World Report college rankings. *Research in Higher Education, 45*(5), 443–461.

Merisotis, J., & Phipps, R. (2000). Remedial education in colleges and universities: What's really going on? *The Review of Higher Education, 24*(1), 67–85.

Merker, B. M., & Smith, J. V. (2001). Validity of the MMPI-2 College Maladjustment Scale. *Journal of College Counseling, 4*(1), 3–9.

Milem, J. F., Chang, M. J., & Antonio, A. L. (2005). *Making diversity work on campus: A research-based perspective.* Retrieved April 23, 2007, from http//:www.aacu.org/inclusive_excellence/

Milem, J. F., Dey, E. L., & and White, C. B. (2004). Diversity considerations in health professions education. In B. D. Smedley, A. S. Butler, & L. R. Bristow (Eds.), *In the nation's compelling interest: Ensuring diversity in the health care workforce* (pp. 345–390). Washington, DC: National Academies Press.

Miller, M. H., Anderson, R., Cannon, J. G., Perez, E. & Moore, H. A. (1998). Campus racial climate policies: The view form the bottom up. *Race, Gender, and Class, 5*(2), 139–157.

Milner, H. R., Husband, T., & Jackson, M. P. (2002). Voices of persistence and self-efficacy: African American graduate students and professors who affirm them. *Journal of Critical Inquiry into Curriculum and Instructions, 4*(1), 33–39.

Milner, R. M. (2004). African American graduate students' experiences: A critical analysis of recent research. In D. Cleveland (Ed.), *A long way to go: Conversations about race by African American faculty and graduate students* (pp. 19–31). New York, NY: Peter Lang.

Mitchell, S. L., & Dell, D.M. (1992). The relationship between Black students' racial identity attitude and participation in campus organizations. *Journal of College Student Development, 33*(1), 39–43.

Moore, J. V., & Rago, M. (2009). The impact of employment on student engagement: Results from NSSE. In B. Perozzi (Ed.), *Enhancing student learning through college employment* (pp. 87–107). Bloomington, IN: Association of College Unions International.

Morehouse College. (n.d.). Mission statement. Retrieved from http://www.morehouse.edu/about/mission.html)

Morris, L. K., & Daniel, L. G. (2008). Perceptions of a chilly climate: Differences in traditional and non-traditional majors for women. *Research in Higher Education, 49*(3), 256–273.

Moses, M. S. (2001). Affirmative action and the creation of more favorable contexts of choice. *American Educational Research Journal, 38*(1), 3–36.

Moses, M. S. (2002). *Embracing race: Why we need race-conscious education policy.* New York, NY: Teachers College Press.

Moses, M. S. (2004). Contested ideals: Understanding moral disagreements over education policy. *Journal of Social Philosophy, 35*(4), 471–482.

Moses, M. S. (2010). Moral and instrumental rationales for affirmative action in five national contexts. *Educational Researcher, 39*(3), 211–228.

Moses, M. S., & Chang, M. J. (2006). Toward a deeper understanding of the diversity rationale. *Educational Researcher, 35*(1), 6–11.

Moses, M. S., & Saenz, L. P. (2008). Hijacking education policy decisions: The case of affirmative action. *Harvard Educational Review, 78*(2), 289–310.

Moses, M. S., Yun, J. T., & Marin, P. (2009). Affirmative action's fate: Are 20 more years enough? *Education Policy Analysis Archives, 17*(17). Retrieved from http://epaa.asu.edu/epaa/v17n17/

Mueller, J. A., & Cole, J. C. (2009). A qualitative examination of heterosexual consciousness among college students. *Journal of College Student Development, 50*(3), 320–336.

Mullen, A. L., Goyette, K. A., & Soares, J. A. (2003). Who goes to grad school? Social and academic correlates of educational continuation after college. *Sociology of Education, 76*(2), 143–169.

Multon, K. D., Brown, S. D., & Lent, R. W. (1991). Relation of self-efficacy beliefs to academic outcomes: A meta-analytic investigation. *Journal of Counseling Psychology, 38*(1), 30–38.

Murnane, R. J., Willett, J. B., & Tyler, J. H. (2000). Who benefits from obtaining a GED? Evidence from high school and beyond. *The Review of Economics and Statistics, 82*, 23–37. doi:10.1162/003465300558605

Murr, C. D. (2010). A scholarship workshop program to improve underrepresented student access to higher education. *Journal of Student Financial Aid, 40*(2), 31–38.

Museus, S. D. (2008). The role of ethnic student organizations in fostering African American and Asian American students' cultural adjustment and membership at predominantly White institutions. *Journal of College Student Development, 49*(6), 568–586.

Museus, S. D. (2009). A critical analysis of the exclusion of Asian American from higher education research and discourse. In L. Zhan (Ed.), *Asian American voices: Engaging, empowering, enabling* (pp. 59–76). New York, NY: NLN Press.

Museus, S. D., & Kiang, P. N. (2009). Deconstructing the model minority myth and how it contributes to the invisible minority reality in higher education research. *New Directions for Institutional Research, 142*, 5-15.

Museus, S. D., & Maramba, D. C. (2011). The impact of culture on Filipino American students' sense of belonging. *The Review of Higher Education, 34*(2), 231–258.

Myers, I. B. (1980). *Gifts differing*. Palo Alto, CA: Counseling Psychologists Press.

Myers, R. D. (2003). *College success programs: Executive summary*. Washington, DC: Pathways to College Network Clearinghouse.

Nadal, K. L. (2004). Pilipino American identity development model. *Journal of Multicultural counseling and development, 32*(1), 45–62.

Nagel, J. (1995). American Indian ethnic renewal: Politics and the resurgence of identity. *American Sociological Review*, 947–965.

Nagel, J. (1997). *American Indian ethnic renewal: Red power and the resurgence of identity and culture*. New York, NY: Oxford University Press.

National Center for Education Statistics (NCES). (1996). *Historically Black colleges and universities: 1976–1994*. Washington DC: Author. Retrieved October 3, 2003, from http://nces.ed.gov/pubs2003/2003161.pdf

National Center for Education Statistics (NCES). (2006). *Descriptive summary of 1989–90 beginning postsecondary students: 5 years later*. Retrieved June 24, 2006, from http://nces.ed.gov/pubs/web/96155t01.asp

National Center for Education Statistics (NCES). (2011). Table 210. Recent high school completes and their enrollment in 2-year and 4-year colleges, by race/ethnicity: 1960–2010. Washington, DC: *Digest of Education Statistics*. Retrieved from http://nces.ed.gov/programs/digest/d11/tables/dt11_210.asp

National Center for Education Statistics (NCES). (2012, June 30). Table 346. Retention of first-time degree-seeking undergraduates at degree-granting institutions, by attendance status, control and level of institution, and percentage of applications accepted: 2006 to 2010. *Digest of Education Statistics*. Retrieved from http://nces.ed.gov/programs/digest/d11/tables/dt11_346.asp

National Survey of Student Engagement. (2009). *Assessment for improvement: Tracking student engagement over time—annual results 2009*. Bloomington: Indiana University Center for Postsecondary Research.

Nelson Laird, T. F., Engberg, M. E., & Hurtado, S. (2005). Modeling accentuation effects: Enrolling in a diversity course and the importance of social action engagement. *The Journal of Higher Education, 76*(4), 448–476.

Ness, E. C. (2010). The politics of determining merit aid eligibility criteria: An analysis of the policy process. *The Journal of Higher Education, 81*(1), 33–60.

Ness, E. C., & Tucker, R. (2008). Eligibility effects on college access: Under-represented student perceptions of Tennessee's merit aid program. *Research in Higher Education, 49*(7), 569–588.

Nettles, M. (1990). Success in doctoral programs: Experiences of minority and White students. *American Journal of Education, 98*(4), 494–522.

Nettles, M., & Millett, C.M. (2006). *Three magic letters: Getting to PhD*. Baltimore, MD: The Johns Hopkins University Press.

Nettles, M. T. (1998). Black and White students' performance and experiences at various types of universities. In M. T. Nettles (Ed.), *Toward Black undergraduate student equality in American higher education* (pp. 57–86). Westport, CT: Greenwood Press.

Neumann, A. (2006). Professing passion: Emotion in the scholarship of professors at research universities. *American Educational Research Journal, 43*(3), 381–424.

Neumann, A. (2009). *Professing to learn: Creating tenured lives and careers in American research universities*. Baltimore, MD: The Johns Hopkins University Press.

Nilsson, J.E., Paul, B.D., Lupini, L.N., & Tatem, B. (1999). Cultural differences in perfectionism: A comparison of African American and White college students. *Journal of College Student Development, 40*(2), 140-150.

Nora, A. (1990). Campus-based aid programs as determinates of retention among Hispanic community college students. *Journal of Higher Education, 61*(3), 312–327.

Nora, A., Barlow, L., & Crisp, G. (2006). An assessment of Hispanic students in four-year institutions of higher education. In A. M. Gloria, J. Castellanos, & M. Kamimura (Eds.), *The Latina/o pathway to the Ph.D.: Abriendo caminos* (pp. 55–78). Sterling, VA: Stylus.

Nora, A., & Cabrera, A. F. (1996). The role of perceptions of prejudice and discrimination on the adjustment of minority students to college. *The Journal of Higher Education, 67*(2), 119–148.

Nora, A., Cabrera, A., Serra Hagedorn, L., & Pascarella, E. (1996). Differential impacts of academic and social experiences on college-related behavioral outcomes across different ethnic and gender groups at four-year institutions. *Research in Higher Education, 37*(4), 427–451.

Noy, S., & Ray, R. (2012). Graduate students' perceptions of their advisors: Is there systematic disadvantage in mentorship? *The Journal of Higher Education, 83*(6), 876–914.

Nuñez, A. (2011). Counterspaces and connections in college transitions: First-generation Latino students' perspectives on Chicano studies. *Journal of College Student Development, 56*(2), 639–655. doi:10.1353/csd.2011.0077

Nyirenda, S. M., & Gong, T. (2009). The squishy and stubborn problem of retention: A study of a mid Atlantic historically black institution with a land-grant mission. *Journal of College Student Retention: Research, Theory and Practice, 11*(4), 529–550.

Oakes, J. (1994). More than misapplied technology: A normative and political response to Hallinan on tracking. *Sociology of Education, 67*(2), 84–88.

Oakes, J. (1995). Two cities' tracking and within-school segregation. *Teachers College Record, 96*(4), 681–690.

Oakes, J., Wells, A. S., Jones, M., & Datnow, A. (1997). Detracking: The social construction of ability, cultural politics and resistance to reform. *Teachers College Record, 98*(2), 482–510.

Obama, B. (2013). *Inaugural address by President Barack Obama.* Retrieved from http://www.whitehouse.gov/the-press-office/2013/01/21/inaugural-address-president-barack-obama

O'Connor, C., Mueller, J., Lewis, R. H., Rivas-Drake, D., & Rosenberg, S. (2011). "Being" Black and strategizing for excellence in a racially stratified academic hierarchy. *American Educational Research Journal, 48*(6), 1232–1257.

O'Connor, N. (2009). Hispanic origin, socio-economic status, and community college enrollment. *The Journal of Higher Education, 80*(2), 121–145.

O'Connor, N., Hammack, F. M., & Scott, M. A. (2010). Social capital, financial knowledge, and Hispanic student college choices. *Research in Higher Education, 51*(3), 195–219.

Ogbu, J. U. (1987). Variability in minority school performance: A problem in search of an explanation. *Anthropology and Education Quarterly, 18*(4), 312–334.

Ogbu, J. U., & Davis, A. (2003). *Black American students in an affluent suburb: A study of academic disengagement.* Mahwah, NJ: Erlbaum.

Ogletree, C. J., & Eaton, S. (2009). Afterword. In E. Zamani-Gallaher, D. O. Green, M. C. Brown, & D. O. Stovall, *The case for affirmative action on campus* (pp. 202–206). Sterling, VA: Stylus.

Okagaki, L., Helling, M. K., & Bingham, G. E. (2009). American Indian college students' ethnic identity and beliefs about education. *Journal of College Student Development, 50*(2), 157–176.

Olivas, M. A. (2011). If you build it, they will assess it (or, an open letter to George Kuh, with love and respect). *The Review of Higher Education, 35*(1), 1–16.

O'Neil, J. M., Egan, J., Owen, S. V., & Murry, V. M. (1993). The gender role journey measure: Scale development and psychometric evaluation. *Sex Roles, 28*, 167–185.

Orentlicher, D. (1998). Affirmative action and Texas' Ten percent solution: Improving diversity and quality. *Notre Dame Law Review, 1*(74), 181–210.

Orfield, G. (1992). Money, equity, and college access. *Harvard Educational Review, 62*(3), 337–373.

Orfield, G., & Lee, C. (2005). *Why segregation matters: Poverty and educational inequality.* Cambridge, MA: The Civil Rights Project.

Orfield, G., & Miller, E. (Eds.). (1998). *Chilling admissions: The affirmation action crisis and the search for alternatives.* Cambridge, MA: Harvard Education Publishing Group.

Orsuwan, M., & Heck, R. H. (2009). Merit-based student aid and freshman interstate college migration: Testing a dynamic model of policy change. *Research in Higher Education, 50*(1), 24–51.

Ortiz, A. M., & Boyer, P. (2003). Student assessment in tribal colleges. *New Directions for Institutional Research, 118,* 41–49.

Ortiz, A. M., & HeavyRunner, I. (2003). Student access, retention, and success: Models of inclusion and support. In M. K. P. Benham & W. J. Stein (Eds.), *The renaissance of American Indian higher education* (pp. 215–240). Hillsdale, NJ: Erlbaum.

Ortiz, A. M., & Rhoads, R. A. (2000). Deconstructing whiteness as part of a multicultural educational framework: From theory to practice. *Journal of College Student Development, 41*(1), 81–93.

Oseguera, L. (2006). Four and six-year baccalaureate degree completion by institutional characteristics and racial/ethnic groups. *The Journal of College Student Retention, 7*(1–2), 19–59.

Oseguera, L., Locks, A. M., & Vega, I. I. (2009). Increasing Latina/o students' baccalaureate attainment: A focus on retention. *Journal of Hispanic Higher Education, 8*(1), 23–53.

Ossana, S. M., Helms, J. E., & Leonard, M. M. (1992). Do "womanist" identity attitudes influence college women's self-esteem and perceptions of environmental bias? *Journal of Counseling & Development, 70,* 402–408. doi:10.1002/j.1556-6676.1992.tb01624.x

Outcalt, C. L., & Skewes-Cox, T. E. (2002). Involvement, interaction, and satisfaction: The human environment at HBCUs. *The Review of Higher Education, 25*(3), 331–347.

Ovink, S. M., & Veazey, B. D. (2011). More than "getting us through": A case study in cultural capital enrichment of underrepresented minority undergraduates. *Research in Higher Education, 52*(4), 370–394.

Owen, S. V., & Froman, R. D. (1988, April). *Development of a college academic self-efficacy scale.* Paper presented at the annual meeting of the National Council on Measurement in Education, New Orleans, LA.

Owens, T. J., & Serpe, R. T. (2003). The role of self-evaluation in identity salience and commitment. In P. J. Burke, T. J. Owens, R. T. Serpe, & P. Thoits (Eds.), *Advances in identity theory and research.* (pp. 85–104). New York, NY: Kluwer Academic/Plenum Publishers.

Oyserman, D., Brickman, D., & Rhodes, M. (2007). Racial-ethnic identity: Content and consequences for African American, Latino and Latina youth. In A. Fuligni (Ed.), *Contesting stereotypes and creating identities: Social categories, social identities and educational participation* (pp. 91–114). New York, NY: Russell Sage.

Oyserman, D., Kemmelmeier, M., Fryberg, S., Brosh, H., & Hart-Johnson, T. (2003). Racial-ethnic self schemas. *Social Psychology Quarterly, 66*(4), 333–347.

Pace, C. R. (1984). *Measuring the quality of college student experiences.* Los Angeles: University of California, Higher Education Research Institute.

Padgett, R. D., Goodman, K. M., Johnson, M. P., Saichaie, K., Umbach, P. D., & Pascarella, E. T. (2010). The impact of college student socialization, social class, and race on need for cognition. *New Directions for Institutional Research, 145,* 99–111. doi:10.1002/ir.324

Padgett, R. D., Johnson, M. P., & Pascarella, E. T. (2012). First-generation undergraduate students and the impacts of the first year of college: Additional evidence. *Journal of College Student Development, 53*(2), 243–266.

Padilla, R. V., Treviño, J., Gonzalez, K., & Trevino, J. (1997). Developing local models of minority students success in college. *Journal of College Student Development, 38*(2), 125–135.

Padula, M., & Miller, D. (1999). Understanding graduate women's reentry experiences. *Psychology of Women Quarterly, 23*(2), 327–343.

Pajares, F. (1996). Self-efficacy beliefs in academic settings. *Review of Educational Research, 6*(4), 543–578. doi:10.3102/00346543066004543

Palmer, R. T., Davis, R. J., & Hilton, A. A. (2009). Exploring challenges that threaten to impede the academic success of academically underprepared Black males at an HBCU. *Journal of College Student Development, 50*(4), 429–445.

Palmer, R. T., Davis, R. J., & Maramba, D. C. (2010). Role of an HBCU in supporting academic success for underprepared Black males. *Negro Educational Review, 61*(1–4), 85–124.

Palmer, R. T., Davis, R. J., & Maramba, D. C. (2011). The impact of family support on the success of black men at an Historically Black University: Affirming the revision of Tinto's theory. *Journal of College Student Development, 52*(5), 577–597.

Palmer, R., & Gasman, M. (2008). "It takes a village to raise a child": The role of social capital in promoting academic success for African American men at a Black College. *Journal of College Student Development, 49*(1), 52–70.

Parham, T., & Helms, J. E. (1981). The influence of Black students' racial identity attitudes on preferences for counselor's race. *Journal of Counseling Psychology, 28*(3), 250–257.

Park, J. J. (2009). Taking race into account: Charting student attitudes towards affirmative action. *Research in Higher Education, 50*(7), 670–690.

Pascarella, E. T., Pierson, C. T., Wolniak, G. C., & Terenzini, P. T. (2004). First-generation college students: Additional evidence on college experiences and outcomes. *The Journal of Higher Education, 75*(3), 249–284.

Pascarella, E. T., & Terenzini, P. T. (1991). *How college affects students: Findings and insights from 20 years of research.* San Francisco, CA: Jossey-Bass.

Pascarella, E. T., & Terenzini, P. T. (2005). *How college affects students: A third decade of research.* San Francisco, CA: Jossey Bass.

Passel, J. S., & Cohn, D. (2008). *U.S. population projections: 2005–2050.* Retrieved from http://pewsocialtrends.org/files/2010/10/85.pdf

Patchner, M. (1982). A decade of social work doctoral graduates: Their characteristics and educational programs. *Journal of Education for Social Work, 18*(2), 35–41.

Pathways to College Network. (2003, August). *A shared agenda: A leadership challenge to improve college access and success.* Washington, DC: Pathways to College Network.

Patton, L. D. (2006). The voice of reason: A qualitative examination of Black student perceptions of Black culture centers. *Journal of College Student Development, 47*(6), 628–646.

Patton, L. D. (2009). My sister's keeper: A qualitative examination of mentoring experiences among African American women in graduate and professional schools. *The Journal of Higher Education, 80*(5), 510–537.

Patton, L. D. (2011). Perspectives on identity, disclosure and the campus environment among African American gay and bisexual men at one historically Black college. *Journal of College Student Development, 52*(1), 77–100.

Patton, L. A., & Bonner, F. A. II (2001). Advising the historically Black Greek letter organization (HBGLO): A reason for angst or euphoria? *National Association of Student Affairs Professional Journal, 4*(1), 17–30.

Patton, L. D., & Harper, S. R. (2003). Mentoring relationships among African American women in graduate and professional schools. In M. F. Howard-Hamilton (Ed.), *Meeting the needs of African American women. New Directions for Student Services* (No. 104, pp. 67–78). San Francisco, CA: Jossey-Bass.

Paulsen, M. B. (2001). The economics of human capital and investment in higher education. In M. B. Paulsen & J. C. Smart (Eds.), *The finance of higher education: Theory, research, policy and practice* (pp. 55–94). New York, NY: Agathon Press.

Pavel, M., & Padilla, R. (1993). American Indian and Alaska Native postsecondary departure: An example of assessing a mainstream model using national longitudinal data. *Journal of American Indian Education, 32*(2), 1–23.

Peppas, N. A. (1981). Student preparation for graduate school through undergraduate research. *Chemical Engineering Education, 15*(3), 135–137.

Perez, P. A., & McDonough, P. M. (2008). Understanding Latina and Latino college choice: A social capital and chain migration analysis. *Journal of Hispanic Higher Education, 7*(3), 249–265.

Peréz, W. (2011). *American by heart: Undocumented Latino students and the promise of higher education.* New York, NY: Teachers College Press.

Peréz, W., & Cortés, R. D. (2011). *Undocumented Latino college students: Their socioemotional and academic experiences.* El Paso, TX: LFB Publishing.

Perna, L. W. (2000). Differences in the decision to attend college among African Americans, Hispanics, and Whites. *The Journal of Higher Education, 71*(2), 117–141.

Perna, L. W. (2001). The contribution of historically Black college and university to the preparation of African Americans for faculty careers. *Research in Higher Education, 42*(3), 267–294.

Perna, L. W. (2006). Understanding the relationship between information about college prices and financial aid and students' college-related behaviors. *American Behavioral Scientist, 49*(12), 1620–1635.

Perna, L. W. (2007). Improving the transition from high school to college in Minnesota: Recommendations based on a review of effective programs. *Growth & Justice.* St. Paul: MN.

Perna, L. W. (2008). Understanding high school students' willingness to borrow to pay college prices. *Research in Higher Education, 49*(7), 589–606.

Perna, L. W., Lundy-Wagner, V., Drezner, N. D., Gasman, M. Yoon, S., Bose, E., & Gary, S. (2009). The contributions of HBCUs to the preparation of African American women for STEM careers: A case study. *Research in Higher Education, 50*(1), 1–23. doi:10.1007/s11162-008-9110-y

Perna, L. W., & Titus, M. A. (2004). Understanding differences in the choice of college attended: The role of state public policies. *Review of Higher Education, 27*(4), 501–526.

Perna, L. W., & Titus, M. A. (2005). The relationship between parental involvement as social capital and college enrollment: An examination of racial/ethnic group differences. *The Journal of Higher Education, 76*(5), 485–518.

Perry, W. (1970). *Forms of intellectual and ethical development in the college years.* New York, NY: Holt, Rhinehart, & Wilson.

Peterson, M., Blackburn, R. T., Gamson, Z., Arce, C. H., Davenport, R. W., & Mingle, J. R. (1978). *Black students on White campuses: The impacts of increased Black enrollments.* Ann Arbor: Institute for Social Research, University of Michigan.

Phinney, J. S. (1992). The multigroup ethnic identity measure: A new scale for use with diverse groups. *Journal of Adolescent Research, 7*(2), 156–176.

Piaget, J. (1952). *The origins of intelligence in children.* New York, NY: International Universities Press.

Picard, I. A., & Guido-DiBrito, F. (1993). Listening to the voice of care: Women's moral development and implications for student affairs practitioners. *Iowa Student Personnel Association Journal, 8*, 21–34.

Pike, G. R., Kuh, G. D., & Gonyea, R. M. (2007). Evaluating the rationale for affirmative action in college admissions: Direct and indirect relationships between campus diversity and gains in understanding diverse groups. *Journal of College Student Development, 48*(2), 166–182.

Pitre, P. E. (2006). College choice: A study of African American and white student aspirations and perceptions related to college attendance. *College Student Journal, 40*(3), 562.

Ponterotto, J. G., Casas, J. M., Suzuki, L. A., & Alexander, C. M. (2001). *Handbook of multicultural counseling.* Thousand Oaks, CA: Sage.

Poock, M. C. (2000). African American students and the decision to attend doctoral programs in higher education administration. *College Student Affairs Journal, 19*(2), 51–59.

Portes, A. (1998). Social capital: Its origins and applications in modern sociology. *Annual Review of Sociology, 24*, 1–24.

Poston, W. (1990). The biracial identity development model: A needed addition. *Journal of Counseling & Development, 69*(2), 152–155.

Prillerman, S. L., Myers, H. F., & Smedley, B. D. (1989). *Stress, well-being and academic achievement in college.* Newbury Park, CA: Sage.

Radford, A., Berkner, L., Wheeless, S., & Shepherd, B. (2010). *Persistence and attainment of 2003–2004 beginning postsecondary students: After 6 years.* NCES 2011-151. Washington, DC: U.S. Department of Education, Office of Educational Research and Improvement.

Ramos-Sanchez, L., & Nichols, L. (2007). Self-efficacy of first-generation and non-first-generation college students: The relationship with academic performance and college adjustment. *Journal of College Counseling, 10*(1), 6–18. doi:10.1002/j.2161-1882.2007.tb00002.x

Rankin, S. R., & Reason, R. D. (2005). Differing perceptions: How students of color and white students perceive campus climate for underrepresented groups. *Journal of College Student Development, 46*(1), 43–61.

Ravitch, D. (1995). *National standards in American education: A citizen's guide.* Washington, DC: The Brookings Institution.

Rawls, J. (1999). *A theory of justice.* Cambridge, MA: Harvard University Press.

Rayle, A. D., Kurpius, S. E. R., & Arredondo, P. (2007). Relationships of self-beliefs, social support, and university comfort with academic success of freshman college women. *Journal of College Student Retention: Research, Theory, and Practice, 8*(3), 325–343.

Reason, R. D., Terenzini, P. T., & Domingo, R. J. (2006). First things first: Developing academic competence in the first year of college. *Research in Higher Education, 47*(2), 149–175.

Redd, K. E. (1998). Historically Black Colleges and Universities: Making a Comeback. In J. P. Merisotis & C. T. O'Brien (Eds.), *Minority-serving institutions: Distinct purposes, common goals.* New Directions in Higher Education, no. 102. San Francisco, CA: Jossey- Bass.

Regents of the University of California v. Bakke, 438 U.S. 265 (1978).

Reid, M. J., & Moore, J. L. (2008). College readiness and academic preparation for postsecondary education: Oral histories of first-generation urban college students. *Urban Education, 43*(2), 240–261.

Rendón, L. I. (1994). Validating cultural diverse students: Toward a new model of learning and student development. *Innovative Higher Education, 19*(1), 3-51. doi: 10.1007/BF01191156

Rendón, L. I. (2002). Community college puente: A validating model of education. *Educational Policy, 16*(4), 642–667.

Rendón, L. I., & Hope, R. O. (1996). *Educating a new majority: Transforming America's educational system for diversity.* San Francisco, CA: Jossey-Bass.

Rendón, L. I., Hope, R., & Associates. (1996). *Educating a new majority: Transforming America's educational system for diversity.* San Francisco, CA: Jossey-Bass.

Rendón, L. I., Jalomo, R. E., & Nora, A. (2000). Theoretical considerations in the study of minority student retention in higher education. In J. M. Braxton (Ed.), *Reworking the student departure puzzle* (pp. 127–156). Nashville, TN: Vanderbilt University Press.

Rendón, L., & Nora, A. (1997). *Student academic progress: Key trends. Report prepared for the national center for urban partnerships.* New York, NY: Ford Foundation.

Renn, K. A. (2000). Patterns of situational identity among biracial and multiracial college students. *The Review of Higher Education, 23*(4), 399–420.

Renn, K. A. (2003). Understanding the identities of mixed-race college students through a development ecology lens. *Journal of College Student Development, 44*, 383–403. doi:10.1353/csd.2003.0032

Renn, K. A. (2004). *Mixed race students in college: The ecology of race, identity, and community on campus.* Albany: State University of New York Press.

Renn, K. A. (2007). LGBT student leaders and queer activists: Identities of lesbian, gay, bisexual, transgender, and queer identified college student leaders and activists. *Journal of College Student Development, 48*(3), 311–330.

Renn, K. A. (2008). Research on biracial and multiracial identity development: Overview and synthesis. *New Directions for Student Services, 123*, 13–21.

Renn, K. A. (2010). LGBT and queer research in higher education: The state and status of the field. *Educational Researcher, 39*(2), 132–141.

Renn, K. A., & Jessup-Anger, E. R. (2008). Preparing new professionals: Lessons for graduate preparation programs from the national study of new professionals in student affairs. *Journal of College Student Development, 49*(4), 319–335.

Reyes, M. E. (2000). What does it take? Successful Alaska Native students at the University of Alaska Fairbanks. *Journal of College Student Retention, 2*(2), 141–159.

Reyes, M.-E. (2011). Unique challenges for women of color in STEM transferring from community college to universities. *Harvard Educational Review, 81*(2), 241–263.

Reynolds, A. L., & Pope, R. L. (1991). The complexities of diversity: Exploring multiple oppressions. *Journal of Counseling & Development, 70*, 174–180. doi:10.1002/j.1556-6676.1991.tb01580.x

Rhoads, R. A. (1994). *Coming out in college: The struggle for a queer identity.* Westport, CT: Greenwood Press

Richardson, R. C., Jr., & Skinner, E. (1990). Adapting to diversity: Organizational influences on student achievement. *Journal of Higher Education, 61*(5), 485–511.

Ridgewell, D. M., & Creamer, E. G. (2003). Institutional culture and the advanced degree aspirations of students attending women's colleges. *College Student Affairs Journal, 23*(1), 77–90.

Rissmeyer, P. A. (1996). *The transition to college for successful African American students on four predominantly white campuses: A grounded theory study* (Doctoral dissertation). State University of New York at Buffalo.

Robinson, J. P. (2008). Evidence of a differential effect of ability grouping on the reading achievement growth of language-minority Hispanics. *Educational Evaluation and Policy Analysis, 30*(2), 141–180.

Robinson, S. J. (2012). Spoketokenism: Black women talking back about graduate school experiences. *Race Ethnicity and Education.* Retrieved from http://www.tandfonline.com/doi/ref/10.1080/13613324.2011.645567#tabModule

Robinson, T. (1993). The intersections of gender, class, race, and culture: On seeing clients whole. *Journal of Multicultural Counseling and Development, 21*(1), 50–58.

Robinson, T. L., & Howard-Hamilton, M. F. (1994). An Afrocentric paradigm: Foundation for a health self-image and health interpersonal relationships. *Journal of Mental Health Counseling, 16*(3), 327–340.

Rockquemore, K., Brunsma, D. L., & Delgado, D. J. (2009). Racing to theory or retheorizing race? Understanding the struggle to build a multiracial identity theory. *Journal of Social Issues, 65*(1), 13–34.

Rodgers, R. F. (1990). An integration of campus ecology and student development: The Olentangy project. In D. G. creamer & Associates, *College student development: theory and practice for the 1990s* (pp. 27–79). Alexandria, VA: American College Personnel Association.

Roebuck, J. B., & Murty, K. S. (1993). *Historically Black colleges and universities.* Westport, CT: Praeger.

Rosa, M. L. D. L. (2006). Is opportunity knocking? Low-income students' perceptions of college and financial aid. *American Behavioral Scientist, 49*(12), 1670–1686.

Rosenbaum, J. (2001). *Beyond college for all.* New York, NY: Russell Sage.

Ross, T., Kena, G., Rathbun, A., Kewal Ramani, A., Zhang, J., Kristapovich, P., & Manning, E. (2012). *Higher education: Gaps in access and persistence study.* Washington, DC: U.S. Department of Education, Institute of Education Sciences, National Center for Education Statistics.

Roueche, J., & Roueche, S. (1999). *High stakes, high performance: Making remedial education work.* Washington, DC: Community College Press.

Rowan-Kenyon, H. T. (2007). Predictors of delayed college enrollment and the impact of socioeconomic status. *The Journal of Higher Education, 78*(2), 188–214.

Rowe, W., & Atkinson, D. R. (1995). Misrepresentation and interpretation: Critical evaluation of White racial identity development models. *The Counseling Psychologist, 23*(2), 364–367.

Rowley, L. L., Hurtado, S., & Ponjuan, L. (2005). *Institutional diversity: The disparities in higher education goals and outcomes.* Unpublished manuscript.

Rubin, B. C. (2003). "I'm not getting any F's": What "at-risk" students say about the support they need. In B. C. Rubin & E. Silva (Eds.), *Critical voices in school reform: Students living through change* (pp. 188–207). London. England: Routledge Falmer.

Rubin, R. B. (2011). The Pell and the poor: A regression-discontinuity analysis of on-time college enrollment. *Research in Higher Education, 52*(7), 675–692.

Ruiz, S., Sharkness, J., Kelly, K., DeAngelo, L., & Pryor, J. (2010). *Findings from the 2009 administration of the your first college year (YFCY): National aggregates.* Los Angeles, CA: Higher Education Research Institute, UCLA.

Rumann, C. B., & Hamrick, F. A. (2010). Student veterans in transition: Re-enrolling after war zone deployments. *The Journal of Higher Education, 81*(4), 431–458.

Ryan, L., & Ryan, R. (1982). *Mental health and the urban Indian.* Unpublished manuscript.

Saenz, V. B. (2005). *Breaking the cycle of segregation: The effects of pre-college racial environments on students' diversity experiences in college* (Unpublished doctoral dissertation). University ot California, Los Angeles.

Sáenz, V. B., Ngai, H. N., & Hurtado, S. (2007). Factors influencing positive interactions across race for African American, Asian, American, Latino, and White college students. *Research in Higher Education, 48*(1), 1–38.

Sallee, M. W. (2011). Performing masculinity: Considering gender in doctoral student socialization. *The Journal of Higher Education, 82*(2), 187–216.

Sánchez, B., Esparza, P., Colón, Y., & Davis, K. E. (2010). Tryin' to make it during the transition from high school: The role of family obligation attitudes and economic context for Latino-emerging adults. *Journal of Adolescent Research, 25*(6), 858–884.

Sander, R. H. (1997). Experimenting with class-based affirmative action. *Journal of Legal Education, 47*, 472–503.

Sander, R. H. (2004). A systemic analysis of affirmative action in American law schools. *Stanford Law Review, 367*–483.

Sankar, C. S., & Raju, P. K. (2011). Use of presage-pedagogy-process-product model to assess the effectiveness of case study methodology in achieving learning outcomes. *Journal of STEM Education, 12*(7 & 8), 45–56.

Santos, J. L., Cabrera, N. L., & Fosnacht, K. J. (2010). Is "race-neutral" really race-neutral?: Adverse impact towards underrepresented minorities in the UC System. *Journal of Higher Education, 81*(6), 675–701.

Sax, L. J., & Arredondo, M. (1999). Student attitudes toward affirmative action in college admissions. *Research in Higher Education, 40*(4), 439–459.

Schaefer, J. L. (2010). Voices of older baby boomer students: Supporting their transitions back into college. *Educational Gerontology, 36*(1), 67–90.

Schapiro, M. O., O'Malley, M. P., & Litten, L. H. (1991). Progression to graduate school from the 'elite' colleges and universities. *Economics of Education Review, 10*(3), 227–244.

Schlossberg, N. K. (1981). A model for analyzing human adaptation to transition. *Counseling Psychologist, 9*(2), 2–18.

Schlossberg, N. K., Waters E. B., & Goodman, J. (1995). *Counseling adults in transition: Linking practice with theory (2nd ed.).* New York, NY: Springer.

Schmidt, P. (2007). *Color and money: How rich White kids are winning the war over college affirmative action.* New York, NY: Palgrave MacMillan.

Schreiner, L. A., Noel, P., & Cantwell, L. (2011). The impact of faculty and staff on high-risk college student persistence. *Journal of College Student Development, 52*(3), 321–338.

Schuh, J., Triponey, V. L., Heim, L. L., & Nishimura, K. (1992). Student involvement in historically Black Greek letter organizations. *National Association of Student Personnel Association Journal, 29*(6), 274–282.

Schwartz, R. A., & Bower, B. L., Rice, D. C., & Washington, C. M. (2003). Isn't I a women, too?: Tracing the experiences of African American women in graduate school. *Journal of Negro Education, 72*(3), 252–268.

Schwartz, R. A., & Washington, C. M. (2002). Predicting academic performance and retention among African American freshmen men. *NASPA Journal, 39*, 355–370. doi:10.2202/1949-6605.1178

Seidman, A. (2005). *College student retention: Formula for student success.* Westport, CT: Greenwood Press.

Sellers, R. M., Rowley, S. A., Chavous, T. M., Shelton, J. N., & Smith, M. A. (1997). Multidimensional Inventory of Black Identity: A preliminary investigation of reliability and construct validity. *Journal of Personality and Social Psychology, 73*(4), 805.

Sewell, W., & Hauser, R. M. (1975). *Education, occupation, and earnings: Achievement in the early career.* New York, NY: Academic Press.

Settles, I. H. (2006). Use of an intersectional framework to understand Black women's racial and gender identities. *Sex Roles, 54*(9), 589–601.

Shapiro, T. M. (2004). *The hidden cost of being African American: How wealth perpetuates inequality.* New York, NY: Oxford University Press.

Shaw, K. M., & London, H. B. (2001). Culture and ideology in keeping transfer commitment: Three community colleges. *The Review of Higher Education, 25*(1), 91–114.

Shields, S. A. (2008). Gender: An intersectionality perspective. *Sex Roles, 59*(5–6), 301–311.

Shih, M., & Sanchez, D. T. (2005). Perspectives and research on the positive and negative implications of having multiple racial identities. *Psychological Bulletin, 131*(4), 569–591.

Shim, S., Barber, B. L., Card, N. A., Xiao, J. J., & Serido, J. (2010). Financial socialization of first-year college students: The roles of parents, work, and education. *Journal of Youth and Adolescence, 39*(12), 1457–1470.

Shotton, H. J., Oosahwe, E., & Cintrón, R. (2007). Stories of success: Experiences of American Indian students in a peer-mentoring retention program. *The Review of Higher Education, 31*(1), 81–107.

Sibulkin, A. E., & Butler, J. S. (2011). Diverse colleges of origin of African American doctoral recipients, 2001–2005: Historically Black colleges and universities and beyond. *Research in Higher Education, 52*(8), 830–852.

Sidanius, J., Levin, S., van Laar, C., & Sears, D. O. (2008). *The diversity challenge.* New York, NY: Russell Sage Foundation.

Sims, S. (1994). *Diversifying historically black colleges and universities: A new higher education paradigm.* Westport, CT: Greenwood Press.

Smedley, B. D., Myers, H. F., & Harrell, S. P. (1993). Minority-status stresses and the college adjustment of ethnic minority freshman. *The Journal of Higher Education, 64*, 434–452.

Smith, A. K., Carmack, H. J., & Titsworth, B. S. (2006). Managing the tension of in(ter) dependence: Communication and the socialization of first-year college students. *Journal of the First-Year Experience & Students in Transition, 18*(2), 83–109.

Smith, D. G. (2009). *Diversity's promise for higher education: Making it work.* Baltimore, MD: Johns Hopkins University Press.

Smith, D. G., Gerbrick, G. L., Figueroa, M. A., Harris Watkins, G., Levitan, T., Cradoc Moore, L., ... Figueroa, B. (1997). *Diversity works: The emerging picture of how students benefit.* Washington, DC: Association of American Colleges and Universities.

Smith, D. G., Turner, C. S., Osei-Kofi, N., & Richards, S. (2004). Interrupting the usual: Successful strategies for hiring diverse faculty. *Journal of Higher Education, 75*(2), 133–160.

Smith, W. A. (1998). Gender and racial/ethnic differences in the affirmative action attitudes of U.S. college students. *Journal of Negro Education, 6*(2), 127–141.

Smyth, F. L., & McArdle, J. J. (2004). Ethnic and gender differences in science graduation at selective colleges with implications for admission policy and college choice. *Research in Higher Education, 45*(4), 353–381.

Snyder, T. D., & Dillow, S. A. (2011). *Digest of education statistics 2011.* National Center for Education Statistics. Washington, DC: U.S. Department of Education.

Snyder, T. D., Tan, A. G., & Hoffman, C. M. (2006). *Digest of education statistics 2005* (NCES 2006–030). U.S. Department of Education, National Center for Education Statistics. Washington, DC: U.S. Government Printing Office.

Sokatch, A. (2006). Peer influences on the college-going decisions of low socioeconomic status urban youth. *Education and Urban Society, 39*(1), 128–146.

Solberg, V. S., O'Brien, K., Villareal, P., Kennel, R., & Davis, B. (1993). Self-efficacy and Hispanic college students: Validation of the college self-efficacy instrument. *Hispanic Journal of Behavioral Sciences, 15*, 180–195. doi:10.1177/07399863930151004

Soliday, M. (2002). *The politics of remediation.* Pittsburgh, PA: University of Pittsburgh Press.

Solórzano, D., Ceja, M., & Yosso, T. (2000). Critical race theory, racial microaggressions, and campus racial climate: The experiences of African-American college students. *Journal of Negro Education,* 69(1/2), 60–73.

Spady, W. (1971). Dropouts from higher education: An interdisciplinary review and synthesis. *Interchange, 1,* 64–85.

Spindler, L., & Spindler, G. (1958). Male and female adaptations in culture change. *American Anthropologist, 60,* 217–233.

St. John, E. P. S. (1991). What really influences minority attendance? Sequential analyses of the high school and beyond sophomore cohort. *Research in Higher Education, 32*(2), 141–158.

St. John, E. P. (2003). *Refinancing the college dream: Access, equal opportunity, and justice for taxpayers.* Baltimore, MD: Johns Hopkins University Press.

St. John, E. P. (2006). *Education and the public interest: School reform, public finance, and access to higher education.* Dordrecht, The Netherlands: Springer.

St. John, E. P. (2012). Academic capital formation: An emergent theory. In R. Winkle-Wagner, P. J. Bowman, & E. P. St. John. *Expanding postsecondary opportunity for underrepresented students: Theory and practice of academic capital formation* (pp. 3–28). Brooklyn, NY: AMS Press.

St. John, E., Cabrera, A., Nora, A., & Asker, E. (2000). Economic influences on persistence reconsidered: How can finance research inform the reconceptualization of persistence models? In J. Braxton (Ed.), *Reworking the student departure puzzle* (pp. 29–47). Nashville, TN: Vanderbilt University Press.

St. John, E. P., Hu, S., & Fisher, A. S. (2011). *Breaking through the access barrier: Academic capital formation informing public policy.* New York, NY: Routledge.

St. John, E. P., Hu, S., Simmons, A., Carter, D., & Weber, J. (2004). What difference does a major make? the influence of college major field on persistence by African American and White students. *Research in Higher Education, 45*(3), 209–232.

St. John, E. P., & Noell, J. (1989). The effects of student financial aid on access to higher education: An analysis of progress with special consideration of minority enrollment. *Research in Higher Education, 30*(6), 563–581.

St John, E. P., Paulsen, M. B., & Carter, D. F. (2005). Diversity, college costs, and postsecondary opportunity: An examination of the financial nexus between college choice and persistence for African Americans and Whites. *The Journal of Higher Education, 76*(5), 545–569.

St. John, E. P., Paulsen, M. B., & Starkey, J. B. (1996). The nexus between college choice and persistence. *Research in Higher Education, 37*(2), 175–220.

St. John, E. P., & Starkey, J. B. (1995). An alternative to net price: Assessing the influence of prices and subsidies on within-year persistence. *Journal of Higher Education, 66*(2), 156–186.

Stage, F. K., & Rushin, P. W. (1993). A combined model of student predisposition to college and persistence in college. *Journal of College Student Development, 34*(4), 276–281.

Stalvey, L. M. (1989). *The education of a WASP.* Madison: University of Wisconsin Press.

Stanton-Salazar, R. D. (1997). A social capital framework for understanding the socialization of racial minority children and youths. *Harvard Educational Review, 67*(1), 1–40.

Stanton-Salazar, R. D. (2001). *Manufacturing hope and despair: The school and kin support networks of U.S.-Mexican youth.* New York, NY: Teachers College Press.

Stanton-Salazar, R. D. (2004). Social capital among working-class minority students. In M. A. Gibson, P. Gándara, & J. P. Koyama (Eds.), *School connections: U.S. Mexican youth, peers, and school achievement* (pp. 18–38). New York, NY: Teachers College Press, Columbia University.

Stater, M. (2009). The impact of financial aid on college GPA at three flagship public institutions. *American Educational Research Journal, 46*(3), 782–815.

Steele, C. M., & Aronson, J. (1995). Stereotype threat and the intellectual test performance of African-Americans. *Journal of Personality and Social Psychology, 69*(5), 797–811.

Steele, C. M., & Aronson, J. (1998). Stereotype threat and the test performance of academically successful African Americans. In C. Jencks & M. Phillips (Eds.), *Black-White test score gap* (pp. 401–428). Washington, DC: Brookings Institution Press.

Steele, C. M., Spencer, S. J., & Aronson, J. (2002). Contending with group image: The psychology of stereotype and social identity threat. *Advances in Experimental Social Psychology, 34*, 379–440.

Stein, E. L., & Weidman, J. C. (1989, November). *Socialization in graduate school: A conceptual framework.* Paper presented at the annual meeting of the Association for the Study of Higher education, Atlanta, GA.

Sternberg, R. J. (2010). *College admissions for the 21st century.* Cambridge, MA: Harvard University Press.

Stevens, M. L. (2009). *Creating a class: College admissions and the education of elites.* Cambridge, MA: Harvard University Press.

Stevens, R. A. (2004). Understanding gay identity development within the college environment. *Journal of College Student Development, 45*(2), 185–206.

Stewart, D. L. (2008). Being all of me: Black students negotiating multiple identities. *The Journal of Higher Education, 79*(2), 183–207.

Stewart, D. L. (2009). Perceptions of multiple identities among Black college students. *Journal of College Student Development, 50*(3), 253–270.

Stoecker, J. L. (1991). Factors influencing the decision to return to graduate school for professional students. *Research in Higher Education, 32*(6), 689–701.

Stonewater, B. B. (1989). Gender differences in career decision making: A theoretical integration. *Initiatives, 52*(1), 27–34.

Strayhorn, T. L. (2011). Singing in a foreign land: An exploratory study of gospel choir participation among African American undergraduates at a predominantly White institution. *Journal of College Student Development, 52*(2), 137–153.

Stryker, S. (1980). *Symbolic interactionism: A social structural version.* Menlo Park, CA: Benjamin/Cummings.

Stryker, S. (1997). In the beginning there is society: Lessons from a sociological social psychology. In C. McGarty & A. Haslam (Eds.), *Message from social psychology: Perspective on mind in society* (pp. 315–327). London. England: Blackwell.

Stryker, S. (2000). Symbolic interaction theory. In E. F. Borgatta & R. J. V. Montgomery (Eds.), *Encyclopedia of sociology, rev. ed.* (Vol. 5, pp. 3095–3102). New York, NY: Macmillan.

Stulberg, L. M., & Weinberg, S. L. L. (Eds.). (2012). *Diversity in American higher education: Toward a more comprehensive approach.* New York, NY: Routledge.

Sulè, V. T. (2009). Oppositional stances of Black female graduate students: Perspectives from social and natural sciences. In M. F. Howard-Hamilton, C. L. Morelon-Quainoo, S. D. Johnson, R. Winkle-Wagner, & L. Santiague (Eds.), *Standing on the outside looking in: Underrepresented students' experiences in advanced degree programs* (pp. 147–168). Sterling, VA: Stylus Publishing.

Svanum, S., & Bigatti, S. M. (2009). Academic course engagement during one semester forecasts college success: England students are more likely to earn a degree, do it faster, and do it better. *Journal of College Student Development, 50*(1), 123–132.

Swail, W. S. (2000). Preparing America's disadvantaged for college: Programs that increase college opportunity. *New Directions for Institutional Research, 107*, 85–101.

Swim, J. K., Hyers, L. L., Cohen, L. L., Fitzgerald, D. C., & Bylsma, W. H. (2003). African American students' experiences with everyday racism: Characteristics of and responses to these incidents. *Journal of Black Psychology, 29*(1), 38–67.

Taylor, C. M., & Howard-Hamilton, M. F. (1995). Student involvement and racial identity attitudes among African American males. *Journal of College Student Development, 36*(4), 330–336.

Taylor, J. D., & Miller, T. K. (2002). Necessary components for evaluating minority retention programs. *NASPA Journal, 39*(3), 266–282.

Taylor, K. B. (2008). Mapping the intricacies of young adults' developmental journey from socially prescribed to internally defined identities, relationships, and beliefs. *Journal of College Student Development, 49*(3), 215–234.

Tekleselassie, A. A. (2010). Demystifying conventional assumptions: Do African American parents anticipate investing less toward their children's college costs than their White peers? *Journal of Student Financial Aid, 40*(2), 5–20.

Terenzini, P. T., Cabrera, A. F., Colbeck, C. L., Bjorklund, S. A., & Parente, J. M. (2001). Racial and ethnic diversity in the classroom: Does it promote student learning? *Journal of Higher Education, 72*(5), 509–531.

Terenzini, P., Rendón, L. I., Upcraft, L., Millar, S., Allison, K., Gregg, P., & Jalomo, R. (1994). The transition to college: Diverse students, diverse stories. *Research in Higher Education, 35*, 57–73. doi:10.1007/BF02496662

Terenzini, P. T., & Wright, T. M. (1987). Influences on students' academic growth during four years of college. *Research in Higher Education, 26*(2), 161–179.

Thoits, P. (2003). Personal agency in the accumulation of multiple role-identities. In P. J. Burke, T. J. Owens, R. T. Serpe, & P. Thoits (Eds.), *Advances in identity theory and research* (pp. 179–194). New York, NY: Kluwer Academic/Plenum Publishers.

Thomas, G. E. (1992). Participation and degree attainment of African-American and Latino students in graduate education relative to other racial and ethnic groups: An update from Office of Civil Rights data. *Harvard Educational Review, 62*(1), 45–65.

Thomas, G. E., Clewell, E. C., & Pearson, W. (1988). Case study of major doctoral producing institutions in recruiting, enrolling and retaining Black and Hispanic graduate students: Student interview protocols. *Graduate Examination Board Grant.*

Thomas, M. E. (1993). Race, class, and personal income: An empirical test of the declining significance of race thesis, 1968–1988. *Social Problems, 40*(3), 328–342.

Thomas, M. E., & Hughes, M. (1986). The continuing significance of race: A study of race, class, and quality of life in America, 1972–1985. *American Sociological Review, 51*, 830–841.

Thompson, J. P., & Tobias, S. (2000). The Texas Ten Percent Plan. *American Behavioral Scientist, 43*(7), 1121–1138.

Thompson, P. F. (2009). On firm foundations: African American Black college graduates and their doctoral student development in the Ivy League. In M. Gasman & C. L. Tudico (Eds.), *Historically Black colleges and universities: Triumphs, troubles, and taboos* (pp. 27–40). New York, NY: Palgrave MacMillan.

Tienda, M., Leicht, K. T., Sullivan, T., Maltese, M., & Lloyd, K. (2003). *Closing the gap?: Admissions and enrollments at the Texas public flagships before and after affirmative action* (Unpublished manuscript). Princeton University, Princeton, NJ.

Tienda, M. & Niu, S. X. (2006a). Capitalizing on segregation, pretending neutrality: College admissions and the Texas Top 10% law. *American Law Economics Review, 8*(2), 3120346. doi:10.1093/aler/ahl006

Tienda, M. & Niu, S. X. (2006b). Flagships, feeders, and the Texas Top 10% law: A test of the "brain drain" hypothesis. *The Journal of Higher Education, 77*(4), 712–739.

Tienda, M., & Sullivan, T. A. (2010). The promise and peril of the Texas uniform admission law. D. L. Featherman, M. Hall, & M. Krislov (Eds.), *The next twenty-five years: Affirmative action and higher education in the United States and South Africa* (pp. 155–174). Ann Arbor: University of Michigan Press.

Tierney, W. G. (1992). An anthropological analysis of student participation in college. *The Journal of Higher Education, 63*(6), 603–618.

Tierney, W. G. (1999). Models of minority college-going and retention: Cultural integrity versus cultural suicide. *The Journal of Negro Education, 68*(1), 80–91.

Tierney, W. G. (2000). Power, identity and the dilemma of college student departure. In J. Braxton (Ed.), *Rethinking the departure puzzle: New theory and research on college student retention* (pp. 259–283). Nashville, TN: Vanderbilt University Press.

Tierney, W. G. (2007). Merit and affirmative action in education: Promulgating a democratic public culture. *Urban Education, 42*(5), 385–402.

Tierney, W. G., Corwin, Z. B., & Colyar, J. E. (Eds.). (2005). *Preparing for college: Nine elements of effective outreach.* Albany, NY: SUNY Press.

Tierney, W. G., & Jun, A. (2001). A university helps prepare low income youths for college: Tracking school success. *Journal of Higher Education, 72*(2), 205–225.

Tierney, W. G., Sallee, M. W., & Venegas, K. M. (2007). Access and financial aid: How American-Indian students pay for college. *Journal of College Admission, 197*, 14–23.

Tierney, W. G., & Venegas, K. M. (2007). The cultural ecology of financial aid. *Readings on Equal Education, 22*, 1–35.

Tierney, W. G., & Venegas, K. M. (2009). Finding money on the table: Information, financial aid, and access to college. *The Journal of Higher Education, 80*(4), 363–388.

Tinto, V. (1975). Dropouts from higher education: A theoretical synthesis of recent research. *Review of Higher Educational Research, 45*, 89–125.

Tinto, V. (1993). *Leaving college: Rethinking the causes and cures of students' attrition.* Chicago, IL: The University of Chicago Press.

Tinto, V. (1997). Classrooms as communities: Exploring the educational character of student persistence. *Journal of Higher Education, 68*(6), 599–623.

Tinto, V. (2000). Linking learning and leaving: Exploring the role of the college classroom in student departure. In J. M. Braxton (Ed.), *Reworking the student departure puzzle* (pp. 213–134). Nashville, TN: Vanderbilt University Press.

Tinto, V. (2012). *Completing college: Rethinking institutional action.* Chicago, IL: The University of Chicago Press.

Titus, M. A. (2006). Understanding the influence of the financial context of institutions on student persistence at four-year colleges and universities. *The Journal of Higher Education, 77*(2), 353–375.

Torres, J. B., & Solberg, V. S. (2001). Role of self-efficacy, stress, social integration, and family support in Latino college student persistence and health. *Journal of Vocational Behavior, 59*(1), 53–63.

Torres, V. (2003a). Influences on ethnic identity development of Latino college students in the first two years of college. *Journal of College Student Development, 44*(4), 532–547.

Torres, V. (2003b). Mi casa is not exactly like your house: A window into the experience of Latino students. *About Campus, 8*(2), 2–7.

Torres, V., & Hernandez, E. (2007). The influence of ethnic identity on self-authorship: A longitudinal study of Latin/a college students. *Journal of College Student Development, 48*, 558–573. doi:10.1353/csd.2007.0057

Torres, V., Howard-Hamilton, M. F., & Cooper, D. L. (2003). Identity development of diverse populations: Implications for teaching and administration in higher education. *ASHE Higher Education Report, 29*(6).

Torres, V., Jones, S. R., & Renn, K. A. (2009). Identity development theories in student affairs: Origins, current status, and new approaches. *Journal of College Student Development, 50*(6), 577–593.

Torres, V., Winston, R. B., Jr., & Cooper, D. L. (2003). Hispanic American students' cultural orientation: Does geographic location, institutional type, or level of stress have an effect? *NASPA Journal, 40*(2). Retrieved from http://publications.naspa.org/naspajournal/vol40/iss2/art10

Toutkoushian, R. K., & Shafiq, M. N. (2010). A conceptual analysis of state support for higher education: Appropriations versus need-based financial aid. *Research in Higher Education, 51*(1), 40–64.

Tovar, E., & Simon, M. A. (2006). Academic probation as a dangerous opportunity: Factors influencing diverse college students' success. *Community College Journal of Research and Practice, 30*(7), 547–564. doi:10.1080/10668920500208237

Trombley, W. (1998). Remedial education under attack. *National CrossTalk, 6*(3), 1.

Turner, A. L., & Berry, T. R. (2000). Counseling center contributions to student retention and graduation: A longitudinal assessment. *Journal of College Student Development, 41*(6), 627–636.

Turner, C. S. V., Garcia, M., Nora, A., & Rendon, L. (Eds.). (1996). The name assigned to the document by the author. This field may also contain sub-titles, series names, and report numbers. *Racial & ethnic diversity in higher education.* ASHE Reader Series. Boston, MA: Person Custom Publishing.

Tuttle, T., McKinney, J., & Rago, M. (2005). College students working: The choice nexus. *IPAS Topics Brief.* Bloomington: Indiana Project on Academic Success.

Tyson, K. (2002). Weighing in: Elementary-age students and the debate on attitudes toward school among Black students. *Social Forces, 80*(4), 1157–1189.

Tyson, K., Darity, W., & Castellino, D. R. (2005). "It's not a "black thing": Understanding the burden of acting white and other dilemmas of high achievement. *American Sociological Review, 70*(4), 582–605.

Uloa, E. C., & Herrerra, M. (2006). Strategies for multicultural student success: What about grad school. *The Career Development Quarterly, 54*, 361–366. doi:10.1002/j.2161-0045.2006.tb00200.x

Umbach, P. D. (2007). How effective are they? Exploring the impact of contingent faculty on undergraduate education. *Review of Higher Education, 30*(2), 91–124.

U.S. Department of Education. (1999, October 20). *The Secretary's recognition of accrediting agencies.* Retrieved September 28, 2003 from http://www.ed.gov/legislation/FedRegister/finrule/1999-4/102099a.html#subpartb

United States Department of Education. (n.d.a) *Developing Hispanic-Serving Institutions Program — Title V.* Retrieved from http://www2.ed.gov/programs/idueshsi/index.html

United States Department of Education. (n.d.b). *United States Department of Education lists of postsecondary institutions enrolling populations with significant percentages of minority students.* Retrieved February 2. 2013, from http://www2.ed.gov/about/offices/list/ocr/edlite-minorityinst.html

U.S. Census Bureau. (2004). *U.S. interim projects by sex, race, age, and Hispanic origin.* Retrieved from: http://www.census.gov/population/www/projections/usinterimproj/natprojtab01a.pdf

U.S. Census Bureau. (2012a). *Table 711. People below poverty level and below 125 percent of poverty level by race and Hispanic origin: 1980 to 2009.* Retrieved from http://www.census.gov/compendia/statab/2012/tables/12s0711.pdf

U.S. Census Bureau (2012b). *Table 231. Educational attainment by selected characteristics: 2010.* Retrieved from http://www.census.gov/compendia/statab/2012/tables/12s0232.pdf

Valadez, J. R. (2008). Shaping the educational decisions of Mexican immigrant high school students. *American Educational Research Journal, 45*(4), 834–860.

Vandiver, B. J., Fhagen-Smith, P. E., Cokley, K., Cross, W. E., Jr., & Worrell, F. C. (2001). Cross's Nigrescence model: From theory to scale to theory. *Journal of Multicultural Counseling and Development, 29*, 174–200. doi:10.1002/j.2161-1912.2001.tb00516.x

Verba, S., & Nie, N. H. (1972). *Participation in America: Political democracy and social equality.* New York, NY: Harper and Row.

Villarejo, M., & Barlow, A. E. (2007). Evolution and evaluation of a biology enrichment program for minorities. *Journal of Women and Minorities in Science and Engineering, 13*(2), 119-144.

Villlarejo, M., Barlow, A. E. L., Kogan, D., Veazey, B. D., & Sweeney, J.K. (2008). Encouraging minority undergraduates to choose sciences careers: Career paths survey results. *Cell Biology Education Life Sciences Education, 7*(4), 394–409. doi:10.1187/cbe.08-04-0018

Walker, G. E., Golde, C. M., Jones, L., Bueschel, A. C., & Hutchings, P. (2009). *The formation of scholars: Rethinking doctoral education for the twenty-first century* (Vol. 11). San Francisco, CA: Jossey-Bass.

Walpole, M. (2003). Socioeconomic status and college: How SES affects college experiences and outcomes. *Review of Higher Education, 27*(1), 45–73.

Walpole, M. (2008). Emerging from the pipeline: African American students, socioeconomic status, and college experiences and outcomes. *Research in Higher Education, 49*(3), 237–255.

Warburton, E. C., Bugarin, R., & Nuñez, A. M. (2001). *Bridging the gap: Academic preparation and postsecondary success of first-generation students* (Report No. NCES 2001-153). Washington, DC: U.S. Department of Education, National Center for Education Statistics.

Watson, L., & Kuh, G. D. (1996). The influence of dominant race environments on student involvement, perceptions, and educational gains: A look at historically Black and predominantly White liberal arts institutions. *Journal of College Student Development, 37*(4), 415–424.

Wei, C. C., Berkner, L., He, S., Lew, S., Cominole, M., & Siegel, P. (2009). *2007–08 National postsecondary student aid study (NPSAS: 08): Student financial aid estimates for 2007–08. First look. NCES 2009-166.* Washington, DC: National Center for Education Statistics.

Weidman, J. C. (1989). Undergraduate socialization: A conceptual approach. In J. C. Smart (Ed.), *Higher education: Handbook of theory and research* (Vol. 5, pp. 289–322). New York, NY: Agathon Press.

Weidman, J. C. (2006). Socialization of students in higher education: Organizational perspectives. In C. Conrad & R. C. Serlin (Eds.), *The Sage handbook for research in education: Engaging ideas and enriching inquiry* (pp. 253–262). Thousand Oaks, CA: Sage.

Weidman, J. C., Twale, D. J., & Stein, E. L. (2001). Socialization of graduate and professional students in higher education: A perilous passage? *ASHE-ERIC Higher Education Report, 28*(3).

Wells, A., Brunson, W. D., Sinkford, J. C., & Valachovic, R. W. (2011). Working with dental school admissions committees to enroll a more diverse student body. *Journal of Dental Education, 75*(5), 685–695.

Wells, R. S., & Lynch, C. M. (2012). Delayed college entry and the socioeconomic gap: Examining the roles of student plans, family income, parental education, and parental occupation. *The Journal of Higher Education, 83*(5), 671–697.

Welner, K. G., & Oakes, J. (1996). (Li)ability grouping: The new susceptibility of school tracking systems to legal challenges. *Harvard Educational Research, 66*(3), 451–471.

West, C. (1993/2001). *Race matters.* New York, NY: Vintage Books.

West, C. (2005). *Democracy matters: Winning the fight against imperialism.* New York, NY: Penguin.

White, J. W., & Lowenthal, P. R. (2011). Minority college students and tacit "codes of power": Developing academic discourse and identities. *The Review of Higher Education, 34*(2), 283–318. doi: 10.1353/rhe.2010.0028

Whitt, E. J., Edison, M. I., Pascarella, E. T., Nora, A., & Terenzini, P. T. (1999). Women's perceptions of a "chilly climate" and cognitive outcomes in college: Additional evidence. *Journal of College Student Development, 40*(2), 163–177.

Wilkerson, I. (2010). *The warmth of other suns: The epic story of America's great migration.* New York, NY: Random House.

Wilkerson, J. M., Brooks, A. K., & Ross, M. W. (2010). Sociosexual identity development and sexual risk taking of acculturating collegiate gay and bisexual men. *Journal of College Student Development, 51*(3), 279–296.

Williams, D. A., Berger, J. B., & McClendon, S. A. (2005). *Toward a model of inclusive excellence and change in postsecondary institutions.* Retrieved June 13, 2007, from http//:www.aacu.org/inclusive_excellence

Williams, D. A., & Clowney, C. (2007). Strategic planning for diversity and organizational change. *Effective Practices for Academic Leaders, 2*(3), 1–16.

Williams, D. A., & Wade-Golden, K. (2007). The chief diversity officer. *College and University Personnel Association Journal, 58*(1), 38–48.

Williams, M. R., Brewley, D. N., Reed, R. J., White, D. Y., & Davis-Haley, R. T. (2005). Learning to read each other: Black female graduate students share their experience at a white research I institution. *The Urban Review, 37*(3), 181–199.

Wilson, W. J. (1978). The declining significance of race. *Society, 15*(5), 11, 16–21.

Winbush, D. E. (2007). Spelman mission was not impossible: How college's fund-raising drive netted $113 million. *Diverse Issues in Higher Education*. Retrieved from http://diverseeducation.com/article/7708/

Winkle-Wagner, R. (2009a). *TheUnchosen Me: Race, gender, and identity among Black women in college*. Baltimore, MD: Johns Hopkins University Press.

Winkle-Wagner, R. (2009b). The perpetual homelessness of college experiences: The tensions between home and campus for African American women. *The Review of Higher Education, 33*(1), 1–36.

Winkle-Wagner, R. (2010). Cultural capital: The uses and abuses of a key theoretical concept in educational research. *ASHE Higher Education Report Series, 36*(1).

Winkle-Wagner, R. (2012a). Academic capital formation: Can it help untangle the confusion about social stratification in the study of college students? In R. Winkle-Wagner, E. P. St. John, & P. Bowman, Eds., *Expanding postsecondary opportunity for underrepresented students: Theory and practice of academic capital formation. Readings on equal education Series, 26*. New York, NY: AMS Press.

Winkle-Wagner, R. (2012b). Self, college experience, and society. *College Student Affairs Journal, 30*(2), 45–60.

Winkle-Wagner, R., Johnson, S. D., Morelon-Quainoo, C., & Santiague, L. (2010). A sense of belonging: Socialization factors that influence the transitions of students of color into advanced-degree programs. In S. K. Gardner & P. Mendoza (Eds.), *On becoming a scholar: Socialization and development in doctoral education*, (pp. 179–202). Sterling, VA: Stylus Publishing.

Winkle-Wagner, R., St. John, E., & Bowman, P. (Eds.). (2012). *Expanding postsecondary opportunity for underrepresented students: Theory and practice of academic aapital formation. Readings on equal education Series, 26*. New York, NY: AMS Press.

Winkle-Wagner, R., Sule, V. T. & Maramba, D. C. (2012). When race disappears: Merit in the college admissions policy decision-making process in the State of Texas. *Educational Policy, 1*–30. doi:10.1177/0895904812465114

Worrell, F. C., Cross Jr., W. E., & Vandiver, B. J. (2001). Nigrescence theory: Current status and challenges for the future. *Journal of Multicultural Counseling and Development, 29*(3), 201–213.

Yancy, D. C, Sutton-Haywood, M., Hermitte, E., Dawkins, P. W., Rainey, K., & Parker, F. E. (2008). The impact of the freshman academy/learning communities on student progression and engagement. *The Journal of Negro Education, 77*(3), 250–263.

Yates, E. L. (2001). Capital campaigns. *Black issues in higher education, 18*(10), 18–25.

Yazedjian, A., Toews, M. L., & Navarro, A. (2009). Exploring parental factors, adjustment, and academic achievement among White and Hispanic college students. *Journal of College Student Development, 50*(4), 458–467. doi:10.1353/csd.0.0080

Yeh, C. J., & Huang, K. (1996). The collectivistic nature of ethnic identity development among Asian-American college students. *Adolescence, 31*(123), 645–661.

Yonezawa, S., Wells, A. S., & Serna, I. (2002). Choosing tracking: "Freedom of choice" in detracking schools. *American Education Research Journal, 39*(37), 37–67.

Yosso, T. J., Parker, L., Solórzano, D. G., & Lynn, M. (2004). From Jim Crow to affirmative action and back again: A critical race discussion of racialized rationales and access to higher education. *Review of Research in Education, 28*, 1–25.

Yosso, T. J., Smith, W. A., Ceja, M., & Solórzano, D. G. (2009). Critical race theory, racial microaggressions, and campus racial climate for Latina/o undergraduates. *Harvard Educational Review, 79*(4), 659–691.

Zamani-Gallaher, E., Green, D. O., Brown, M. C., & Stovall, D. O. *The case for affirmative action on campus*. Sterling, VA: Stylus Publishing.

Zajacova, A., Lynch, S. M., & Espenshade, T. J. (2005). Self-efficacy, stress, and academic success in college. *Research in Higher Education, 46*(6), 677–706. doi:10.1007/s11162-004-4139-z

Zeldin, A. M., & Pajares, F. (2000). Against the odds: Self-efficacy beliefs of women in mathematical, scientific, and technological careers. *American Educational Research Journal, 37*(1), 215–246. doi:10.3102/00028312037001215

Zhang, L. (2005). Advance to graduate education: The effect of college quality and undergraduate majors. *Review of Higher Education, 28*(3), 313–338.

Zhang, L. (2011). Does merit-based aid affect degree production in STEM fields?: Evidence from Georgia and Florida. *The Journal of Higher Education, 82*(4), 389–415.

Zhang, L., & Ness, E. (2010). Does state merit-based aid stem brain drain. *Educational Evaluation and Policy Analysis, 32*(2), 143–165.

Zimmerman, B. J. (1990). Self-regulating academic learning and achievement: The emergence of a social cognitive perspective. *Educational Psychology Review, 2*(2), 173–201. doi:10.1007/BF01322178

Zimmerman, B. J., Bandura, A., & Matinez-Pons, M. (1992). Self-motivation for academic attainment: The role of self-efficacy beliefs and personal goal setting. *American Educational Research Journal, 29*(3), 663–676.

Zinn, M. B., & Dill, B. T. (Eds.). (1994). *Women of color in US society*. Philadelphia: Temple University Press.

Zúñiga, X., Nagda, B. A., Chesler, M., & Cytron-Wlaker, A. (2007). Intergroup dialogue in higher education: Meaningful learning about social justice. *ASHE-ERIC Higher Education Report, 32*(4).

INDEX